World Entertainment Media

This new book offers an insightful guide into the complex tapestry of global entertainment media markets. It features analyses and case studies from leading international media scholars, who explore the causes and effects of globalization upon this ever-evolving industry.

There are still opposing and restraining forces to globalization processes taking place in media, and the global mediascape comprises international, regional and local markets, and global and local players, which in recent years have evolved at an uneven pace. By analyzing similarities and differences in a landscape where driving forces of globalization meet locally situated audiences and institutions, this volume unveils a complex, contested space comprising global and local players, whose success is determined by both their national and international dimensions. It guides its readers to the geographical and intellectual exploration of the international media landscape, analyzing the global and local media players and their *modus operandi*.

Editor Paolo Sigismondi's insightful, engaging collection presents a compelling and novel approach to the analysis of global entertainment media. *World Entertainment Media: Global, Regional and Local Perspectives* is an ideal starting point for students and practitioners alike looking to build a solid understanding of the global mediascape, and a great resource for instructors and scholars in global media entertainment.

Paolo Sigismondi, MBA, PhD, is a Clinical Associate Professor at the Annenberg School for Communication and Journalism of the University of Southern California. He has a background as a global media executive, and his research has been presented at international conferences and published in leading academic journals, including *Communication Theory* and the *International Journal of Communication*. He is the author of the book *The Digital Glocalization of Entertainment: New Paradigms in the 21st Century Global Mediascape* and the translator of its Italian edition *La Glocalizzazione Digitale dell'Audiovisivo: Nuovi Paradigmi nel Panorama Mondiale*.

World Entertainment Media
Global, Regional and Local Perspectives

Edited by Paolo Sigismondi

NEW YORK AND LONDON

First published 2020
by Routledge
52 Vanderbilt Avenue, New York, NY 10017

and by Routledge
2 Park Square, Milton Park, Abingdon, Oxon, OX14 4RN

Routledge is an imprint of the Taylor & Francis Group, an informa business

© 2020 Taylor & Francis

The right of Paolo Sigismondi to be identified as the author of the editorial material, and of the authors for their individual chapters, has been asserted in accordance with sections 77 and 78 of the Copyright, Designs and Patents Act 1988.

All rights reserved. No part of this book may be reprinted or reproduced or utilised in any form or by any electronic, mechanical, or other means, now known or hereafter invented, including photocopying and recording, or in any information storage or retrieval system, without permission in writing from the publishers.

Trademark notice: Product or corporate names may be trademarks or registered trademarks, and are used only for identification and explanation without intent to infringe.

Library of Congress Cataloging-in-Publication Data
Names: Sigismondi, Paolo, editor.
Title: World entertainment media : global, regional and local perspectives / edited by Paolo Sigismondi.
Description: New York, NY : Routledge, 2020. | Includes bibliographical references and index.
Identifiers: LCCN 2019014882 (print) | LCCN 2019019236 (ebook) | ISBN 9781315106298 (eBook) | ISBN 9781138094017 (hardback) | ISBN 9781138094024 (pbk.) | ISBN 9781315106298 (ebk.).
Subjects: LCSH: Mass media and globalization. | Glocalization.
Classification: LCC P94.6 (ebook) | LCC P94.6 .W69 2020 (print) | DDC 302.23—dc23
LC record available at https://lccn.loc.gov/2019014882

ISBN: 978-1-138-09401-7 (hbk)
ISBN: 978-1-138-09402-4 (pbk)
ISBN: 978-1-315-10629-8 (ebk)

Typeset in Times New Roman
by Swales & Willis Ltd, Exeter, Devon, UK
Printed and bound by CPI Group (UK) Ltd, CR0 4YY

In memory of my father

Contents

List of Illustrations	x
List of Contributors	xi
Acknowledgments	xvii

1 Introduction: Entertainment Media as a Lens to Probe the Twenty-First-Century Global Landscape   1
PAOLO SIGISMONDI

PART I
The Americas   9

2 Canadian TV Goes Global: Within and Beyond Cultural Imperialism   11
TANNER MIRRLEES

3 U.S. Entertainment Media: Expansion Across Platforms, Industries and Borders   19
PAUL TORRE

4 Mexico: A Historically Asymmetrical Media Context   29
HUMBERTO DARWIN FRANCO MIGUES AND GUILLERMO OROZCO GÓMEZ

5 Subjective Camera, Direct Address, and Audience Participation: *Velho Chico* and a New Brazilian Telenovela Aesthetics   39
SAMANTHA NOGUEIRA JOYCE AND ANTONIO LA PASTINA

PART II
EMEA (Europe, Middle East, Africa)   47

6 Media Policy in the European Union: A Synoptic Overview of the Legislative Framework and a Critical Review of Some Current Issues   49
PAUL CLEMENS MURSCHETZ

7   The Entertainment Landscape of the United Kingdom: Exploring
    British Television, Radio, and Film   58
    JEFFREY L. GRIFFIN

8   Entertainment Industries in France   68
    PHILIPPE BOUQUILLION

9   German Entertainment Media Industry: Characteristics and
    Market Break-Down   77
    GIANNA L. EHRLICH AND M. BJØRN VON RIMSCHA

10 From Bootlegging Hollywood to Streaming Battle Rap:
    The Transformation of the Russian Entertainment Industry   87
    ANNA POPKOVA

11 The Entertainment Industry in Spain   96
    JUAN PABLO ARTERO MUÑOZ

12 Entertainment: The Golden Resource of Italian Cultural
    and Media Industries   106
    MARIO MORCELLINI, MIHAELA GAVRILA AND SIMONE MULARGIA

13 Turkey in Global Entertainment: From the Harem to
    the Battlefield   116
    SENEM B. ÇEVIK

14 Entertainment Media Industry in Egypt: Overview, Challenges
    and Future Performance   124
    RASHA ALLAM

15 Nollywood: Prisms and Paradigms*   135
    JUDE AKUDINOBI

16 Entertaining the Nation: Incentivizing the Indigenization of Soap
    Opera in South Africa   142
    SARAH GIBSON, LAUREN DYLL AND RUTH TEER-TOMASELLI

PART III
Asia and Oceania   153

17 Media Culture Globalization and/in Japan   155
    KOICHI IWABUCHI

| 18 | China's Entertainment Industry | 164 |

YING ZHU

| 19 | Beyond *Hallyu*: Innovation, Social Critique, and Experimentation in South Korean Cinema and Television** | 173 |

JEONGMEE KIM, MICHAEL A. UNGER AND KEITH B. WAGNER

| 20 | The Marketization of Bollywood*** | 182 |

SOMJIT BARAT

| 21 | Australian Entertainment Industries | 193 |

TERRY FLEW AND CHRISTY COLLIS

| 22 | Conclusion: A Snapshot and a Springboard for the Exploration of World Entertainment Media | 201 |

PAOLO SIGISMONDI

Index 205

* First published as the article: "Nollywood: Prisms and Paradigms" by Jude Akudinobi, *Cinema Journal* 54:2, Winter 2015, pp. 133–140. Copyright © 2015 by the University of Texas Press. All rights reserved.

** First published as the article: "Beyond *Hallyu*: Innovation, Social Critique, and Experimentation in South Korean Cinema and Television" by Jeongmee Kim, Michael A. Unger and Keith B. Wagner, *Quarterly Review of Film and Video* (2017) 34:4, pp. 321–332.

*** First published as the article: "The Marketization of Bollywood" by Somjit Barat, *Quarterly Review of Film and Video* (2018) 35:2, pp. 105–118.

Illustrations

Figures

3.1	Film and television companies in U.S. entertainment media	21
3.2	Emergent companies in U.S. entertainment media	23
12.1	Italian TV audience's evolution (%)	108
12.2	Households with broadband access, 2016 (as % of all households)	113

Tables

4.1	Open Television National Networks in Mexico	31
4.2	Main National Radio Networks in Mexico	32
4.3	The Main Pay-Television Companies in Mexico	33
4.4	Main Cellular Telephony Companies in Mexico	33
4.5	Main Landline Telephone Companies in Mexico	34
4.6	Main Mobile and Landline Broadband Companies in Mexico	34
8.1	Direct Revenues of the Sector in France in 2013 in Billions of Euros	69
11.1	Audience Share of National Television Groups and Channels in 2014–2016	97
11.2	Pay-TV Subscribers and Revenues by Companies 2012–2016	98
11.3	Online Video Genres in 2015–2016	99
11.4	Main Film Distribution Companies in 2016	100
11.5	Videogames Industry in 2016	101
11.6	Audience of National Radio Groups and Channels in 2014–2016	102
11.7	Recorded Music Industry in 2016	103
11.8	Revenue Forecasts for the Entertainment Industry in 2017–2021	104
12.1	Distribution of Advertising Revenue (Mil €)	109
12.2	Share of the Main Subjects Operating in the Integrated Communications System (%)	110
14.1	Daily Average of Television Transmission Hours, in Central and Local Channels, by Subject of Program (2005–2016) – Unit: Hour	125
14.2	Daily Average of Television Transmission Hours of Nile Specialized Channels (2005–2016)	126
14.3	Number of Published and Printed Books and Booklets Written and Translated by Subject (2013–2015)	131
20.1	Indian Movie Stats: Top Five Grossing Movies	188
20.2	Total 2006–2011 Box Office Revenue for the Top Six Countries (US $ Millions)	190

Contributors

Jude Akudinobi earned his PhD in cinema-television from the University of Southern California, and teaches in the Department of Black Studies at the University of California, Santa Barbara. His works on African cinema have appeared in various journals, anthologies and other publications.

Rasha Allam, Assistant Professor and Associate Chair at the Department Journalism and Mass Communication, is a graduate of the Department of Journalism and Mass Communication, School of Global Affairs and Public Policy at The American University in Cairo. She is an Honorary Alumni of the Annenberg school for Communication, University of Pennsylvania and an associate of the Oxford University program of Media Laws and Regulations. Her BA and MA are in Journalism and Mass Communication and her Doctorate is in Business Administration, with specialization in Media Management from Maastricht School of Management.

Allam's areas of teaching include media management, media economics, and mass media policies, laws and regulations. Allam's research record includes conference presentations on local, regional and global levels; and publishing book chapters and reports with specific reference to media in the Middle East.

Dr. Juan Pablo Artero Muñoz is an Associate Professor of Journalism at the University of Zaragoza, Spain. He has been an executive board member at the European Media Management Association (2008–2012) as well as a regular participant at the World Media Economics and Management Conference community. His research interests are focused on media economics, management and policy. His academic publications account for more than 60 books, book chapters and journal articles, both in Spanish and English. He has attended conferences, seminars and professional meetings in more than 30 countries.

Dr. Somjit Barat (PhD in Marketing, University of North Texas) is an Associate Professor in the School of Business at the Pennsylvania State University. He teaches several marketing courses at the Mont Alto campus, which is located in South Central Pennsylvania. He also conducts research in the areas of consumer behavior, banking, ethics, economics and Bollywood and disseminates his research findings through national and international conferences. In addition, Dr. Barat is actively involved in global marketing and promoting Study Abroad programs for students. He currently resides in Hagerstown, Maryland with his wife and two kids. Dr. Barat enjoys playing the drums, listening to music and cooking food of different flavors.

Philippe Bouquillion, Professor of Communication Sciences in the university Paris13, is a researcher at the Laboratory of Excellence "Cultural Industries and Artistic Creation" and at the Laboratory of Information and Communication Sciences. He is coordinator of the axis "Cultural Industries and Arts" at the Maison des Sciences de l'Homme Paris Nord. His work focuses on the cultural and creative industries. His most recent research work has focused on digital platforms in Europe and India as well as regulatory and public policy issues.

Senem B. Çevik is a lecturer at the University of California, Irvine at the International Studies Program. Her research focus is public diplomacy and strategic communication with an emphasis on Turkey. She is a blogger at the University of Southern California Center on Public Diplomacy. Çevik is a fellow with the International Dialogue Initiative and staff member of The Olive Tree Initiative.

Christy Collis is Director of Research Quality and Coordinator of Entrepreneurship and Industry-Integrated Learning in the Creative Industries Faculty at Queensland University of Technology in Brisbane, Australia. In 2006, she launched Australia's first university Entertainment Industries degree program. She is one of three commissioning editors of the Palgrave Entertainment Industries book series.

Dr. Lauren Dyll is a Senior Lecturer in the Centre for Communication, Media and Society at the University of KwaZulu-Natal. She lectures and supervises in media theory and social change communication. Adopting a cultural studies perspective, her research interests include critical indigenous qualitative methodologies with the aim to signal strategies that facilitate participatory and transformative aspects of the research encounter and relations within society. She is particularly interested in this relationship within the field of social change communication with multiple partners, including indigenous communities. As tourism is often a significant part of indigenous communities' political economies, the ways in which indigenous knowledge and development-as-cultural-tourism is mobilized are studied. Related to this are issues of culture and identity. More recently, research interests include media theory, particularly local (South African) television. She is currently a principle investigator on the research project, "Representing and consuming the local: Exploring the production and reception of *Uzalo*: *Blood is Forever*."

Gianna L. Ehrlich is a research associate and PhD student at the Department of Communication of Johannes Gutenberg University in Mainz, Germany. Her research interests include advertising research and media branding with a focus on customer-based brand equity. She is a co-speaker of MedienökonomieJR (Media EconomicsJR), which is a network for early-career researchers who address scholars who are interested in a variety of issues in the field of media economics and media management and search for an informal, uncomplicated and interdisciplinary exchange.

Terry Flew is Professor of Media and Communication in the Creative Industries Faculty at the Queensland University of Technology, Brisbane, Australia. He is the author of *Understanding Global Media* (Palgrave, 2018), *Politics, Media and Democracy in Australia* (Routledge, 2017 – with Brian McNair, Stephen Harrington and Adam Swift), *Global Media and National Policies: The Return of the State* (Palgrave, 2016 – with Petros Iosifidis and Jeanette Steemers), *Media Economics* (Palgrave, 2015 – with Stuart Cunningham and Adam Swift), *Global Creative Industries* (Polity, 2013) and *The Creative Industries, Culture and Policy* (Sage, 2012). He is President-Elect of the International Communications Association (ICA), becoming ICA President in 2020, and has been an Executive Board member of the International Communications Association since 2013. He is on the editorial boards of 13 academic journals, and was the founding Editor-in-Chief of *Communication Research and Practice*, an ANZCA journal established in 2016 and published by Taylor & Francis.

Prof. Mihaela Gavrila, PhD, is Professor in Television Studies and Sociology of Cultural and Communicative Processes at the Department of Communication and Social Research of Sapienza University of Rome (Italy).

On December 13, 2017, with the Decree of the Minister of Economic Development, she was nominated as an effective member of the Media and Minors Committee representing the Italian institutions.

Over time, she has been carrying out teaching activities in University master, research doctorate and advanced training courses on subjects such as communication, media and technologies. She has been collaborating as Professor in Communication and Security Studies with the Italian national police academies Scuola Superiore di Polizia and Scuola Interforze di Polizia for many years. Furthermore, she is a member of the Advisory Board of Studies for *Visual Arts and Communication – an International Journal* (Romania), *RESED – Revista de Estudios Socioeducativos* (Spain), and *Rivista Trimestrale della Scuola di Perfezionamento per le Forze di Polizia and Rivista Sociologia Italiana – AIS Journal of Sociology,* Egea Editore Milano (Italy).

Dr. Sarah Gibson is a senior lecturer in the Centre for Communication, Media and Society (CCMS) at the University of KwaZulu-Natal in South Africa. She previously worked at Surrey University and Lancaster University in the United Kingdom. She has published in journals such as the *Journal of African Cinema, Journal for Cultural Research, Space and Culture, Tourist Studies* and *Third Text*, and has co-edited *Mobilizing Hospitality: The Ethics of Social Relations in a Mobile World* (Ashgate, 2007).

Guillermo Orozco Gómez is a full Professor and Director of the Social Communication Studies Department, University of Guadalajara; Communicator, MA and Doctor of Education, Harvard; Member of the Mexican Academy of Sciences and the National System of Researchers; and Director of the UNESCO chair: Media and Information Literacy and Intercultural Dialogue for Latin America. His academic work has been developed for 30 years along the lines of Media Literacy, TV Fiction and Audience Analysis. He created and directed the Institutional Research Program (PROIICOM) and the series Communication and Social Practices Notebooks, Iberoamerican University, Mexico. Coordinator of the book series of the International Forum TVMORFOSIS. Author of 80 articles and book chapters, co-author of 18 books. His latest books: *Viewership: Communication, Education and Citizenry*, translated into Portuguese: *Recepção Midiática, Aprendizagens e Cidadania*, 2014; *At the Edge of Screens*, Ed. (La Crujía, Argentina, 2015); *TvMorphosis 6: Management and Consumption of Digital Contents. New models* (Tintable, Mexico, 2017).

Dr. Jeffrey L. Griffin is an associate professor in the Department of Communication at the University of Dayton in Dayton, Ohio, USA. His specialties are international communication, intercultural communication and classic film. His research interests include the globalization of television and film and the spread of English as a global language. Dr. Griffin has published articles in *English Today, Film International, Gazette, International Communication Bulletin, Journal of Popular Film & Television, Journalism Quarterly, Mass Comm Review, Newspaper Research Journal* and *Visual Communication Quarterly*.

Koichi Iwabuchi is Professor of Media and Cultural Studies and Director of the Monash Asia Institute, Monash University, Australia. His main research interests are media and cultural globalization, trans-Asian cultural flows and connections, and multicultural questions and cultural citizenship in the Japanese and East Asian contexts. His recent English publications include *Resilient Borders and Cultural Diversity: Internationalism, Brand Nationalism and Multiculturalism in Japan* (Lexington Books, 2015); *Multiculturalism in East Asia: A Transnational Exploration of Japan, South Korea and Taiwan* (co-eds, Rowman & Littlefield International, 2016); *Handbook for East Asian Pop Culture* (co-eds, Routledge). Iwabuchi is the editor of the book series, *Asian Cultural Studies: Transnational and Dialogic Approaches* (Rowan & Littlefield International).

Samantha Nogueira Joyce is Assistant Professor of Communication at Saint Mary's College of California. She studies media history, theory and criticism with concentrations in cultural studies, critical theory and Latin American and Brazilian Media and Cultural Studies.

Her research covers a range of contemporary as well as historical topics in order to understand the many ways in which people's identities are constituted by and through the media, especially television. In addition to her book *Brazilian Telenovelas and the Myth of Racial Democracy* her research has appeared in *International Journal of Communication, Brazilian Journalism Research, Rumores*, and others.

Jeongmee Kim is Senior Lecturer in Film and Television Studies at Manchester Metropolitan University. She has published in such academic journals as *Critical Studies in Television and Media, Culture & Society* and is the editor of *Reading Asian Television Drama: Crossing Borders and Breaking Boundaries* (I.B. Tauris, 2014).

Antonio La Pastina is an Associate Professor in the Department of Communication at Texas A&M University. His research focuses on the longitudinal understanding of how communities engage with mediated forms of communication. Utilizing ethnography, he has conducted research in rural northeast Brazil, southern Italy and along the Texas–Mexico border. He has also written extensively on telenovelas and representation of otherness in that genre.

Humberto Darwin Franco Migues is a journalist; MA of Communication and Doctor of Education. University of Guadalajara; Member of the National Researcher System; Full Professor and Researcher at the Social Communication Studies Department, University of Guadalajara; Member of the UNESCO-UNAOC Chair: Media Information Literacy and Intercultural Dialogue for Latin America; Researcher for the Iberoamerican Television Fiction Observatory (OBITEL); and Member of the Mexican Association of Communication Researchers (AMIC) and the Mexican Association for the Right to Communication (AMEDI). In addition to his academic work, he works as a journalist specializing in issues of social violence and disappearances. His works have been published in local, national and international media. Winner of the Jalisco Award of Journalism in 2014 in the Written Press Category. His latest books are: *Citizens' Literacy Handbook: A Pedagogical Guide to Empower the Citizen Before Electoral Publicity* (U. de G., 2016), and *At the Edge of Screens* (La Crujía, 2014) co-authored with Guillermo Orozco Gómez.

Tanner Mirrlees is the Director of the Communication and Digital Media Studies program at the University of Ontario Institute of Technology (UOIT). Mirrlees's current research focuses on the political economy of the U.S. Empire and the cultural industries, media work and labor, and the nexus of the alt-right and social media. Mirrlees is the author of *Hearts and Mines: The U.S. Empire's Culture Industry* (University of British Columbia Press, 2016) and *Global Entertainment Media: Between Cultural Imperialism and Cultural Globalization* (Routledge, 2013).

Mario Morcellini, member of the Board of Autorità per le Garanzie nelle Comunicazioni (AGCOM) (Authority for Communications Guarantees), elected by the Senate of the Italian Republic (Senato della Repubblica) in February 2017. He has been Full Professor in Sociology of Cultural and Communicative Processes at Sapienza – University of Rome. In the same university, he has been Director of the Communication and Social Research Department (2010–2016), Vice-Rector for Institutional Communication (2014–2016) and Dean of the Communication Sciences Faculty from 2004 to 2010.

He carried and still carries out counseling and scientific direction activities for: MIUR (Italian Minister of University and Research); CRN (National Council of Research); RAI (Italian Public Television); ONG (National Order of Journalists); FNSI (National Federation of the Press).

He carried out studies and researches on TV and press information, on audiovisual cultural consumption and on Italian media system, with particular attention to television scheduling and the answers of the television public in the mixed system. He then focused his research interest on socialization of children and young people, and on the role played in this field by the media system, realizing studies on the relationships between communication and formation.

Simone Mulargia, PhD, has been Postdoctoral Research Fellow in the Department of Communication and Social Research (CORIS), Sapienza University of Rome, since 2010. His research and publications study the relationship between culture, technology and society, focusing on the role of digital media. His work is published in journals such as *Games and Culture*, *Media Culture and Society* and *The Sociological Review*.

Paul Clemens Murschetz, PhD, is Professor in Media and Communication Studies at Berlin University of Digital Sciences. He has published widely in journals such as: *The International Journal on Media Management*, the *European Journal of Communication* and the *Annals of the International Communication Association*. He edited two volumes on international media policy: *State Aid for Newspapers – Theories, Cases, Action* (Media Business and Innovation, Springer International Publishing 2014) and *The Handbook of State Aid for Film. Finance, Industries, Regulation* (together with R. Teichmann, & M. Karmasin), (Media Business and Innovation,, Springer International Publishing 2018).

Anna Popkova is Assistant Professor at Western Michigan University School of Communication. Her research examines the relationships between media institutions, media discourses, policymakers, various publics and communication technologies as these apply to such issues as the politics of national identity at national and transnational levels, state and non-state public diplomacy, and the role of culture, technology and communication in shaping the traditions of public participation and civic discourse worldwide. Most of Dr. Popkova's work focuses on Russia and Russia–U.S. relations and has been published in the *Journal of Communication Inquiry*, *International Journal of Communication*, *International Communication Gazette* and elsewhere.

Dr. M. Bjørn von Rimscha is professor of media business at the Department of Comunication, Johannes Gutenberg University, Mainz, Germany, where he heads the media management study program. His research interests are in the structural, organizational and individual influences on media and entertainment production. His research has been published, e.g. in *Media Culture and Society*, *International Journal on Media Management* and *Media Industries*. He also acts as associate editor of the *Journal of Media Business Studies*.

Prof. Ruth Teer-Tomaselli is the Director of the Centre for Culture and Media in Society (CCMS) at the University of KwaZulu-Natal, South Africa. She holds the UNESCO Chair in Communications for Southern Africa. Her research interests are in the political economy and history of the media, in television and radio studies and in memory studies. Her recent publications include a co-edited book with Donal McCracken, *Media and the Empire* (London: Routledge, 2016) to which she contributed chapters on the role of the SABC during World War II, and a comparative study of broadcasting in the interwar years in three British Dominion countries – South Africa, Australia and Canada. Public service broadcasting is a continuing area of interest, with recent articles on language and propaganda in broadcasting, as well as the introduction of commercialization in PSB. In her spare time, she gardens and grows bonsai trees.

Paul Torre teaches and researches in the Digital Media Leadership program at the University of Northern Iowa. His entertainment industry experience includes positions addressing film and television production management, business and legal affairs, and global marketing and distribution. His research explores entertainment industry structures and practices, media regulations and policies, the interplay between U.S. and global media markets, and how new technologies are shaping the media business models of the future.

Michael A. Unger is an Assistant Professor of Film at Sogang University's Graduate School of Media in Seoul, South Korea. He is a writer, director and editor of documentaries, shorts, music videos and experimental work screened and broadcast in the United States, Europe and Asia.

His documentary *Far From Forgotten*, which he co-directed with Jia Lim, is part of the permanent collection at the National Museum of Korean Contemporary History in Seoul. He has published work on documentaries, film directors and Korean popular culture in *Journal of Film and Video*, *Journal of Popular Music Studies*, *Visual Communication*, *Quarterly Review of Film and Video*, *Asian Cinema*, *Studies in Documentary* and other periodicals in the United States, the United Kingdom and Asia.

Keith B. Wagner is an Assistant Professor of Global Media and Culture in the Centre for Multidisciplinary and Intercultural Inquiry and Director of the Graduate Program in Film and Media Studies at University College London. He is the co-editor of *Neoliberalism and Global Cinema: Capital, Culture and Marxist Critique* (2011) and *China's iGeneration: Cinema and Moving Image Culture for the Twenty First Century* (2014). His monographic study entitled *Living with Uncertainty: Neoliberal Societies and Precarity in Global Cinema* will be published in 2020 by the University of Michigan Press. He is currently co-editing three new collections, devoted to diverse areas of study: *Asian Media Conglomerates*, *Fredric Jameson and Film Theory* and *Global London on Screen*.

Ying Zhu is a Professor of Cinema Studies in the Department of Media Culture at the City University of New York, College of Staten Island. A leading expert in Chinese film and Television, she has published eight books, including *Two Billion Eyes: The Story of China Central Television* (2014) and *Art, Politics, and Commerce in Chinese Cinema* (2010). Her first research monograph, *Chinese Cinema during the Era of Reform: The Ingenuity of the System* (2003) initiated the study of Chinese cinema within the framework of political economy. Her second research monograph, *Television in Post-Reform China: Serial Drama, Confucian Leadership and the Global Television Market* (2008), together with two edited books in which her work featured prominently – *TV China* (2009) and *TV Drama in China* (2008) – pioneered the subfield of Chinese TV drama studies in the West. She is currently working on a Fulbright sponsored book, *The Sino-Hollywood Courtship*, that parallels Hollywood's contemporary China engagement with the dominance and local resistance of American films in China during China's Republican era.

Acknowledgments

An edited book on global media entertainment is an exploration above and beyond one's own boundaries, and probing the ever-changing features of the world through the lens of media entertainment provides an opportunity for new encounters and discoveries at almost every turn. It has truly been a pleasure to work on this project for the last two years with the authors who contributed to this volume. I am delighted to have had the opportunity to collaborate with such an outstanding group of international authors, with deep knowledge of the countries they analyze in their chapters stemming from years of research on the distinctive features of these media landscapes in addition to having lived and worked in these specific cultural environments. Their analyses allow the reader to explore the unique features of their respective media entertainment environments and, as a result, their countries. I would like to take the opportunity to thank them for their time, wisdom, generosity, enthusiasm and patience during the different phases of the publication of this book.

The idea of editing this volume originated during a conversation with Erica Wetter, publisher in media studies at Routledge, with whom I exchanged views on the status of academic publications on global entertainment at the annual International Communication Association conference in Fukuoka, Japan in 2016, and in particular on the potential value of a collection of essays focusing on different media landscapes around the world. I want to thank her for following up on the original idea and for her gracious, professional and constant support throughout all the different stages of the publication of this volume, and her staff at Routledge, in particular Emma Sherriff, for their commitment to this project.

I am indebted, and have been for more than a decade, to the community of the Annenberg School for Communication and Journalism of the University of Southern California, which provides an ideal environment to teach, learn and conduct research to shed light on the evolution of the global mediascape. I would like to express my gratitude to the school leadership guiding this academic institution over the years, to my colleagues and to the students coming from all over the world for the insightful discussions and intellectual exchanges on the topic, and to the doctoral student Do Own Kim for her research assistance on this project. The twenty-first-century global landscape is undergoing significant transformations ushered in by the unfolding digital revolution and contested phenomena of globalization. This volume suggests entertainment media as a lens to probe the landscape, offering global, regional and local perspectives.

Los Angeles, CA Paolo Sigismondi

1 Introduction
Entertainment Media as a Lens to Probe the Twenty-First-Century Global Landscape

Paolo Sigismondi

Entertainment Media in a Complex and Dynamic Twenty-First-Century Global Landscape

An unprecedented avalanche of entertainment media content is available to viewers worldwide with access to the Internet. The leading social media platforms (which did not exist only 15 years ago) report astounding data at the time of this writing: Facebook has on average 1.4 billion daily active users, whereas a billion hours of videos are watched on YouTube every single day by more than a billion viewers. As these numbers indicate, both platforms have established a global footprint, above and beyond their country of origin – the US mediascape – exceeding the one billion regular user threshold with localized versions around the world. YouTube has for example launched local versions in more than 88 countries in 76 different languages covering 95% of the Internet population (Facebook 2018; YouTube 2018).

These platforms are increasingly funding and distributing media entertainment content in competition with legacy media and other internet-based platforms, such as Netflix, Amazon and Hulu, which have also reached a critical mass of viewers and are situated at a pivotal nexus in the evolving entertainment landscape, as analyzed by scholars (see for example Lotz, 2017 and Lobato, 2019) and monitored by trade journals tracking their increasingly relevant role in financing original creative content (see for example Jarvey, 2017). The unprecedented availability of entertainment media content ushered in by the rise of internetbased media platforms is just one aspect of the unfolding phenomena of globalization, which are irreversibly shaping the international media landscape on multiple levels, impacting the activities of financing, producing and distributing media content while offering new ways for audiences to access, retrieve and interact with entertainment media.

In the current chapter of the evolution of globalization processes international trade in services and intangible assets is increasingly significant, and current estimates of the value of cross-border flows of free digital services (ranging from e-mail to mapping, search and social media from companies such as YouTube and Facebook), currently untracked by trade statistics as they are free for global consumers, indicate it could be worth up to 3 trillion USD annually (McKinsey Global Institute, 2019, pp. 50–52). Within these unfolding processes Wolf (2003) has convincingly argued that the industry of creating, distributing and exhibiting entertainment media is a key driver of the current post-industrial economy, defined as an *entertainment economy*.

Entertainment media plays a central role in human communication and has gained a pivotal role in societies around the world. Why is it so relevant and worth investigating? Huizinga (1949) insightfully pointed out the central role of *play* in human development over the centuries, tracing the evolution of *homo ludens* since ancient Rome and Greece through the Middle Ages, the Renaissance and the early modern world. For example, in ancient Rome *panem et circenses* [bread and circuses] were deemed by the poet Juvenal essential needs to be satisfied in order to prevent social unrest, positioning entertainment at the same level as the physiological desire for food in the hierarchy of needs, as both basic human necessities to be provided in functioning societies. Media entertainment, in all the old and new emerging forms, has been in many aspects overlapping with and replacing in the twenty-first century most of what used to belong within the realm of play, amplified in engagement power and planetary reach by evolving communication technologies. How the entertainment media landscape is evolving both in global and local terms represents a central theme of investigation to analyze society, and the relevance of media entertainment has not gone unnoticed in scholarly conversations from different strands of inquiry and in public discourse, generating an evolving body of literature.

Specifically probing and explicating the appeal of media entertainment, communication scholars have proposed theoretical frameworks, such as the role of transportation into narrative worlds (Green, Brock & Kaufman, 2004) and enjoyment at the heart of media entertainment (Vorderer, Klimmt and Ritterfeld, 2004), which contribute to the understanding of the deep linkages between audiences and entertainment. Moreover, Zillmann and Vorderer (2000) suggest we have entered an *entertainment age*, such is its central role in society, investigating the psychology of its appeal.

The international dimensions of entertainment media are fascinating, yet complex to ascertain. International media landscapes, from a competitive standpoint, are becoming more and more intertwined and it is therefore essential for all entities operating in the twenty-first century to consider positioning themselves above and beyond their national borders. Global leaders in the international mediascape have, over time, built a competitive advantage, being able to capture additional revenue streams from international distribution, which allow them in turn to fund popular culture artifacts with a higher production value (Sigismondi, 2017). Legacy media players, such as the Hollywood studios, have, through successful international distribution of entertainment productions, both feature-length motion pictures and TV series, created and sustained a global competitive advantage in the twentieth century and continue to hold their primacy at the turn of a new millennium. At the same time, new entities in the field of non-scripted entertainment ("reality" TV programmes, quiz shows, etc.), such as the European-based players Endemol and FremantleMedia, have been challenging, in the last decade, Hollywood's competitive advantage in television outlets around the world by introducing programmes like "reality TV" shows, which are able to create and capture economic value both in the traditional, linear landscape and the new digital environment, successfully adapting their formats internationally (Sigismondi, 2012). Also new media players, such as the aforementioned global social media platforms, are adapting their content to better intercept the needs and expectations of locally situated audiences. To better compete in the changing landscape, legacy global players are undergoing processes of mergers and consolidations leading to the creation of increasingly larger global media conglomerates, and are constantly scanning the globe to monetize their content, facing rising competition from the corporate giants emerging from the digital revolution, sometimes referred to as *FAANG*, an acronym indicating the best performing tech stocks, namely Facebook, Apple, Amazon, Netflix and Google, all competing in the media landscape at global level as well.

The international media scene, however, is far from being a uniform landscape. It represents a mosaic comprising regional and local markets with distinct unique features including local players, which in recent years have evolved at an uneven pace, oftentimes taking advantage of the opportunities ushered in by the Information and Communication Technology (ICT) revolution while branching outside their local media ecosystems. Notwithstanding (or precisely as a result of) the acceleration of phenomena of globalization, there are opposing and restraining forces to globalization processes taking place in media, ranging from national controls to local preferences or just downright opposition to phenomena of internationalization, when local audiences, noticing the increased loss of sovereignty of their nations, fear the unfolding dissipation of local cultures in danger of being swept away by a foreign-originated avalanche of media content to which they feel oftentimes disconnected.

Two events in the past years brought to the fore in the US and internationally how uncomfortable, if not plain hostile, a large portion of citizens within different countries and cultures are when confronted with phenomena of globalization: the 2016 presidential elections in the US and the United Kingdom European Union membership referendum, which have set in motion the exit of this country from the European Union, the so-called "Brexit." Both events can be explicated, in their complexities, also as backlashes against globalization, identified as a culprit, if not the scapegoat, of the *malaise* of affluent twenty-first-century societies with uneven distribution of resources and access to globalization rewards. It is worth noting that these pushbacks take place in countries that retain a pivotal role in these processes and overall economically benefit from globalization and, not surprisingly, there are even more signs of growing opposition in countries marginalized at the periphery of globalization, which are left behind and perceive their relevance increasingly diminished in the international arena.

Within these unfolding, contested phenomena of globalization, this book aims at providing a geographical and intellectual exploration into the complexities of global entertainment media, revealing an evolving tapestry of diversity. It intends to shed light on the multifaceted international media landscape, analyzing the global trends as well as the distinctive features of local and regional media landscapes, their players and their *modus operandi*. The book is intended for those interested and curious to deepen their knowledge of the cultural, economic and political forces shaping the media playing field around the world, ranging from students and scholars in different disciplines, such as communication and media studies, international relations and public diplomacy, media economics and business, to practitioners operating in the media industries in non-profit or profit oriented entities, or policy makers at local, regional and international level, interested in learning more about the different activities of production, distribution and exhibition of media entertainment around the world.

Entertainment media is specifically utilized to probe the twenty-first-century global landscape, as a unique prism to analyze similarities and differences in a globalized world where driving forces of globalization meet locally situated audiences and institutions to unveil an evolving, contested space comprising global, regional and local players, whose success (or lack thereof) is determined by both their national and international dimensions. The twenty-first-century global mediascape is located at a particular juncture within the multifaceted phenomena of globalization. It is being impacted by the globalization processes of which at the same time it constitutes a major driver. The technological drivers – such as the digital revolution ushered in by the Internet – and the political drivers – such as international trade agreements – at the center of globalization processes are globalizing the media sectors not unlike other industries. At the same time, however, the increased international interconnections of the media landscapes also contribute to accelerate the other processes of globalization via the increased flows of media content facilitated by the more-and-more globalized conduits, the international distribution platforms.

Entertainment media can indeed provide a unique intellectual entry point to analyze phenomena of globalization, focusing on entertainment flows at all different levels, as these flows can be considered simultaneously a unique driver and a major consequence of globalization. An exploration on a country-by-country basis of the development of different media ecosystems can shed light on how phenomena of globalization materialize in local contexts, and to what extent different players around the world currently are, or have the potential of, successfully distributing their content internationally.

Theoretical Frameworks on Global Media Entertainment

A Brief Overview

The analyses presented in this volume aim at contributing to conversations and discussions on global media entertainment, whose academic debates in the last decades have focused on many different aspects of the international flows of media entertainment content crossing national and cultural boundaries. The collection of chapters in this volume intends to do so by focusing on 20 different media landscapes and analyzing how these conversations and debates, and the diverse theoretical lenses shaping them, materialize in different mediascapes. It is beyond the scope of this introduction to conduct a thorough literature review on all the themes investigated by the different academic voices interested in international media entertainment analyzing the topic with their own theoretical lenses and intellectual vantage points. A brief overview is offered instead, with the goal of situating the analyses presented in this volume within broader scholarly conversations.

A central aspect of the analyses conducted by an evolving body of literature on global media entertainment, within the different research foci adopted, has been to shed light on and explicate the phenomenon of the international trade imbalances of cultural goods between the West and the rest of the world, and in particular, the role of US global media conglomerates. The concept of *cultural imperialism* was introduced in scholarly conversations, within different academic fields of inquiry, when analyses of the international entertainment landscape revealed a significant imbalance generated by the flow of exports from Western economies, and the US in particular, vastly exceeding the imports from the rest of the world in all the different sectors of entertainment.

Since the 1970s research conducted by UNESCO – the United Nations Educational, Scientific and Cultural Organization – helped raise international awareness on the issue and contributed to this debate, providing voices and intellectual ammunition to the concerns and demands originating from the developing countries of the world, specifically analyzing the relationship between international communication and national development, and demanding a New World Information and Communication Order (NWICO), as indicated for example by the 82 recommendations on global communication issues provided by the MacBride Report (1980, pp. 191–233). At the same time different strands of inquiry in academia within the fields of communication, business and economics, political science and cultural studies have been analyzing and dissecting different issues in global entertainment ever since.

Within these debates Herbert Schiller's seminal works *Mass Communications and American Empire* (1992) and *Culture Inc.* (1989) identified the rise of the American *empire* as the modern reincarnation of former European colonial empires (mainly British, French and Dutch), including its primacy in the cultural industries worldwide, raising concerns of global homogeneity within a consumerist culture. Within critical studies conversations, the Frankfurt School theorists' Marxist critique of capitalism focused on the culture industry as a key component of the capitalistic economy producing culture as a commodity (Adorno & Horkheimer, 1979). Along these theoretical lines scholars analyzed the "dependence effect" (Galbraith, 1959, 1998) linking powerful and developing economies, whereas others brought to the fore and explicated the role of entertainment media in manufacturing consent internationally and generating new phenomena of imperialism in popular culture and international homogeneity as a result (see for example Galtung, 1971; Herman & Chomsky, 1988; Tomlinson, 1991; Ritzer, 1993).

Over the years many different areas of inquiry have attracted the attention of scholarly analysis, ranging from the export of US-originated TV series in Latin America and its impact (Wells, 1972) to the international diffusion of Disney comics in reproducing capitalistic values worldwide (Mattelart, 1979), for example. The central role of transnational media corporations, and Hollywood in particular (Wasko, 2003; Miller, Govin, McMurria, Maxwell & Wang, 2005), whose reach has increasingly expanded globally in the last decades, has generated multiple discussions (see for example Herman & McChesney, 1997; Demers, 2002; Thussu, 2006; Bielby & Harrington, 2008; Birkinbine, Gómez & Wasko, 2016) within the multifaceted issues originating in the analysis of the global political economy of entertainment analyzed over time by an evolving body of literature (see for example Guback, 1969; Jarvie, 1992; Vasey, 1997; Trumpbour, 2002; Havens, 2006; Straubhaar, 2007; Mirrlees, 2013; Artz, 2015; Noam, 2016; Miller & Kraidy, 2016). These conversations have raised, among other issues, the concern that cultural globalization generated by the uneven international distribution of media entertainment artifacts would be detrimental to worldwide diversity leading toward a homogenized consumer culture revolving around Western values, which would endanger local cultures around the world.

While the globalization processes unfold, local differences remain. States still matter, as pointed out by Waisbord and Morris (2001), and indeed local governments have been trying to exert their influence in shaping the flows of import and export of the creative industries, adopting specific policies (Flew, 2012; Murschetz, Teichmann & Karmasin, 2018). The regulatory framework is also in a state of flux in the new global digital mediascape as the informal media economy, operating outside the parameters indicated by international and local legislative frameworks and thriving under the radar of regulations, challenges public and private players around the world (Lobato & Thomas, 2015). Furthermore, as a result of the central role of the cultural industries both domestically and internationally in shaping the current *zeitgeist*, soft power dimensions are generated and sustained, with or without the support of local governments, within the international flow of audiovisual artifacts when images and ways of life are transported outside their original cultural *milieu* (Sigismondi, 2009 and 2018), while locally situated audiences continue to enjoy both international and locally produced entertainment.

Oftentimes globalization and localization forces intersect, and phenomena of hybridization can occur (Garcia Canclini, 1995; Kraidy, 2005), fostering transterritiorial and mulitilinguistic identities in postmodern societies and cultures around the world. These aforementioned approaches help explicate the current dynamic global cultural landscape where the end result is generated by competing and oftentimes conflicting forces, as in the case of cultural homogenization and hybridization, and successful transnational media corporation also localize their offerings to meet the demands and expectations of the local audiences within the recipient markets. In fact, within the flows of entertainment a relevant portion of content proposed to local audiences is glocalized, and academic research has analyzed and explicated relevant business practices in producing and distributing popular culture artifacts globally, such as the local adaptations of global media formats (Sigismondi, 2012; Chalabi, 2015). Within these complex dynamics, Thussu (2007) specifically brings to the fore the relevance and the impact of the emerging trends of contra-flows of non-Western media in the global landscape arena, identifying and contrasting "the 'dominant flows', largely emanating from the global North, with the United States at its core [and the] contra-flows, originating from the erstwhile peripheries of global media industries—designated 'subaltern flows'" (p.10).

The theoretical positions sketched above, and the debates stemming from these, urge us to explore an evolving landscape where transnational and local media and entertainment conglomerates play essential roles in shaping global contemporary culture, while at the same time active and culturally situated audiences meet, modify and adapt the popular culture artifacts proposed by an increasing number of delivery channels. An investigation of local cultural industries provides, then, a central piece of the international media mosaic, and a specific analysis of the most relevant media markets is necessary to paint a more complete picture of the global mediascape. Following the aforementioned conversations and debates on flows and contra-flows of entertainment, this book aims at exploring the current dynamics of the "new cartography of global communication" (Thussu, 2007, p. 26), focusing on 20 different media landscapes and their players operating at global, regional and/or local level.

In media terms "international" does not necessarily mean nor imply "global," as oftentimes cultural artifacts increasingly find in the new digital environment novel outlets of international distribution, reaching culturally and geographically distant audiences. It is necessary to conduct with magnifying glasses the analysis of different media landscapes to explore what unfolds in the international flows and contra-flows of entertainment where in addition to global players, local and regional contenders operate and coexist locally and in the crevasses between local and global. New internet-based platforms allow original distribution of entertainment, connecting distant cultures and creating consistent flows or just occasional encounters between different cultures through the production, distribution and exhibition of media entertainment. This volume aims at contribute to the understanding of the evolving global mediascape by bringing to the fore different global, regional and local perspectives operating, and thriving, in world entertainment media on a country by country basis.

World Entertainment Media: Global, Regional and Local Perspectives. Organization of the Book

Ensuing this introduction, different media landscapes are analyzed in distinct chapters organized geographically in regions – The Americas; Europe, Middle East and Africa; Asia and Oceania – followed by a final chapter drawing the conclusions and offering final thoughts and reflections. Some of the authors shared key quantitative data from the media landscape of their country when deemed appropriate to capture distinctive aspects and dimensions, while others preferred to offer an anumerical critical perspective, oftentimes presenting a specific case study to illustrate a particular uniqueness of the local cultural industry, reflecting the different approaches to the analysis of media entertainment, which comprises and benefits from different theoretical lenses and background. Media landscapes can be analyzed through economic, political, social and cultural lenses, and the approach of the different contributors underlines the variety and complexities of media entertainment in the different phases of production, distribution and exhibition.

The chapters guide the reader into a world exploration of media entertainment, delving into and analyzing the specific features of the most relevant media landscapes, including some emerging countries in the following geographical order: The Americas (Canada, US, Mexico and Brazil); Europe, Middle East and Africa (the European Union, the UK, France, Germany, Russia, Spain, Italy, Turkey, Egypt, Nigeria, and South Africa); Asia and Oceania (Japan, China, South Korea, India and Australia). While this project has solicited, and benefits as a result from, 19 original chapters (including this introduction and the concluding chapter) created specifically for this book analyzing different media landscapes, the collection includes also three previously published articles as Chapters 15, 19 and 20 (illustrating Nigeria, South Korea and India respectively) to analyze the phenomena of "Nollywood" in the Nigerian mediascape, the Korean wave [*Hallyu*] originating from South Korea, and "Bollywood" within the Indian media landscape. While there are evolving bodies of literature in academia and beyond delving into these three topics in more detail, it was deemed appropriate to insert also an overview of these unique media phenomena, whose international presence is increasingly noticeable, in this volume. An exploration of the global entertainment landscape would be less exhaustive omitting these phenomena, which contribute to the diversity of flows of entertainment crossing the globe.

The media landscapes analyzed include all the most relevant ones in economic terms: in particular, the chapters analyze the top 15 markets in the world, considering as a point of reference the box office receipts indicated by the latest available MPAA (Motion Picture Association of America) data of top international box office markets in their *THEME* (Theatrical and Home Entertainment Market Environment) comprehensive report for 2017 (MPAA, 2018, pp. 7–10). It is worth pointing out that, in economic terms, the theatrical markets (that is, revenues generated by paid admissions in theatres) are evolving unevenly around the world, with revenues in the mature US market not increasing in the past years, whereas China has been growing and poised to surpass the US. While theatrical numbers are still a key point of reference for the industry, to paint a more complete picture of the entertainment industry it is however necessary to consider also the other revenue streams generated by entertainment content (both feature-length motion pictures and TV content) distributed via multiple media platforms above and beyond movie theatres. In these dimensions, at the time of writing, the US still holds the lead in global home-entertainment consumer spending, with a significant shift from "physical" to "digital," as the number of subscriptions to online video services has been notably increasing in the past few years (MPAA, 2018, pp. 11–13), revealing the shift in entertainment consumption habits and the new preferred modalities for twenty-first-century audiences to access and enjoy media entertainment content.

The economic dimensions of the different media markets were considered in the selection of the different countries included in this volume with the intent to make sure not to omit any significant economic evolution in the global landscape, but they do not represent – of course – an evaluation of the relevance of the different landscapes nor are they meant to indicate in this book any rankings for importance among regions or countries, as the economic dimension is deemed just one of the many different aspects to be included in the analysis of media entertainment and its complex socio-political and cultural multifaceted repercussions. As a result, media landscapes currently not in the top 20 in economic terms were included in this collection (such as Egypt and South Africa, for example) to intentionally incorporate different geographical regions and their specific cultural productions.

At the end of the intellectual journey presented by the 20 different chapters, each dedicated to a specific media landscape, the final one draws the conclusion of the book, summarizing the findings of the analyses presented and identifying common trends among the different local media landscapes, with all their distinct features notwithstanding, while acknowledging the limitations of the project and suggesting future research trajectories in the study of the evolutions of the global entertainment landscape.

References

Adorno, T. & Horkheimer, M. (1979). *Dialectic of enlightenment*. London: Verso.
Artz. L. (2015). *Global entertainment media: A critical introduction*. Malden, MA: Wiley.
Bielby, D. D. & Harrington, C. L. (2008). *Global TV: Exporting television and culture in the world market*. New York: New York University Press.
Birkinbine, B., Gómez, R. & Wasko, J. (Eds.) (2016). *Global media giants*. New York: Routledge.
Chalabi, J. K. (2015). *The format age: Television's entertainment revolution*. Cambridge, UK: Polity Press
Demers, D. (2002). *Global media: Menace of messiah?* Cresskill: NJ. Hampton Press.
Facebook (2018). *Company Info: Stats*. Retrieved on March 14, 2018 from: http://newsroom.fb.com/company-info/
Flew, T. (2012). *The creative industries, culture and policy*. London: Sage.
Galbraith, J. K. (1959, 1998). The dependence effect. In J. B. Schor & D. B. Holt (Eds.). *The consumer society* (2000). New York: The New Press.
Galtung, J. (1971). A structural theory of imperialism. *Journal of Peace Research*, 8(2), 81–117. DOI:10.1177/002234337100800201
Garcia Canclini, N. (1995). *Hybrid cultures: Strategies for entering and leaving modernity*. Minneapolis, MN: University of Minnesota.
Green, M. C., Brock, T. C. & Kaufman, G. F. (2004). Understanding media enjoyment: The role of transportation into narrative worlds. *Communication Theory*, 14(4), 311–327. DOI:10.1111/j.1468-2885.2004.tb00317.x
Guback, T. (1969). *The international film industry: Western Europe and America since 1945*. Bloomington, IN: Indiana University Press.
Havens, T. (2006). *Global television marketplace*. London: BFI Publishing.
Herman, E. & Chomsky, N. (1988). *Manufacturing consent: The political economy of the mass media*. New York: Pantheon.
Herman, E. & McChesney, R. (1997). *The global media: The new missionaries of corporate capitalism*. London: Cassell.
Huizinga, J. (1949). *Homo ludens: A study of the play-element in culture*. London: Routledge.
Jarvey, N. (2017, August 23). How streaming giants are spending money for tv push. *The Hollywood Reporter*. Retrieved on May 29, 2018 from: www.hollywoodreporter.com/news/how-streaming-giants-are-spending-money-tv-push-1031885
Jarvie, I. (1992). *Hollywood's overseas campaign: The North Atlantic movie trade, 1920–1950*. Cambridge, UK: Cambridge University Press.
Kraidy, M. M. (2005). *Hybridity, or the cultural logic of globalization*. Philadelphia, PA: Temple University Press.
Lobato, R. & Thomas, J. (2015). *The informal media economy*. Cambridge, UK: Polity Press.
Lobato, R. (2019). *Netflix nations: The geography of digital distribution*. New York: NYU Press.
Lotz, A. D. (2017). *Portals: A treatise on internet-distributed television*. Ann Arbor, MI: Michigan Publishing, University of Michigan Library. DOI: http://dx.doi.org/10.3998/mpub.96996

MacBride Report (1980). *Many voices, one world: Communication and society today and tomorrow.* International Communication for the Study of Communication Problem. Paris: UNESCO.

Mattelart, A. (1979). *Multinational corporations and the control of culture: The ideological apparatuses of imperialism.* Brighton, UK: Harvester Press.

McKinsey Global Institute (2019). *Globalization in transition: The future of trade and value chains.* New York: McKinsey & Company.

Miller, T., Govin, N., McMurria, J., Maxwell, R. & Wang, T. (2005). *Global Hollywood 2.* London: British Film Institute.

Miller, T. & Kraidy, M. M. (2016) *Global media studies.* New York: Polity.

Mirrlees, T. (2013). *Global entertainment media: Between cultural imperialism and cultural globalization.* New York: Routledge.

Murschetz, P. T., Teichmann, R. & Karmasin, M. (Eds.) (2018). *Handbook of state aid for film: Finance, industries and regulation.* Cham, Switzerland: Springer International Publishing AG.

Noam, E. M. (Ed.) (2016). *Who owns the world's media? Media concentration and ownership around the world.* New York: Oxford University Press.

MPAA (2018). *THEME (Theatrical and Home Entertainment Market Environment) Report 2017.* Retrieved on May 29, 2018 from www.mpaa.org/wp-content/uploads/2018/04/MPAA-THEME-Report-2017_Final.pdf

Ritzer, G. (1993). *The McDonaldization of society.* Thousand Oaks, CA: Sage.

Schiller, H. I. (1989). *Culture Inc.: The corporate takeover of public expression.* New York: Oxford University Press.

Schiller, H. I. (1992). *Mass communications and American empire.* New York: Westview Press.

Sigismondi, P. (2009). Hollywood piracy in China: An accidental case of US public diplomacy in the globalization age? *Chinese Journal of Communication, 2*(3), 273–287. DOI:10.1080/17544750903209002

Sigismondi, P. (2012). *The digital glocalization of entertainment: New paradigms in the 21st century global mediascape.* New York: Springer Science + Business Media

Sigismondi, P. (2017). The digital transformation of international entertainment flows. In P. Messaris and L. Humphreys (Eds.) *Digital media: Transformations in human communication 2nd ed.* (pp. 247–254). New York: Peter Lang.

Sigismondi, P. (2018). Exploring translation gaps: The untranslatability and global diffusion of "cool", *Communication Theory, 28*(3), 292–310. DOI: 10.1093/ct/qtx007

Straubhaar, J. (2007). *World television: From global to local.* London: Sage.

Thussu, D. K. (2006). *International communication: Continuity and change.* New York: Oxford University Press.

Thussu, D. K. (Eds.) (2007). *Media on the move: Global flow and contra-flow.* London: Routledge.

Tomlinson, J. (1991). *Cultural imperialism.* Baltimore, MD: The John Hopkins University Press.

Trumpbour, J. (2002). *Selling Hollywood to the world: US and European struggles for mastery of the global film industry, 1920–1950.* New York: Cambridge University Press.

Vasey, R. (1997). *The world according to Hollywood.* Madison, WI: University of Wisconsin Press.

Vorderer, P., Klimmt, C. and Ritterfeld, U. (2004) Enjoyment: At the Heart of Media Entertainment, *Communication Theory, 14*(4), 388–408. DOI:10.1111/j.1468-2885.2004.tb00321.x

Waisbord, S. & Morris, N. (Eds.) (2001). *Media and globalization: Why the state matters.* Lanham, MA: Rowman & Littlefield

Wasko, J. (2003). *How Hollywood works.* London: Sage Publications.

Wells, A. (1972). *Picture tube imperialism? The impact of US television on Latin America.* New York: Orbis.

Wolf, M. (2003). *The entertainment economy: How mega-media forces are transforming our lives.* New York: Three Rivers Press.

YouTube (2018). *Press room.* Retrieved on March 14, 2018 from: www.youtube.com/yt/press/

Zillmann, D. and Vorderer, P. (eds.) (2000). *Media entertainment: The psychology of its appeal.* Mahwah, NJ: Lawrence Erlbaum Associates.

Part I
The Americas

2 Canadian TV Goes Global

Within and Beyond Cultural Imperialism

Tanner Mirrlees

Introduction: "Canadian Content: Clearly, We Want to Export"

For much of Canadian media history, the story of American cultural imperialism has pervaded critical communications research, cultural policy discourse and public common sense. Yet, for the past two decades, Canadian media executives and Federal government officials have championed the globalization of the Canadian cultural industries. In a speech entitled "Positioning Canadian Content in a Global Digital World," Quebecor Inc's CEO Pierre Karl Peladeau says: "We need to reorient our funding infrastructure from being strictly locally focused to also being export-focused" (QMI Agency, 2012). Gearing Canada's cultural industries to take on the world market, Canadian Heritage Minister Mélanie Joly concurs: "2017 will be the year of Canadian content; clearly, we want to export" (Lewis, 2017). Eager to accelerate the flow of Canadian cultural products to the US, Europe, and even China and India, Joly declares: "We are moving away from protectionism to promotion" (Lewis, 2017). Peladeau and Joly's comments point to cultural industries in Canada that are not weak and inward, but strong and rapidly expanding.

While the old and familiar story of American cultural imperialism in Canada can be told, this chapter narrates a new and less conventional story—one about the globalization of the Canadian cultural industries. It does so by way of an up-to-date overview of the national strength and international scope of the Canadian cultural industries, focusing on the economic and cultural power of the TV sector in particular. Although the story of American cultural imperialism in Canada continues to be persuasive, it fails to address changes in the current political economy of Canada's TV sector. The US is the world's strongest media centre, but Canada is much more than a weak media periphery; Canada's TV sector is substantial, prosperous and growing. There is a near one-way flow of TV shows from the US to Canada; yet, Canada's TV sector is producing TV shows with partners across borders and exporting them to the US market, and elsewhere. US-based global media giants and the US government push for and pursue cultural free trade with Canada to tear down its protectionist barriers; yet, the Canadian State protects the Canadian TV sector locally from free trade while simultaneously promoting the sector's business globally.

The Story of American Cultural Imperialism in Canada: Continuity and Change

In 1949, the Canadian Federal Government commissioned Vincent Massey's "Royal Commission on National Development in the Arts, Letters, and Sciences to assess the condition of Canada's mass media (radio, film, TV and books), arts and cultural institutions, and higher education system. In this report, American TV was described as "essentially a commercial enterprise, an advertising industry" (p. 47) and said not to serve Canada's "national needs" of "unity and understanding, and education in the broad sense" (p. 47). The Massey Commission advised the Federal Government build public institutions that would assist Canadian TV's development while protecting it "from excessive commercialization and Americanization" (Massey Commission, 1951, p. 58). In 1953, the historian Arthur R.M. Lower said: "There is no doubt in my mind that if we Canadians allow television to pass under American control and with American programs, our future will be American" (Vipond, 2011, p. 107). In 1961, CBC Radio aired a program hosted by Sydney Lamb that asked listeners: "Does watching American TV make you less Canadian?" (CBC, 2018).

From the late 1960s to early 1980s, many researchers in the political economy of communications would likely answer Lamb's question with a "yes." Observing an asymmetrical US–Canada media power relationship and a near one-way flow of TV shows from the US to Canada, they described Canada as a victim of American cultural imperialism. In *Mass Communications and American Empire*, Schiller (1969) highlighted the "domination" of Canada's "television air waves by American programs" (p. 79). In The *Geopolitics of Information: How Western Culture Dominates the World*, Smith (1980) described how "the culturally and politically debilitating effects of media dependency" were "most eloquently illustrated" by Canada, which was treated by the US as "part of a large North American market for films, television programmes and other media products" (p. 52). In *Dependency Road*, Smythe (1981) conceptualized Canada as the "world's most dependent 'developed' country" and called for the protection of Canada's "cultural screens" against "disruptive intrusion" by the US's "consciousness industries" (p. 232). For that generation of critical scholars, Canada was a case in point of the validity of the cultural imperialism paradigm. Canada seemed to already be what poorer countries might become if they failed to shield their TV broadcasters and national cultures from the US Empire's expansive cultural industries.

In addition to being a critical research paradigm, the story of American cultural imperialism has been part of TV broadcasting policy discourse in Canada. The policy story stresses that "a televisual border of difference" needs to be maintained so that Canadian citizens can see "themselves as a unique imagined community" (Tinic, 2013, p. 37). By pitting a fledgling Canadian TV industry and a benign Federal State against an ever-expanding US media Empire whose commercial TV shows threaten to erode Canadian culture, the story buttresses collaborations between the private owners of Canadian TV networks and the public officials of the Canadian State to ensure that Canadian TV firms will remain Canadian owned, and that TV broadcasters will defensively schedule Canadian TV programs that represent Canada to Canadians (Attalah, 2007, p. 325).

The story of American cultural imperialism has furthermore appeared in some recent American Studies textbooks: "the impact of American cultural imperialism is enormous—so powerful so powerful, in fact, that it frequently displaces the stories that Canadian tell themselves" (MacLean, 2010, p. 393). Although the story of American cultural imperialism in Canada continues to be told, it is not the only or best story available to tell. Over the past decade, scholars have complicated the story with fresh research on Canadian TV broadcasting policies, industries, technologies, texts and viewers (Attalah, 2007, 2009; Beaty and Sullivan, 2006; Tinic, 2005, 2013; Wagman, 2010). In this spirit, the chapter's remaining sections highlight continuity in the story of American cultural imperialism in Canada while also emphasizing significant changes to it.

Canada: A Media Periphery of Empire and a Peripheral Media Centre

The story of American cultural imperialism in Canada represents the US as a strong media centre and Canada as a weak media periphery. This is not an unreasonable premise, as the US is the world's largest media centre. According to the 2017 Forbes Global 2000 list of the world's biggest companies, seven of the world's top ten Broadcasting and Cable TV companies are based in the US: Comcast (#31), Walt Disney (#71), Charter Communications (#107), Time Warner (#153), Dish Network (#393), CBS (#459) and Viacom (#538) and Liberty Global (#591) (Forbes, 2018). Large and vertically integrated US-based globalizing media conglomerates such as Walt Disney and Time Warner are the top producers, distributors and exhibitors of TV shows around the world. Relative to the size and strength of the US media centre, Canada is a weaker and smaller periphery. Yet, this centre–periphery binary is complicated when taking stock of the powerful corporations and cultural industries based in Canada.

Presently, Canada is the globe's tenth largest economy and home to 50 of the world's biggest 2000 corporations (Forbes, 2018). The cultural industries in Canada are booming. These refer to all of the big, small and medium-sized corporations operating in Canada that produce, distribute and exhibit copyrighted cultural products for the market (with the goal of private profit) instead of for social need using capital goods (technology) and waged labour power (manual and mental skills). The core sectors include: advertising (e.g., BBDO Canada and Leo Burnett); film and TV production (e.g., Muse Entertainment, eOne, Nelvana), radio and TV broadcasting (e.g., CBC/Radio-Canada, Global TV and CTV), music (e.g., Universal Music Canada, Sony Music Canada, and Arts & Crafts), Publishing (Random House of Canada and Torstar), digital games (e.g., Capcom Vancouver, Ubisoft Quebec, and Rockstar Toronto), Telecommunications (e.g., BCE and Rogers Communications) and the Internet-Web (e.g., Google.ca and Netflix.ca). Presiding over the cultural industries are five vertically integrated corporations: BCE, Rogers, Telus, Shaw and Quebecor (CMCRP, 2017). These corporations are owned and operated by a Canadian business class, have significant links and ties to the Canadian State, employ a Canadian workforce and sell media goods and services to Canadian consumers. In 2015, 18 convergent telecom, media and internet companies accounted for 90% of all revenue; in that same year, the big five took nearly three-quarters (71.1%) of the total revenue (CMCRP, 2017). The big five companies are also global and appear on the 2017 Forbes Global 2000 list (Forbes, 2018).

Due to years of untrammeled ownership concentration, Canada's big five media conglomerates have gotten bigger, and now they exert much more power over the structure of Canada's TV sector than US companies do. BCE, Rogers, Shaw and Quebecor control almost all of the TV broadcast and pay-per-view market in Canada. Their power extends to production, as they source the creation of TV shows to in-house studios and also outsource it to a network of independents. They hold sway over the TV sector's value chain, where many types of affiliated firms interact in overlapping stages. Their production studios organize the financial and physical infrastructure for making TV shows; their distribution companies buy the rights to distribute TV shows from studios and then wholesale these rights to exhibition companies for set periods of time in specific territories and windows; their exhibition companies—TV broadcasters, pay-per-view cable firms and video-on-demand services—make TV shows available to watch by viewers through a variety of commercial windows. Most Canadians continue to watch broadcast TV on a TV set, but many are "cutting the cord" to digital stream TV shows, anytime, anywhere. Whether they are owned by one of the big five or linked to them contractually, all companies in Canada's TV sector are market oriented and pursue profit: production studios make money by selling content rights to distribution companies; distribution companies make money from selling rights to exhibitors; exhibitors make money by selling copies to consumers (and by selling access to consumer attention to advertisers).

In 2015–2016, $2.6 billion was spent on TV production in Canada, and 709 TV series were made at an average cost of $1.43 million per hour episode. In that same year, Canada's private TV broadcasters generated $7.1 billion in revenues (CMPA, 2016, p. 107). The US continues to be world system's media centre, but Canada is emerging as a peripheral media centre. Canada is currently home to powerful cultural industries, big media conglomerates and a flourishing TV sector. Canada's TV sector does not rival the US's, but this sector is nonetheless productive and prosperous.

Canadian Cultural Industries Crossing Borders: TV Exports and TV Co-Productions

The story of American cultural imperialism in Canada dramatizes a near one-way flow of media products from the US to Canada, with little to no counter-flow or audio-visual trade reciprocity.

There is some truth to this story. In 2016, the top ten TV shows watched in English Canada were American hits like *Big Bang Theory, The X-files, NCIS, Grey's Anatomy, Criminal Minds: Beyond Borders, NCIS: New Orleans* and *Quantico* (CMPA, 2016). Hollywood films usually take 94% to 99% of the Canadian box office each year and in 2015, Canadian films accounted for a little over 1% of the total box office (CMPA, 2016). The top 15 most visited websites in Canada are American, and digital giants like Google and Facebook are without rival (Alexa, 2018). Netflix and Amazon Prime Video rule the video streaming services sector in Canada, and national upstarts like BCE's Crave TV never came close to rivalling the size of their subscriber base or revenues. There is no TV trade reciprocity between Canada and the US, and Canada is probably the only country in the world where most citizens consume more foreign—American—TV than they do domestic TV shows. Lots of Canadians watch America on their screens; few Americans watch Canada on theirs. The US Empire leaves a big cultural footprint in Canada, no doubt.

Yet, there is more to the story than a one-way flow of products from the US to Canada because reverse and multi-directional media flows between Canada and the US, and Canada and other countries have been growing. Each year, the Canadian TV sector sells exhibition rights to its shows to national TV exhibitors at global TV trade fairs such as NATPE (National Association of Television Programming Executives), MIPCOM (Marché International des Films et des Programmes pour la Télévision, la Video, le Cable et le Satellite), MIPTV (Marché International des Programmes de Télévision), ATF (Asia Television Forum) and HKIFTM (Hong Kong International Film and TV Market). Next to the US, the United Kingdom, Netherlands and France, Canada is one of the world's biggest exporters of TV shows. In 2015–2016, the export value of Canadian film and TV productions increased to an all-time high of just over $3.3 billion (CMPA, 2016, p. 28). Between 2006 and 2016, the Canadian TV sector's major export markets were the US (50%), the UK (29%), France (8%) and Ireland (7%), Switzerland (2%), Netherlands (2%), Germany (1%) and Australia (1%). Although Canadian TV shows were also exported to Brazil, South Africa, Japan, India, Malaysia, Mexico and numerous other countries, the top eight export markets represent nearly 99% of all pre-sale exports of Canadian TV shows (MDR, 2016, p. 34).

Over the past 15 years, the Canadian TV sector has produced a variety of globally popular and profitable TV series. *Degrassi: The Next Generation* is "a critical and commercial success on national and international fronts" that resonated with trans-national youth culture (Levine, 2009, p. 516). *Corner Gas* not only aired in the US but was also broadcast in 26 more countries, and was acclaimed. *Little Mosque on the Prairie* debuted in 2007 and ran for six seasons in Canada and 90 other countries (Volmers, 2012). In 2016, the export value of Canadian-produced films and TV shows increased to an all-time high of just over $3.3 billion (CMPA, 2016, p. 28). In that same year, made-in-Canada TV shows such as *American Gods, Hemlock Grove, The Handmaid's Tale* and *12 Monkeys* were big in the US while Canadian sci-fi (e.g., *Orphan Black, Dark Matter, Van Helsing*), comedies (e.g., *Schitt's Creek*) and kids shows (e.g., *Johnny Test, Wild Kratts, Camp Lakebottom*) were being watched all over the world (CMPA, 2016, p. 13). In 2017, *Cardinal*, a new Canadian crime drama, was exported to hundreds of countries (Wong, 2017).

In addition to exporting TV shows worldwide, the Canadian TV sector is also producing TV shows across borders. Canada is widely recognized as a major magnet of Hollywood "runaway productions." US-based globalizing Hollywood studios have contracted out Canada's independent film and TV studios to work on thousands of entertainment products. The Canadian government, TV sector elites and sometimes even below-the-line cultural workers pull TV productions across the border with subsidies, favorable currency exchange rates, locations that are easily made to look like American locales and low labour costs. Cities such as Toronto and Vancouver are sometimes described as "Hollywood North" because of the volume of Hollywood TV production happening there. International TV hits such as *Covert Affairs, Beauty and the Beast, Nikita, The Flash, Flashpoint, Hannibal, Hemlock Grove, The Transporter* and *Lost Girl* were made in Canada, as were high-profile blockbuster films like *X-Men: Apocalypse, Deadpool* and *Suicide Squad*. In 2015–2016, Canada hosted foreign location shoots for 156 TV series. Three quarters of these were US productions. The UK and France accounted for 5% and 3% respectively, with Germany and a handful other countries accounting for the rest (CMPA 2016, p. 89). Hollywood North creates thousands of jobs for Canadian workers but Hollywood South reaps the biggest rewards of this cross-border production relationship by controlling the copyright, and the revenue. In the new international division of cultural labour, Canada is a choice service destination for Hollywood.

However, Canada is much more than an attractive production locale for footloose Hollywood studios. Canada's TV studios are also going global too, producing TV shows across borders with studios elsewhere. Many Canadian cross-border TV productions are governed by treaty co-productions, or formal partnerships bring together the studios and States of two or more countries. At present, Canada has TV co-production treaties with 54 countries including Australia, Brazil, Chile, China, Colombia, Cuba, Czech Republic, Denmark, Finland, France, Germany, Greece, Hungary, Ireland, Italy, Japan, Mexico, New Zealand, Russia, Senegal, South Africa, South Korea, Spain, Sweden, the United Kingdom and Venezuela. Treaty co-productions enable Canadian TV studios to combine their financing and creative resources with resources made available in other countries. By teaming up with studios in other countries, Canadian TV studios are able to finance and make high-budget and high-quality TV shows that flow across borders. Between 2006 and 2016, Canadian screen studios participated in over 700 treaty co-productions and in 2015, Canadian TV studios were part of 58 TV and feature film treaty co-productions. The United Kingdom, France, Australia, Germany and Ireland are Canada's main treaty coproduction partners (CMPA, 2016, p. 69). In addition to participating in treaty co-productions, Canadian TV studios also co-produce TV shows through non-treaty co-ventures.

The flow of TV shows between the US and Canada is not balanced or reciprocal, but it is not just one-way. Canada is much more than a passive importer of TV shows and subordinate service provider for Hollywood. The Canadian TV sector is strong and growing with the global media flow, exporting TV shows to the US and around the world while co-producing TV shows across borders with many partners.

The Canadian State, Policy and Regulation: A Political Boon to TV Business

The story of American cultural imperialism in Canada sometimes tells of the US State's support for the globalization of US-based media giants and its enthusiasm for seeing American TV shows travel the world. In some Canadian-inflected versions of this story, the Canadian State and media CEOs are compliant compradors to the US State and media giants: they "sellout" Canadian culture by lowering national barriers to the free-flow of American TV and reap rewards for doing so. In others, the Canadian political and business class are powerless to curb cultural free trade. Yet, Canadian political and economic elites do not simply collude with or bow down to the US State and media giants. Since the 1960s, the Canadian State's cultural policy and regulatory regime has facilitated the growth and prosperity of the privately owned cultural industries and legitimized this to the public as an expression of cultural national security (Edwardson, 2008). Presently, the Canadian State protects the Canadian TV sector from direct competition with the US-based global media giants while promoting this sector's own profit interests around the world.

The Canadian State is a boon to the business of TV. The Canadian Radio-Television and Telecommunication Commission (CRTC) protects the Canadian broadcasting sector from foreign competition by prohibiting foreign companies from owning more than 20% of one broadcaster. Furthermore, the CRTC compels TV broadcasters to daily schedule Canadian TV shows, and by regulating into existence a captive market for such products, it enables the growth of Canada's TV production sector. Telefilm Canada supports Canadian TV production with the Canada

Media Fund (CMF), which in 2015–2016, contributed $286 million to support $1.3 billion in TV production (CMPA, 2016, p. 39). Additionally, the Canadian State allocates subsidies to the TV sector. The Canadian Film or Video Production Tax Credit (CPTC) provides certified Canadian TV productions with a fully refundable tax credit, available at a rate of 25% of the expenditure on labour, so long as that labour-power is sold by Canadian workers. Provincial governments give further assistance to the TV sector. For example, the Government of Ontario's Ministry of Tourism and Sport, with its Ontario Media Development Corporation (OMDC) being "the central catalyst for the province's cultural media cluster," offers a variety of grants and tax credits to TV studios (OMDC, 2017). The Ontario Film & Television Tax Credit covers 35% of the eligible Ontario labour costs on qualifying TV shows produced in Ontario. The Ontario Production Services Tax Credit refunds 21.5% of all qualifying production costs incurred in Ontario by a TV studio. The Ontario Computer Animation & Special Effects Tax Credit cuts off another 18% of animation and special effects labour costs incurred by a company (OMDC, 2018). In 2016–2017, Ontario allocated over 500 million dollars in tax credits to 2,500 TV and film productions. Federal and provincial subvention agencies combine with municipal agencies across the major cities of Canada to give even more support the business of Canadian TV. Toronto is North America's third largest TV production centre, and the Toronto Film & Television Office is a one-stop shop for Canadian and transnational production studios searching for information about TV sector connections, subsidies, services, talent, crew and locations to shoot.

In addition to regulating and subsidizing the TV sector, the Canadian State helps this sector to go global. Since 1990s, the State has pushed for the internationalization of the cultural industries (Milz, 2007; Pennee, 1999) and presently, it works to boost Canadian cultural exports worldwide, including TV shows. Global Affairs (Government of Canada: Global Affairs, 2013) and Canadian Heritage (Government of Canada: Heritage, June 2016, August 2016)—major Federal Government agencies—try to strengthen the Canadian cultural industries globally by opening markets for them, increasing cultural exports and providing trade advice to key export-oriented firms. The State is developing an export strategy for Canadian cultural products, and the TV industry is keen to see this happen. As a recent TV industry research report titled "Exporting Canadian Television Globally" puts it: the strength of "federal and provincial agencies in promoting Canadian television programs, encouraging greater coproduction and attracting inward investment" forms "the basis for creating a robust approach to export development, one that could propel the Canadian industry forward with confidence on the global stage" (MDR, 2016, p. 4).

While the Canadian State promotes Canadian TV around the world, it also protects the TV sector from free trade. Since the early 1980s, it has fought to exempt the Canadian TV from the Canada–United States Free Trade Agreement (FTA), the North American Free Trade Agreement (NAFTA), the General Agreement on Tariffs and Trade (GATT) and the World Trade Organization (WTO). In the fall of 2005, delegates from over 180 countries (led by Canada and France) approved the UNESCO Convention on the Protection and Promotion of Diversity of the Cultural Expressions (CPPDCE), which enabled the Canadian State to exempt cultural goods (including TV shows) from free-trade agreements with the US. Some journalists frame the CPPDCE as Canada "taking a swipe at US cultural imperialism" (Henley, 2005), but it also shores up the market power of big Canadian media firms by shielding them from being taken over by bigger US media firms.

While the US State pushes audio-visual free trade around the world on behalf of the profit-interests of US-based global media giants, Canada's TV sector is not a victim of US-led cultural free trade. Rather, the Canadian State has supported the national and international economic interests of Canadian TV firms by protecting them from free trade while promoting their exports around the world.

Conclusion: Within and Beyond Cultural Imperialism

In the early twenty-first century, the US is still an Empire, and the US-based globalizing media giants are a significant source of US economic, military and cultural-ideological power worldwide (Mirrlees, 2016). The story of American cultural imperialism in Canada may continue to be told, and for good reason. The US Empire's cultural industries are larger, wealthier and more powerful than Canada's and an asymmetrical economic and cultural relationship between the US and Canada exists. One wonders how the gargantuan US security State, media-corporate sector and population would react if the situation were reversed, if the US were on the receiving end, and TV shows and films about Canada filled US screens and displaced the stories that Americans tell themselves.

Although the story of American cultural imperialism in Canada continues to be persuasive, it glosses over significant changes in the current political economy of Canada's TV sector. Canada is home to powerful national and globalizing media companies engaged in cross-border TV production, distribution and exhibition activities with firms in the US and around the world. The Canadian State oversees a formidable cultural policy and regulatory apparatus committed to assisting the Canadian TV sector's capitalist development, protecting this sector from a US takeover, and promoting its exports globally. In the early twenty-first century, Canada exists within the sphere of American cultural imperialism, but it also pushes beyond it. In this regard, Canada is neither a rival to American cultural imperialism nor a passive victim of it. Perhaps it is little bit of a cultural imperialist too.

References

Alexa. (2018, January 2). Top Ten Websites in Canada. www.alexa.com/topsites/countries/CA

Attalah, P. (2007). A Usable History for the Study of Television. *Canadian Review of American Studies*, 30 (3), 325–345.

Attalah, P. (2009). Review Essay: Reading Television. *Canadian Journal of Communication*, 34 (1), 163–170.

Beaty, B., & Sullivan, R. (2006). *Canadian Television Today*. Calgary, AB: University of Calgary Press.

CBC (2018, January 1). Does Watching American TV Make you Less Canadian? CBC News. Retrieved from www.cbc.ca/archives/entry/does-watching-american-tv-make-you-less-canadian

CMPA (Canadian Media Producers Association). (2016). *Profile 2016: Economic Report on the Screen-Based Media Production Industry in Canada*. Retrieved from https://telefilm.ca/en/studies/profile-2016-economic-report-screen-based-media-production-industry-canada

Edwardson, R. (2008). *Canadian Content: Culture and the Quest for Nationhood*. Toronto: University of Toronto Press.

Forbes (2018, January 1). Global 2000 List: 2017. *Forbes*. Retrieved from www.forbes.com/global2000/#5db50b89335d

Government of Canada: Global Affairs. (2013, June 6). Culture. Retrieved from www.international.gc.ca/trade-agreements-accords-commerciaux/topics-domaines/ip-pi/culture.aspx?lang=eng

Government of Canada: Heritage. (2016, August 23). Strengthening Canadian Content, Discovery and Export in a Digital World. Retrieved from www.canada.ca/en/services/culture/consultations/pre-consultation.html

Government of Canada: Heritage. (2016, May 27). Canadian Films' Share of the Box Office Revenues. Retrieved from http://canada.pch.gc.ca/eng/1464190351879

Henley, J. (2005, October 19). Global Plan to Protect Film Culture. *The Guardian*. Retrieved from www.guardian.co.uk/world/2005/oct/19/artsnews.filmnews

Levine, Elana. (2009). National Television, Global Market: Canada's Degrassi: The Next Generation. *Media, Culture & Society*, 31(4): 515–531.

Lewis, M. (2017, February 13). All the World's a Stage for Canadian Culture. *Toronto Star*. Retrieved from www.thestar.com/business/2017/02/13/all-the-worlds-a-stage-for-canadas-culture-says-joly.html

MacLean, A. (2010). Canadian Studies and American Studies. In J.C. Rowe (Ed.), *A Concise Companion to American Studies* (pp. 387–406). Malden, MA: Blackwell Publishing.

MDR (Maria De Rosa). (2016). Exporting Canadian Television Globally: Trends, Opportunities and Future Directions. Retrieved from https://trends.cmf-fmc.ca/research-reports/exporting-canadian-television-to-international-markets-trends-opportunities

Milz, S. (2007). Canadian Cultural Policy-Making at a Time of Neoliberal Globalization. ESC: *English Studies in Canada*, 33 (1–2), 85–107.

Mirrlees, T. (2016). *Hearts and Mines: The US Empire's Culture Industry*. Vancouver: UBC Press.

OMDC (Ontario Media Development Corporation). (2017). Year in Review: 2016–2017. Retrieved from www.omdc.on.ca/Assets/Communications/Year+in+Review/OMDC+Year+in+Review+2016–17.pdf

OMDC (Ontario Media Development Corporation). (2018, January 4). Tax Credit Statistics for 2016–17. www.omdc.on.ca/Assets/Tax+Credits/English/Tax+Credit+Statistics/Tax+Credit+Applications+Received+and+Certificates+Issued+in+2016-17_en.jpg

Pennee, D. (1999). Culture as Security: Canadian Foreign Policy and International Relations from the Cold War to the Market Wars. *International Journal of Canadian Studies*, 20(1), 191–213.

QMI Agency. (2012, October 8). Canada's TV Industry Could "Face Extinction": Peladeau. *Toronto Sun*. Retrieved from http://torontosun.com/2012/10/08/canadas-tv-industry-could-face-extinction-peladeau/wcm/25e5de16-3540-47ef-9943-4135811986a9

Royal Commission on National Development in the Arts, Letters and Sciences [Massey Commission] (1951). Report: Royal Commission on National Development in the Arts, Letters, and Sciences, 1949–1951. Ottawa: Edmond Cloutier.

Schiller, H.I. (1969). *Mass Communications and American Empire*. Boston, MA: Beacon Press.

Smith, A. (1980). *The Geopolitics of Information: How Western Culture Dominates the World*. Oxford, UK: Oxford University Press.

Smythe, D. (1981). *Dependency Road: Communications, Capitalism, Consciousness, and Canada*. Norwood, NJ: Ablex.

Tinic, S. (2005). *On Location: Canada's Television Industry in a Global Market*. Toronto: University of Toronto Press.

Tinic, S. (2013). The Borders of Cultural Difference: Canadian Television and Cultural Identity. In K. Conway and T. Pasch (Eds.), *Beyond the Border: Tensions across the Forty-Ninth Parallel in the Great Plains and Prairies*. Montreal: McGill-Queen's University Press.

Vipond, Mary. (2011). *The Mass Media in Canada*. Toronto: Lorimer.

Volmers, E. (2012, June 13). Little Mosque on the Prairie's Legacy Lives on. *Calgary Herald*. Retrieved from www.calgaryherald.com/entertainment/Little+Mosque+Prairie+legacy+lives/6771522/story.html

Wagman, I. (2010). On the Policy Reflex in Canadian Communication Studies. *Canadian Journal of Communication*, 35 (1), 619–630.

CMCRP (The Canadian Media Concentration Research Project). (2017). *Media and Internet Concentration in Canada Report, 1984–2016*. Retrieved from www.cmcrp.org/wp-content/uploads/2017/11/CMCR_Media__Internet_Concentration_27112017_Final.pdf

Wong, T. (2017, December 24). Who Says Canadian TV is Dead? 2017 Was Best Year Ever for Drama. *Toronto Star*. Retrieved from www.thestar.com/entertainment/television/2017/12/24/who-says-canadian-tv-is-dead-2017-was-best-year-ever-for-drama.html

3 U.S. Entertainment Media

Expansion Across Platforms, Industries and Borders

Paul Torre

Introduction

James Cameron's *Avatar* was released by 20th Century Fox in 2009, and launched the most recent expansion of 3-D technologies for feature films, with *Avatar* besting Cameron's *Titanic* to become the highest grossing film ever. In 2011, Disney CEO Bob Iger and COO Tom Staggs met with the *Avatar* film director, and producer Jon Landau, to discuss incorporating the world of *Avatar* into a Disney theme park. Cameron and Landau worked with Disney over the next few years, and *Pandora—The World of Avatar* opened in May, 2017 in the Animal Kingdom theme park in Orlando, Florida. In September of 2017, Cameron began production on the first of four sequels to *Avatar*, with the films set to open during December holiday weekends from 2020 to 2025. The stories, creatures, look and feel of the feature film sequels will be incorporated into *Pandora* at Disney's Animal Kingdom, and throughout Disney's global network of theme parks in the years to come (Sposato, 2018). In the summer of 2018, Disney and 21st Century Fox arrived at an acquisitions agreement, where Disney purchased select 21st Century Fox divisions and intellectual properties, and the $71 billion package included the rights to the *Avatar* universe. Initially, Disney was licensing the rights to *Avatar*, but through a merger and acquisition, Disney owns and controls an even broader array of intellectual properties ready-made for ongoing exploitation.

In the past few decades, both consolidation in the United States media industry and an influx of new competitors have been significant drivers affecting market structure and production outcomes (Crawford, 2013). In this chapter, we will discuss how U.S. entertainment media content is generated by converging industries, is transferred between platforms and across borders, and spans technologies and geographies. Traditional U.S. media companies, such as film and television studios, are now competing with the technology companies they previously relied upon, with all media companies using the Internet, and a plethora of connected devices, to reshape the entertainment media landscape.

In 1983, 50 media companies controlled 90% of the entertainment industry landscape in the United States, but by 2011 that number had collapsed to just six media companies (Holt, 2011). In 2018, just five companies controlled nine of the ten most watched U.S. cable television channels, and Disney, with its acquisition of assets from 21st Century Fox, generated half of the North American box office revenues for that year. Disney acquired select Fox media assets because they needed additional content to supply their new streaming service to compete with market share leader Netflix. A new distribution platform requires new product, and intellectual property, created or acquired, is a necessity to drive early consumer adoption and guarantee loyal customers (Havens & Lotz, 2017).

Entertainment media in the United States has expanded across platforms, industries and borders, and recent developments in the media sectors demonstrate the significance of each of these expansions. The entertainment industry in the United States began with film, incorporated over-the-air broadcasting with radio and television, and now distributes its content across technologies and industries, via cable, the Internet and mobile (Croteau & Hoynes, 2019). A historical recounting of the U.S. industry includes the development of small companies that grew organically, and/or large companies that grew through mergers and acquisitions. Some media companies have concentrated in one entertainment sector, and other companies have expanded across multiple U.S. entertainment media sectors. U.S. media industry expansion across platforms, industries and borders has been affected by changing business models, rivalry with new competitors, and shifting approaches to governmental regulation of media companies.

In analyzing entertainment media in the U.S. I will be utilizing several different disciplinary approaches, including those from media economics and critical political economy. The U.S. media industries are an amalgam of corporate and consumer practices and behaviors, with complicated market dynamics impacted by media regulation and transnational media trade (Birkinbine, Gomez & Wasko, 2017; Lee & Jin, 2018; Meehan & Torre, 2011). In this chapter, I will examine U.S. entertainment media expansion across platforms, industries, and borders, exploring past patterns and future directions.

Entertainment Media in the United States

The United States media system, broadly conceived, can be analyzed by attention to various industrial sectors. The audiovisual category includes radio, film, broadcast, cable, satellite television and streaming services. Telecommunications media includes wireline and wireless (mobile) services. Online media includes Internet service providers (ISPs) and search engines (Noam, 2016). These demarcations often distinguish between content and delivery industries, or media products vs. media infrastructures.

In focusing on entertainment media, this chapter will explore the U.S. film and television industries, and how filmed entertainment is also carried along online distribution pathways, pathways with their own designs and mandates. The media companies located in these sectors, and those contributing to this enterprise, may be legendary, or they may be relatively recent upstarts. Their interconnectedness is evidenced both by their reliance on one another, and by their inevitable competition with each other.

Studies of any manufacturing industry include value chain analysis, where the stages of research and development, production, and distribution and retail sales, are initiated according to core competencies of the firm, and then assessed for their productivity and efficiency (Kung, 2017). Entertainment products and services emerge from a manufacturing process and move to and through a distribution phase. In the film and television sectors many products are developed and produced by the major studios based in Los Angeles and New York. Some of these companies originated as traditional film studios that have retained similar functions for a century, but most of these have evolved over time (Noam, 2016). These studios have expanded and contracted, and have regularly undergone ownership and management changes. They vary in their past and present stability.

Per Figure 3.1, Disney has always been owned by the Walt Disney Company, and in 2018 it acquired 21st Century Fox, one of the original studios and a direct competitor. Columbia Pictures, founded in 1918, was sold to Coca-Cola in the 1980s, and was acquired and renamed Sony Pictures by Japanese electronics manufacturer Sony in 1989. NBCUniversal represents the 2004 combination of one of the "Big Three" television networks and a major film studio that was fully acquired by cable giant Comcast in 2013. After a failed merger with America Online (AOL) in 2000, Warner Bros. was acquired by another telecom company, AT&T, in 2017. CBS and Viacom, once conjoined and then separated, are both controlled by National Amusements. The film studio (Paramount) and television studio (CBS) may reunite in order to survive the battle for market share and scale. A relative newcomer, Lionsgate was founded in 1997, and increased its media assets with the 2012 acquisition of Summit Entertainment.

Studio Moniker	Film Unit	TV Unit	Parent Company
Disney	Walt Disney Studios	Walt Disney Television	Walt Disney Company
21st Century-Fox	20th Century-Fox Film	20th Century-Fox Television	Walt Disney Company
Sony Pictures	Sony Pictures (Columbia)	Sony Pictures Television	Sony Corporation
NBCUniversal	Universal Pictures	NBC-Universal Television	Comcast
Warner Bros.	Warner Bros. Pictures	Warner Bros. Television	AT&T
CBS		CBS Television	National Amusements
Viacom	Paramount Pictures		National Amusements
Lionsgate	Lionsgate Film	Lionsgate Television	Lions Gate Entertainment

Figure 3.1 Film and television companies in U.S. entertainment media.
(Author research based on public reporting.)

Each of the configurations and reconfigurations in Figure 3.1 indicate how the entertainment media landscape is constantly in flux, as media conglomerates jockey for position. Even as Disney initiated its play for the Fox film and television assets in 2017, Comcast, the parent company of NBC-Universal, was readying a competing offer. As discussed, Fox controlled intellectual properties based on the feature film *Avatar*, and Fox and Disney had a pre-established relationship via the *Pandora: World of Avatar* themed area in Disney's Animal Kingdom theme park. Comcast NBCUniversal had the similar basis for a deal with Fox, since Fox's television series *The Simpsons* had generated themed areas in Universal Parks and Resorts in Hollywood and Florida. Entertainment media companies in the U.S. are constant competitors, and yet constructed and positioned for occasional cooperation.

How a media conglomerate structures itself internally indicates its external business pursuits. For instance, as part of its 21st Century Fox acquisition process, the Walt Disney Company announced a strategic reorganization of its businesses into four distinct segments. The long-standing film and television segment, Studio Entertainment and Media Networks, was joined by a newly combined Parks, Experiences and Consumer Products segment, and newly formed Direct-to-Consumer and International segments. These four divisions reflect the historical evolution of the Walt Disney Company's multiple core competencies, from film to television, from theme parks to global expansion, and onto its new streaming service to counter Netflix. Disney's evolution, and corporate realignment also demonstrates the current strategy of U.S.-based entertainment media companies, a strategy predicated upon expansion across platforms, industries and borders.

U.S. Entertainment Media Expands Across Platforms

U.S. entertainment media expands across platforms via simple or complicated distribution pathways. Such distribution platforms present media content to consumers for their selection. Content that originated on one platform may migrate to another, as another iteration of that content, and another consumption opportunity. The movement may be from a traditional media platform to a newer or emerging media platform, from a feature-film theatrical exhibition space to a personal digital device, for instance. Creators of content and controllers of intellectual property may drive the distribution, or consumer preference may provide the impetus.

Entertainment products may be destined for a primary retail platform, but carefully calibrated exploitation may include secondary distribution windows, where consumers and audiences are offered another purchase opportunity. The success of entertainment media is predicated upon encouraging purchase of essentially the same product multiple times (Ulin, 2013). Entertainment media studios and other companies create products and services for media markets, and they hope that their exploitation of intellectual property generates revenues over a long period of time, across platforms, and in many markets.

Entertainment media products are costly to produce, and so a multi-stage distribution process is planned for. The distribution process for feature film offers an appropriate example. The major studios in the United States release more than 100 films per year, and they vary between films designed for broad audiences and those destined to garner a niche following. They are released into movie theaters following wide or more limited release patterns, and this theatrical release is the first platform for film distribution. Subsequent media platforms include hotels, airlines, pay-per-view, video-on-demand, pay cable channels, physical disc releases, Internet streaming, etc. This distribution pattern across media platforms is intended to offer purchase opportunities and additional revenue generation over time and space, in various retail contexts, across digital devices (Landry & Greenwald, 2018). In this process, the consumer experience changes, the price of entry fluctuates, the product shelf life is extended and the product lifecycle continues on.

For many decades the process followed a pattern of sequential distribution windows, where a specific film was available in one *exclusive* window after another. Any overlap in distribution windows would result in lost revenues, where one possible purchase might eat into another, resulting in so-called cannibalization. This careful plan to maximize revenue has significantly and rapidly changed, however. In recent years, audiences have demanded that films be available on more platforms sooner, and simultaneously. This has led to a proliferation of film distribution platforms, with films available in theaters and via Internet streaming simultaneously, for instance. With the introduction of digital platforms, and without the essential element of exclusivity, however, studios have seen a reduction in revenues across platforms (Ulin, 2013). The decline of DVD sales, which peaked in 2004, was the result of an increase in cable channel offerings, in addition to an increase in piracy, each of which negated exclusivity. Subsequent developments in online distribution platforms, such as Netflix, which launched streaming in 2007, offered video on-demand features that consumers began to expect.

With respect to television distribution, there has been an expansion across platforms, with U.S. television content available on Hulu, Amazon, Netflix and other streaming services. Digital distribution allows for direct-to-consumer business models that eliminate the "middleman" and cultivate a relationship between content controllers and customers. Consumers desire content that is available always and everywhere, across platforms and devices. An increase in audience fragmentation means that companies needs to find and woo prospects. U.S. media companies succeed when they focus on direct user relationships, by forging commercial bonds with fans, by converting data into an excellent user experience (Littleton, 2018). It is essential that media companies create compelling advertising products, and also leverage the loyalty and engagement through quality content.

In some cases, television distribution is driven by traditional content producers seeking subsequent platforms, as another stage in distribution process they initiate and control, from the original run to re-runs, or to off-network syndication, perhaps. In other cases, this form of television distribution is instigated by a new competitor, who may have initially provided a platform for others, but is now using their platform for their own original content (Basin, 2019). Netflix, which was originally a physical media delivery service competing with local

Company/Service	Year est.	Steps towards media production/distribution
Netflix Netflix streaming Netflix Originals	1997 2007 2012	First mover in online streaming. Global expansion in 2016. Content budget rises from $9 bil in 2017, to $12 bil in 2018, to a projected $15 bil in 2019.
Hulu Hulu with Live TV Disney's Hulu	2007 2017 2019	Joint venture with U.S. television program producers. Produced original programming beginning in 2011. Content budget of $2.5 bil in 2017. Disney, with 60% ownership, plans to triple spending by 2022.
Amazon Amazon Prime Amazon Instant Video	1994 2006 2011	Pre-existing audience of Amazon Prime members. Global expansion in 2016. Dozens of streaming partners through Amazon Channels. More than $5 billion was budgeted in 2018 for original content and for sports rights, with $1 bil to acquire rights and produce a *Lord of the Rings* series.
YouTube YouTube Premium YouTube TV	2005 2015 2017	Originally distributes short form videos, primarily user generated content. Premium service with ad-free access to original series and films by YouTube personalities. Also offers live television.
Facebook Facebook Watch	2004 2017	Ad revenue split with partner producers (barter system). Facebook Watch global launch in 2018. Budget of $1 bil through 2018
Apple Computer Apple streaming	1976 2019	Streaming content from $1 bil budget, featuring top talent: Oprah Winfrey, Reese Witherspoon, and Steven Spielberg. Projected spend on content of $4 bil by 2022. Streaming partners a la Amazon.
Disney Plus	2019	Contains content from Disney's family-friendly IP: Pixar, Marvel, Lucasfilm, etc. Original content budget at more than $1 bil. In tandem with Hulu (for Disney's R-rated content).
Warner Media	2019	Building on content from HBO Now and DC Universe, including the *Harry Potter* franchise, and consolidating the DramaFever, Boomerang and Filmstruck sub-scale direct-to-consumer offerings.

Figure 3.2 Emergent companies in U.S. entertainment media.
(Author research based on public reporting and analyst projections.)

video stores, successfully transitioned to an online streaming service, eventually expanding its operations around the world. Online streaming functions as another platform for distribution of television content. U.S. television producers and rights holders license content to Netflix as a domestic or global distribution platform.

Other services in the U.S. media market provide a similar service for cross-platform distribution. Hulu was developed as a partnership, with content provided by NBC, FOX, and then ABC, as well as programming from a number of cable networks. Initially and primarily functioning as a "catch-up" service, Hulu collects content from program providers, who saw the limits of their proprietary online services, and sought scale through a joint online venture. Amazon Prime, building upon the history and success of the online retailer, provides access to a deep catalog of film and television content. Some streaming services have not proven successful with U.S. audiences, including niche services like Seeso and Filmstruck. Other streaming services, from Disney, Warner Media, represent the newest competitors within the U.S. market for online television content. Figure 3.2 includes companies engaged in media distribution across platforms and industries, and media production and distribution actions taken or anticipated.

Companies that provide online distribution of film and television content do so as an extension of the original producer or rights holder. They license distribution rights for limited times, extending the reach of traditional media companies. And yet, these same distribution platforms have also developed into competitors, as Netflix, followed by Amazon and Hulu, have created their own original content. These online streaming companies have seen their licensed offerings shrink, as distribution contracts end and content is pulled from their services. Producing original content means that a streaming company can guarantee a steady supply of attractive programming, building a library and solidifying a secure business model.

U.S. Entertainment Media Expands Across Industries

The U.S. entertainment media system is structured into industrial sectors and the companies that operate within them. Media companies can be situated according to the entertainment products or services they produce or distribute. There is inevitable crossover between sectors, however, as companies expand their core business and industrial reach. At the center of the entertainment media industry there are the major studios and networks, which were originally devoted to film and then television. More recently, Internet streamers are distributing entertainment media content, as well as producing their own content. A historical recounting of the U.S. industry includes the development of small companies that grew organically, and large companies that grew through mergers or acquisitions. Some media companies have concentrated in one entertainment sector, and other companies have transitioned across multiple entertainment media sectors, expanding across media industries.

As discussed, the U.S. film studio system included a number of major and minor studios: Columbia, Disney, Paramount, 20th Century Fox, Universal, and Warner Bros. Beginning in the early 1900s, these motion picture studios established a presence on the west coast, with their soundstages and production facilities located in Hollywood and Los Angeles. Paramount Pictures, founded in 1916, launched its studio by focusing on filmmaking, but the company acquired film theaters soon thereafter, building its capabilities from production to distribution via its network of theatrical exhibitors. Expanding across industries offered access to new markets, and through vertical integration allowed for the benefits of corporate synergies along the media industries value chain.

Beginning in 1954, Walt Disney promoted its film and theme-park developments on Sunday evening broadcasts on network television, as *Walt Disney's Disneyland, Walt Disney Presents* and *The Wonderful World of Disney*. In 1996, Disney acquired Capital Cities/ABC (including the cable network ESPN), and was able to create and distribute content for television.

In 1999, Viacom, a pay-TV network company, acquired the broadcaster CBS. As with Disney's acquisition of ABC, and then FX and the National Geographic cable channels, the key is distribution and the ability to create a pipeline that delivers advertising, along with programming, all across the demographic spectrum. For Viacom, this capability extended from young to old, from their youth-oriented cable channel, MTV, to the oldest-skewing television network, CBS. Viacom's media empire reaches across multiple industries: movies, broadcast television, cable television, radio, billboards and the Internet.

More recent expansions across industries include Comcast's purchase of NBC-Universal in 2011, and AT&T's move to buy Time Warner in 2017. AT&T's acquisition of Warner Bros. was a cross-sector expansion, where a media-related company in the business of telephony and cable television shifted its efforts up the entertainment media value chain, from distribution to production to development. The benefits and synergies of entertainment media expansion across industries is clear in the joint efforts of AT&T and Warner Bros. to promote the second *Fantastic Beasts* film, *The Crimes of Grindelwald*. Prior to the opening, in November of 2018, the marketing and distribution support included AT&T retail stores with *Fantastic Beasts* posters and interactive displays; a dedicated DirecTV on-demand channel for Warner Bros. *Harry Potter* and *Fantastic Beasts* movies; sweepstakes for tickets and travel to the Hollywood premiere; advance screenings for AT&T customers in major cities; and exclusive film-related content across AT&T's digital channels (Spangler, 2018). In many ways, as with the Disney–Fox merger, these recent expansions across industries are attempts to reconfigure and reboot the traditional media landscape to combat the rise of streaming media competitors.

Beyond the major studios and their film and television divisions, and in addition to the cable companies and the streaming media companies, there are four technology companies that are exerting increasing influence in the U.S. entertainment media landscape. Alphabet (Google), Amazon, Apple and Facebook are playing an ever-larger role in the production and distribution of entertainment media content, functioning as partners and competitors of film and television producers and distributors. Figure 3.2 displays these companies and the steps they have taken in their expansion across industries.

In 2017, Apple hired two Sony Pictures Television executives, setting them up as heads of worldwide video programming with a $1 billion budget to develop original programming for a Subscription Video on Demand (SVOD) service. For this initial foray, Apple planned to launch up to ten shows in the first year, working with Jennifer Aniston, Reese Witherspoon, Steven Spielberg, Damien Chazelle, Kristen Wiig and M. Night Shyamalan (Goldberg, 2018). In addition to the executives hired away from Sony, Apple poached executives from a number of other traditional and streaming media companies, including talent versed in international television development, as Apple is focused on global television distribution. The category of entertainment media in the United States has expanded to include technology-based companies, and multiple companies now bridge the creativity/technology divide.

Regulation of U.S. Entertainment Media Expansion

The entertainment industry in the U.S. is regulated by several key government agencies, including the Federal Communications Commission (FCC), the Federal Trade Commission, the Department of Justice, and the U.S. Congress. Nonetheless, the entertainment industry wields significant power within the U.S. political economy. For instance, the 1996 Telecommunications Act, passed by the U.S. Congress, adjusted television broadcast station ownership caps, leading to a series of mergers, allowing film studios to merge with TV networks, TV networks to acquire cable channels, and electronics manufacturing companies to expand into media. This deregulatory action, allowing for new pairings, included Disney and ABC, and Westinghouse and CBS.

From 2011 to 2013, the FCC and Department of Justice, approved the Comcast–NBCUniversal merger in stages. In 2018, however, that merger was subject to renewed scrutiny, with rival cable operators charging Comcast with anti-competitive misconduct. Restrictions were put in place when the merger was initially approved, but the restrictions governing corporate behavior were short-lived and expired. Subsequently, Comcast was accused of questionable business tactics, such as withholding NBC's television programming from competing cable providers.

During the 2017 review of the merger between AT&T and Time Warner, the U.S. Justice Department argued against the coupling, claiming that control of Time Warner, and HBO and TBS, would allow AT&T to charge its rivals more for channel carriage. In the assessment of the Justice Department, this would limit the growth of innovative, next-generation entrants that could offer alternatives and substitutes to AT&T's traditional pay-TV model. In evidence presented at the trial, the Justice Department argued that AT&T would have greater bargaining leverage since the company could threaten to retract Time Warner content, pulling it from rival distributors during negotiations. In this scenario, customers would be inclined to drop their current providers and switch to AT&T services like DirecTV in order to watch its content. The Justice Department claimed that the AT&T–Time Warner merger would restrict competition and negatively impact American consumers.

Nonetheless, the AT&T–Time Warner merger was allowed to proceed, with the Department of Justice overruled by a Circuit Court ruling. In November of 2018, HBO pulled its content from DISH and DISH-Sling, the main competitors to AT&T's DirecTV and DirecTV Now, underscoring the Justice Department concerns about the merger. U.S. entertainment media expansions across industries are subject to regulatory approval, but in recent decades deregulatory policies have been more prevalent, underscoring the significant impact of entertainment industry lobbying efforts.

U.S. Entertainment Media Expands Across Borders

The history of film and television distribution across borders has always included attention to U.S. entertainment media content as a dominant force throughout the world. During the last few decades, however, we have seen increased influence and inroads from other regional and global players across the entertainment media landscape (Lee & Jin, 2018). Nowadays, expansion across borders means reaching out to new markets that may or may not be receptive to U.S. entertainment media. Defining and limiting the borders and boundaries of U.S. entertainment media presents another challenge, considering the evolution of entertainment media sectors and the transnational flow of media content.

Comcast was Disney's chief rival in pursuing a merger with 21st Century Fox. For Comcast, seeking to acquire the Fox assets, with its European satellite services, was principally about building Comcast's international businesses. In the end, Comcast was able to acquire a majority stake in Sky Broadcasting, giving the U.S. cable provider, film studio and television company access to satellite and streaming television services across borders. With Sky, Comcast secured one of Europe's largest media companies, expanding its reach to 23 million customers across five countries, including Britain, Germany and Italy.

There are numerous recent examples of U.S. entertainment media expanding across borders. Beginning in 2010, Warner Brothers Television purchased a majority stake in the U.K. production studio Shed Entertainment, and by 2014 it had taken full control and renamed the unit Warner Brothers Television UK. The television studio continued its acquisition streak by spending $273 million for Eyeworks, a coalition of international television production units based in the Netherlands that same year. Also in 2014, 21st Century Fox engineered a merger between the U.K.'s Shine and the Netherlands' Endemol, acquiring the new entity and rechristening it, EndemolShine Group. These acquisitions by Warners and Fox of these international assets provided these companies with new development activities, new content and new international expertise in entertainment media production and distribution. These expansions across borders also made both companies more attractive acquisition targets, as AT&T bought Time Warner, and Disney purchased the Fox assets. Warners' HBO unit also expanded across borders into Canada in 2018, with a direct-to-consumer, over-the-top (OTT) package. Previously HBO was tethered to a cable service, but with this freestanding offering, HBO was better positioned to directly compete with Netflix and Amazon Prime.

In 2014, Netflix debuted in six European nations: Germany, France, Luxembourg, Belgium, Austria and Switzerland. The streaming service expanded into southern Europe in 2015, with launches in Italy, Spain and Portugal, and in January of 2016 Netflix announced new service in 190 additional countries. Netflix may be available globally, but it has struggled to license content globally. Netflix offered 8,500 titles available on Netflix in the U.S. in 2016, but only 3,000 in the U.K. Series offered in one country are often not available in others, and Netflix establishes separate packages for each territory. The push to develop original content is directly connected to the importance of controlling worldwide rights to programming.

As they have expanded abroad, Netflix and other U.S.-based streaming services faced pragmatic distribution challenges, depending upon the condition of the territory's Internet infrastructure. Australia, India, Cuba and many other territories did not have sufficient broadband service at the time of the launch. When Netflix launched in Russia in 2015, the company discovered that while customers in Moscow had high-speed broadband service, in many other parts of the country potential Netflix customers had Internet service far below Netflix's technical requirements for stable streaming.

Amazon Prime Video expanded around the globe in 2016 extending its reach beyond the U.S., the U.K., Germany, Austria and Japan to 200 territories, where the service was included with Prime or as a low-cost add-on subscription service. In the U.S., Amazon Prime Video offered 18,000 titles in 2016, but as with Netflix, Amazon did not have the rights to the vast majority of those titles.

Media companies based in the United States expand across borders and acquire assets abroad as a way to breach barriers to entry, and extend their reach into international markets. As they reach new markets, U.S. media companies encounter new challenges, and are required to develop innovative strategies.

Challenges Facing U.S. Entertainment Media

In this chapter, I have examined U.S. entertainment media expansion across platforms, industries and borders, exploring these past patterns. With respect to future directions, entertainment media companies are facing two important challenges as they expand and compete across these barriers.

First, there is the pressure on U.S. entertainment media companies to achieve appropriate scale. Developing critical mass and acquiring requisite assets is key to the ability to expand across platforms and industries. This is exemplified by Disney's multiple acquisitions, of Pixar, then Marvel, then LucasFilm, then BamTech, and then the Fox assets. Each step provided Disney with content for expansion across platforms, and each represented a movement across industries: to 3-D animation, comics, special effects, Internet distribution, and theme park expansion.

Second, the competitive arena for entertainment media within the United States is increasingly a zero-sum game, as there is little room to grow in the saturated domestic media market (PricewaterhouseCoopers, 2018). The merger landscape has turned into a fight for assets, with Disney CEO Bob Iger, New Fox's Rupert Murdoch, Comcast's Brian Roberts, and AT&T leadership, scrambling to acquire the few businesses remaining that will help their companies beat back Netflix and Google and Facebook, and allow them to expand across borders to less saturated media markets. Global expansion requires new and innovative strategies and U.S. media companies may not find immediate success in reaching audiences abroad.

The new wave of consolidation, and the strategy of expansion across platforms, industries and borders, indicates that large companies that choose to compete will have to develop ever greater breadth and depth. This is what undergirds the Disney–Fox and AT&T–Time Warner mergers, and the ongoing merger talks between CBS and Viacom. Partnerships with technology companies are also essential, even as those technology companies expand into traditional entertainment media industries, as Apple has, with its $1 billion war chest. As U.S. entertainment media moves towards the 2020s, it is likely that additional mergers will occur, with smaller companies, like Sony and Lionsgate, becoming acquisition targets. Competition within the streaming sphere will also increase, as services from Apple, Disney/Hulu and WarnerMedia clash with Netflix and Amazon. In the battle to attract audiences, control of entertainment distribution is equally as essential as control of entertainment content.

References

Basin, K. (2019). *The business of television*. New York: Routledge.
Birkinbine, B. J., Gomez, R., & Wasko, J. (Eds.). (2017). *Global media giants* (1st ed.). New York: Routledge.
Crawford, S. (2013). *Captive audience: The telecom industry and monopoly power in the new gilded age*. New Haven, CT: Yale UP.
Croteau, D. & Hoynes, W. (2019). *Media/society: Technology, content, and users*. Los Angeles, CA: Sage Publications.
Goldberg, L. (2018, June 28) Apple's big TV push: A comprehensive guide to all its programming (so far). Retrieved from www.hollywoodreporter.com/live-feed/apples-tv-push-a-guide-all-programming-far-1123806
Havens, T. & Lotz, A. D. (2017). *Understanding media industries* (2nd ed.). New York: Oxford University Press.
Holt, J. (2011). *Empires of entertainment: Media industries and the politics of deregulation, 1980–1996*. New Brunswick: Rutgers University Press
Kung, L. (2017). *Strategic management in the media: Theory to practice* (2nd ed.). Los Angeles, CA: Sage Publications.
Landry, P. & Greenwald, S. (2018). *The business of film* (2nd ed.). New York: Routledge.
Lee, M. & Jin, D.Y. (2018). *Understanding the business of global media in the digital age*. New York: Routledge.
Littleton, C. (2018, August 21). How Hollywood is racing to catch up with Netflix. Retrieved from https://variety.com/2018/digital/features/media-streaming-services-netflix-disney-comcast-att-1202910463/
Meehan, E. & Torre, P. (2011). Markets in theory and markets in television. In J. Wasko, G. Murdock, & H. Sousa (Eds.), *The handbook of political economy of communication*. Maldon, MA: Wiley-Blackwell.
Noam, E. M. (2016). *Who owns the world's media? Media concentration and ownership around the world*. New York: Oxford University Press.
PricewaterhouseCoopers (2018). Perspectives from the global entertainment and media outlook 2018–2022. Retrieved from www.pwc.com/gx/en/entertainment-media/outlook/perspectives-from-the-global-entertainment-and-media-outlook-2018-2022.pdf
Spangler, T. (2018, October 17) AT&T cranks up promo engine for "Fantastic Beasts: The Crimes of Grindelwald". Retrieved from https://variety.com/2018/film/news/att-fantastic-beasts-the-crimes-of-grindelwald-jk-rowling-1202983215/
Sposato, S. (2018, August 13). Interview: "Avatar" film producer Jon Landau talks sequels & Pandora – The World of Avatar at Walt Disney World. Retrieved from https://insidethemagic.net/2018/08/interview-avatar-film-producer-jon-landau-talks-sequels-pandora-the-world-of-avatar-at-walt-disney-world/
Ulin, J. (2013). *The business of media distribution: Monetizing film, TV, and video content in an online world* (2nd ed.). Waltham, MA: Focal Press.

4 Mexico

A Historically Asymmetrical Media Context

Humberto Darwin Franco Migues and Guillermo Orozco Gómez

Mexico is, and will be until 2020, the second largest telecommunications and broadcasting business market in Latin America, second only to Brazil. In 2016, for example, this sector obtained profits of 22.8 billion dollars (PwC, 2017). One of its main attractions lies in the total portion of the population that can access not only the traditional media, but also the "new" communication platforms. In Mexico, a country with 120 million inhabitants, at least 63% of the population (70 million Mexicans approximately) are Internet users (AMIPCI, 2017), while the radio and open TV audiences reach 86% of the population, that is, 103 million people (IFETEL, 2017).

This penetration capacity has made of the telecommunications sector one of the country's economic pillars, at least for the last federal administration (2012–2018), which bet on it and in 2014 passed and promulgated a structural telecommunications and broadcasting reform. The reform replaced the dated "Ley de Medios" (Media Law), which had been in effect since the moment it was enacted in 1967.

The most important changes of this reform that gave rise to the new "Ley Federal de Telecomunicaciones y Radiodifusión" ("Federal Telecommunications and Broadcasting Law") were: 1) creating an autonomous and independent body to regulate the sector: the Instituto Federal de Telecomunicaciones (Federal Telecommunications Institute), IFETEL. Side by side the Comisión Federal de Competencia Económica (Federal Commission of Economic Competition) (COFECO) was founded, which can intervene economically in the monopolistic structures in the sector. Both bodies represent a significant step forward since it is no longer the executive that regulates the sector directly, but rather specialized autonomous bodies; 2) removing the prohibitions against foreign investors participating within the sector, since it now allows investment that is 100% foreign in telecommunications and 49% in broadcasting; provided that there is a certain measure of reciprocity with the countries involved; and 3) establishing conditions for competition to prevent the preponderance of any company; that is, the law establishes that no single company can hoard more than 50% of the market.

This, no doubt, meant a fundamental change in the Mexican media context which had historically been characterized by having monopolistic figures (Orozco, 2005). On the one hand, the company Televisa hoards over 80% of the broadcasting market, which includes the radio, open and private television and, on the other hand, Carlos Slim (one of the wealthiest men in the world, according to *Forbes* magazine) through his company América Móvil owns over 90% of the telecommunications sector, clearly dominating the services of landline and mobile telephony and the Internet (Orozco and Hernández, 2011).

The Ley Federal de Telecomunicaciones y Radiodifusión (The Federal Telecommunications and Broadcasting Act) was enacted on June 10, 2013 and it came into effect on August 13, 2014. One of the first actions of the IFETEL, the new regulating body on the subject of telecommunications and broadcasting, was to declare Televisa and América Móvil "predominant economic agents" (Orozco and Franco, 2015), which is why they have been compelled to disintegrate (defragment) to yield the way to new competitors. Although this is not yet happening, it would mean that the two great Mexican media monopolies are coming to an end, at least as we have known them. This loss of "preponderance" in a sector, however, opened up the possibility for the media companies to participate in other sectors where they had been forbidden to invest. For example, since the reform, Televisa has a presence in the telecommunications market and they provide Internet and landline/cellular telephony through their company Izzy. In turn, now has the power to invest in private television, which it does through its multiplatform ClaroTV.

Despite the prohibition in the Act, both companies continue to be predominant, since in legal reforms that occurred between 2014 and 2016 amendments were made for predominance to be in a company's overall participation in the market and not just in a single sector, which cause Televisa and America Móvil to be predominant in their sectors but not in the overall set of services they provide. This means that the monopolies they own not only remain intact but also have diversified and increased in other sectors and services (OBITEL, 2016).

The reform also passed measures known as "must offer" and "must carry", which compel the open TV networks to give their free signals to those cable systems that request them, and the company then asks them all, without exception, to broadcast all the open television national and local channels in the cities where they offer their services. This measure put an end to the dispute between open TV networks and the cable or satellite television systems, because since 2011 both Televisa and TV Azteca had charged excessive fees for airing their signals on these systems.

The reform also provided for the opening up of competition, with new tenders for the 700 MHz band and open digital television, which paved the way for the tender of two new national television networks. That is how on October 17, 2016 the third national open television network, Imagen TV, started airing. This company belongs to Grupo Imagen, one of the most important radio consortiums in Mexico.

There was an important change in the system of concessions as well, because the model of concessions (trade usufruct) and permissions (non-profit conditioned usufruct) was changed to a modality of "single concessions", thereby broadening the possibility for concessionaires to be able to "provide all kinds of services through their networks". This allowed, for example, Televisa to enter the telephony market, and América Móvil the television market, thus putting an end to the dispute that both monopolies maintained with each other and with the government, who for years had refused to modify the concession deeds of both monopolies.

Another factor that also modified the Mexican media system was that the reform now recognizes four different models of communication: commercial, public, social and private. However, the radioelectric spectrum was not modified – as in other Latin American legislations – so that each model could have an equal percentage; that is why public/citizen communication has remained outside this new legislation, because

> the reform deprives non-corporate actors of favorable conditions to access radio and television concessions –which are, consequently, not very competitive in commercial terms, even though they are relevant in the social sphere– such as universities, state and municipal governments and aboriginal communities.
>
> (La Jornada, 2013)

According to the Federal Government, the Telecommunications Reform brought about a reduction of the prices of landline and cellular telephony, since it eliminated long distance rates, roaming and interconnection rates. This meant yearly savings totaling 20billion pesos for Mexicans. Another benefit that the Mexican State boasts about is the fact that the penetration level of wireless broadband has doubled, going from 23 to 43 users per 100 inhabitants, one of the highest in Latin America.

In the ceremony celebrating the fourth anniversary of this reform, Mexican President Enrique Peña Nieto (2012–2018) pointed out that the sector showed a sustained increase of 10% annually, greater than that which the Mexican economy as a whole experienced (6% yearly) (Sánchez, 2017).

Despite the apparent bright outlook of this reform, authors such as Gómez and Sosa (2010), explain that the problem about legislation that aims to regulate the media and telecommunications in Mexico is that:

> there have not been any democratic mechanisms and channels that allow participation of the different social agents – since the civil society is excluded –, to take part in the processes and contribute to the construction of public policies on the subject of audiovisual and communication systems in general.
>
> (Gómez, 2008, p. 203)

And that is explained by the fact that the changes in form and content in the radio telecommunications sector have been motivated by political circumstances rather than by the acknowledgement of communication as a fundamental right in the country's democratic development (Orozco, 2012).

An X-Ray of the Mexican Media Ecosystem

Along with the telecommunications reform, on December 31, 2015 the "analog switch-off" was implemented in the country, thus putting an end to traditional television and yielding the way to Digital Terrestrial Television (DTT), which meant a significant change in the Mexican media context because it multiplied the number of television channels and radio stations by defragmenting analog signals. The standard that was chosen for DTT was ATSC (promoted by the USA in countries such as South Korea, Canada and Taiwan).

The implementation of this transition entailed the Mexican state delivering ten million TV sets that were distributed to low-income households; today IFETEL explains that 93% of households in Mexico have a digital TV set and/or a set-top box signal converter. The government's investment, so that no Mexican was left without television, was 19 billion pesos (IFETEL, 2017).

After the "analog switch-off", there were 821 open television channels and 1,745 radio stations; a historical figure for the country, which before 2015 only boasted 149 television channels and 1,352 radio stations.

In the case of television, of the 821 TV channels, 672 correspond to digital channels, while 149 correspond to open signal television. Of these TV stations, 460 have a concession (all of them DTT); 328 are licensees (184 DTT and 144 open signal); 20 are public (15 in DTT and 5 open signal) and just 3 are social media. All of them air digitally.

Table 4.1 Open Television National Networks in Mexico

Private Networks *(Channels 6)*	*Public Networks* *(Channels 3)*
Televisa (Channels 2, 5 and 9)	Once Tv (Channel 11)
TV Azteca (Channels 1 and 7)	Conaculta (Channel 22)
Imagen Tv (Channel 3)	Una voz con todos (Channel 14)
Total number of TV networks = 9	

Source: OBITEL (2017).

As to the radio, of the 1,745 stations, 1,345 air on Frequency Modulation (FM) and 393 on Amplitude Modulation (AM). Of the total number of stations, 1,307 are concessional; 416 are licensees; 14 have a social character; and 8 have a public profile.

Both in radio and television, and despite the "analog switch-off", the monopoly and oligopoly scheme continues to predominate, both in terms of ownership of signals and market presence; in the case of television, the emergence of the third national network, Imagen TV, has not meant actual competition in terms of ratings for the two already existing networks, Televisa and TV Azteca, since the latter two continue to predominate in audience preference in the two most important TV formats on Mexican television: sport and fiction.

In the specific case of TV fiction and, according to Observatorio Iberoamericano de Ficción Televisiva (OBITEL), during 2016 and 2017 there was an evident difference between both networks, since no TV Azteca fiction production ranked among the 20 most viewed shows, because its series or telenovelas did not surpass six ratings points. In turn, Televisa continues to dominate this sector and its productions boast a viewership average ranging from 14 to 20 points; TV Azteca continues to have preference levels ranging from 9 to 14 points. Both networks have made up what has been called the Mexican "TV duopoly" since 1997 (Sinclair and Straubhaar, 2013).

Televisa and TV Azteca together not only concentrate 70% of TV signals in Mexico, but they are also the only companies to reach 97% national coverage. Recently, public channels such as TVUNAM, Canal 22, OnceTV and the recently created Sistema Mexicano de Radiodifusión (Mexican Broadcasting System) (SMR), have attained a veritable feat: their signals reach 65% of the country. This means a historical achievement, which opens up unheard-of possibilities of non-commercial TV presence in most of the Mexican territory.

In the field of the radio, the story is very similar, except that instead of a predominant presence of two companies there are nine corporate groups who have more than 50% of the country's radio stations in their power. Among them, the following stand out: Acir Group, Radiorama, CMR Group, Ramsa Group and Radio Centro Group. The latter even tried to obtain the fourth national television network; however, their economic solvency could not be proved to ensure the survival of this new TV network and, consequently, the concession was refused to them.

This oligopolistic organization of radio has remained almost intact in Mexico, since the main modifications on the subject of broadcasting have concentrated on television and there are few regulations in this sector. According to the Asociación de Agencias de Medios (Media Agency Association), the radio concentrates between 9% and 10% of the advertising market in Mexico,

Table 4.2 Main National Radio Networks in Mexico

Radio Groups	Number of Stations
Acir Group	169
Radiorama	116
CMR Group	94
Ramsa Group	74
Radio Centro Group	68
Televisa Radio	64
Corporadio	52
Grupo Fórmula	52
MVS Radio	27
Radio México Group	27
Multimedios Group	21
Total of networks: 11	**Stations:764**

Source: Our table, content from IFETEL (2017).

Table 4.3 The Main Pay-Television Companies in Mexico

Paid-For TV Companies	Number of Subscribers
Televisa Group	
Cablecom	
Cablemas	
Cablevisión	
Cablevisión RED	
SKY	10,598,262
TI	3,264,285
DISH/MVS	2,929,993
Megacable	437,380
Total Play	123,882
MaxCom	43,436
TvRey	23,052
Ultravisión	24,436
Axtel	17,733
AireCable	
Total of companies: 9	**17,452,459**

Source: Our table, content from IFETEL (2017).

in such a way that every year they obtain profits of between approximately five and six billion pesos (AAM, 2016).

As for pay-television, both cable and satellite TV, there are nine companies that dominate nationwide, which render this service to 17,452,459 households. This means that 66% of households in Mexico already boast a private television service, and it has happened this way because policies such as Triple Play (integrated services of paid-television, landline telephony and the Internet) have favored its growth (LAMAC, 2017). In fact, the Competitive Intelligence Unit (CIU), has described Mexico as the Latin American country with the lowest cost for this service, since here – as an average – people pay 26.3 dollars, while the average for the region is 42.7 dollars (CIU, 2017); that is why pay-television is the telecommunications business that has grown the most in the last few years.

Televisa, through companies such as Cablemás, Cablevisión and Sky, owns 61% of the market, which makes them predominant but also monopolistic enterprises; nevertheless, Televisa Group has not been punished in any way, shape or form.

Landline and mobile telephony markets, and Internet services do not escape these asymmetrical practices, since multinational América Móvil hoards the sector, which, through its companies Telmex and Telcel dominates both landline and cellular telephony services.

Table 4.4 Main Cellular Telephony Companies in Mexico

Telephony Companies	Number of Users
Telcel	72,641,312
Telefónica	25,096,517
AT&T	12,669,857
Total of companies: 3	**Stations: 110,407,686**

Source: Our table, content from IFETEL (2017).

Table 4.5 Main Landline Telephone Companies in Mexico

Telephone Companies	Number of Users
Telmex	19,297,968
Megacable	1,249,848
Telefónica	791,391
Total of companies: 3	**Stations: 20,548,998**

Source: Our table, content from IFETEL (2017).

In the case of cellular telephony, there are 111,565,582 active lines in Mexico; this means that 92% of the country's population has access to a cell phone. Of these active lines, 65% have the service provided by Telcel (América Móvil); 22% through the Spanish enterprise, Telefónica; while AT&T provides the service for 11% of the users. These three companies concentrate 98% of the cellular telephony in Mexico.

In landline telephony, monopolistic practices tend to repeat themselves, since two companies monopolize the entire operation for 70% of the landlines since they own collectively 19,297,052 active lines, of which TELMEX owns 12,333,698 lines and Megacable, 1,249,848.

The main broadband Internet (both landline and mobile) service providers in Mexico are again Telcel, Telefónica and AT&T, since they own 54,503,017 of the 55,852,061 subscriptions existing in Mexico.

Despite all the growth, and according to the Asociación Mexicana de Internet (Mexican Internet Association) (AMIPCI), Internet penetration in Mexican society is 63%. Of this percentage, 52% stays logged onto the Internet – as an average – for eight hours a day, which exceeds the three hours dedicated to television and two hours fifty minutes to the radio. The most common, repeated practice among Mexican Internet users is accessing social networks, specifically Facebook, Twitter and WhatsApp (AMIPCI, 2017).

Table 4.6 Main Mobile and Landline Broadband Companies in Mexico

Mobile Broadband	
Telephone Companies	Number of Users
Telcel	54,503,017
Telefónica	1,018,886
AT&T	1,0899,214
Total of companies: 3	**55,852,061**

Source: Our table, content from IFETEL (2017).

Landline Broadband	
Telephone Companies	Number of Users
Telmex	8,293,725
Cablemás	609,187
Cablevisión	555,373
Total of companies: 3	**55,667,577**

Source: Our table, content from IFETEL (2017).

The Rights of the Audience: A Future in the Hands of the Media

In Mexico, the executives of large media organizations have historically and systematically brandished the labels of censorship and freedom of expression as a means of exerting pressure when a regulatory and/or legislative framework seeks to regulate practices that are in violation of citizens' and audiences' rights. This has occurred not only with the different modifications that preceded the 2013 Reforma en Telecomunicaciones y Radiodifusión (Reform in Telecommunicatios and Broadcasting), but also with respect to the modifications to the Reglamento de Radio y Televisión en Materia Electoral (Radio and Television Regulations for Electoral Matters) proposed by the extinct Instituto Federal Electoral (Federal Electoral Institute) (IFE) in 2008.

The truth is that this was not an attempt against freedom of expression but rather a regulation that modified, among other things, the acquisition of electoral publicity, by third parties granting to IFE the unique faculty to acquire airtime during the electoral processes.

One of the main legal setbacks occurred during 2017, when the Union Congress decided unilaterally to modify the rights of audiences, which, for the first time, were provided for in the Ley Federal de Telecomunicaciones y Radiodifusión (Federal Law on Telecommunications and Broadcasting), modified in such a way that their observance and enforcement will now involve a process of self-regulation by the media rather than being part of an observance exercise by the regulatory bodies and, indirectly, by the citizenry. This entails leaving in the hands of the media two very important issues: 1) the process for electing the audience ombudsman, and 2) determining rights by virtue of the ethical codes that each medium in particular builds; that is, even though there already are parameters and rights that are perfectly well described in law, a "vote of confidence and good faith" would be given to the media owners so that each medium make their own adjustments.

The audience ombudsman of the Sistema Universitario de Radio, Televisión y Cinematografía de la Universidad de Guadalajara (University System of Radio, Television and Cinematography of the University of Guadalajara), Gabriel Sosa Plata, pointed out, with respect to these changes:

> This way, if any of the audiences' rights is violated, the IFT will not be able to interfere. At the same time, the audiences' ombudsmanship of the station where the violation occurred, will be able to analyze the case and if necessary give some recommendations to repair the damage, but no matter its seriousness, it might go unattended by the concessionaire without any consequences whatsoever. In addition to the latter factor, with the reform it is more likely for there to be ombudsmanships in name only, without the autonomy or resources for undertaking their function; figureheads.
>
> (Sosa, 2017, p. 2)

The legislation, in the words of Sosa Plata, would be a beautiful letterhead under which the relevance of the rights of audiences is made public, but in practice it is little, or no, good advocating their rights. The most important among these rights is that they be told the truth without manipulation, but this is a right that will not be guaranteed because the reform itself decided to eliminate the criteria that compelled the media, specifically in the area of news, to differentiate clearly between information and publicity, and between information and personal opinion.

In the second of these cases, article 15 of the Lineamientos de los Derechos de las Audiencias (Guidelines for the Audiences' Rights) that had been proposed by IFETEL was never passed due to the controversies presented against it, both in the Senate and by the Republic's Presidency. In these legal processes – which will now be very difficult to reverse – it has been established that:

> To differentiate clearly news information from its presenter's opinion, the person who is providing that information should warn the audiences at the moment it is presented, in a clear and explicit manner, that the statement made or to be made is an opinion and it is not part of the news information presented.
>
> (Sosa, 2017, p. 2)

This would be a way of differentiating, and not a previous measure to censor, as the TV networks have wanted to assume. It was discarded simply because it was considered to be an attempt against the media's and the communicators' freedoms of expression.

That is how they also discarded the the right of Mexican audiences to be told sufficiently clearly whether what is being aired is reported news information or simply paid-for publicity. With the objective of not having to make these differences transparent, the senators declared that this measure was unfeasible, which, to begin with, makes it easier for the "right to veracity" to be violated. And since this violation will be at the mercy of self-regulation, it is not possible to imagine any medium pointing out that their news programs include "paid advertising".

Today's Mass Media Crisis and the Migration/Evolution of Audiences

The goal of reaching new audiences, mainly young people, compelled the TV networks to make changes in recent years. For example, Televisa, in addition to presenting itself to audiences "as something more than just a TV channel", decided to change their entire programming grid so as to prove that the change was not only in form but also in content. Their "Canal de Las Estrellas" ("the Stars Channel") was publicized as a platform that was simply called: "Las Estrellas" (The Stars") (Franco and Orozco, 2015).

A significant change for this company occurred in their star news show, which was always anchored by a man – Joaquín López Dóriga – and, before that, for many years by another man – Jacobo Zabludosky: the former was replaced by a female reporter, Denise Maerker. This also meant the end of the one-hour evening news shows, giving way to a more dynamic model, which synthesizes the news in half an hour using a narrative informative style similar to the one used on the Internet. However, this change in the news did not have the expected success and, even though it has remained on air, has not reached the expected ratings.

Other failures also occurred in the night-time slot on this channel, where they sought to implement a format similar to the *Late Night Shows* that are aired in the United States (like those hosted by David Letterman or Conan O'Brien); however, the show entitled "Esta Noche con Arath" – hosted by comedian Arath de la Torre – did not work and had to be taken off air after two months.

This programming crisis is due, mainly, to the drop in ratings not only of the shows aired in prime time but also in the programming grid as a whole. According to the results that OBITEL has collected systematically for over a decade about the most viewed shows on national television – which are, most of the time, either a soccer match or fiction – film, series or telenovela – it can be observed that in 2008 the highest ratings in Mexico ranged from 34 to 36 points; just a decade later, the highest ratings are around 18 to 21 points. The downturn, then, has been 15 points (OBITEL, 2017).

Back to the Future

In a significant decline, private (commercial) television in Mexico is facing a growing double competition. First, the one posed by that "other television", the so-called public, university, state, regional or community TV, which has increased the number of channels with the analog switch-off and diversified their programming, but above all, it has decided to produce fiction; a programming genre that it always disdained because it was considered banal (only thinking of the subjugating model imposed by the typical telenovelas produced by Televisa and TV Azteca). The case of Channel 11, a university TV station belonging to the Instituto Politécnico National (National Polytechnic Institute), which has been producing fiction of their own for a decade, is an illustrative, promising example of a change in Mexican television, since the fiction produced by Channel 11 involves new, attractive issues, which includes fiction for children: *El Diván de Valentina, Kipalta* or *Yo Soy Yo* (the two latter focusing on bullying) and historical fiction, such as the series *Los Minondo* and the miniseries *Juana Ines*, by the renown Mexican TV director, Patricia Arriaga, which was bought by Netflix and, after being aired in Mexico, can be enjoyed on that platform from all over the world.

Second, competition with the traditional television model in Mexico (with the almost exclusive Televisa–TV Azteca duopoly) comes from abroad: precisely from the growing expansion of OTT services, which do not respect borders and can be accessed by an ever-growing number of audiences at lower costs, and which provide greater, more widely varied programming (Calleja, 2017).

The growing preference of audiences for international TV fiction in the formats of series and miniseries rather than those of the telenovela or the soap operas, opens up an opportunity to increase the ratings of other media in Mexico, inasmuch as they produce fiction; what can be called the "Mexican telenovela and Latin-American empire" is coming to an end and new fiction is arising, with current issues and creative treatments, that comes above all from Brazil, Mexico, Argentina and Colombia and, of course, from Spain. These products attract other sectors in the audiences. Many of these fiction contents are short- and medium-length videos, which makes them easier to access in a generalized manner from different devices and by different sectors in the audiences (Torres, 2017).

In addition to the above tendency, la Asociación Mexicana de Productoras y Televisoras Universitarias (Mexican Association of University Producers and TV Stations) (AMPTU) – which also includes the Canal del Congreso and Canal Judicial (Channel of the Congress and Judicial Channel), which are Mexican government official channels, created in 2017 at the initiative of Canal 44 from Universidad de Guadalajara (University of Guadalajara) – has arisen as a legitimate national interlocutor in the definition of the Mexican media arena. This association could work as a hinge between commercial media and other media in the transformation of telecommunications.

Only the future will tell whether the internal changes in audience taste and the subsequent drop in historical ratings – along with the new, creative program definitions of the "other media" and their growing associative power, in conjunction with the external changes, especially those brought about by the digital technology tendencies – will shape up a new media-networks technological context that is less asymmetrical than the one that has prevailed in Mexico so far.

References

Mexican Media Agency Association (AMM) (2016). *Valor de la mercadotecnia en México*. Retrieved from www.aamedios.com/docs/Valor_de_la_inversion_mercadotecnica_en_mexico_2015.pdf

Mexican Internet Association (AMIPCI) (2017). *13 Estudio sobre los Hábitos de los Usuarios de Internet en México 2017*. Retrieved from www.asociaciondeinternet.mx/es/component/remository/Habitos-de-Internet/13-Estudio-sobre-los-Habitos-de-los-Usuarios-de-Internet-en-Mexico-2017/lang,es-es/?Itemid=

Calleja, A. (2017). Ignoran y reprimen a radiodifusoras. *Revista Zócalo*. Retrieved from www.revistazocalo.com.mx/archivo/45-zocalo/1380-pag4243112.html

Gómez, R. (2008). Políticas e industrias audiovisuales en México: apuntes y diagnóstico. *Comunicación y Sociedad*, 10: 191–206. Retrieved from www.comunicacionysociedad.cucsh.udg.mx/index.php/comsoc/article/view/1848/1627

Gómez, R. and Sosa, (2010). La concentración en el mercado de la televisión restringida en México. *Comunicación y Sociedad*, 14: 109–142.

Federal Institute of Telecommunications (IFETEL) (2017). *Banco de Información de Telecomunicaciones*. Retrieved from https://bit.ift.org.mx/BitWebApp/

La Jornada (March 23, 2013). Editorial. Retrieved from www.jornada.unam.mx/2013/03/23/edito

Latin American Multichannel Advertising Council (LAMAC) (2017). *Penetración de la televisión de paga en México*. Retrieved from www.lamac.org/mexico/metricas/total-por-tv-paga

Observatorio Iberoamericano de Ficción Televisiva (OBITEL) (2016). *(Re) invención de géneros y formatos de la ficción televisiva*. Sao Paulo, Brasil: Sulina.

Observatorio Iberoamericano de Ficción Televisiva (OBITEL) (2017). *Una década de ficción televisiva en Iberoamérica. Análisis de 10 años de Obitel (2007–2016)*. Sao Paulo, Brasil: Sulina.

Orozco, G. (2005). Mexico. In Cooper-Chen, A. (Ed.), *Global, entertainment, media. Content, audiences, issues*, pp. 203–220. Mahwah, NJ: Lawrence Erlbaum Associates.

Orozco, G. (2012). Televisión y producción de interacciones comunicativas. *Comunicación y Sociedad*, 18: 39–84. Retrieved from www.comunicacionysociedad.cucsh.udg.mx/index.php/comsoc/article/view/190/225

Orozco, G. and Franco D. (March 5, 2015). ¿Ganan audiencias y consumidores con Preponderancia? *Revista Zócalo*. Retrieved from www.revistazocalo.com.mx/archivo/45-zocalo/5541-ganan-audiencias-y-consumidores-con-preponderancia.html

Orozco, G. and Hernández, F. (2011). *Televisiones en México. Un recuento histórico*. Guadalajara, México: Universidad de Guadalajara.

PwC (2017). Entertainment and Media Outlook México 2016–2020. Retrieved from www.pwc.com/mx/es/publicaciones/c2g/entertainment-and-media-outlook-mexico-2016-2020.pdf

Sánchez, E. (July 26, 2017). Peña celebra logros en telecomunicaciones. *Excélsior*. Retrieved from www.excelsior.com.mx/nacional/2017/06/27/1172148

Sinclair, J. and Straubhaar, J. (2013). *Latin American Television Industries*. London: British Film Institute.

Sosa, G. (October 31, 2017). Derecho a distorsionar el periodismo. *SinEmbargo*. Retrieved from www.sinembargo.mx/31-10-2017/3340731

The Competitive Intelligence Unit (CIU) (2017). *Telecomunicaciones en México: 2017 y Pronósticos 2018*. Retrieved from www.theciu.com/publicaciones-2/2018/1/22/telecomunicaciones-en-mxico-2017-y-pronsticos-2018

Torres, G. (2017). Gestión y consumo de contenidos digitales: ¿qué se produce para los contenidos de corta y mediana duración? In Orozco, G. (Ed.), *TvMorfosis 6. Gestión y consumo de contenidos digitales. Nuevos modelos*, pp. 29–41. Guadalajara, México: Universidad de Guadalajara/Tintable.

5 Subjective Camera, Direct Address, and Audience Participation

Velho Chico and a New Brazilian Telenovela Aesthetics

Samantha Nogueira Joyce and Antonio La Pastina

Introduction

The Brazilian media is marked by a strong dynastic patriarchal character. Virtual and horizontal integration has led to the development of a monopoly in the broadcasting industry. The two new major players in "pay TV" are TVA (owned by the publishing group Abril) and Globosat (TV Globo). Additionally, Globo's signal can be picked up in 99.5% of the Brazilian territory, and, for over 30 years, its own international channel, Globo Internacional, has distributed programs to more than 130 countries (over 300 telenovelas). Additionally, in 2007, 25,000 hours of programming were licensed to over 50 countries and translated into 24 different languages, reaching an average audience of 100 million viewers worldwide every day (Globo in The World).

Notably, the most important change in media regulations in Brazil is the Civil Rights Framework for the Internet. While it does not solve the problem of media concentration, this act works as a rule-book for networks, establishing guaranties, principles, rights, and obligations for both companies and Internet users. Its main value revolves around "net neutrality" and is of interest to TV Globo, as its telenovelas are headed towards transmediation (Lopes & Gómez, 2017, p. 28–34).

A key characteristic of Brazilian telenovelas is referred to as "the open text" – the ongoing daily production that leaves the narrative open to last-minute changes based on audience participation, ratings, etc. The technique was made even more relevant in 2016, with the tragic death of Domingos Montagner. The actor played the romantic lead – Santo – in TV Globo's telenovela *Velho Chico*. Montagner drowned in a river days before the final scenes were shot. This research is a case study investigating the ways in which the "open text" was used in a new and disruptive way: with a subjective camera. *Velho Chico* provides a key example of how producers deal with these kinds of crisis moments and how they aimed to address the audience and bring them into the program in a new participatory way.

Velho Chico was a rural telenovela (from March, 2016 to September, 2016) that can be described as a type of Shakespearean family saga. Filled with family rivalries, regional beliefs, and political conflicts, the plot was set in three different time periods by the São Francisco River (*Velho Chico*). But more than just a setting, the river was a character with personality and whims, responsible for mystical events.

The innovative aesthetic strategy used in *Velho Chico* – a post-mortem subjective camera – was possible due to the "open text". However, key to our analysis is the fact that it positioned viewers in the place of the leading actor. In other words, when characters in the program talked to Santo, they were in fact talking to the audience via direct address. The subjective camera disrupted traditional ways of making telenovelas and represented a new and interesting type of audience inclusion that represents, aesthetically, what has been suggested in general about Brazilian telenovelas: that as an open text, the program is in direct and constant conversation with the audiences that watch them, and that these strategies change and adapt to current events, as we will demonstrate below.

Contextualizing Brazilian Television, and the (In)famous Telenovelas

Brazilians love the *telinha*[1]. Regardless of the ever-changing technological formats of content viewing, the television screen is still the number one source of entertainment and information in that country. While the country has not been left behind as far as technological innovations in regard to the production and delivery of content, the (in)famous telenovelas are still the number one genre of consumption and production in Brazil. Recent technological advances include the online companion platforms *Globo Play, Now*, and *Vivo Play*. But, when it comes to Brazil, the *telinha* still holds a place of prominence in most living rooms (Lopes & Gómez, 2016, p. 135).

A recent report by Obitel (Observatório Ibero-Americano de Ficção Televisiva – "Ibero-American Observatory of Television")[2], shows that television remains the predominant means of communication in Brazil. According to that survey, 95% of respondents watch TV, and 73% of them do so daily. The research shows that on average, Brazilians spend 4 hours and 31 daily minutes exposed to the TV set, Monday through Friday, and 4 hours and 14 minutes on the weekend. These numbers were higher than in the previous year (3 hours and 29 minutes and 3 hours and 32 minutes respectively). This suggests that in Brazil, Internet use is not leading to the abandonment of the television screen, and instead, we see a transmediation between "old and new media" (Joyce & Martinez, 2016, p. 89).

These numbers keep growing. In 2016 there was a 4.7% increase in television viewing, with the telenovela being the absolute leader format in Brazil, and for the past ten years, the top ten titles have always been national productions by TV Globo. The first fiction by another broadcaster to appear in the most viewed list – *Os Dez Mandamentos* (The Ten Commandments) by TV Record – ranked 34th overall. Ultimately, TV Globo has consistently had the highest number of titles in the top ten as far as fictional productions in Brazil, occupying the first place within the 12 countries monitored by Obitel (Lopes & Gómez, 2017, pp. 114, 125).

Thus, for over six decades, every evening, millions of viewers throughout Brazil have tuned into TV Globo's telenovelas[3] and the textual "openness" has been one of the key ingredients to the lasting success of the genre (Mattelart and Mattelart, 1990; Joyce, 2013; LaPastina & Joyce, 2015). The "open text" allows telenovelas to be constructed in a more complex manner, permitting writers and producers to use this characteristic of "openness" to create an alliance with a broadly diverse audience.

Distinct from U.S. soap operas, Brazilian telenovelas have a cultural-socio-economical-political weight that is intrinsic to that country. Lopes (2009) argues that the telenovela has conquered the public's recognition as an aesthetic and cultural product, becoming a force in the country's culture and identity. In our analysis of *Velho Chico*, we highlight a key difference in an important production aesthetic device – the subjective camera – which broke away from the audience's familiarity with the traditional form of the genre, and the genre itself, by repositioning a character's point of view and by inviting the audience to become a participant in the plot through POV and direct address. Key to this innovation in the production and consumption of *Velho Chico* is another key production technique: the open text – which allowed for this innovation to take place during a time of crisis: the death of the leading romantic actor/character.

Scheduled time and length are other characteristics that distinguish Brazilian telenovelas from American soaps. Telenovelas are broadcast daily, several times a day, but primarily during prime time. They have definitive endings that permit narrative closure usually after 180 to 200 episodes. They discuss current events and are designed to attract a wide viewing audience of men, women, and children (Hamburger, 2005; Lopes, 2009; Joyce, 2013).

Mazziotti (1993) argues that telenovelas "allow for the viewers an emotional participation in a set of fictitious powers that play with elemental human questions: honor, goodness, love, villainy, life, death, virtue, and sin, that in definite ways have something to do with the viewer". A key production ingredient heightens this participation: the open text (p. 11).

"Open Texts" as a Production Strategy in Search of Profit

The open text is key to Brazilian telenovelas longevity. As Joyce (2012) explains,

> Because the story is written at the same time that chapters are shown, the public's reaction to the telenovelas is taken into account by the writers in the chapters to come. It is this integration between the writers and the public that characterizes the telenovelas as an "open art form." And to channel this large viewer participation (with the aim of maintaining a high audience share), TV Globo constantly conducts surveys and focus groups to ensure that the viewers are happy with stories and plot lines.
>
> (Joyce, 2012, p. 9)

Porto (2008) describes the relationship between all those involved in the production and consumption of the telenovela text as a "mass ceremony" (p. 2). The intense close relationship between audience and writers is related to daily involvement between these social actors, but also due to the very nature of the production of this cultural/television product. In other words, how a telenovela is actually *made*, matters.

Telenovelas operate like a revolving carousel. In other words, when the final episode of a telenovela is broadcast on Saturday evening, a brand-new telenovela starts on the following Monday. Preparations for the next telenovela start as soon as the preceding one airs: like an assembly line, production never stops.

The assembly line also creates flexibility in the production, allowing episodes to be edited moments before the broadcast. This can happen for various reasons: pressure from the public, to create suspense, or due to other unexpected events. Writers are responsible for writing six episodes every week, and producers are responsible for taping blocks of six episodes weekly. This corresponds to an average of 40 pages per day (Hamburger, 2005; Joyce, 2012).

While it is clear that "open text" is a production element that operates as a commercial strategy that develops a captive audience as well as profit, this research is interested in shedding light on how it ignited a creative novel aesthetic to making telenovelas, inviting yet a different form of participation, as discussed below.

Previous Protagonist's Deaths and the "Open Text"

The first time a protagonist died during the time a telenovela was airing was in 1972, with the telenovela *O Primeiro Amor* ("The First Love"). Actor Sérgio Cardoso (47 years old), who played professor Luciano Limo, passed away after a heart attack just 28 days before the final episode was about to air and the program was still in production, as is customary. The "open text" solution to the tragic event was to substitute the actor with his real-life best friend, Leonardo Villar:

> The cast of 'The First Love' suffered a severe blow on August 18, 1972, only 28 episodes from the end of the telenovela: Sérgio Cardoso, the protagonist of the program, died a victim of a heart attack. The death of the actor generated a national commotion. To replace him, Leonardo Villar was summoned. His first scene aired in Episode 200, with a simple homage to Sérgio Cardoso. The image on the screen was frozen after the actor left a room. Meeting with the rest of the cast on the stage of the Phoenix Theater, actor Paulo José read a text announcing the change and recalling Sergio Cardoso's trajectory in theater and television, and explained that from that moment on, Leonardo Villar, personal friend of Sérgio Cardoso's, from the times of the Brazilian Theater of Comedy, would begin to replace his colleague, as a way of paying homage to him. Then the scene went on, and when the door of the room opened again, Leonardo Villar came on the scene, already portraying Professor Luciano.
>
> (O Meu Primeiro Amor, para. 1)

Perhaps the most well-known real-life tragedy involving a Brazilian telenovela comes from the 1992 *De Corpo e Alma* ("Of Body and Soul") by writer Glória Perez. The event caused the entire country to mourn the death of the twenty-two-year-old "Brazilian Sweetheart" Daniela Perez, the writer's daughter, who was assassinated in a morbid case that overshadowed a major political event in the country – the news of the impeachment of then-president Fernando Collor de Mello.

Thanks to the "open text", the production for the program was not halted. In fact, the telenovela, with scenes of a break-up between the fictional character played by Daniela and her on-screen boyfriend (and number one suspect of her real-life assassination) followed the nightly news – *Jornal Nacional* – which had been covering the actress's death. Grossi (1993) describes the relationship between the audience and news of her death as a "collective delirium" (p. 166). The author notes the public's sheer incredulity:

> On both sides of the screen, people thought: "It can not be true. This guy has confused fiction with reality". In the episode of 'Body and Soul' that aired after her death we watch in disbelief, scenes of jealousy of Bira towards Yasmin, as if we already knew the end of the story, without however wanting to believe it. The telenovela, incidentally, had begun immediately after the *Jornal Nacional*, without any commercial break, further confusing our parameters between fiction and reality.
>
> (p. 166)

A study-abroad trip was the solution found by the authors to explain Yasmin's departure from the story. Bira simply ceased to exist (Veja 10 Mudanças, 2014). The telenovela production went on as usual[4]: the show's main screenwriter, Gloria Perez, was in fact Daniella's mother, and she continued the story for two months after her daughter's death, with Daniella appearing in flashbacks from already-shot footage (Bellos, 2007, para. 20).

What all of these have in common is the fact that while the open-text type of production allowed for a rewrite of the narrative, the aesthetic values of the show were not altered drastically. The telenovela's form was not altered. The innovation in *Velho Chico* came in the form of the production element (subjective camera) that disrupted the traditional way of making and seeing telenovelas, as we will discuss below.

A New Aesthetic: Subjective Camera, and a New Type of Audience Participation

It is safe to say that *Velho Chico* had in fact two protagonists – Santo, played by Montagner, and the São Francisco River (*Velho Chico* or "Old Chico"). Discovered 515 years ago, the river cuts through five states and 505 Brazilian municipalities, and has been losing its vitality due to pollution, industrialization, and a lack of governmental policies to protect its waters.

Velho Chico was thus a telenovela, a fictitious beloved character, and a real life villain, credited for "taking the life" of actor Domingos Montagner, who died after drowning in its water on September 15, 2016, while going for a swim with his co-star (actress Camila Pitanga) just moments after shooting a scene for one of the upcoming final episodes of the telenovela. A strong undercurrent pulled both actors under water. Camila Pitanga was able to hold on to a rock and save herself. Montagner was unfortunately taken under. His body was found hours later at a river beach, where they had been shooting previously that day. In a telenovela marked by folklore and mysticism, the day of Montagner's tragic death was also marked by morbid coincidences approximating the lines between reality and fiction. That night, during the telenovela's broadcast, his on-screen mother tried to kill herself by drowning in that river.

Contrary to the previous examples where the codes of the telenovela were maintained intact after the death of a protagonist, the production team chose not to eliminate the actor from the narrative. Production-wise, this creative choice disrupted the way scenes were produced and consumed. Because writers chose not to rewrite the final scenes of the saga, they opted to shoot Santo's final scenes with a subjective camera, with the audience accompanying and seeing everything through Santo's "eyes", and hearing the dialogue "for" Santo.

Characters – his love interest, daughter, brothers – talked and looked straight at/to the camera (or to Santo and/or viewers). Consequently Santo "responded" with camera movements, blurs representing emotional situations and/or tears, and muddled vision, along with pre-recorded audio by Montagner.

Actor Gabriel Leone, who played his son Miguel, explained the new way of shooting scenes in a telenovela as a way to make the actor and the character present in the narrative as the team's idea to give continuity to the work and to character, and to finish telling the story (Santos, 2016, para. 2).

The sequences with the characters "looking" at Santo and the viewers "looking" at Santo, thrilled viewers, who commented online. In fact, the actor's name, along with comments regarding the "subjective camera", became a trending topic on Twitter during the broadcast (Dos Santos, 2016, para. 2). Ratings were also strong, with IBOPE marking a 30-point[5] range, the second-best average after Montagner's death: 34.8 IBOPE points in the greater São Paulo area. The highest audience had been 37 points, recorded on the day of the actor's death on September 15 (Medina, 2016, para 3).

The subjective camera was the subject of a column by TV writer Flávio Ricco (2016), who viewed the technique as a "demonstration of what Brazilian television professionals are capable of, facing the most different situations or, as is the case, in the face of the tragic disappearance of one of its protagonists" (para. 1). The author added that he had "goosebumps" with the solution found by the director to make the actors stare at, and talk directly into, the camera, stating that the camera was "poetically and delicately placed in Santo's place, providing moments that no viewer will be able to forget any time soon" (para. 2).

The recourse of using Santo's point of view through the camera made it possible for Santo to be at his son's wedding on the final day of the broadcast. According to his fictional son Miguel (actor Gabriel Leone), the "camera was completely alive, as if he was with us in our wedding scene" (Elenco e autor, 2016, para. 2). Additionally, Leone stated that the subjective camera was operated by the person who had been shooting Santo since the beginning of the program:

> He is a cameraman that had been working with us in *Velho Chico* from the beginning, who had a lot of familiarity with him, (Domingos Montagner), and had shot him many times. He had the responsibility of being, not only his eyes, but of feeling for him, relating, and acting with us.
> (Elenco e autor, 2016, para. 3)

Finally, another aesthetic innovation, was the use of pre-recorded audio by Montagner. For example, in the episode that aired on September 26, 2016, his daughter looks at the camera and tells Santo: "It is so good to have you here with me, my father. I love you." And Santo replies, "I love you." At first, critics and viewers were skeptical of the new subjective approach adopted by the production team. As Braz Jr. (2016) states:

> At first, when the director announced that he would use this feature, I was a little skeptical, mainly because Montagner had a very strong screen presence. Could a camera possibly replace it? It was obviously not the same thing, but the alternative has proven itself to have worked. Seeing the actors all opposite Santo in this way was really quite exciting for the audience. There was also the voice of the character, which was taken from dialogues of past episodes of the telenovela. This recipe made everything very delicate and impactful at the same time. You can imagine the difficulty and the emotion of the actors to work this way. Especially Camila Pitanga, who seemed to be very touched by it all.
> (Braz Jr., 2016, para. 2)

Another aesthetic innovation was the fact that the word "*Fim*" ("The End") that appears at the end of all telenovelas, signifying the much-anticipated resolution to all conflicts, was clearly omitted. As one news article noted:

> Unlike the customary endings, the word(s) "The end" did not appear at any time written on the screen. In addition, the river, the boat and the presence of an absence were felt in the form of homage [. . .] After all, life does not stop and the telenovela didn't either [. . .] the final chapter of "Velho Chico" had something that the telenovela often loses when it falls into the banality of the genre: the power to affect the public.
>
> (Santo (Domingos Montagner), 2016)

Interestingly enough, without the traditional definitive ending marked by "*Fim*", the production team, which was the first to implement the use of the subjective camera in a telenovela, highlighted once again the fact that the telenovela is an open text.

Conclusions

Every evening millions of viewers throughout Brazil tune in their television sets to TV Globo's telenovelas. The present research aimed to shed new light into one of the key characteristics of the program – the "open text" – and how it has evolved over the years during a particular situation – the death of a protagonist during the production. We chose to compare and contrast a recent example – the death in 2016 of actor Domingos Montagner amidst the final days of taping of *Velho Chico* – with a few previous examples of telenovelas where key actors had died.

While we understood from the start that this versatile characteristic and "way of doing" – is used in many instances as a tool to keep and/or boost ratings, we also saw it as a practice that changed and disrupted the very way this established genre was made. Additionally, we discussed how "open texts" encourage blending the boundaries between fact and fiction. Furthermore, we demonstrated how, coupled together, these two factors have contributed to the longevity and popularity of the genre.

The innovation brought about the daily open-ended production/open text, was in the form of a subjective camera that looked for the character but also placed viewers in the place of the character, through the camera's POV. For the first time in the history of Brazilian telenovelas, characters in the program talked to the audience via direct address. The subjective camera disrupted traditional ways of making telenovelas and represented a new kind of audience inclusion that represents aesthetically what had been suggested in general about Brazilian telenovelas: that as an open text, the program is in direct and constant conversation with its audience.

Our intent was not to make a value judgment on the artistic, narrative, and creative developments utilized previously by each author. Instead, we proposed to explicate this flexible production tool. While traditionally the "open text" characteristic permitted the adaptation of the text in a short time, more recently, in *Velho Chico*, it also allowed for a creative outcome that disrupted the traditional way of making telenovelas by introducing the "subjective camera" tool. As Braz Jr. (2016) states:

> It is worth saying that what happened with *Velho Chico* is something unprecedented on Brazilian TV. The telenovela lost its protagonist in its final stretch, which leaves an irreparable gap, even more so because they did not choose to put another actor in his place. The subjective camera was a way to keep the character alive, even if in a different and strange way.
>
> (para. 5)

Our research traced the deaths of other protagonists during a telenovela's production and investigated how the "open text" had been utilized in order to deal with the tragic event at hand: by substituting the protagonist with another actor in order to make a love story come to fruition (*Meu Primeiro Amor*, in 1972), or a study-abroad trip and the use flashbacks to deal with the character's disappearance from the plot (*De Corpo e Alma*, 1992).

But the above examples did not disturb traditional modes of making telenovelas. In other words, the codes of television were not changed and the production and aesthetic values were not drastically altered. We demonstrated that in the past, adjustments were made to the script, actors were replaced, but ultimately the telenovela's form had stayed intact. However, *Velho Chico* did disrupt the program's form when the production team chose to keep the character alive through a subjective camera with Santo's point of view, and used playback recordings to stand in for his voice.

Another innovation in regard to form that was implemented in *Velho Chico* was the careful omission of the much-anticipated word "*Fim*" ("The End") following the program's final scene. Finally, what we discovered was that this simple word, which traditionally carries the responsibility of sealing the concrete ending of the program, did not fulfill its legacy to close something once and for all but, instead, left the text even more "open".

Fim.

Notes

1 "Telinha" refers to the way in which Brazilians describe the television screen. The sufix "*inha*" means small, but there are also affectionate undertones to the suffix "*inha*".
2 Obitel is comprised of a ten-year network of researchers from 12 countries in the Ibero-American regions: Argentina, Brazil, Chile, Colombia, Ecuador, Spain, United States, Mexico, Peru, Portugal, Uruguay, and Venezuela.
3 Globo has traditionally dominated the market with many of their telenovelas leading the ratings. Although since the late 1980s other Brazilian networks, such as (the now extinct) Manchete, SBT, and Record, have conquered a slice of the market, reducing Globo's penetration, telenovelas are still very profitable. Other technologies such as cable and streaming services have also has changed the dynamics of ratings, especially among urban upper classes. However, Globo's telenovelas are still the audience leaders.
4 During the seven days immediately after the crime, writers Leonor Bassères and Gilberto Braga assumed the responsibility of writing the following episodes and presenting an alternative for the disappearance of the two characters. After just one week, Gloria Perez resumed her work until the end of the telenovela (Veja 10 Mudanças, 2014, 20para. 12]
5 Each IBOPE point represents 69,400 households.

References

Globo in the World. *Globo.com*. Retrieved February 1, 2018 from http://redeglobo.globo.com/Portal/institucional/foldereletronico/ingles/g_globo_mundo.html

O Meu Primeiro Amor. Tendo como cenário principal uma escola, O Primeiro Amor trazia um víuvo no centro de um triângulo amoroso. *Memóriaglobo.com.br*. Retrieved February 6, 2017 from http://memoriaglobo.globo.com/programas/entretenimento/novelas/o-primeiro-amor/curiosidades.htm

Santo (Domingos Montagner) (2016) apareceu na cena final da trama, navegando pelo rio São Francisco próximo ao Gaiola Encantado ao som do refrão 'Adeus, Velho Chico'. *Purepeople.com.br*. Retrieved February 7, 2017 from http://www.purepeople.com.br/noticia/fim-da-novela-velho-chico-comove-com-chuva-de-lagrimas-e-adeus-a-santo-no-rio_a138116/1

(August 12, 2014). Veja Dez Veja 10 mudanças que a Globo foi obrigada a fazer em suas novelas. O caso envolvendo Drica Moraes e Marjorie Estiano não é o primeiro. *TribunadaBahia.com.br*. Retrieved February 8, 2017 from http://www.tribunadabahia.com.br/2014/12/08/veja-10-mudancas-que-globo-foi-obrigada-fazer-em-suas-novelas

Bellos, A. (2007). Telenovelas: the story so far. Telegraph.co.uk. Retrieved July 1, 2015 from www.telegraph.co.uk/culture/3662430/Telenovelas-the-story-so-far.html

Braz Jr. O. (2016). Domingos Montagner faz chorar em Velho Chico. Retrieved February 7, 2017 from http://entretenimento.r7.com/blogs/odair-braz-jr/criticas/domingos-montagner-faz-chorar-em-velho-chico-27-09-2016/

Dos Santos, F. (2016). Câmera substitui Domingos Montagner em "Velho Chico" e comove internautas. www.otvfoco.com.br. Retrieved September 29, 2016 from www.otvfoco.com.br/camera-substitui-domingos-montagner-em-velho-chico-e-comove-internautas/#ixzz4LabBIJaB

Elenco e autor de "Velho Chico" comentam sobre câmera subjetiva. (September 29, 2016). Uai.com.br. Retrieved February 7, 2017 from www.uai.com.br/app/noticia/series-e-tv/2016/09/28/noticias-series-e-tv,194932/elenco-e-autor-de-velho-chico-comentam-sobre-camera-subjetiva.shtml

Gregolin, M. V. (2008). *Viver a Vida* no limiar da tela: A narrative transmidia chega à novella. *Revista Geminis* 1(1), 53–57.

Grossi, M. P. (1993). De Angela Diniz a Daniela Perez: A Tragetória da impunidade. *Estudos Feministas* 1 166–169.

Hamburger, E. (2005). *O Brasil antenado. A sociedade na novela.* Rio de Janeiro, Brasil: Jorge Zahar Editor.

Joyce, S. N. (2012). *Brazilian Telenovelas and the Myth of Racial Democracy.* Lanham, MD: Lexington Books.

Joyce, S. N. (2013). A kiss is (not) just a kiss. Heterodeterminism, homosexuality and TV Globo telenovelas. *International Journal of Communication* 7 (2013), 48–66.

Joyce, S. N. & Martinez, M. M. (2016). Brics and mediated narratives: The proximity between Brazilian news and telenovelas. *Brazilian Journalism Research* 12(1), 78–97.

LaPastina, A. & Joyce, S. N. (2015). Changing GLBTQ representations: The Sexual Other in Brazilian Telenovelas. *Lumina* (lumina.ufjf.emnuvens.com.br), 1–28.

Lopes, M. I. V. (2009). Telenovelas as a communicative resourse. *Matrizes* 3(1), 21–47.

Lopes, M. I. V. & Gómez, G. O. (2016). *Ibero-American observatory of television fiction Obitel 2016 (Re) invention of TV fiction genres and formats.* Retrieved November 12, 2017 from www.obitel.net/wp-content/uploads/2017/09/obitel-2017-ingles.pdf

Lopes, M. I. V. & Gómez, G. O. (2017). *Ibero-American observatory of television fiction obitel 2017. One decade of television fiction in Ibero-America: An analys of ten years of Obitel (2007–2016).* Retrieved September 11, 2017 from www.obitel.net/wp-content/uploads/2017/09/obitel-2017-ingles.pdf

Mattelart, M., & Mattelart, A. (1990). *The carnival of images: Brazilian television fiction.* New York: Bergin & Garvey.

Mazziotti, N. (1993). El estado de las investigaciones sobre telenovela lationoamericana. *Revista de ciencias de la informacion* 8, 45–59.

Medina, A. (2016). Com efeitos especiais para substituir Domingos Montagner, Velho Chico tem boa audiência. Veja.abril.com.br. Retrieved February 7, 2017 from http://veja.abril.com.br/blog/radar-on-line/audiencia/com-efeitos-especiais-para-substituir-domingos-montagner-velho-chico-tem-boa-audiencia/

Porto, M. (2008). Telenovelas and National Identity in Brazil. Paper presented to the IX International Congress of the Brazilian Studies Association (BRASA), New Orleans, March 27–29, 2008. Retrieved February 2, 2017 from www.brasa.org/wordpress/Documents/BRASA_IX/Mauro-Porto.pdf

Ricco, F. (2016). "Velho Chico" é prova da capacidade da TV do Brasil. Uol.com.br. Retrieved February 7, 2017 from http://tvefamosos.uol.com.br/colunas/flavio-ricco/2016/09/28/velho-chico-e-prova-da-capacidade-da-tv-do-brasil.htm

Santos, R. (2016). Atores se emocionaram com câmera no lugar de Montagner: "Seguimos o trabalho com ele e por ele". www.otvfoco.com.br. Retrieved September 27, 2016 from www.otvfoco.com.br/atores-se-emocionaram-com-camera-no-lugar-de-montagner-seguimos-o-trabalho-com-ele-e-por-ele/#ixzz4Laar7Bgk

Part II
EMEA (Europe, Middle East, Africa)

6 Media Policy in the European Union

A Synoptic Overview of the Legislative Framework and a Critical Review of Some Current Issues

Paul Clemens Murschetz

The EU's Audiovisual and Media Policy

The European Union (http://europa.eu/) is a unique economic and political union between 28 countries that together cover much of the European continent. The predecessor of the EU was created in the aftermath of the Second World War. The first steps were to foster economic cooperation: the idea being that countries that trade with one another become economically interdependent and are so more likely to avoid conflict. The result was the European Economic Community (EEC), created in 1958, and initially increasing economic cooperation between six countries: Belgium, Germany, France, Italy, Luxembourg and the Netherlands. Since then, 22 other members joined and a huge single market (also known as the "internal" market) has been created and continues to develop towards its full potential. What began as a purely economic union has evolved into an organization spanning many policy areas, from human rights to transport and trade. The EEC changed its name to the European Union (EU) in 1993.

Like any other goods and services, audiovisual media – film, TV, video – are subject to certain EU-wide rules to ensure they can circulate freely and fairly in the single European market, regardless of how they are delivered (traditional TV, video-on-demand, internet, etc.). This is the aim of the EU's audiovisual and media policy, and more particularly the audiovisual media services directive (see in more detail later). Together, the EU media policy landscape is built on a complex set of regulatory areas (European Union, 2018).

Although there is a growing body of research literature in EU media policy, showing that there is an increasing interest in the field (e.g., Iosifidis, 2011; Lunt & Livingstone, 2012; Puppis, Simpson, & van den Bulck, 2016; Picard & Pickard, 2017), critical analyses into the structures, processes, efficacies, challenges and controversies of EU media policy formulation, implementation and practice is sparse. This entry will address this void. It shall provide a synoptic overview of the legislative framework of the EU's audiovisual and media policy and look to some of the most important challenges it is facing with regard to maintaining an effective aggregate transnational policy universe that lives up to its promise of promoting cultural diversity and the economic prosperity of media in Europe. Certainly, this is a daunting task given the changing nature of current environmental challenges on the media industries at large, notably through digitization, convergence, globalization, market concentration, audience fragmentation and intensified competition through digitally based companies such as Google, Apple, Facebook and others as significant content and service providers diversifying into and attacking the traditional media domains from outside the EU. Nonetheless, research on these macro-level challenges and how they affect the efficacy of policy instruments applied has become ever more important should the "European project" survive its institutional crisis and hence overcome the general atmosphere of disillusionment on many levels.

The Legislative Framework

The EU's legislative media policy framework, consisting of institutional bodies, rules, instruments, actors, capacities, venues and effects, hence a whole "ecosystem", is implemented by the European Commission (EC), which represents the interests of the EU, and is one of the three main institutions involved in EU legislation besides the European Parliament (which represents the EU's citizens and is directly elected by them) and the Council of Europe (which represents the governments of the individual member countries), in the following four main areas (European Parliament, 2017; Donders, Pauwels, & Loisen, 2014):[1]

1) Articles 167 and 173 of the Treaty on the Functioning of the European Union (TFEU) govern the EU's media. The key piece of legislation in this field is the Audiovisual Media Services Directive (AVSMD).[2] AVMSD aims at creating an effective single European market for audiovisual media. It aims at harmonizing the rules of the 28 national and subnational jurisdictions. Their objective is to achieve an internal market in audiovisual (AV) media services while protecting the interests of children and minors and enforcing public interest objectives, such as diversity and quality;
2) Media-specific funding programs to stimulate the production and distribution of AV media services, for example, Creative Europe programme, to complement national support systems, that is state aid schemes for print and audiovisual media, instruments that are confronted with the difficulty in balancing economic goals in European media policy issues with cultural and public interest objectives (diversity, pluralism, universality);
3) Policies to enforce media literacy and media pluralism (under the responsibility of the member states). The EU considers media literacy to be an important factor for active citizenship in today's information society. The Council conclusions on developing media literacy and critical thinking through education and training of 30 May 2016 underline that media literacy is more important than ever in the age of the internet and social media and that it needs to be an integral part of education and training at all levels. Media pluralism calls for the need for transparency, freedom and diversity in Europe's media landscape and is explicitly laid down in Article 11 of the Charter of Fundamental Rights of the European Union which asks for respect of "freedom and pluralism of the media"; and
4) Policies to promote online distribution of content to improve the environment for online creative content and promote the digital single market, whereby the EC's role is to support and protect users and owners of media content; ensure that intellectual property rights are fair for all; promote the growth of digital distribution. This is done by: liaising with stakeholders; developing new policies; encouraging the adoption of appropriate laws across the EU; and providing training and support for the creative sector via the Creative Europe programme.

The Audiovisual Media Services Directive

The opening of the television market to different operators (with the consequential end of national monopolies), the need to face international competition and to protect consumers throughout Europe in a similar manner, as well as the extraordinary evolution of audio-visual and communication services caused by the spread of the internet, have laid the foundation for strong European intervention in this field, which is traditionally managed only through national policies. During the 1980s, new developments in broadcasting technologies led to an increase in the number of commercial TV stations in Europe and to their broadcasts being able to be received in several countries. This gave rise to a need for common minimum standards, which were first laid out in the "Television without frontiers" (TVwF) Directive (89/552/EEC). The first revision, in 1997, put in place the "country of origin" principle. The principle states that, where an action or service is performed in one country but received in another, the applicable law is the law of the country where the action or service is performed.

New services, such as Video on Demand (VOD) available over the internet, were added in the 2007 revision. The directive was codified in 2010 and renamed the "Audiovisual Media Services" (AVMS) Directive. The audiovisual media services directive requires EU countries to coordinate national legislation with each other to:

- create comparable conditions in all countries for emerging audiovisual media
- protect children and consumers
- safeguard media pluralism
- combat racial and religious hatred
- preserve cultural diversity
- ensure national media regulators remain independent.

Methodically, each of the 28 EU member states is encouraged to follow minimum standards for the following:

- Advertising – rules and restrictions in place for certain products (e.g., alcohol, tobacco, medicines) and no more than 12 minutes' advertising per hour
- Major events – events like the Olympics or the football World Cup must be available to a wide audience, not just on pay-TV channels
- Protecting children – violent or pornographic programmes scheduled late at night or limited access through parental controls
- Promotion of European films and audiovisual content – at least half of TV broadcasting time should be allocated to European films and television programmes. Video-on-demand services should also promote European works
- Accessibility – media companies should make their audiovisual content accessible to people with visual or hearing impairments.

Media-Specific Funding Programmes

While the print media in Europe have traditionally enjoyed a great degree of autonomy and self-regulation, audiovisual, film and broadcast media has attracted state intervention because of technical matters (spectrum scarcity), but also because of its capability regarding its relevance to the formation of public opinion and the public interest at large and across Europe. However, the organization and functioning of the media systems are not the same across Europe, for they vary in the way they are funded and structured, their political independence, and so on (Iosifidis, 2011). These large variations among the media systems stem from different traditions, political cultures as well as regulatory systems that exist across Europe (European Union, 2017; 2018).

Creative Europe and MEDIA

Creative Europe is the European Commission's framework programme for support to the culture and audiovisual sectors. The MEDIA sub-programme of the Creative Europe programme is the fifth multiannual programme since 1991 in support of the audiovisual industry. It builds on the success of its predecessors, the MEDIA and MEDIA Mundus program (2007–2013). The total budget of the Creative Europe programme amounted to EUR 1.46 billion (2014–2020), a budget increase of 9% compared to the previous programme. At least 56% of that sum is set aside for the MEDIA sub-programme. MEDIA provides support and funding opportunities for film and TV projects, cinema networks, film festivals, audience development, training measures for audiovisual professionals, access to markets, distribution, video game development, online distribution and international co-production funds (European Union, 2016a; 2016b).

Financial Subsidies for Print

Public intervention in press economics takes place against the background of constitutional guarantees for press freedom within most liberal democracies of Western Europe, according to which freedom of opinion is protected and an individual's right to publish and disseminate information freely without prior restraint through any state authority is safeguarded (Murschetz, 2014; Nielsen, & Linnebank, 2011). In contrast to the Anglo-Saxon minimalist approach to press regulation, which depends on general competition law and the publishers' voluntary adherence to ethical standards under the supervision of an independent watchdog commission, the continental-style authorities in Austria, France, Norway and Sweden, for example, have opted for far more interventionist public policies into press economics, in the belief that this is the best way to safeguard plurality of titles and diversity of opinion.

Still, these mechanisms of intervention to provide economic support for journalistic diversity are currently undergoing changes in various countries. While interventionist measures such as direct cash payments to selected projects or general incentives such as postal subsidies or VAT rates on printed matter still play a vital role in providing conditions conducive to economic stability of the industry and, importantly, promote a public interest culture in journalism, their efficacy is being reviewed to reduce their costs. As a result, European regulators of print media are navigating among the contradictions of general expenditure-cutting public austerity budgets to act as a brake on continuing cash subsidies, anti-trust laws and publicly funded operational funds open to public-interest journalism, including special grants for new journalistic ventures and start-up companies (Murschetz, 2018).

State Aid for Film and TV

In Europe, public authorities are generously funding the European film industry. The many schemes offered aim at strengthening artistic talent and creativity, safeguarding cultural diversity, fostering European integration and improving the economic wealth of the film industry and its stakeholders at large (European Commission, 2014a, 2014b; Murschetz, Teichmann, & Karmasin, 2018). In 2016, the European Audiovisual Observatory, part of the Council of Europe in Strasbourg, published a report that analyzed the development of public measures designed to foster the film and audiovisual sectors, and film production in particularly, between the years 2010 and 2014, from an aggregate European perspective. The report covers direct public funding, fiscal incentives, legal obligations for broadcasters to invest in film and audiovisual content as well as guarantee facilities (loan guarantees) for securing access to private financing. Overall, results show that Europe is more actively engaged in supporting its film industry than ever:

- There were 250 film funds active between 2010 and 2014, a very stable figure considering that 20 new funds were created and 21 shut down during the period
- The yearly average income of film and AV funds in Europe was EUR 2.53 billion (the sum of all profiles of film funds, at national/federal, sub-national/regional and local and supranational/EU level)
- The number of fiscal incentive (tax credits, rebates and tax shelter) schemes more than doubled between 2008 and 2014 (up from 12 to 26 schemes)
- The average yearly spent for film and AV funds in Europe totaled EUR 2.29 billion, a rise of 13.4 % over the time covered.

Notably, France alone accounted for a massive 42% of the incoming resources for film and audiovisual funds in Europe (followed at a great distance by the other four big markets in the EU). This is mostly due to massive mandatory contributions from broadcasters to the CNC, the country's national film fund. Contributions from the national/federal government and broadcasting levies were the two main sources of financing for film and audiovisual funds in Europe. Contributions from the administration at all geographical levels had hardly compensated for the steady decline of income from levies on broadcasters. In fact, direct public funding seems to play an ever more important role in financing European theatrical works, as broadcaster investments seem to have declined and pre-sales/minimum guarantees have reportedly become more difficult to obtain, particularly for small- and medium-budget films. This leads to the important question: Is there a financing gap emerging for European film production which cannot be filled by public funds? If so, how can access to private financing be improved? (Talavera Milla, Kanzler, & Fontaine, 2016).

Public Service Broadcasting

EU countries are committed to public broadcasting services – the 1999 Treaty of Amsterdam recognized their role in providing for democratic, social and cultural needs that are not met by the market, and preventing the industry from being dominated by one or more big players.

Government grants to public broadcasters are therefore exempt from the EU's strict rules on state subsidies, if the funding is used for public service goals and does not unfairly disadvantage private sector broadcasters. As it stands, government policies in TV broadcasting are principally related to (European Commission, 2013; European Parliament, 2013):

- Citizens' rights and consumer protection (e.g., protection of minors, privacy, advertising and personal data)
- Issues related to EU single market and cultural policies (e.g., technical standards, interoperability, access to broadband interactivity), and
- Anti-trust and competition issues (e.g., monopolies and abuse of dominant position, competitive bottlenecks).

In fact, many established media firms and, notably, public service media are experiencing moments of considerable instability when financial pressures grow and challenges exhibited by new competitors emerge, content proliferates, audience behavior shifts, advertising revenue declines and budgets allocated to public media services are reduced. This is crucial as the public interest and service function of media, namely to ensure every citizen has easy access to diversified information, to stimulate their participation in public debate and to strengthen democracy, is critically endangered (European Commission, 2012; European Union, 2015; Mansell, 2014).

Media Literacy and Media Pluralism

Media literacy is the ability to access the media, to understand and to critically evaluate different aspects of the media and media content and to communicate in a variety of contexts. It is a fundamental skill for the younger generation and for adults. The EU considers media literacy to be an important factor for active citizenship in today's information society. The Council's conclusions on developing media literacy and critical thinking through education and training of 30 May 2016 underline that media literacy is more important than ever in the age of the internet and social media and that it needs to be an integral part of education and training at all levels. Media pluralism calls for the need for transparency, freedom and diversity in Europe's media landscape. At the beginning of 2012 the EU established the Centre for Media Pluralism and Media Freedom (CMPF) at the Robert Schuman Centre for Advanced Studies, a research initiative within the European University Institute in Florence, with co-funding from the EU (RSCAS, 2014; HLGMFP, 2013). The CMPF is a further step in the Commission's continuing effort to improve the protection of media pluralism and media freedom in Europe, and to determine the actions that need to be taken at European or national level to foster these objectives.

Policies to Promote Online Distribution

In the context of "connected TV", that is, new television services at the convergence of broadcast and broadband connectivity, government policies face the challenging task of securing a variety of choice for consumers, warranting identical conditions for the competition of platforms while at the same time taking the specificities of each use into consideration regarding its relevance to the formation of public opinion and the public interest (European Parliament, 2013; Murschetz, 2016; Nicoltchev, 2011; Valcke & Ausloos, 2014). In this context, the European Commission first launched a public stakeholder consultation in 2015 and then carried out an ex-post evaluation (so-called "REFIT") on the implications of the convergence between traditional TV and the internet. The latter assessed the effectiveness, efficiency, relevance, coherence and EU added-value of the AVMSD. It concluded the following: (1) changing the limit for commercial communications from 12 minutes per hour to 20% per day between 7a.m. and 11p.m.; (2) protecting minors from content that "may impair" them, with the same regulation applying to traditional broadcasts and on-demand services; (3) extending the provisions on European works to on-demand services providers, which have to ensure that European works make up at least 20% of their catalogues and give these works due prominence; and (4) bringing video-sharing platforms (VSPs) under the scope of the AVMSD for the purposes of combating hate speech and protecting minors from harmful content.

On 25 April 2017, the European Parliament's Committee on Culture and Education voted to amend the proposal for an updated EU Audiovisual Media Services Directive, presented by the Commission on 25 May 2016. The overarching goal of the proposal was to bring about a balance between competitiveness and consumer protection. It therefore aimed to introduce flexibility when restrictions only applicable to TV are no longer justified, promote European films, protect minors and tackle hate speech more efficiently. The new AVMSD also reflects a new approach to online platforms (European Parliament, 2017).

Conclusion: A Critical Review of Some Current Issues

Given the findings of this research, we can reasonably conclude the following: First, it is argued here that EU media policy is greatly challenged by issues of media convergence. Convergence is a complex process of transformation which can only be understood when its dynamisms of, and among, technological, industrial, organizational, politica and socio-cultural factors are taken into account. While asking how convergence adds value to media industry's players' corporate strategies is legitimate and important, one must remain skeptical, however, as to what effectively is to be gleaned from convergence when the socio-cultural dimensions are unresolved, and the strategies of audiences sold as mere commodities to advertisers and the media without considering its public value in the sense of benefitting the common good are critical.

Certainly, the disruptive potentials arising from convergence in its full dimensionality evoke a nexus of policy research dimensions. These span issues of technology change and innovation, effects of the convergence on journalism, effects of convergence on changes in the industry structure and the competitive behavior of incumbent media players and their new rivals from outside the industry, the evermore important changes in audience behavior, and any needs for public policy to protect consumers. Eventually, it is noteworthy to stress the importance of intensifying research into the need of policy convergence with a view to understanding its implications for a unified system of governance of the telecommunications, media and information technology sectors, and the various and often divergent ambitions of the stakeholders involved. An example is the new AVMSD. Although its increased protection for vulnerable viewers in VOD platforms has been greeted with satisfaction, the new rules on promoting European works and commercial communications have received mixed views from stakeholders. Still, the danger remains that governance actors will simply consider the issues as too difficult, too politically complex and too sensitive to confront. If they do so, they risk ignoring a central means through which governance outcomes in the media domain will be shaped in the twenty-first century.

Second, EU media policy's grand idea is to achieve a balance between competitiveness, cultural diversity and consumer protection. Keeping up this balance has become even more prominent in the twenty-first century with the shift towards convergent digital media, the associated rise of user-created content, multi-platform content distribution, and moves away from the mass communications paradigm that dominated twentieth-century media policy. Undeniably, media regulation has always been controversial, since it assumes state intervention, which limits freedom of expression and the right to communication. Globalization, technological convergence and other structural changes such as privatization, commercialization, industry consolidation and reregulation (referring to the relaxation of strict rules for broadcasting and telecommunications and the introduction of "light touch" regulatory frameworks) have had an impact that affects media policymaking and regulation. Many commentators attempt to elaborate on the theoretical foundations for understanding the ongoing developments in communications policy and regulatory aspects by providing definitions of the concept of the "public interest". Seen from an institutionalist perspective, Europe is built on a large framework of support to audiovisual and media across the continent. In total, these schemes account for (federal and regional) subsidies of more than 300 million euros per year. Support schemes come as direct subsidies supporting national film culture. State film support is organized on federal, regional and local levels, through either conditionally (i.e., when films are successful at the box office) repayable loans or as non-repayable grants (including prizes). However, while these schemes guarantee that the cultural film heritage of Europe is safeguarded and promoted, they seem to be biased towards safeguarding the economic well-being of these industries rather than promoting cultural innovation, and media literacy and pluralism.

And finally, in this chapter, it was argued that profound changes in the media ecosystem as such are taking place – for example those driven by convergence – which have important implications for effectively governing EU media policy. However, these impacts are complex, contrary and, of course, highly context-specific. Hence, various strands of scholarly research in current and emerging developments of media policy should be applied to various questions surrounding the fundamental transformation of the European media sector as driven by the paradigms of neoliberalism, privatization, commercialization and the bespoken convergence in media. Critically, on the level of principles, interventionist schemes of EU media policy are under pressure as government protection and support is a controversial means to regulate media markets and seem to have in-built biases towards failure in that they: (a) do not avoid the fundamental economic problem of market failure in the media industries; (b) are considered as economically ineffective as "free markets" work more efficiently; (c) are a waste of taxpayers' money, that is, cost to taxpayers exceeds benefit to consumers and producers; (d) do little to help adapt to future changes needed to get media suited to the needs of the market; (e) are considered to be politically challenging as far as they require consent across opposing political forces backed up by a solid and impartial method of selecting companies and channeling the money to them; (f) cannot create long-term sustainability but instead create dependence on the handouts of the state; (g) do not improve the working conditions of journalists; and (h) neither incentivize news consumption of audiences nor improve their satisfaction with content. Indeed, a combination of complexity, uncertainty and volatility is characteristic and explains a lot of what is unique about today's media life in practice and therefore why policy is distinctively challenging. Public policy (including media policy) in a globalized world is informed by multiple actors, although there are three that stand out above all others. These are the state (the core executive), the market (private and business actors including the media) and civil society (voluntary and community sector actors).

To conclude, it needs to be emphasized that building bridges from traditional media policy research to new theoretical perspectives such as research to media governance and policy formulation is inevitable (Turnpenny & Jordan, 2015). These new perspectives may offer a broader yet deeper understanding of emergent mechanisms and modes of operation. Policy analysis would learn a great deal from integrating these perspectives. These new perspectives may not only remain scientific research programmes (SRP) in the sense of Lakatos (1977), but also political actions programmes (PAP). Governance theory and policy formulation research then allows for situations in which a particular theory is simultaneously a "degenerating" SRP and a "progressive" PAP, that is, one that offers governments an expanding agenda of policy analysis, formulation, implementation and evaluation (Lakatos, 1977).

Notes

1 Additionally, the EU is party to the UNESCO Convention on the Protection and Promotion of the Diversity of Cultural Expressions and has secured an exemption from the WTO's free-trade rules (the "cultural exception"), that entitles EU countries to limit imports of cultural items like films. Further, during the Cannes Film Festival the EU organizes discussions and panels on various topics such as film financing, film distribution, audience development and innovation. The European Film Forum was launched in 2015 and is a platform for structured dialogue between policymakers and the audiovisual sector. A "New talent in the EU" award was introduced in 2004 to publicize young European directors who have followed MEDIA-sponsored training. The European Border Breakers Award is a prize for emerging artists, co-funded by the Creative Europe programme.
2 Jurisdiction over media policy is rather drawn from various articles within the TFEU to construct policies for the various media and communication technology sectors. This is a necessity arising from the complex nature of media goods and services, which can be defined neither solely as cultural goods nor simply as economic goods. The legal basis is contained in the TFEU in the form of Articles 28, 30, 34, 35 (free movement of goods); 45–62 (free movement of persons, services and capital); 101–109 (competition policy); 114 (technological harmonization, or the use of similar technological standards, for instance, in internet productions); 165 (education); 166 (vocational training); 167 (culture); and 173 (industry).

References

Donders, K., Pauwels, C., & Loisen, J. (Eds.) (2014). *The Palgrave Handbook of European Media Policy*. Houndmills: Palgrave Macmillan.
European Commission (2012). Fast-forward Europe 8 solutions to thrive in the digital world. http://ec.europa.eu/information_society/media_taskforce/doc/pluralism/forum/report.pdf
European Commission (2013). Preparing for a Fully Converged Audiovisual World: Growth, Creation and Values. Brussels, 24.4.2013, COM(2013)231 final. http://eur-lex.europa.eu
European Commission (2014a). State aid rules for film and other audiovisual works. Competition policy brief, issue 13, September, http://ec.europa.eu/competition/publications/cpb/2014/013_en.pdf.
European Commission (2014b). European film in the digital era: Bridging cultural diversity and competitiveness. Final report, COM(2014)272F. Brussels, Belgium.
European Parliament (2013). The challenges of Connected TV. www.europarl.europa.eu/RegData/etudes/note/join/2013/513976/IPOL-CULT_NT%282013%29513976_EN.pdf.
European Parliament (2017). Audiovisual and media policy. Fact Sheet on the European Union www.europarl.europa.eu/atyourservice/en/displayFtu.html?ftuId=FTU_5.13.2.html.
European Union (2015). Digital agenda scoreboard 2015: Most targets reached, time has come to lift digital borders. https://ec.europa.eu/digital-agenda/en/news/digital-agenda-scoreboard-2015-most-targets-reached-time-has-comelift-digital-borders.
European Union (2016a). EU MEDIA Programme 1991–2016. https://ec.europa.eu/digital-single-market/en/news/eu-MEDIA-programme-1991-2016.
European Union (2016b). Factsheet. 25 years of the MEDIA Programme. 13 May 2016. http://europa.eu/rapid/press-release_MEMO-16-1709_en.htm.
European Union (2017). Audiovisual and media. https://europa.eu/european-union/topics/audiovisual-media_en.
European Union (2018). The EU in brief. https://europa.eu/european-union/about-eu/eu-in-brief_en

HLGMFP (2013). A free and pluralist media to sustain European democracy: The report of the High-Level Group on media freedom and pluralism. https://ec.europa.eu/digital-agenda/sites/digital-agenda/files/HLG%20Final%20Report.pdf.

Iosifidis, P. (2011). *Global Media and Communication Policy*. Basingstoke: Palgrave Macmillan.

Lakatos, I. (1977). *The Methodology of Scientific Research Programmes: Philosophical Papers Volume 1*. Cambridge: Cambridge University Press.

Lunt, P., & Livingstone, S. (2012). *Media Policy Media Regulation: Governance and the Interests of Citizens and Consumers*. London, UK: Sage.

Mansell, R. (2014). Here comes the revolution — the European digital agenda. In K. Donders, C. Pauwels, & J. Loisen (Eds.), *The Palgrave Handbook of European Media Policy* (pp. 202–217). London: Palgrave Macmillan.

Murschetz, P. C. (Ed.) (2014). *State Aid for Newspapers: Theories, Cases, Actions*. Cham: Springer International Publishing.

Murschetz, P. C. (2016). Connected television: media convergence, industry structure and corporate strategies. In E. L. Cohen (Ed.), *Communication Yearbook* 40 (pp. 69–93). New York: Routledge.

Murschetz, P. C., Teichmann, R., & Karmasin, M. (Eds.) (2018). *The Handbook of State Aid for Film: Finance, Industries, Regulation*. Cham: Springer International Publishing.

Murschetz, P. C. (2018). State supported journalism. In T. P. Vos, & F. Hanusch (Eds.), *The International Encyclopedia of Journalism Studies*. Hoboken, NJ: Wiley-Blackwell.

Nicoltchev, S. (Ed.) (2011). Iris special: The regulation of on-demand audiovisual services: Chaos or coherence?. Observatoire européen de l'audiovisuel: Strasbourg, 53–56.

Nielsen, R. K., & Linnebank, G. (2011). *Public Support for the Media: A Six-Country Overview of Direct and Indirect Subsidies*, Oxford: Reuters Institute for the Study of Journalism.

Picard, R. G., & Pickard, V. (2017). *Essential Principles for Contemporary Media and Communications Policymaking*. Oxford: Reuters Institute for the Study of Journalism. https://reutersinstitute.politics.ox.ac.uk

Puppis, M., Simpson, S., & Van den Bulck, H. (2016). Contextualising European media policy in the twenty-first century. In S. Simpson, M. Puppis, & H. Van den Bulck (Eds.), *European Media Policy for the Twenty-First Century: Assessing the Past, Setting Agendas for the Future* (pp. 1–23). London: Routledge.

RSCAS – Robert Schuman Centre for Advanced Studies (2014). The evolving regulation of the media in Europe as an instrument for freedom and pluralism (by Elda Brogi and Pier Luigi Parcu). Florence: EUI Working Paper RSCAS 2014/09.

Talavera Milla, J., Kanzler, M., & Fontaine, G. (2016). Public financing for film and audiovisual content – The state of soft money in Europe. Strasbourg: European Audiovisual Observatory.

Turnpenny, J. R., & Jordan, A. J. (Eds.) (2015). *The Tools of Policy Formulation: Actors, Capacities, Venues and Effects* (pp. 3–33). Cheltenham: Edward Elgar Publications.

Valcke, P., & Ausloos, J. (2014). Audiovisual media services 3.0: (Re)defining the scope of European broadcasting law in a converging and connected media environment. In K. Donders, C. Pauwels, & J. Loisen (Eds.), *The Palgrave Handbook of European Media Policy* (pp. 312–328). Basingstoke: Palgrave Macmillan.

7 The Entertainment Landscape of the United Kingdom

Exploring British Television, Radio, and Film

Jeffrey L. Griffin

Introduction

This chapter will examine the entertainment landscape of the United Kingdom and consider the impact that the British television and film industries have on the rest of the world. Any overview of the British entertainment sector must include consideration of political, geographic, and cultural factors that have affected its development.

Background

The United Kingdom, which consists of England, Wales, Scotland, – the three countries of the island of Great Britain – and Northern Ireland, is a parliamentary constitutional monarchy with the monarch serving in the symbolic role of head of state and a prime minister as head of government. The UK joined the European Union in 1973, but in a popular referendum held in December 2016, UK citizens voted to leave the EU, the so-called Brexit, by a vote of 52% to 48% (Kennedy, 2017). Prime Minister Theresa May formally triggered the split in March 2017 by signing a letter invoking Article 50 of the Lisbon Treaty and submitting it to EU President Donald Tusk, ushering in two years of negotiations on the UK's departure. The UK is a member of the Commonwealth, a voluntary political association of 52 independent states that was founded in 1949 (The Commonwealth, n.d.). An outgrowth of the British empire, the Commonwealth primarily consists of former British colonies. Slightly smaller than Oregon, the United Kingdom has a population of nearly 65 million (CIA World Factbook, n.d.). While English is not designated as the official language of the UK, it is the de facto official language. Recognized regional languages are Scots, spoken by about 30% of the people of Scotland; Scottish Gaelic, spoken by about 60,000 people in Scotland; Welsh, spoken by about 20% of the people of Wales; Irish, spoken by about 10% of the Northern Ireland populace; and Cornish, spoken by 2,000 to 3,000 people in Cornwall (CIA World Factbook, n.d.). The UK economy is healthy, having recovered well from the prolonged economic downturn of 2008–09. In 2016, the UK had a gross domestic product of $2.648 trillion, the fifth biggest in the world (World Bank, n.d.). The gross domestic product grew 0.4% in the third quarter of 2017, and it was up 1.7% compared to one year earlier (Office for National Statistics, 2017). The production sector, agricultural sector, and services industry were the main engines of GDP growth.

Television in Britain: The Basics

Television is all but ubiquitous in UK homes, with 26.7 million of the 28 million homes being TV households (Broadcasters' Audience Research Board, n.d.-a). Furthermore, all TV households have some sort of digital television. Digital terrestrial platforms have the largest share of households, followed by digital satellite, with digital cable a distant third (Broadcasters' Audience Research Board, n.d.-b). Brits watch a considerable amount of television – slightly more than three and a half hours a day per person (Broadcasters' Audience Research Board, 2017), but that pales in comparison to the five hours four minutes of television that the average American watches (Koblin, 2016).

The television landscape is dominated by five entities, all of which operate multiple channels: the British Broadcasting Corporation (BBC), ITV, Channel 4, Channel 5, and Sky. Public broadcaster BBC, which operates nine television channels, including the flagship broadcast networks BBC One and BBC Two, leads the pack in terms of viewership. The BBC's networks collectively accounted for 32% of all viewing in 2016 (Broadcasters' Audience Research Board, 2017). The ITV raft of networks, consisting of flagship commercial broadcast network ITV and a dozen spinoff channels, accounted for 21% of viewing. Commercial broadcaster Channel 4 and its eight spinoff networks commanded 10%, while Sky, which operates a raft of 38 satellite networks, accounted for 8% of viewing. In fifth place was Channel 5, which operates commercial broadcaster Channel 5 and seven other networks, collectively accounting for 6% of viewing. It is noteworthy that the terrestrial broadcasters have been so successful at adapting to the increasingly competitive, fragmented television landscape, retaining viewership on their original networks, while at the same time taking advantage of the possibilities afforded by the digital era to create new companion offerings.

As noted earlier, more Brits access television through a digital terrestrial platform than any other method. A digital television service called Freeview, owned and operated by the BBC, ITV, Channel 4, Sky, and Arqiva (a communications infrastructure company), launched in 2002 (Freeview, n.d.-a). With more than 19 million homes using Freeview, it is the most watched digital platform in the UK. A free service, as the name implies, Freeview provides more than 70 standard-definition channels and 15 high-definition channels (Freeview, n.d.-b). Freeview can be accessed through a rooftop antenna, or aerial, as the British call it. Televisions sold in the UK that were manufactured after 2010 have Freeview built in and only need the aerial to be connected.

While watching live television through a TV set remains the overwhelmingly dominant way that Brits access television, increasingly people watch programs on demand. A study of long-form viewing across all devices indicates that people spend 80% of their time watching live television, compared to 12% watching recorded programming and 8% watching on-demand programming (Ofcom, 2017). Streaming, both of programming on traditional networks and over-the-top services such as Netflix and Amazon Prime, is gaining popularity. A report issued in August 2017 by Ofcom, the country's regulatory body for television and radio, showed that 67% of adults use the online services of the main British broadcasters – BBC iplayer, ITV Hub, All4, and My5 – while 45% use a subscription streaming service such as Netflix or Amazon Prime (Ofcom, 2017).

Profiling the Leading Television Networks

BBC One and its companion network, BBC Two, are commercial-free channels. Like other BBC television networks and the public broadcaster's radio services, they are funded through the proceeds of a license fee. Every television household is required to pay an annual license fee. Similarly, the license fee must be paid to watch or download BBC programs through the BBC iPlayer streaming service. In April 2019, the license fee was raised to £154.50 pounds, which is about $197 (BBC, 2019). The BBC, which began a regular television service in 1936, – making it the first broadcaster in the world to do so – operates under a royal charter. It is accountable to the public through Parliament and must periodically justify that it is serving the public and making good use of the license-fee revenue. The previous royal charter expired at the end of December 2016 and was renewed through the end of December 2027 (BBC, 2016).

BBC One is a general-interest network aimed at a mainstream audience. As such, it offers a range of popular fare, including fictional programming such as dramas and sitcoms, light-entertainment programs, and sporting events. News and public-affairs programs are also prominently featured on the schedule. Seven-part nature series *Blue Planet II* was the most-popular television show in 2017, with an episode that attracted 14 million viewers (Taylor, 2018). Reality-competition series *Strictly Come Dancing* was the BBC One's second-most popular program in 2017, with one episode attracting 13 million viewers. The most-watched fictional shows on BBC One in 2017 were the detective drama *Sherlock*, a modern-day updating of Sherlock Holmes, and *Call the Midwife*, a drama about midwives set in the East End of London in the late 1950s and early 1960s (IMDb, n.d.-a). Both are veteran dramas. Four seasons – or *series*, as the British say – of *Sherlock* have aired since the show began in 2010 (IMDb, n.d.-b). *Call the Midwife* aired its seventh season in early 2018. Also popular on BBC One in 2017 was the miniseries drama *The Moorside*, about the abduction of a schoolgirl. Venerable science-fiction series *Doctor Who*, which the BBC revived in 2005, has slumped in recent years but remains a hit. The 2017 season averaged 5.5 million viewers, the fewest of the ten seasons that have aired since the show was revived (Doctor Who ratings, 2017). A further sign of attrition is that the 2017 Christmas special was watched by 7.9 million viewers (Call the Midwife wins Christmas, 2018), a hefty total, but one that pales in comparison to the 13.3 million who watched the 2007 Christmas special. This signature BBC property is getting a reboot, with a new showrunner coming aboard in 2018 and a new doctor. For the first time in the franchise's history, the time lord Doctor Who regenerated as a woman at the end of the 2017 Christmas special. Reporting on the show's viewership decline but cultural importance nonetheless, *The Guardian* wrote:

> *Doctor Who* is not the cultural juggernaut it once was: in the David Tennant era of the mid-late 2000s, the BBC One show regularly attracted more than 10 million live viewers; with Peter Capaldi as the Doctor, the audience sunk to under half that figure, the lowest ratings since it returned to television in 2005 . . . But, when it is firing, *Doctor Who* is still one of the only programmes – and perhaps the only drama – that can draw a genuine family audience, sitting together in one room at the moment of transmission.
>
> (Lewis, 2017)

But the news that a woman would play Doctor Who shocked many, both in Britain and around the world. As *The Guardian* noted, "The headline that, after half a century of white men there would at last be a female Doctor Who, was reported around the world" (Lewis, 2017). BBC One fares well with police procedurals, including veteran *Death in Paradise*, which started in 2011. Set on a fictional Caribbean island, *Death in Paradise* offers viewers a "blend of relentlessly upbeat whimsy" (O'Donovan, 2017). Another popular, long-running BBC One crime drama is forensic-pathologist series *Silent Witness*, which started in 1996. A further example is *Shetland*, set on Scotland's remote Shetland islands. Based on a series of novels by Ann Cleeves, *Shetland* revolves around Detective Inspector Jimmy Perez. Airing its fourth season in 2018, the show has been described as a "brooding dark cop drama – Celtic noir" (Wollaston, 2016). Another type of drama that BBC One is known for is period dramas. A current example is *Poldark*, a remake of a 1970s series set in eighteenth-century Cornwall. Based on a series of novels by Winston Graham, *Poldark* debuted in 2015 with an eight-episode run and was an instant hit (Sweney, 2015). The third series aired in summer 2017, and a fourth was slated for 2018. One of the mainstays in the BBC One prime-time lineup, soap *EastEnders*, is no longer the ratings powerhouse that it long was, but remains a popular series. The venerable soap, which airs four times a week, premiered in 1985. Comedy has historically been a strength of BBC One. The sitcom *Peter Kay's Car Share* burst onto the scene in 2015, becoming an instant hit. Starring comedian Peter Kay, the show, which revolves around two supermarket employees who commute to work together, had the most-watched premiere of any sitcom on any channel since 2011 (Conlan, 2015). The show's six-episode first season was followed by a four-episode second season in 2017, after which Kay announced he intended to stop the series. Fans were overwrought by the show's demise and unresolved storyline, with more than 100,000 even signing a petition demanding a new conclusion to the series, and, ultimately, Kay relented, agreeing to bring the series back in 2018 for an improvised episode and for a new finale (Doran, 2017). Critics have lavished praise on *Car Share*, with *The Independent* calling it "a welcome remedy to modern-day burnout" (Brown, 2017) and the *New Statesman* proclaiming that "it has the ability briefly to restore one's faith in human beings" (Cooke, 2017). *Car Share* has also won numerous awards, including the National Television Award in 2016 for Most Popular Comedy Series, the BAFTA TV Award in 2016 for Best Scripted Comedy, and a Broadcast Award in 2016 for Best Original Programme (IMDb, n.d.-c).

BBC Two, which launched in 1964, is not aimed at mainstream viewers in the same way that BBC One is. The diverse slate of programming spans the same categories, but the emphasis is different. Factual programming, such as documentaries, looms large in the schedule. For example, a six-part 2018 documentary series titled *A Vicar's Life* examined the clergy (Braxton, 2018). Similarly, a three-part 2018 documentary called *Surgeons: At the Edge of Life* profiled surgeons who are on the cutting edge of medical science (Rackham, n.d). The biggest current drama hit is *Peaky Blinders*, which revolves around an English gangster family in the 1920s. The fourth season averaged 3.3 million viewers per episode, the most of any BBC Two drama in 2017, and a fifth season is slated for 2019 (Deen, 2018). Comedy is another strength of BBC Two, ranging from panel shows to sitcoms. A popular veteran sitcom is *Episodes*. *Episodes*, which debuted in 2011, is a fish-out-of-water comedy revolving around a husband-and-wife team of writers who go to Hollywood for an American remake of a sitcom they created. BBC Two is also known for programs centering on such things as antiques, gardening, and cars. Shows about antiques include *Celebrity Antiques Road Trip*, while a popular gardening series is *Gardeners' World*. Auto show *Top Gear*, which was revived in 2002, has been a key performer for BBC Two, although viewership has declined since popular host Jeremy Clarkson was fired in 2015. Now hosted by American Matt LeBlanc, the actor best known for his role in *Friends*, the motoring show was slated to air its twenty-fifth series in 2018 (Karasin, 2018).

ITV is a mainstream commercial network that began broadcasting in 1955. ITV is made up of 15 regional franchises, originally all owned by separate companies, but now 13 of which are owned by ITV plc (ITV plc, n.d.). ITV does especially well with fictional programs. Drama is a strength, particularly police procedurals. Popular ITV police series include *Midsomer Murders, Vera,* and *Broadchurch. Midsomer Murders*, which debuted in 1997, is a veritable institution on British television that shows no signs of slowing down. It has continued to generate strong viewership, even weathering the replacement of the lead character, DCI Tom Barnaby, after 2011 (IMDb, n.d.-d). Now another Barnaby, Tom's cousin John, is the DCI solving murders in fictional Midsomer County. *Vera*, which began in 2011, stars renowned actress Brenda Blethyn as DCI Vera Stanhope, who investigates murders in Northumberland (IMDb, n.d.-e). The return of *Broadchurch* for its third and likely final season in 2017 fared well, with the final episode attracting 11.6 million viewers, the biggest audience for any drama on British television that year (Taylor, 2018). Set in a coastal South West England town, *Broadchurch* revolves around DCI Alec Hardy, portrayed by noted British actor David Tennant, known for his starring role in *Doctor Who*. A popular ITV period drama is *Victoria*, which focuses on the early years of Queen Victoria's reign. *Victoria* premiered in 2016. Comedy-drama is another strength of ITV, and a successful, long-running example is *Doc Martin*, which centers on a brilliant doctor who lacks social skills and suffers from a blood phobia. Set in a coastal Cornish village, *Doc Martin*, which premiered in 2004, aired its eighth season in 2017. Another key comedy-drama for ITV has been *Cold Feet*, a series exploring the bonds between three couples in Manchester that had a very successful five-season run from 1997–2003. During that time, the acclaimed series won numerous prestigious awards, including Best TV Comedy Drama at the British Comedy Awards in 1999, 2000, and 2003, a BAFTA Award for Best Drama Series in 2002, and a National Television Award for Most Popular Comedy Programme in 2002 (IMDb, n.d.-f). Thirteen years after it originally ended, *Cold Feet* was revived, returning with new seasons in 2016 and 2017. The show remains a solid performer, with the 2017 season averaging 5.1 million viewers per episode, and another season is slated for 2018 (More Cold Feet, 2017). Prime-time soaps perform well for ITV, year in and year out. *Coronation Street*, which debuted in 1960, is perennially one of the most-watched shows on British television. Revolving around the Rovers Return pub in the fictional Northern England town of Weatherfield, *Coronation Street* currently airs six episodes a week, two each on Monday, Wednesday and Friday. In 2016, the show hosted a royal guest, as Queen Elizabeth's daughter, Princess Anne, visited the set, alongside a group of 50 Commonwealth leaders from the business, governmental, and non-governmental organization sectors (Cliff, 2016). *Emmerdale*, a soap set in the Yorkshire Dales, has been another reliable hit since its launch in 1972. *Emmerdale* also airs six episodes weekly, with one episode Monday, Tuesday, Wednesday, and Friday and two on Thursday. ITV also airs popular reality fare such as *I'm a Celebrity. . .Get Me Out of Here, The Voice UK*, and *The X Factor*. The initial episode of the 2017 installment of *I'm a Celebrity. . .Get Me Out of Here* was watched by 12.7 million viewers, the biggest audience of the year for ITV (Jefferies, 2018).

Channel 4 is a publicly owned, not-for-profit, commercial broadcaster. Channel 4, which launched in 1982, describes its remit as "to deliver high-quality, innovative, alternative content that challenges the status quo" (Channel 4, n.d.). The crown jewel in Channel 4's lineup is a cooking competition, *The Great British Bake Off*. The immensely popular show was poached from BBC One in a 2016 deal, and new episodes began airing on Channel 4 in 2017. Ten million viewers watched the 2017 finale, and, although that was six million fewer than the 2016 finale on BBC One, it was still the fourth-biggest audience in Channel 4 history (Jefferies, 2018). The shift of the show to Channel 4 was a remarkably big deal in the UK. As *The Atlantic* wrote:

> It's hard to accurately convey how well-loved The Great British Bake Off is in the U.K., just as it's difficult to explain the appeal of the somewhat eccentric televised baking contest—in which a contestant once fashioned a cake re-creation of his near-death experience—to someone who's never seen it. When news broke last year that the series had been purchased by a rival network, after airing on the BBC for all of its seven seasons, a fit of something akin to national hysteria broke out.
>
> (Gilbert, 2017)

Fears that Channel 4 "might hipsterize a show that was defiantly un-hip at best" did not prove to be founded, and the show has continued to be a cultural force in a way that few TV shows ever are (Gilbert, 2017). *The Atlantic* noted

> Britain may be divided by Brexit, and by national politics, and even by the cultural merit of Celebrity Love Island, but #GBBO, as it's referred to on Twitter, is a great uniter. Popular among men and women, young and old, it keeps what's left of Britain's tattered dream of pluralism and equality alive.
>
> (Gilbert, 2017)

Other reality television programs perform well for Channel 4, particularly the oddly premised *Gogglebox*, which features people watching television shows in their homes, reacting to what they are watching and giving their opinions of the shows. In 2017, *The Telegraph* reflected on the surprising success of *Gogglebox*:

> Who would have predicted that watching other people watching TV would become such a ratings-gobbling, award-grabbing phenomenon? Yet that's precisely the pitch for Gogglebox, which returns for its ninth run this week. The Channel 4 hit won its third consecutive National Television Award last month, to add to a groaning mantlepiece that already holds a Bafta and half-a-dozen other gongs.
>
> (Hogan, 2017)

Channel 4 also airs comedies, including *Derry Girls*, which debuted in January 2018 and immediately became a sensation. Set in the 1990s in the Northern Ireland city of Derry, the sitcom emerged as Channel 4's biggest comedy hit in years, averaging about 2.5 million viewers per episode (Derry Girl Tara celebrates "whole female-led TV Show", 2108). Travel shows are also popular on Channel 4. Examples from 2017 include *Coastal Railways with Julie Walters* and *Travel Man: 48 Hours in Tenerife* (Broadcasters' Audience Research Board, n.d.-c).

Channel 5, which is owned by American media conglomerate Viacom, is perennially the least watched of the five big terrestrial broadcasters. Channel 5, which launched in 1997, was purchased in 2014 by Viacom, which paid nearly $760 million to acquire it from Richard Desmond's Northern & Shell Media Group (James, 2014). Channel 5's lineup is a low-budget mix of imported programming, reality fare, and old films, with a dose of sports thrown in. American imports such as crime series *NCIS* and science-fiction series *The X-Files* help anchor prime time, as do Australian soaps *Neighbours* and *Home and Away*. Reality programs such as *GPs: Behind Closed Doors*, which centers on a local medical practice, and *Police Interceptors*, which revolves around high-speed police units, also dot the lineup.

The flagship network of satellite provider Sky, which is owned by 21st Century Fox, is Sky One. In December 2017, global media baron Rupert Murdoch announced the sale of most of his entertainment assets, including a controlling share of most 21st Century Fox properties, Sky among them, to American media conglomerate Disney (Sweney, 2017). Sky One programming includes original fiction series such as the historical drama *Jamestown*, which revolves around three British women in the New World in the early seventeenth century. Another original, which premiered in 2018, is the comedy-drama *Bliss*, which focuses on the moral dilemma of a travel writer who is a bigamist (Dowell, 2018). A leading original is superhero crime drama *Stan Lee's Lucky Man*, which debuted in 2016. First-season episodes were watched by a cumulative average of 1.9 million viewers per episode, making the show the most successful drama series ever on Sky One (Tartaglione, 2016). A third season is slated for 2018. Sky One also airs lots of U.S. fare, including comedy series *The Simpsons* and *Modern Family*, crime dramas *NCIS: Los Angeles* and *Hawaii Five-O*, and action series *MacGyver*.

British Television Exports

Britain consistently ranks as the world's second-biggest exporter of television programs. In the one-year period from April 2015 through March 2016, British program exports amounted to $1.7 billion, a 10% jump over the previous year (Barraclough, 2017). Sales to the United States, the UK's biggest export market, hit $624 million, reflecting a 16% increase. The leading scripted shows in 2015–16 sales were mystery series *Sherlock* and sci-fi series *Doctor Who*, both of which sold in more than 200 territories (Pact, n.d.). Natural-history series *Planet Earth II* was sold in 154 territories (BBC Worldwide, n.d.).

Another popular British show in foreign markets is *Downtown Abbey*, a recent costume drama about the lives of an aristocratic family and its staff. *Downtown Abbey* airs in 250 territories worldwide (Scott, 2017). Detective drama *Midsomer Murders* has sold in more than 220 territories, while *Vera*, another detective drama, has sold in over 290 territories.

The growth of streaming services has opened up new horizons for fans of British television. Not only do mega-streamers such as Netflix, Amazon Prime, and Hulu offer some British fare, but there are also streaming services in some markets aimed at Anglophiles. For example, in the United States, Acorn TV, owned by RLJ Entertainment, launched in 2013 and a rival service, BritBox, backed by BBC commercial arm BBC Worldwide and broadcaster ITV, started in 2017. Acorn TV, which costs $49.99 per year or $4.99 per month, had about 430,000 subscribers at the end of 2016. *The Hollywood Reporter* described Acorn TV as "the glorious streaming service specializing in all things British television (and now beyond)," and went on to anoint it as perhaps "the best platform you've never heard of and thus aren't using" (Goodman, 2017). BritBox, which is priced at $6.99 per month, had not yet released subscriber numbers as of early 2018.

Radio in Britain

Radio remains a popular, almost universally utilized medium in Britain. About 90% of people listen to the radio at least once a week (Ofcom, 2017). Furthermore, the amount of time spent listening has actually increased and now stands at 21 hours 24 minutes per week on average. The BBC is the dominant player in radio, with its stations collectively accounting for 53% of listening in 2016, while commercial stations collectively accounted for 45% of listening (Ofcom, 2017). Technological advances have also affected the radio landscape. For example, 57% of homes have a digital radio receiver, and 31% of households have a car with digital radio. Furthermore, 46% of listening now takes place on a digital platform, that is, through a digital radio receiver, online, or through a TV set. Another sign of the impact of newer technologies is that 8% of UK adults listen weekly to podcasts (Ofcom, 2017).

Film in Britain

Cinema-going remains a popular entertainment option for Brits despite the increasing competition from home entertainment. UK cinemas grossed £1.2 billion at the box office in 2016, and that was the second-biggest total on record, eclipsed slightly by the 2015 haul (British Film Institute, 2017). Altogether, 168.3 million movie tickets were sold in 2016, reflecting a drop of 2% from the year before. Movie fans had lots to choose from: 821 films were released at cinemas in 2016 in the UK and Republic of Ireland (British Film Institute, 2017). However, as in most countries, U.S. films are a major force, accounting for 26% of all film releases in 2016 (217 films) and 59% of the total box office. Still, the vitality of the British film industry cannot be denied, both in terms of the number of films made and their impact at the box office. In 2016, 176 British films were released at the cinema, and they accounted for 36% of the total box-office take. The four highest-grossing films at the UK box office in 2016 were all international coproductions, but all qualified as UK films: *Rogue One: A Star Wars Story, Fantastic Beasts and Where To Find Them, Bridget Jones's Baby*, and *The Jungle Book* (British Film Institute, 2017). British-qualifying films are eligible for generous tax breaks under The Creative Industries Tax Reliefs, which started in 2007 (Elliott, 2017). This tax-relief scheme has encouraged big Hollywood studios to make films in Britain, boosting the country's film industry. According to the Office for National Statistics, the film and television industries contributed £7.7 billion to the British economy in 2016 – reflecting an 80% increase over five years (2017). Spending on film production is soaring: in 2017, a record £1.9 billion was spent on film production, a jump of 12% compared to the previous year (British Film Institute, 2018). Four of the five highest-grossing films at the box office in 2017 were made in the UK: *Star Wars: The Last Jedi, Beauty and the Beast, Dunkirk*, and *Paddington 2*.

Global Dimensions of British Film

Britain is significant in a global context both as a film market and as a country whose film exports greatly exceed its imports. An analysis of the global film market in 2016 ranked the United Kingdom as the fourth-largest filmed entertainment market in the world, trailing only the United States, China, and Japan (British Film Institute, 2017). The analysis of film revenues by PricewaterhouseCoopers calculated the global share that countries/regions had. The $3,908 million in filmed entertainment revenues of the United Kingdom accounted for 5.8% of the global total. While this was dwarfed by the $21,199 million in revenues and 31.4% share of the

United States, it still exceeded the revenues and shares of such countries/regions as Germany (ranked 5), France (6), and other Western European countries (7). The vitality of Britain's film industry is reflected in the export market – in 2015, the UK film industry exported nearly £2 billion worth of services, taking into account both intellectual property and audiovisual and related services (British Film Institute, 2017). Furthermore, when film imports are taken into account, Britain had a positive balance of trade of £1.2 billion in 2015.

References

Barraclough, L. (2017, February 2). British Television exports rise 10% to $1.66 Billion. *Variety*. Retrieved from http://variety.com/2017/tv/global/british-television-exports-rise-ten-per-cent-1201976483/

Braxton, M. (2018, January 26). A Vicar's Life on BBC2: so much more than collars and cassocks. *Radio Times*. Retrieved from www.radiotimes.com/news/tv/2018-01-26/a-vicars-life-bbc-2-review/

BBC Worldwide. (n.d.). Transformation: Annual Review 2016–2017. Retrieved from www.bbcworldwide.com/media/2176/bbcw_annual_report_16-17.pdf

British Broadcasting Corporation. (2019, May 13). Where can I find information about the licence fee?. Retrieved from www.bbc.co.uk/faqs/general/licence_fee

British Broadcasting Corporation. (2016, December). Copy of Royal Charter for the continuance of the British Broadcasting Corporation. Retrieved from http://downloads.bbc.co.uk/bbctrust/assets/files/pdf/about/how_we_govern/2016/charter.pdf

British Film Institute. (2017). BFI Statistical Yearbook 2017. Retrieved from www.bfi.org.uk/sites/bfi.org.uk/files/downloads/bfi-statistical-yearbook-2017.pdf

British Film Institute. (2018, January 31). BFI press release: BFI statistics for 2017 show new record for UK film and high-end TV production spend. Retrieved from www.bfi.org.uk/sites/bfi.org.uk/files/downloads/bfi-press-release-bfi-statistics-new-record-uk-film-high-end-tv-production-spend-2018-01-31.pdf

Broadcasters' Audience Research Board. (2017, March). Trends in television viewing 2016. Retrieved from www.barb.co.uk/download/?file=/wp-content/uploads/2017/03/BARB-Trends-in-Television-Viewing-2016.pdf

Broadcasters' Audience Research Board. (n.d.-a). TV ownership: Television ownership in private domestic households 1956–2017 (millions). Retrieved from www.barb.co.uk/resources/tv-ownership/

Broadcasters' Audience Research Board. (n.d.-b). Universes. Retrieved from www.barb.co.uk/resources/universes/

Broadcasters' Audience Research Board. (n.d.-c). Monthly top 10 programmes. Retrieved from www.barb.co.uk/viewing-data/monthly-top-10/

Brown, J. (2017, April 13). Series 2 of Car Share ups the romance and the laughs. *The Independent*. Retrieved from www.independent.co.uk/arts-entertainment/series-2-car-share-peter-kay-bbc-a7681861.html

Call the Midwife wins Christmas TV ratings battle once again. (2018, Jan. 2). *The Telegraph*. Retrieved from www.telegraph.co.uk/news/2018/01/02/call-midwife-wins-christmas-tv-ratings-battle/

Channel 4. (n.d.). What is Channel 4?. Retrieved from www.channel4.com/corporate/about-4/who-we-are/what-is-channel-4

CIA World Factbook. (n.d.). United Kingdom. Retrieved from www.cia.gov/library/publications/the-world-factbook/geos/uk.html

Cliff, M. (2016, April 14). Did she have a drink in the Rovers? Princess Anne follows in the Queen's footsteps with a visit to Coronation Street. *The Daily Mail*. Retrieved from www.dailymail.co.uk/femail/article-3539810/Princess-Anne-follows-Queen-s-footsteps-visit-Coronation-Street.html

Conlan, T. (2015, May 22). BBC's Car Share is highest-rated sitcom to premiere on any channel. *The Guardian*. Retrieved from www.theguardian.com/media/2015/may/22/car-share-becomes-highest-rated-sitcom-to-premiere-on-any-channel

Cooke, R. (2017, April 28). Peter Kay's Car Share will restore your faith in human beings. *New Statesman*. Retrieved from www.newstatesman.com/culture/tv-radio/2017/04/peter-kays-car-share-will-restore-your-faith-human-beings

Deen, S. (2018, January 12). Tom Hardy's Peaky Blinders death helps show become most-watched drama on BBC Two in 2017. *Metro*. Retrieved from http://metro.co.uk/2018/01/12/tom-hardys-peaky-blinders-death-helps-show-become-watched-drama-bbc-two-2017-7223490/

Derry Girl Tara celebrates 'whole female-led TV Show'. (2018, February 4). Raidió Teilifís Éireann. Retrieved from www.rte.ie/entertainment/2018/0204/938224-derry-girl-tara-celebrates-whole-female-led-tv-show/

Doctor Who ratings for last series lowest since it returned to TV in 2005. (2017, July 10). *The Irish News*. Retrieved from www.irishnews.com/magazine/entertainment/2017/07/10/news/doctor-who-ratings-for-last-series-lowest-since-it-returned-to-tv-in-2005-1080816/

Doran, S. (2017, November 17). Peter Kay confirms Car Share will return in 2018. *Radio Times*. Retrieved from www.radiotimes.com/news/tv/2017-11-17/peter-kay-confirms-car-share-will-return-in-2018/

Dowell, B. (2018, January 6). First look at Stephen Mangan and Heather Graham in new Sky 1 comedy Bliss. *Radio Times*. Retrieved from www.radiotimes.com/news/2018-01-26/bliss-sky-1-stephen-mangan-heather-graham-pictures/

Elliott, L. (2017, December 14). The force is strong with British film industry as revenues soar. *The Guardian*. Retrieved from www.theguardian.com/film/2017/dec/14/the-force-is-strong-with-british-film-industry-as-revenues-soar

Freeview. (n.d.-a). About us. Retrieved from www.freeview.co.uk/about-us#uGSVeB2fGoc5wl4T.97

Freeview. (n.d.-b). Retrieved from www.freeview.co.uk/why-freeview#u0tk9vYplD9fltXA.97

Gilbert, S. (2017, August 30). The Great British Bake Off keeps the dream alive. *The Atlantic*. Retrieved from www.theatlantic.com/entertainment/archive/2017/08/the-great-british-bakeoff-returns-on-channel-4/538419/

Goodman, T. (2017, January 20). Critic's notebook: On the wonders of little-known streaming service Acorn TV. *The Hollywood Reporter*. Retrieved from www.hollywoodreporter.com/bastard-machine/acorn-tv-streaming-966641?utm_source=twitter&utm_source=t.co&utm_medium=referral

Hogan, M. (2017, February 24). From the "end of civilisation" to the talk of Westminster: is Gogglebox truly Britain at its best? *The Telegraph*. Retrieved from www.telegraph.co.uk/tv/0/end-civilisation-talk-westminster-gogglebox-truly-britain-best/

IMDb. (n.d.-a). Call the Midwife. Retrieved from www.imdb.com/title/tt1983079/

IMDb. (n.d.-b). Sherlock. Retrieved from www.imdb.com/title/tt1475582/

IMDb. (n.d.-c). Car Share. Retrieved from www.imdb.com/title/tt4635922/awards?ref_=tt_ql_op_1

IMDb. (n.d.-d). Midsomer Murders. Retrieved from www.imdb.com/title/tt0118401/

IMDb. (n.d.-e). Vera. Retrieved from www.imdb.com/title/tt1693592/

IMDb. (n.d.-f). Cold Feet. Retrieved from www.imdb.com/title/tt0168596/

ITV plc. (n.d.). About ITV/ History. Retrieved from www.itvplc.com/about/history/2017

James, M. (2014, May 1). Viacom buys Britain's Channel 5 Broadcasting for $760 million. *The Los Angeles Times*. Retrieved from www.latimes.com/entertainment/envelope/cotown/la-et-ct-viacom-buys-britains-channel-5-20140501-story.html

Jefferies, M. (2018, January 10). BBC shrugs off loss of The Great British Bake Off to broadcast most-watched TV show of 2017. *The Mirror*. Retrieved from www.mirror.co.uk/tv/tv-news/bbc-shrugs-loss-great-british-11830831

Karasin, E. (2018, January 26). How YOU doin'? Beaming Matt LeBlanc gets behind the wheel and tests out a flying car in action-packed trailer for Top Gear's new series. *The Daily Mail*. Retrieved from www.dailymail.co.uk/tvshowbiz/article-5317593/Top-Gear-Matt-LeBlanc-tests-flying-car-trailer.html

Kennedy, S. (2017, March 20). Brexit timeline: From the referendum to Article 50. Bloomberg. Retrieved from www.bloomberg.com/news/features/2017-03-20/brexit-timeline-from-eu-referendum-to-theresa-may-and-article-50

Koblin, J. (2016, June 30). How much do we love TV? Let us count the ways. *The New York Times*. Retrieved from www.nytimes.com/2016/07/01/business/media/nielsen-survey-media-viewing.html?_r=0

Lewis, T. (2017, December 23). Jodie Whittaker: regenerating as a woman – the new Doctor Who. *The Guardian*. Retrieved from www.theguardian.com/tv-and-radio/2017/dec/24/jodie-whittaker-regenerating-as-doctor-who-will-be-life-changing

More Cold Feet to air on ITV in 2018. (2017, October 31). BBC.com. Retrieved from www.bbc.com/news/entertainment-arts-41821738

O'Donovan, G. (2017, January 6). Death in Paradise's upbeat whimsy is just the thing to beat the January blues – review. *The Telegraph*. Retrieved from www.telegraph.co.uk/tv/0/death-paradises-upbeat-whimsy-just-thing-beat-january-blues/

Ofcom. (2017, August 3). Communications market report United Kingdom. Retrieved from www.ofcom.org.uk/__data/assets/pdf_file/0017/105074/cmr-2017-uk.pdf

Office for National Statistics. (2017, December 14). Paddington, Star Wars and the rise of the UK film industry. Retrieved from https://visual.ons.gov.uk/paddington-star-wars-and-the-rise-of-the-uk-film-industry/

Office for National Statistics. (2017, December 22). Quarterly national accounts: July to September 2017. Retrieved from www.ons.gov.uk/economy/grossdomesticproductgdp/bulletins/quarterlynationalaccounts/julytoseptember2017

Pact. (n.d.). UK Television Exports 2015/16. Retrieved from www.pact.co.uk/asset/6E7181A3%2D728C%2D4C93%2D8F2642627AF8E036/

Rackham, J. (n.d.). Surgeons: At the Edge of Life. *Radio Times*. Retrieved from http://www.radiotimes.com/tv-programme/e/f5rvnz/surgeons-at-the-edge-of-life--s1-e3-the-pioneers/

Scott, K. (2017, November 15). The British TV shows that are watched all over the world. CNN. Retrieved from www.cnn.com/2017/11/14/entertainment/gallery/biggest-british-television-exports/index.html

Sweney, M. (2015, April 27). BBC's Poldark finale attracts 5.9 million viewers. *The Guardian*. Retrieved from www.theguardian.com/media/2015/apr/27/bbc-poldark-finale-viewers-aidan-turner

Sweney, M. (2017, December 14). Rupert Murdoch reshapes media empire with $66bn Disney deal. *The Guardian*. Retrieved from www.theguardian.com/media/2017/dec/14/rupert-murdochs-60bn-disney-deal-reshapes-his-media-empire

Tartaglione, N. (2016, March 24). "Stan Lee's Lucky Man": Hit Sky1 crime drama gets second season order. Deadline Hollywood. Retrieved from http://deadline.com/2016/03/stan-lees-lucky-man-renewed-second-season-sky1-1201725714/

Taylor, F. (2018, January 11). Blue Planet II beats Strictly Come Dancing to become most watched TV show of 2017. *Radio Times*. Retrieved from www.radiotimes.com/news/tv/2018-01-11/most-watched-tv-shows-2017/

The Commonwealth. (n.d.). About us. Retrieved from http://thecommonwealth.org/about-us

The World Bank. (n.d.). Retrieved from https://data.worldbank.org/indicator/NY.GDP.MKTP.CD?locations=GB

Wollaston, S. (2016, January 16). Shetland review – wildness, beauty and a damn good yarn. *The Guardian*. Retrieved from www.theguardian.com/tv-and-radio/2016/jan/16/shetland-review-wildness-beauty-and-a-damn-good-yarn

8 Entertainment Industries in France

Philippe Bouquillion

Background

Market dynamics and public intervention have been closely linked throughout the history of the entertainment industries in France. Since the seventeenth century, monarchical power has taken regulations or developed institutions to regulate and control these activities and to place them at the service of royal power. The aim was to promote national culture against other European cultures. In many ways, these goals are still relevant today.

With the development of the cultural industries of the twentieth century (recorded music, cinema, television, video games) in addition to the previous cultural industries (book and press), complex games are at work between public intervention and market regulation. Of course, these games are different according to the sectors and the times.

During the first half of the twentieth century, the State intervened mainly in sectors of political or cultural importance that needed public support to subsist in a market economy. In 1958, when General De Gaulle came back to power, the will was to restore a strong central State (and in particular a strong executive power). Cultural policy was at the service of this objective. A Ministry of Culture was been created fort the first time in France. The National Centre for Cinematography (CNC) was reinforced in order to defend artistic quality in French cinema. In addition, the public broadcasting sector (radio and television) has been developed because the government wished to develop a television that would be under its power to relay its political action. Therefore, television and radio have been under public monopoly until 1982.

After 1981, with the coming to power of François Mitterrand and his emblematic Minister of Culture, Jack Lang, public policies towards cultural industries began to change. Economic objectives have gradually been added to cultural or political objectives. Cultural industries, and especially television, are now considered as the vector of the industrialization and commercialization of the whole culture. Reflections on the economic impacts of culture are multiplying. Culture is considered as an economic sector in itself, as a creator of wealth and as a vector for French exports. Three public policy axes were then put in place. First, liberalization measures have been taken, particularly in the audio-visual sector, with the abolition of the public monopoly and the creation of private channels. The aim was to promote the competitiveness of these industries on a transnational scale. Second, a complex set of measures has been taken in favour of film, television and book in order to overcome market failures and to allow cultural industries to maximize production, product distribution and valorization capacities, including exports. The audio-visual sector was at the heart of this policy. In this field, three measures have been articulated: taxes on the revenue of television channels to finance the production of television programs and cinema films; broadcasting quotas for original French and European content; a chronology of media, distinguishing various windows of valorization for cinema movies then released in theatres until their diffusion in free VOD 48 months later. Third, the government tried to favour the development of French industrial champions as for instance Canal+ (the historical pay-TV player in France) later included in Vivendi Universal, which was the world number two in the entertainment industry by the end of the 1990s.

Entertainment Landscape

Cultural industry markets are difficult to assess because there are no recent statistics that capture the whole industry. The latest statistics are for 2013. They have been produced by a consulting agency, France Créative, on behalf of the Ministry of Culture and services of the Ministry of Economy and Finance.

The visual arts is a very heterogeneous set that gathers together crafts, architecture, design, photography, the art market, museums, 3-D printing, photographic equipment, drawing equipment, art fairs, comics, books and the fine arts press. Cultural industries represent only a minority of the so-called creative economy. Of a total of €72.7 billion, cultural industries (press, television, books, music, video games, cinema and radio) represent only €31.3 billion (or 43.05%) of the total.

The creative economy taken as a whole is expanding but to a limited extent. "Between 2011 and 2013, the cultural economy outperformed the national economy, with a 1.2% increase in total revenues (while GDP grew by 0.9% over the period) and direct jobs of + 1.5% (against 0.2% for the national average)."[2]

For its part, the study department of the Ministry of Culture, which has a more restrictive vision of the cultural field than France Créative, has calculated various indicators reflecting the weight of culture throughout the French economy. According to this point of view, in 2015, the cultural economy only represented a value of €43 billion, or only 2.2% of the French economy. Moreover, this weight has been declining since 2003, when it stood at 2.54%.[3] This decline is explained in particular by the deployment of digital. Broadband connections, and with them the whole economy of the Internet, only started in France in 2003–04.

The sectorial evolutions are contrasted. The sectors which are the most concerned by the deployment of digital are experiencing the greatest difficulties.

> Direct revenues of four sectors have increased between 2011 and 2013: the visual arts (+ 8%), music (+ 3%), live entertainment (+ 2%) and advertising (+ 1%). The direct revenues of four other sectors have declined during the same period: film (–9%), press (–6%), television (–4%) and book (–3%).[4]

Entertainment industries in France, as in many other geographical areas, are structured as an oligopoly with fringes. Big actors coexist with smaller ones.

Table 8.1 Direct Revenues of the Sector in France in 2013 in Billions of Euros[1]

Sector	Revenues
Visual arts	20.4
Advertising and communication	14.4
Press	10.5
Television	10.2
Music	5.3
Performing arts	6.6
Book	4.6
Video game	3
Cinema	2.9
Radio	1.4

Three actors dominate the book industry, in terms of turnover and because they control book diffusion. Hachette, which belongs to Lagardère, generated a turnover of €2.26 billion in 2016; Editis, which is a subsidiary of Planeta, the number one publisher in Spain, is the second largest player with a turnover in 2016 of €816 million; Madrigall, the group controlled by Antoine Gallimard, (the Gallimard family has played an important role in the French book industry during the twentieth century), had a turnover of €437 million in 2016.[5] Then come smaller groups, of average size on the French scale: Bayard, owned by a Catholic congregation, €353 million in 2016[6]; Media-Participations, €355; La Martinière group, €206 million.[7]

Likewise, the recorded music market is in the hands of the three international majors: Universal Music Group, Sony Music Entertainment and Warner Music Group, which control between 70% and 80% of the market.

Television includes the pay and commercial television markets and also a still-important public sector. In 2014, revenues of television channels were estimated at €9 billions, taking into account public funding. Advertising (sponsorship included) accounted for 35.4%, subscriptions for 34.4% and contribution to public broadcasting and the budget allocation of the State for 30.2%.[8] The audience and advertising revenues of major commercial channels have declined because of the emergence of digital terrestrial television channels, competition from the Internet and the development of various forms of non-linear television. The turnover of pay television, €3 billion, was divided between Canal+'s channels, €1.8 billion, and other channels, €1.2 billion. All markets combined in the main industrial groups (with turnover in 2016 in billion of euros) are: Canal Plus Group (Vivendi), 5.25, of which Canal+, 1.63; France Télévisions (a state-owned company, 3.39); TF1 Group (Bouygues Group), 2.06; M6 (RTL-Bertelsmann), 1.27; Lagardère Active, 0.915.[9]

The press industry is highly segmented and these segments are undergoing different developments – in particular between the daily news press and the magazine press. However, common trends can be identified. Fierce competition has developed since the 2000s between the so-called paid press and the so-called free press. In the same way, the pure players of the Web have strongly developed and today capture a significant amount of advertising budgets dedicated to online information, as well as readers' time.

The dual-market system (sales and advertising) is therefore in deep crisis. This crisis adds to structural difficulties. For several decades press groups have been underfunded and have not been able to lead the investments that would be necessary to avoid a decline in readership and to face the challenges raised by digital technology and major players such as Google. In this difficult situation, the press market has been highly concentrated. The main industrial groups (with turnover in 2016 in million of euros) are: Groupe Figaro (Dassault family), 550; Hachette Filipacchi Associés (Lagardère), 446; Prisma Press (Bertelsmann), 384; Group The World, 327.[10]

The cinema market is dominated by a duopoly formed by Pathé, which achieved a turnover of €905 million in 2016. Pathé is one of the most important actors in cinema in France and in Europe (in production, distribution but especially cinematographic exploitation).[11] The second player in the duopoly is Gaumont, with a turnover in 2016 of €188 million.[12]

France is the country of cultural exception. Public intervention plays a central role in structuring the entertainment industries although cultural industries represent only a minor share of the Ministry of Culture's expenditure (16%)[13]. Today, public policies towards cultural industries are based on the founding principles defined by Jack Lang in the early 1980s. The main orientations of the public policies in favour of the cultural industries have hardly been affected by the industrial and technological transformations although these are today radical, with notably the digital transition and the reinforcement of the transnationalization notably related to the digital platforms. In the sectors of cinema, television, books and the press, which are the sectors where public intervention is the strongest, a set of measures are thought about and articulated according to an "ideal" operation of the sector as considered by the Ministry of Culture.

Nowadays, this policy suffers from complexity, is poorly structured and is only maintained thanks to its inertia and the lobbying of the industrial players who benefit from it. Measures can be of three types: fiscal, regulatory and financial (subsidies). These very numerous measures are difficult to identify and therefore are not thought about in relation to each other. The Ministry of Culture has only a rough vision of its own measures and a weak vision of the action of other organizations. Thus, several factors combine to explain the difficulty of coordinating public action towards culture and entertainment.

First, cultural enterprises can benefit from aid non-specific to culture. For example, a start-up in the field of information and communication technologies or video games trying to raise funds can solicit both the Institute for Financing Culture and Cultural Industries (IFCIC), founded in 1983, which offers bank loan guarantee services to cultural enterprises, and the Public Investment Bank (BPI), which finances innovation.

Second, tax expenditures play an important role and represent very large financial amounts (€1.5 billion in 2017, mainly 93% – for the cultural industries).[14] In addition tax revenues are directly allocated to corporations. It represents an amount of €770 million in 2017.

> Two taxes account for more than 80% of this total: the television service tax due by publishers and distributors of television services on the one hand, and the tax on admissions to the cinema. These two taxes go into the cinema and audio-visual aid funds managed by the National Centre for Cinematography and Moving Image (CNC) to support audio-visual creation.[15]

Households are also involved in the financing of culture through the audio-visual levy (€3.9 billion in 2017)[16].

Third, several ministries are involved in culture and entertainment industries. The budget of the Ministry of Culture and Communication for 2017 is €3.6 billion. However, the expenditure of the other ministries in the direction of culture represents greater public expense than that of the Ministry of Culture: "In 2017, the cultural spending of other ministries is estimated at 4 billion euros, of which 73% for the Ministry of Education, Higher Education and Research".[17]

Fourth, territorial communities contribute centrally to cultural public spending. In 2014, they spent more than €9.3 billion on culture. More than three quarters of these expenditures are made by municipalities and groups of municipalities.

Fifth, measures towards cultural industries that are under the responsibility of the Ministry of Culture are managed by specialized operators by sector. The two most important institutions are the National Centre for Cinematography and Animated Image (CNC), competent for cinema, television and video games and the National Book Centre (CNL) for the book sector. These two operators administer most of the measures in their area of expertise. These institutions are, de facto, largely autonomous with regards to their supervisory authority, the Ministry of Culture. They drive the action and they also set objectives and main modalities of intervention. This situation presents great inconvenience: public policy is partitioned by sector. Therefore, in the digital and trans-nationalization era, where French actors in cultural industries are confronted with transnational actors, such as GAFAM, whose size is global and whose strategies impact all cultural content, there is no institution within the Ministry of Culture able to think about the transnational dimensions.

In addition, the application of the regulation of the entertainment industries is ensured by two specialized institutions, the Higher Audio-visual Council (CSA) for television and the Regulatory Authority for Electronic Communications and Post (ARCEP) for telecommunications. These two institutions share also the regulation of the Internet. Their intervention has various impacts on the activity of the industrial players. The CSA plays a more important role in ensuring the respect of pluralism (balance of speaking time between the various political parties, in particular). ARCEP, on the other hand, in the field of telecommunications and therefore in the field of the Internet, plays a more central economic role. For example, ARCEP assures the defence of net neutrality and thus plays a central role in the relations between telecommunication operators and industry players using bandwidth, such as Netflix or YouTube.

Cross-Border Links and Connections

French policy towards entertainment and especially cultural industries since the 1980s has aimed at maximizing exports. In general this is aimed at supporting production, but there are also more specific measures. For example, the CNL supports the translation of French books into foreign languages. In addition, the European Union has long developed a policy to support cultural exchanges between the various member countries of the European Union. However the results of this policy are mixed.

First, French exports of cultural products are weak. France is not one of the most exporting countries of cultural products. Considered as a whole, in 2014

> The share of export turnover of cultural enterprises is only 9%, compared with an average of 16% in all market sectors. In addition, exports are concentrated in a few sectors. The share of export turnover is very variable from one sector to another: it reaches 64% for video game publishing, 35% for news agencies, 28% for edition of thematic channels, but remains negligible for almost half of cultural activities, especially for live performance, architecture and cultural education.[18]

In recent years, exports within several sectors of the cultural industries have declined. In 2015, the external trade balance is positive in books (+€16 million) but negative in the press (–€46 million euros), musical instruments (–€93 million) and phono-videograms (–€167 million).

Second, entertainment productions from abroad play an important role in France. In the field of cinema, foreign films make up the biggest part of theatrical releases (200 million admissions in 2015): 52% for American films, 36% for French films and 12% for films from other countries. Among the ten films that crossed the threshold of four million admissions in 2015, there are seven Hollywood films and only two French films.

Foreign fiction, especially American fiction, is highly appreciated by French television viewers and, as such, it is very present in French TV channels. The importance of foreign fiction among the top 50 has grown over the period from 2005 to 2015 (+4 programs out of 50).

Similarly, the majority of films sold in the two video markets (DVD and VOD), are American films (64% for the physical market and 44% for VOD).

Francophone recorded music productions accounted for half of album sales in 2015 and francophone artists are behind nine of the top ten album sales. However, there are only two French titles in the top ten.

Third, the industrial players, and in particular the American ones, play a central role in several domains of the entertainment industries. French socio-economic players play a dominant role only in the markets of commercial television, cinemas, press, books, telecommunications and Internet access. In the field of pay television, the balance of power between French and American players is changing in favour of the latter since Netflix entered the French market. In recorded music, the three majors are very dominant. However, the world number one, Universal Music, is the subsidiary of a French group, Vivendi.

US Web industry players occupy an extremely dominant position in several areas. Thus, in January 2017, the search engine Google exceeded 93% of market share in France, all media combined. French actors are totally absent. On the mobile, the dominance of Google is even more overwhelming with 98% of market share. The market of browsers is dominated by American players: Chrome (47%), Safari (20%) and Firefox (15%).

French actors are also dominated in digital activities closer to content. The deployment of digital has favoured the domination of foreign actors in the downstream of the sector. For example, Amazon is responsible for 62% of online sales of CDs, ahead of the French platform, Fnac.com (26%). In the music download market, 79% of revenue is generated by iTunes in 2015 and its main competitor is an American player, Google (11% in 2015). One of the few areas where a French player occupies a significant position is the streaming of music. Despite the arrival of new players and a loss of more than 20 points of market share in two years, in 2015, Deezer remains in the lead with 43% of revenues from this market, followed by Spotify (21%) and Napster (14%).

Digital Transformation

The use of digital technologies and devices has experienced very strong development in France since the early 2000s, when the broadband Internet network developed (ADSL) with a flat-fee subscription. Moreover, during the 2000s, a rich content offer was developed, driven in particular by the massive deployment of major transnational industrial players (in particular the GAFA).

In 2016, 87% of French people over the age of 12 were Internet users (55% in 2006). Most of them logged on every day. The gap between women and men has decreased: in 2006, 61% of men were Internet users but only 50% of women. They are respectively 89% and 85% in 2016. The average number of hours spent each week on the Internet, excluding video viewing, has increased significantly since 2012: it went from 13 hours in 2012 to 18 hours in 2016. It is now closer to the average number of hours spent watching television (more than 20 hours in 2016). The computer remains the main mode of access but mobiles play a growing role: 78% of French people use mobile devices to connect to the Internet. The 12 to 24-year-olds are the only ones for whom the rate of use of mobile devices is higher than the use of the computer.[19]

Legal content offers continue to grow. Consumption of catch-up TV has increased by a factor of 2.8 between 2011 and 2015 (5,085 billion videos viewed in 2015). Similarly, there is a strong increase in the offer. In 2015, free channels offered 17,110 hours of television programs in catch-up TV, an increase of 62% compared to 2011. In 2016, the advertising revenue of catch-up TV is estimated at €105 million, compared with €60 million in 2013.[20] Similarly, 55% of French people have listened to or downloaded music over the Internet in the last 12 months, a rate that has increased significantly since 2010 (+18%). This practice concerns almost all 12 to 24-year-olds (more than 95% of them), then decreases sharply with age. Participation in social networks (like Facebook, LinkedIn) is observed at comparable rates: 56% of French people have participated in the last 12 months and the 18 to 24-year-olds are the main users (94%). The proportion of people using the Internet to follow the news is progressing: 59% in 2016 (49% in 2012).

In 2016, online advertising investments in France were estimated at 3.5 billion euros. This amount is €1.9 billion for search and €1.2 billion for display (+15% since 2015). The increase of display is due to the strong growth of video display (€417 million). In terms of media chosen by advertisers, the share of advertising expenses grew sharply for mobile in 2016 (€1,264 million), and mobile now accounts for 41% of total advertising expenditure on line.[21]

One of the main challenges for the entertainment industries of this digital boom lies in the decline in revenues in some markets. This trend can be observed in various sectors including television and video but is also very strong and even older in the press and recorded music.

Thus, with a turnover of €7.5 billion in 2015, newspaper publishers have lost 42% of their revenues since 1990. This decrease is explained by the decline in sales of paper copies, cumulative to that advertising revenue. Over the period 1990 to 2015, advertising investments decreased overall by 61%. Between 2009 and 2014, the general information press saw its sales fall by 15%. However, the overall audience of the press is increasing, thanks to the consultation of newspaper websites. Experts from the Ministry of Culture have conducted a study on a set of 30 newspapers that shows that the audience (paper and Internet) increased by 21% between April 2014 and January 2015. The share of digital consultations represents 56% of the total audience in January 2015 against 46% in April 2014.

Similarly, revenues from the recorded music market decreased from €797 million in 2007 to 426 in 2015. Losses in the physical market are not offset by gains in the digital market (€57 million to €152 million from 2007 to 2015).

A Case Study: The French OTT Market, Between Global and National

As a conclusion, I propose to focus on the development of Over-The-Top (OTT) audio-visual offers. This case illustrates many of the issues we have already examined: challenges of digital deployment, relations between French and transnational actors and content, and the ability or inability of public policies to respond to these new challenges.

VOD market was estimated at €492 million at the end of 2017, including 259 million for the SVOD, which is the most dynamic component of VOD market.[22] Even if this market is still small, its development is questioning the pay-TV market, which is decreasing. Its main player, Canal+, is in great difficulty and lost many of its subscribers in 2016 and 2017. Thereby, this actor is less and less able to fulfill its regulatory obligations, especially to finance the production of French films, while the whole regulation in favour of audio-visual and cinema is threatened. Canal+ plays a very special role in the French audio-visual and cinematographic economy. This company was created in 1984 by the personal will of the President François Mitterrand. The central objective was to build a large private pay-TV channel whose dominant position would be protected from both French and foreign competition and which, in return, would bring significant resources to French film production. The dominant position of Canal+ has, to a greater or lesser extent, been preserved for a long time. Its offering includes: a paid terrestrial channel (Canal+), a satellite package (Canal Sat), a SVOD offer (Canal Play) and film and television production activities, notably Group Canal.

These changes are related to the strong market power of the new entrants in the French audio-visual market. Canal+ has four main competitors: Netflix, leader of the French OTT market, which launched its offer in France in September 2014 and had almost two million subscribers at the beginning of 2018; Orange Cinéma Séries (OCS), a subsidiary of Orange, the incumbent French telecommunications operator, with 2.6 million subscribers (March 2017) in its bouquet of pay channels and its SVOD service (which has just started, at the beginning of 2018); SFR Play, launched in November 2015, a subsidiary of Altice, a group present in telecommunications, cable networks and media; Amazon Prime Video, launched in December 2016 (8% of market at the end of 2017). These four players are in a strong position with regard to Canal+.

Indeed, stakeholders in the communication industries, such as Amazon, Orange or Altice, and foreign players from the cultural industries, such as Netflix, have more capacity than Canal+ to raise funds, to acquire the most strategic content or to transform content into joint-products. Thus, transnational actors and communication industry players have developed aggressive strategies to acquire the most strategic content in order to recruit new subscribers. This content is mainly sport and exclusively American films and TV series. Netflix benefits from a rich catalogue of American series. On the other hand, the rules on media chronology prevent Netflix from distributing recent films that have been released for less than 36 months. Similarly, Netflix has also developed an offer of French content. This company plans to invest $8 billion in the creation of original series and films in 2018 so that 50% of its catalogue will be composed of exclusive content by the end of 2018. In comparison, Canal+ has invested only €500 million in content in 2017. Amazon does not have a very strong content offer on the French market but the company claims to have spent $4.5 billion in 2017 for its programs. Similarly, Altice SFR Play and Orange OCS are challenging the leading position of Canal+ in sports and also in American movies and series. SFR and more OCS managed to sign agreements with major American studios to obtain the rights of series or films. These actors can drive such strategies in content for several reasons.

First, Amazon and Netflix have a financial capacity that is not comparable with those of Canal+. One indicator of the financial strength of these players is that Netflix's market value is $60 billion against €5 billion for Vivendi. Second, Amazon, Orange and Altice, as players in the communication industries, are able to transform audio-visual content into joint-products. The main objective of Orange or Altice is not to win money directly with OTT offers but to distinguish their Triple Play offer from those of competitors. Thus, these players can both offer very low rates and buy expensive content. Orange's contracts with American studios are very expansive (for HBO's content, Orange has to pay $30 million each year). Therefore, Orange is losing money with this pay-TV activity. In this game, of course Amazon is the strongest because of its tremendous financial strength and global size. Amazon is offering audio-visual content in order to bring consumers to its e-commerce and cloud computing services and to generate user data. As a result, the price of its OTT offer is very low, €49 per year, and is included in its more general offer, "Amazon Prime". On top of that, Canal+, in order not to compete with its main pay-TV services, does not include the best series and films in its OTT offer (Canal Play). Thereby, an avenue is open for its competitors.

The deployment of the OTT offers increases tension and opposition already present regarding regulation. Many French TV players want an end to the financing obligations of audio-visual and cinematographic production. Foreign players refuse to submit to these financing obligations, as well as to broadcasting quotas, which creates a distortion of competition. Media chronology is also a sensitive question. The vast majority of film producers back media chronology. On the other hand, players of the communication industries present in OTT have an inverse interest. For example, Orange has appealed for a much shorter chronology. Similarly, Netflix announced during the most recent Cannes Film Festival its intention to no longer respect it. Canal+ has a more intermediate position. These rules help Canal+ to reserve the most recent films for its pay channel and satellite package, which are more profitable than its OTT offer.

Faced with these challenges, the French government has nevertheless decided to maintain the main lines of current regulation. Therefore, Françoise Nyssen, Minister of Culture in 2018, has welcomed the draft revision of the European directive "Audio-visual Media Services" presented in May 2017; this includes quotas for the distribution of European and national works in the catalogues of non-linear audio-visual services and Member States the possibility of applying their funding mechanisms for creation to services targeting their territory, even if they are established in another country of the European Union.

Notes

1. France Créative (2015). "Création sous tension. 2e Panorama de l'économie de la culture et de la création en France", October 9. Retrieved from www.ey.com/Publication/vwLUAssets/EY-2e-panorama-de-l-economie-de-la-culture-et-de-la-creation-en-France/$FILE/EY-2e-panorama-de-l-economie-de-la-culture-et-de-la-creation-en-France.pdf
2. France Créative, 2015, 11.
3. Ministère de la Culture et de la Communication (2017). *Chiffres clés, statistiques de la culture et de la communication 2017*. Paris: Ministère de la Culture – DEPS.
4. France Créative, 2015, 8.
5. La Dépêche (2017). "L'année 2016 a été bénéfique pour l'édition française", June 16. Retrieved from www.ladepeche.fr/article/2017/06/16/2595224-l-annee-2016-a-ete-benefique-pour-l-edition-francaise.html
6. Bayard. Retrieved from www.groupebayard.com/index.php/fr/articles/rubrique/id/4
7. Yahoo actualités. Retrieved from https://fr.news.yahoo.com/%C3%A9dition-n%C3%A9gociations-rapprochement-entre-martini%C3%A8re-media-participations-145444216--finance.html
8. CNC (2015). "L'économie de la télévision. Financements, audience, programmes", December 7. Retrieved from www.cnc.fr/web/fr/etudes/-/ressources/8236155

9 Stratégies. Retrieved from www.strategies.fr/entreprises-du-secteur/les-200-premiers-medias-en-france-en-2016
10 Stratégies. Retrieved from www.strategies.fr/entreprises-du-secteur/les-200-premiers-medias-en-france-en-2016
11 Pathé. Retrieved from www.pathe.com/sites/default/files/PATHE_2016_FR_PLANCHES_OK.pdf
12 Yahoo Finance. Retrieved from https://fr.finance.yahoo.com/quote/GAM.PA/financials?p=GAM.PA
13 Ministère de la Culture et de la Communication (2017).
14 Ministère de la Culture et de la Communication (2017).
15 Ministère de la Culture et de la Communication (2017).
16 Ministère de la Culture et de la Communication (2017).
17 Ministère de la Culture et de la Communication (2017).
18 Ministère de la Culture et de la Communication (2017).
19 Ministère de la Culture et de la Communication (2017).
20 Ministère de la Culture et de la Communication (2017).
21 Ministère de la Culture et de la Communication (2017).
22 ZDNET. Retrieved from www.zdnet.fr/blogs/digital-home-revolution/le-marche-video-francais-au-dessus-du-milliard-d-euros-grace-a-netflix-39862152.htm

9 German Entertainment Media Industry
Characteristics and Market Break-Down

Gianna L. Ehrlich and M. Bjørn von Rimscha

Background

The German media and entertainment industry had a total turnover of 76.2 billion euros in 2016. This figure puts it on a par with the UK market and in fourth place in the world (PwC, 2017).

Historical Background of German Entertainment Media

The media and thus also the entertainment industry in its current form in Germany developed after World War II. During the Nazi regime, entertainment was highly politicized and part of the regime's Arian supremacy propaganda. Therefore, restructuring the media system to prevent another totalitarian rule was high on the agenda of the Allied control authorities. Most media and entertainment producers were banned from working in the industry again and production facilities were seized. In western Germany, newspapers and magazines were operated under Allied licenses. Due to the lack of advertising money as well as radio frequencies in post-war Germany, politically independent broadcasters were set up as a public service modeled after the British Broadcasting Corporation. In the eastern part of Germany, media and entertainment companies from the Nazi era were also closed and new ones created with untainted staff, however, the new system was again commissioned to serve the state ideology – only this time a socialist one. The lack of its own production facilities meant there was a strong market position for foreign productions in both parts of Germany, also with the objective of reeducation (Fay, 2008).

The entertainment market in Germany is still shaped by these origins. There is a strong public service sector, on the one hand, and commercial media conglomerates, most of which have their historical roots in the print sector, on the other hand. However, in the meantime, companies traditionally focused on the media market in Germany have strongly internationalized their activities and are active in many parts of the world (Dreier, 2009). International influence is strong in terms of content (especially in film and music) and structures (Public Service Broadcaster – PSB), but it is much less pronounced in terms of ownership.

Political Characteristics

Germany is a federal parliamentary republic in central-western Europe consisting of 16 federal states. It is part of the European Union and the European single market. Thus, media and entertainment companies face legislation on three levels: European, federal, and state.

The central legal basis for entertainment and media regulation is the German constitution which states seven basic legal provisions, the so-called communication freedoms: freedom of expression, freedom of opinion distribution, freedom of information, press freedom, freedom of broadcasting, film freedom, and freedom from censorship. Different from, for example, the USA, freedom of speech in Germany is slightly more limited by competing basic rights that prohibit racism and protect personal rights of individuals. These limits also apply to entertainment.

The promotion of culture is deemed an important policy objective in Germany, hence numerous schemes offer subsidies for cultural and entertainment production such as public film funds, support for museums and theaters. Competition, for example in the book market, is limited, to foster diversity, and strong PSBs should contribute to cultural life. While the cultural objective is usually at the heart of public funding schemes, regional economic policy often also plays its part.

Due to its affiliation with the EU, European legislation such as the Audiovisual Media Services Directive (AVMSD) (Directive 2010/13/EU, 2010) also applies in Germany, including quotas for European content. However, the aim to protect local production via quotas is much less prominent in Germany compared to other European countries such as, for example, France.

Economic Characteristics

Germany has the world's fourth largest economy by gross domestic product in current prices (International Monetary Fund, 2018). It features a high standard of living and a tradition of developed public services, also in the media sector. The average German household (2.0 members) in 2015 has spent 252 euros per month on "leisure, entertainment, and culture" excluding telco services. That equals 10.5% of household consumption (Statistisches Bundesamt, 2017). According to latest available data from Eurostat (2016), Germany ranks slightly above the EU average percentage household spend on recreation and culture, but considerably lower than, for example, the UK and Scandinavia.

Cultural Characteristics

Stereotypic descriptions of German evoke the image of rule-oriented controllers or smart but stiff engineers. That is exaggerated; however, Germans are not the most entertainment-oriented people, neither as consumers nor as producers. In surveys, recipients play down their entertainment consumption and media managers disproportionately emphasize the information products in their portfolios. A successful but trivial light entertainment show on German television is not hailed as a commercial success but publicly denounced as problematic lowbrow entertainment.

For audiovisual content, Germans love to be entertained in their own language. That means apart from few arthouse offerings, imported content is lip-sync dubbed. Dubbing is an additional cost and time factor when importing content, but as a result, the dubbed content feels less foreign for German audiences. Even before the age of TV-formats, Germans loved to have their own national remakes of internationally successful entertainment offerings. The Donald Duck Universe of the mid-twentieth century, for example, found its German equivalent in the Fix & Foxi Universe – a pretty blunt copy, albeit with an educational claim.

With the experiences of two totalitarian regimes in the twentieth century, Germans are quite wary when it comes to disclosing personal data. Thus, while they acknowledge the added comfort in individualization based on user tracking, they are also reluctant to provide this data in the first place (Krasnova, Veltri, & Günther, 2012).

Entertainment Market Segments

The sectors that essentially make up the entertainment media industry, and conversely, where entertainment is particularly important, are the television, home entertainment, film, games, and music industry. Theatre and show production in Germany are largely funded by public money and thus will not be disussed here. The following chapter provides an overview of the different regulations and policies as well as the executive government agencies and associations that shape the areas of the entertainment media industry in Germany. In addition, the most important companies in each field are presented.

Television/Home Entertainment

Regulative Environment

Parent guidelines for the structure of the German broadcasting law consist mainly in the form of the AVMS Directive of the European Union. Its objective is the alignment of national legislation in the field of television and the regulation of television in the framework of the EU-wide freedom to provide services. On the national level, the constitution sets the legal framework for radio and television as mentioned earlier.

Interstate treaties create a uniform normative basis important for national players. Most important among these are the Interstate Treaty on Broadcasting and Telemedia (Rundfunkstaatsvertrag RStV) and the amended state treaties on the three PSBs (Arbeitsgemeinschaft der öffentlich-rechtlichen Rundfunkanstalten der Bundesrepublik Deutschland – ARD, Zweites Deutsches Fernsehen – ZDF and, DeutschlandRadio) (Beck, 2012, p. 39). In Germany, cultural policy is in the competence of the federal states, thus each state has its own media laws. These direct the admission and supervision of commercial broadcasters and are implemented by the respective state media authorities. Together they are responsible for, for example, the licensing and supervision of commercial broadcasters, compliance with the provisions on diversity of opinion in national commercial television, and fundamental aspects of media policy, such as those relating to technology, convergence and media law (die medienanstalten [ALM], 2018). In addition to the state media authorities, there is the Voluntary Self-Monitoring Television (FSF) as the supervisory body of commercial broadcasters, which defines the age rating for TV programs.

The mandate for PSBs in Germany is a broad universal service including (quality) entertainment and the obligation to commission programs from German producers. Commerical broadcasters also have to contribute to funding German fiction productions via the film levy. The relevant regulations are laid out in the interstate treaties (Beck, 2012, p. 229).

The PSBs are primarily funded by the licence fee of 17.50 euros per month and household, which constitutes 85% of their revenues. In addition, a small proportion of revenue is generated through restricted advertising and sponsorship as well as trade in program rights (Mitteldeutscher Rundfunk, 2016, p. 18). The fee is set by the independent Commission for the Determination of the Financial Requirements of the PSBs (Kommission zur Ermittlung des Finanzbedarfs der Rundfunkanstalten [KEF], 2016, p. 6), thus the influence of politics on the fee is only indirect by setting the broad objectives of the public broadcasters.

Commercial broadcasting is financed mainly by advertising revenues. The limitations on advertising in commercial broadcasting are governed by the Interstate Treaty on Broadcasting and Telemedia. A maximum of 20% of the broadcasting time may be attributed to advertising; a separation of advertising and program as well as the labeling of advertising are required. In addition to advertising revenues, commercial operators also generate income from commercial holdings; some of them are home shopping channels (e.g. QVC) or pay-TV providers (e.g. Sky) (Dreier, 2009).

Market Players

The largest public broadcaster is the ARD, a consortium of state-level public service braodcasters (PSBs). The fee-funded network has a budget of approximately 6.9 billion euros and about 20,000 employees (Mitteldeutscher Rundfunk, 2016, pp. 15–17). The ZDF is also funded by the licence fee. In 2017, ARD, the state-level PSBs, and the ZDF had a cumulative audience share of about 41% (AGF & GfK, 2018).

In commercial TV, primarily advertising-funded, entertainment-oriented channel formats prevail (ALM, 2017, pp. 24–25). Two multinational media groups dominate: the RTL Group, owned by Bertelsmann (RTL Group, 2017, p. 58), and the ProSiebenSat.1 SE, listed in the German stock index DAX (ProSiebenSat.1 Media SE, 2017, p. 64). Foreign ownership in commercial TV in Germany is fairly limited. Discovery, Comcast, Time Warner, and Viacom each are represented only with niche programs, some of which are only available in TV packages (Kommission zur Ermittlung der Konzentration im Medienbereich [KEK], 2017). In 2017, the Mediengruppe RTL with its several channels had a market share of 22.9% and the ProSiebenSat.1 group reached 17.5% of the audience market (AGF & GfK, 2018). In the advertising market, ProSiebenSat.1 group accounted for 40% and the RTL group for 37% of gross advertising revenues in 2016 (Heffler & Höhe, 2017, p. 164).

In addition to these market leaders, there are special interest channels, including sport, news, children's, teleshopping, and music channels. Although the overall number of broadcasters is high, the market is oligopolistic due to the dominance of the two public broadcasters and the two commercial broadcasting groups, so the relative journalistic concentration is high (KEK, 2017).

Regarding the share and the type of entertainment content, there are major differences between public service and commercial broadcasters. While 37% and 43% respectively of the total broadcasting time of ARD and of ZDF is informational content such as magazines and news, there is also a high share of fictional (one third) and non-fictional entertainment (a tenth), especially during prime time (Krüger, 2017, pp. 187–189). Within the entertainment category, the focus is on television movies (ARD: 14%, ZDF: 7% of total broadcasting time), television series (ARD: 14%, ZDF: 21%), and feature films (ARD: 9%, ZDF: 7%) (Krüger, 2017, p. 191). For the ARD, the financially most important program area is sport, with prime costs of 461.8 million euros in 2014, followed by politics and society, teleplay, entertainment like quiz shows, and feature films. Similarly, the ZDF spent 368 million euros on sport in the same period, followed by TV films, politics and news (KEF, 2016, p. 47). For the big commercial broadcasters, reality TV formats account for a large share of air time (RTL 28% and Sat.1 36%) while ProSieben concentrates on TV series (ALM, 2017, p. 218).

Concerning commercial pay-TV and pay-TV-on-demand, Sky Deutschland is the most important platform in the German market with a turnover of 2 billion euros in 2015/16 (KEK, 2017, p. 139) and 4.6 million subscribers, which corresponds to a share of 1.5% in the audience market (AGF & GfK, 2018). Due to a great variety of entertainment in free-to-air television, the pay-TV penetration in Germany is much lower than in other markets. However, Germans seem to have an appetite for pay-TV in the form of streaming services.

The currently rapidly growing VoD market is dominated by international companies such as Amazon Prime (32% of VoD users) and Netflix (17% of VoD users). Runnerups include the platform Maxdome (11%), owned by the ProSiebenSat.1 group, and the Sky Go service (12%), owned by Sky Deutschland (Goldhammer & Wiegand, 2016).

Overall, the home entertainment market is worth 1.8 billion euros. While the sales (1.2 bn) are still dominated by DVDs (58%) compared to Blu-Ray (32%) and only 10% electronic sell through, rentals (0.6 bn) are dominated by online subscription (SVoD, 56%) and transactional video on demand (TVoD, 17%) (Berauer, 2017, pp. 55–59).

TV production in Germany is essentially a national market dominated by a few high-turnover companies: The latest study focusing on the German producer market (Castendyk & Goldhammer, 2012) found that approximately 5% of the companies had a turnover of more than 5 million euros and accounted for more than three quarters of the industry turnover; 95% of the companies had a turnover of a maximum of 5 million euros and generated just under a quarter of the industry turnover; 81% of TV producers generated more than 90% of their 1.82 billion euros total revenue from domestic revenues; and only 4% of companies earned at least half their revenues in foreign markets. The 1.82 billion euros industry turnover of the TV production was generated by approximately 60% on orders of public broadcasters and 37% on orders of commercial channels. Many of the large production companies are associated with a TV channel, which acts as key commissioner. For example, UFA is part of the RTL Group (RTL Group, 2017) and ZDF Enterprises is a subsidiary of the ZDF (ZDF, 2017). Admittedly, the market power of the demand side, that is, the TV broadcaster, is greater than that of the production companies (Castendyk & Goldhammer, 2012, p. 45). However, especially for successful international formats, channels have to deal with international partners that often have more clout.

Film

Regulative Environment

Important statutory framework conditions for the film industry include copyright, the Youth Protection Act, and the Film Funding Act. The regulations and the associated relevant institutions are briefly described.

German copyright law includes the lawful exploitation of the works of an author. On the European level, the Copyright Directive was harmonized in 2001. The Second Act for Governing Copyright in the Information Society includes a ban on the circumvention of copyright protection procedures. To clarify the legal situation and display of copyright infringement, the Society for the Prosecution of Copyright Infringements is being funded by film and entertainment software manufacturers and supported by the German Federal Film Board (Beck, 2012, p. 169).

According to the criteria of the Youth Protection Act, the possible age ratings of films are 0, 6, 12, 16, and 18 years (§14 para. 2 JuSchG). The voluntary self-control of the film industry (FSK) acts as the supervisory body. It is run by the umbrella industry association SPIO (Beck, 2012, p. 167).

Central to the German film industry are public funding schemes at national and federal level. Film funding is a legal measure aimed at improving the quality[1] of German film productions and financially supporting a considerable proportion of German films. The state's commitment is intended to counteract a market failure of the cultural-asset film in the face of strong international – mainly American – competition. In the context of project film funding, "artistically valuable" films that increase the quality of national filmmaking can benefit from public funds. In reality, public support for film production is largely also motivated by regional economic policy, especially in thoses states that are home to larger production facilities. Overall, public film funding amounted to 361 million euros in 2016 (Berauer, 2017).

While many state-level funding schemes are tax funded, the federal film board (FFA) is funded largely by a film levy payable by cinemas, home entertainment distributors, and broadcasters. Thus, successful foreign productions indirectly help to fund German film productions. The total volume of film levy in 2015 amounted to more than 58 million euros (Filmförderungsanstalt [FFA], 2016, p. 11).

Market Players

In the German film industry, the distribution of the market shares of companies is in line with the box-office success of the films: A small number of market participants captures a large share of the market. Film distribution is dominated by the local distribution outlets of the six American major studios: Warner Bros., Walt Disney Motion Pictures Group, Sony Pictures Entertainment, 20th Century Fox, Universal Studios, and Paramount Pictures, which only represent 5% of distributors but account for a cumulative 65% of revenues (Berauer, 2017), so the relative concentration in the market is very high.

As in most countries, distribution is the bottleneck of the German film industy: For each distribution company there are about 25 production companies (Wirtz, 2016, pp. 335–337). The distributors have considerable bargaining power due to their market position and represent a market entry barrier. However, audiovisual producers in Germany generally do not rely solely on cinema productions, but generate additional revenue from the production of TV content. On average, cinematic exposure accounts for only 55% of those producers whose main activity is in this area (Seufert, 2002, p. 90).

Film production in Germany is characterized by small companies. With an average of 11 permanent and 69 freelance employees, 2.3 films were produced per year in 2000 when the last industry survey was conducted (Seufert, 2002, p. 92). Companies with only one or two employees and an irregular output of feature-length films less than once a year are not uncommon. In 2016, 80% of German production companies reported to have an output of only one feature film (Berauer, 2017, p. 15) The German film production market is regionally structured and clustered in Berlin-Potsdam, Munich, and Hamburg (Beck, 2012, p. 173). Bavaria Film, Constantin Film, Wild Bunch, Tele München Gruppe, and UFA Film & TV Produktion are amongst the more than 1,500 German-registered production companies (Wirtz, 2016, p. 335). In 2015, the German film industry employed approximately 77,000 people, which represented 0.17% of the German workforce (Berauer, 2017, p. 95).

While there were many smaller film theaters with a single or a few showrooms in Germany until the 1990s, multiplex cinemas with at least eight screens are also widespread today and have partially supplanted the smaller providers. However, a large number of the film theaters are still organized in small and medium-sized enterprises and family businesses. In 2016, of the total of 4,739 screens in Germany, 29.4% were at multiplex cinemas, and 70.6% at regular cinemas and in special forms (FFA, 2017). Together, the top five cinema groups generate one third of the total industry turnover (Berauer, 2017, p. 31). The five companies Cineplex, Cinestar, Cinemaxx, UCI Kinowelt, and Kinopolis are each subsidiaries of a foreign parent company. Cinemas in Germany recorded 121.1 million visitors in 2016, equivalent to 1.47 visits per inhabitant. In terms of visitors, films produced in Germany reached a market share of 22.7%, while US productions dominated with a share of 64.5%. Overall, sales of 1,023 million euros were generated (FFA, 2017).

Computer and Video Games

Regulative Environment

Technological advances are driving changes in both the German hardware and software markets. Above all, the regulative environment focuses on the content of the games rather than the platform and therefore has a particular impact on the production and distribution of software (Wirtz, 2016, p. 679). In Germany, regulation at the legal level mainly takes place through the application of criminal law (StGB), youth protection law (JuSchG), and copyright law (UrhG).

By international standards, youth protection legislation in Germany is very restrictive. At times, a special version of a game is distributed in German with human opponents being replaced by robots (Wirtz, 2016, p. 681). Computer games have the same age ratings as films which are also granted by a self-regulatory body (Unterhaltungssoftware Selbstkontrolle). If a title lacks a rating, distribution is strictly limited.

The computer games industry in Germany currently does not benefit from public funding at national level. Nevertheless, there are several funding institutions of the federal states focusing on project-based funding in the form of conditionally repayable loans (Castendyk & Müller-Lietzkow, 2017, pp. 152–156). Industry associations are calling for a state funding system for developers because of the cultural significance of electronic games (GAME Bundesverband, 2017). The association is also co-organizer and sponsor of gamescom, the world's largest trade and consumer fair for consumer electronics with a focus on gaming hardware and software that takes place annually in Cologne.

Market Players

In the core market of the computer and video game industry, companies based in Germany generated a cumulative turnover of 2.88 billion euros in 2015. Of these, 54% were generated in Germany and 46% abroad (Castendyk & Müller-Lietzkow, 2017).

Regarding game consoles, three players in Germany – as well as worldwide – constitute an oligopolistic market: Sony, Nintendo, and Microsoft. In terms of devices sold, Sony had a market share of 47%, Nintendo 41%, and Microsoft 12% (VGChartz, 2018). Because consoles are proprietary systems, gaming software sales are also in line with the sales share in the hardware market, so there is also considerable concentration: 4% of the companies generate 79% of the total industry turnover (Castendyk & Müller-Lietzkow, 2017, p. 99).

Both in the area of publishers and of software producers, international companies play the biggest role on the German market. They usually work closely with local developer studios. The largest publishers in terms of sales both internationally and in Germany are Tencent, Sony, Activision Blizzard, Microsoft, Apple, and Electronic Arts (Newzoo, 2017).

In Germany, the games industry employed approximately 14,100 people in 2015, 47% of which were working in games production and 32% in the publishing sector. On average, there were 21.4 employees per company (Castendyk & Müller-Lietzkow, 2017, p. 108). The developer studios are mostly smaller companies; only a dozen have more than 100 employees. The ten biggest developers in Germany are InnoGames, Bigpoint, Goodgame Studios, Gamigo, Crytek, Blue Byte, Gameforge, Wooga, Travian Games, and Gameduell. They employ as many people as the rest of the top 50 (Games Wirtschaft, 2017). In 2015, the development turnover of German game developers amounted to 549 million euros (Castendyk & Müller-Lietzkow, 2017, p. 94).

Music

Regulative Environment

The music market in Germany has little specific regulation, most importantly, of course, copyright law. At the beginning of the century there was an intense public debate about whether to introduce a so-called "Radioquote" that would have obliged radio stations to reserve at least 35% of air time for domestic artists. While the federal parliament called for a commitment of the radio industry to realize such a quota, the federal states as responsible authorities did not implement such a quota. Latest available data show that without a quota, the share of German production is about 30% of air time (Deutsches Musikinformationszentrum [MIZ], 2017).

The market for recorded music in Germany has a volume of 1.6 billion euros, with more than 60% still deriving from sales of physical media such as CD and vinyl. Thus, compared to the global market, Germany is a late adopter of digital music; however, since 2014, audio streaming is growing fast, with yearly growth rates of about 25%. The physical share is especially high in the segments of audio books, classical music, and kids. For pop music, digital distribution is most advanced, especially for international artists. This indicates an age gap, since domestic artists usually have a somewhat older audience (Bundesverband Musikindustrie [BVMI], 2017). The recorded music audience is predominantly male; across all genres only 36% of the customers are female.

Most popular genres are Rock and Pop music (74%), followed by Oldies & Evergreens (66%), German schlager (52%), and musicals (45%) (MIZ, 2017, multiple choices possible). Annually some 120,000 new titles are released, 17% of which physically. Overall, the number of titles released is declining and successively being replaced by tracks made available for streaming (BVMI, 2017).

Market Players

The international big three dominate the German market for recorded music: Sony Music Entertainment, Universal Music Group, and Warner Music group. Independent labels account for only 31% of the market (Worldwide Independent Network).

Seufert (2015, p. 16) states that recorded music accounts for only 22% of the 3.92 billion euros gross value of music industry. Other sectors are music instruments (19%), music lessons (10%), artists (15%), and, most importantly, live music (27%). In 2014, German consumers spent 2.8 billion euros on concerts and other music events. While it is evident that live music is of ample importance for the industry, detailed analysis of the respective shares of genres or industry players (venues vs. organizer vs. artists) are not available.

The public sector of live music is minuscule in pop genres; however, in classical music the relevance of publicly funded venues is high. Publicly funded operas, ballets, and musical had a combined audience of 7.5 million in 2016. Typically, the ticket sales in these venues cover only about 18% of the cost and each ticket is subsidized by the state with 124 euros (MIZ, 2017).

The music industry 2015 employs approximately 45,000 individuals, that is, 0.1% of the German workforce (MIZ, 2017).

Cross-Border Links and Connections

Cross-border flow of entertainment media is notoriously hard to quantify. Official statistics are not especially helpful, since the cross-border flows are usually captured in the customs statistic. However, custom tariffs are based on the weight of the traded good, and in this context, any entertainment is light and the value of entertainment import and exports is hard to pin down.

Nevertheless, cross-border links can also be identified in the share of foreign products in the entertainment supply (imports) or in the annual reports of major industry players (export). In 2016, German films (including co-productions) accounted for only 22.7% of the total film theater audience. European production accounted for another 11.5%; thus the market is clearly dominated by films of US origin with an audience market share of 64.5%. Films with neither European nor US-American origin had only 1.3% of the audience (FFA, 2016, 2017).

For feature films on television, the significance of imported productions is even higher. German productions account for only 14% of the total number of films on TV. However, with US American production accounting for 54% of the total, the diversity of the countries of origin is higher than in the cinemas (Berauer, 2017, p. 90). Krüger (2017) notes that the PSBs and RTL easily fulfill the quota for European content suggested by the Audiovisual Media Services Directive for fiction content, while Sat.1 and ProSieben clearly fail to meet it. For entertainment content beyond feature films and for home entertainment, market shares by country of origin are not registered.

In terms of TV format trade in recent years, Germany has become more successful in selling formats abroad; nevertheless imports still clearly outnumber exports, with the Netherlands, UK, and Scandinavia as the most important sources of format imports. When it comes to exporting TV content, German producers are more successful in TV movies and fictional series. Especially, crime series from the PSB with high production values are exported; nonetheless the German TV market by and large remains an import market (Mikos, 2016).

Domestic artists are well represented in the German recorded music market; however, there are large differences depending on the respective genre and format. While two thirds (2016) of the long-play charts stem from German productions (up from only 20% at the turn of the century), the single charts are dominated by two thirds of foreign artists (down from 50% at the beginning of the century) (MIZ, 2017).

Beyond import and export of content, German media companies are active as investors in other countries. For example, the RTL group owns TV broadcasters in nine European countries and German publishers are important players in most European magazine markets, however actual revenue figures or market shares are not disclosed.

Summary

Overall Germany is one of the largest markets for entertainment in the world. The market is fairly regulated and there is a strong public service element in most market segments. German entertainment producers have intensified their efforts to export; the domestic demand is still dominated by foreign content, in some segments overwhelmingly so.

Note

1 Although it is in regular use, the term "quality" remains fuzzy and its meaning is not clearly defined in the conditions for grants.

References

AGF, & GfK. (2018). *Marktanteile der AGF- und Lizenzsender im Tagesdurchschnitt 2017*. Retrieved from www.agf.de/daten/tvdaten/marktanteile/?name=marktanteile#

Beck, K. (2012). *Das Mediensystem Deutschlands*. Wiesbaden: VS Verlag für Sozialwissenschaften.

Berauer, W. (2017). *Filmstatistisches Jahrbuch 2017*. Baden-Baden: Nomos.

Bundesverband Musikindustrie (BVMI). (2017). *Musikindustrie in Zahlen 2016*. Berlin.

Castendyk, O., & Goldhammer, K. (2012). *Produzentenstudie 2012: Daten zur Film- und Fernsehwirtschaft in Deutschland 2011/2012*. Berlin: Vistas.

Castendyk, O., & Müller-Lietzkow, J. (2017). *Die Computer- und Videospielindustrie in Deutschland Daten – Fakten – Analysen*. Retrieved from www.hamburgmediaschool.com/fileadmin/user_upload/Dateien/Forschung/FoKo/Abschlussbericht_Games-Studie_V1.2_2017-12-05.pdf

Deutsches Musikinformationszentrum (MIZ). (2017). *Statistiken*. Retrieved from www.miz.org/statistiken.html

die medienanstalten (ALM) (Ed.). (2017). *Content-Bericht 2016: Forschung, Fakten, Trends*. Leipzig: Vistas.

die medienanstalten (ALM). (2018). *Über uns*. Retrieved from www.die-medienanstalten.de/ueber-uns/

Dreier, H. (2009). Das Mediensystem Deutschlands. In C. Matzen (Ed.), *Internationales Handbuch Medien* (28th ed., pp. 257–272). Baden-Baden: Nomos.

Directive 2010/13/EU, European Parliament; Council of the European Union 2010.

Eurostat. (2016). *Mean consumption expenditure of private households on cultural goods and services*. Retrieved from http://appsso.eurostat.ec.europa.eu/nui/show.do?dataset=cult_pcs_hbs&lang=en

Fay, J. (2008). *Theaters of Occupation: Hollywood and the Reeducation of Postwar Germany* (2nd ed.). Minneapolis, MN: University of Minnesota Press.

Filmförderungsanstalt (FFA). (2016). *Geschäftsbericht 2015*. Berlin.

Filmförderungsanstalt (FFA). (2017). *FFA info* (No. 1/2017). Berlin.

GAME Bundesverband. (2017). *Förderkonzept des GAME Bundesverband e.V*. Retrieved from http://game-bundesverband.de/wp-content/uploads/2017/05/F%C3%B6rderkonzept-GAME_Rev2.pdf

Games Wirtschaft. (2017). *Die 50 größten Games-Entwickler in Deutschland*. Retrieved from www.gameswirtschaft.de/wirtschaft/50-groesste-games-entwickler-studios-deutschland-august-2017/

Goldhammer, K., & Wiegand, A. (2016). *Pay-VoD in Deutschland 2016-2021*.

Heffler, M., & Höhe, D. (2017). Werbemarkt 2016 (Teil 1): Steigerung der Werbeerlöse. *Media Perspektiven*, (3), 157–169.

International Monetary Fund. (2018). *World economic and financial surveys: World economic outlook database – entire dataset*. Retrieved from www.imf.org/external/pubs/ft/weo/2018/02/weodata/download.aspx

Kommission zur Ermittlung der Konzentration im Medienbereich (KEK). (2017). *19. Jahresbericht 2016/2017*. Berlin: die medienanstalten – ALMKommission zur Ermittlung des Finanzbedarfs der Rundfunkanstalten (KEF). (2016). *20. Bericht*. Mainz.

Krasnova, H., Veltri, N. F., & Günther, O. (2012). Self-disclosure and privacy calculus on social networking sites: The role of culture. *Business & Information Systems Engineering*, *4*(3), 127–135.

Krüger, U. M. (2017). Profile deutscher Fernsehprogramme – Angebotsentwicklung zur Gesamt- und Hauptsendezeit. *Media Perspektiven*, (4), 186–205.

Mikos, L. (2016). Germany as TV show import market. In L. Powell & R. R. Shandley (Eds.), *German television: Historical and theoretical approaches* (pp. 155–174). New York: Berghahn.

Mitteldeutscher Rundfunk. (2016). Bericht über die wirtschaftliche und finanzielle Lage der Landesrundfunkanstalten gemäß § 5a Rundfunkfinanzierungsstaatsvertrag. Retrieved from www.ard.de/download/1015988/Bericht.pdf

Newzoo. (2017). Top 25 companies by game revenues. Retrieved from https://newzoo.com/insights/rankings/top-25-companies-game-revenues/

ProSiebenSat.1 Media SE. (2017). Geschäftsbericht 2016. Retrieved from www.prosiebensat1.de/uploads/2017/05/09/P7S1_GB16_DE_GB_2017-05-08.pdf

PwC. (2017). German entertainment and media outlook 2017–2021. Düsseldorf.

RTL Group. (2017). Annual Report 2016. Retrieved from http://www.rtlgroup.com/en/investors/financial_publications/annual-reports.cfm

Seufert, W. (2002). *Film- und Fernsehwirtschaft in Deutschland 2000/2001: Beschäftigte, wirtschaftliche Lage und Struktur der Produktionsunternehmen*. Berlin: Vistas.

Seufert, W. (2015). Musikwirtschaft in Deutschland: Studie zur volkswirtschaftlichen Bedeutung von Musikunternehmen unter Berücksichtigung aller Teilsektoren und Ausstrahlungseffekte. Retrieved from www.musikindustrie.de/fileadmin/bvmi/upload/06_Publikationen/Musikwirtschaftsstudie/musikwirtschaft-in-deutschland-2015.pdf

Statistisches Bundesamt. (2017). *Laufende Wirtschaftsrechnungen: Einkommen, Einnahmen und Ausgaben privater Haushalte 2015*. Wiesbaden. Retrieved from www.destatis.de/DE/Publikationen/Thematisch/"EinkommenKonsumLebensbedingungen/EinkommenVerbrauch/EinnahmenAusgabenprivaterHaushalte2150100157004.pdf?__blob=publicationFile

VGChartz. (2018). Germany yearly chart: The year's top-selling games at retail ranked by unit sales. Retrieved from www.vgchartz.com/yearly/2018/Germany/

Wirtz, B. W. (2016). *Medien- und Internetmanagement* (9th ed.). Wiesbaden: Springer Gabler.

Worldwide Independent Network. WINTEL market report 2017. Retrieved from http://winformusic.org/files/WINTEL%202017/WINTEL%202017.pdf

ZDF. (2017). Beteiligungen und Kooperationen. Retrieved from www.zdf.de/zdfunternehmen/zdf-beteiligungen-und-kooperationen-100.html

10 From Bootlegging Hollywood to Streaming Battle Rap

The Transformation of the Russian Entertainment Industry

Anna Popkova

Brief History of Russian Post-Soviet Entertainment

The history of post-Soviet Russian entertainment in many ways mirrors the history of the country itself. Like all other domains of life and culture, the entertainment industry had to switch from a government-regulated and government-funded model to a free-market model, which assumed self-sufficiency. In a country undergoing a major economic crisis, this was a challenge.

The film industry was hit particularly hard because of the sharp decrease in government funding that affected both film production and film exhibition. Muravina (1999) writes of the "destruction of film industry in Russia" (p. 829) in the 1990s, describing, among other things, the mass closures of the movie theaters across the country and instances of some movie theaters having to rent their space to car dealerships to generate profit. To be sure, film production was robust at the very beginning of the decade, with film producers excited to make films on a greater variety of subjects than during the USSR. However, the economic collapse took its toll and by 1996 various sources reported the production of films having gone down to somewhere between 20 and 50 films a year (as opposed to 470 films produced in 1991) (Frumes, 1999, p. 844).

Another major challenge for the film industry in Russia was piracy. Pirated videotapes of foreign films were widely available on the Russian market. The so-called "cloth" tapes (videos shot from the projection screen) were of poor quality but Russians, hungry for foreign entertainment, were not concerned. People often gathered at the "videotecs" to watch these films while the movie theaters scrambled to attract viewers. Frumes (1999) wrote:

> by 1994, there were 64 million blank video cassettes imported into Russia, but only 7500 pre-recorded tapes. We do not know for sure what those blank cassettes were used for, but there appears to be a relationship between large numbers of blank videos and fewer theatres.
> (p. 845)

The problem of piracy significantly affected Russian music industry in the 1990s as well. The emerging Russian show business was already full of problems such as the low level of professionalism of artists and the exploitation of artists by produces. Piracy exacerbated these issues by making it difficult for artists to profit from album sales. Sometimes even the official recording companies produced pirated CDs and audiocassettes in addition to the legal production (Yarotskiy, 2000). The problem persisted throughout the 1990s and into the early 2000s. For example, the International Federation of the Phonographic Industry reported that in the late 1990s the share of pirated music on the Russian market was between 60 and 75 percent (Preobrazhenskiy & Latov, n.d.).

An important step for the Russian music industry in the 1990s was the emergence of MTV Russia in 1998 as a result of the agreement between MTV Networks and one of Russia's music TV channels, BIZ-TV. MTV Russia significantly influenced the development of the Russian music industry, especially during the first several years when the channel successfully "glocalized" MTV, combining "the particularities of the [Russian] national culture and humor with the spirit of original [American] MTV" (Sukhanov, 2012).

The emergence of MTV Russia also connected the Russian music industry with Russian television – an industry that adapted to the challenges of the 1990s fairly well. Having inherited the infrastructure, the resources and, most importantly, the model under which over 95 percent of Russians had free access to leading television channels, television quickly became an attractive platform for advertisers. Advertising created revenue that in turn could be used to produce national and purchase foreign content. Television entertainment in Russia in the 1990s was dominated by foreign content. Frumes (1999) cites statistics that illustrate well the differences between the dynamics in film and television industries: "In 1994, [the American Film Marketing Association reported that of the total $5.5 million in film sales to Russia], over $4.2 million was from licensing free television rights" (p. 847).

In addition to showing many foreign films, Russian television channels purchased foreign soap operas, with Mexican soap operas becoming incredibly popular among Russian viewers. Closer to the end of the decade, however, Russian television started producing domestic serials, with the first one, *Ulitsy Razbitykh Fonarei* (*Streets of Broken Lights*), which came out in 1997, becoming incredibly successful. The success of this serial inspired the production of many more new ones, with their numbers increasing well into the 2000s (Beumers, 2009). Russian television of the 1990s also introduced such new formats as game shows and entertainment-centered talk shows. Some were licensed foreign shows, others were Russian adaptations of the foreign (predominantly American) shows. The most famous one was *Pole Chudes* (*The Field of Miracles*). The show's creators illegally appropriated the *Wheel of Fortune* format but subjected it to "radical change and adaptation" (Hutchings & Rulyova, 2009, p. 161), making the show one of the prime popular-culture examples of the interplay between the national and the global in early post-Soviet Russia (Hutchings and Rulyova, 2009).

By the early 2000s, the Russian economy had stabilized and various sectors of the entertainment industry could invest more resources in production, distribution and promotion of entertainment content. Russian consumers had more disposable income to spend on entertainment. Russia also established itself as a nation state, which also informed the push for producing domestic content. The improvement of the Russian economy and the overall professionalization of the Russian entertainment industry attracted foreign investment, and more global entertainment conglomerates became interested in the Russian market. The interplay of these factors was evident in all sectors of the Russian entertainment industry throughout the 2000s.

The Russian film industry "has risen . . . like the phoenix from the ashes" (Beumers, 2008, p. 208). If in 1997, the box office turnover in Russia was $6 million, by 2007 Russia was "the fifth highest grossing cinema market with an estimated $580 million box office" (Beumers, 2008, p. 208). One reason for this dramatic transformation was an increase, as a result of mostly private initiatives, in the quantity and the quality of Russian movie theaters. Second, a combination of private initiatives and state support created conditions and incentives for boosting domestic film production. A common approach involved major television channels developing film production arms and investing the profits gained from showing television serials in the production of films that could be later aired on television. The production of Russian blockbusters and sequels took off as well, with such major hits as *Bumer* (*Bimmer*), *Bumer 2* (*Bimmer 2*), *Nochnoi Dozor* (*Night Watch*), *Dnevnoi Dozor* (*Day Watch*), *Turetskiy Gambit* (*Turkish Gambit*) and *Statskiy Sovetnik* (*Counsellor of State*), to name a few, becoming incredibly popular.

In tune with "a common tendency in global TV network development" (Mikhailova, 2010, p. 177), Russian television of the 2000s started to be dominated by entertainment content. Russian-made serials started to push out previously popular Mexican soap operas and significantly outnumbered American serials also popular in the 1990s. For example, Vartanova and Smirnov (2010) report that in 1997 the number of Russian serials was 103 ... and by 2005 it had grown to 538. The number of American serials on Russian TV ... in 1997 [was] 87 ... in 2005, 153. A negative dynamic is apparent in ... serials produced ... in Latin America: in 1997 there were 38 ... but in 2005, the number dropped to seven.

(p. 32)

Some Russian serials were produced by the TV channels themselves and others by professional serial and film production companies (Beumers, 2009). In addition to serials, internationally licensed game and reality shows became highly popular. Compared to the 1990s, the quantity of the domestic entertainment content on Russian television had gone up but the quality of most of that content had been criticized by scholars and TV critics for lacking taste and catering to the lowest common denominator (Arutunyan, 2009).

Present-Day Entertainment Landscape: Key Trends and Major Players

The current state of the Russian entertainment industry reflects the continuation of the trends that started in late 2000s – consolidation of the market, conglomeration and commercialization. Five major corporations are responsible for the production and distribution of most entertainment in Russia.

The first, Gazprom-Media is a subsidiary of Gazprom – Russia's largest producer and exporter of natural gas. Though formally a private corporation, Gazprom is owned by the Russian government. A media corporation of modest size at the time of its founding in 1998, Gazprom-Media acquired its most valuable assets in 2001–2002 during a controversial "deal" that involved another corporation – Media-Most. Media-Most's TV channel NTV was highly critical of the Russian government and President Putin pressured Media-Most's owner to sell the company to Gazprom. After acquiring all of Media-Most's media assets, Gazprom-Media became "a leading player in the [Russian] media market" (Our History, n.d.), pursuing business opportunities in all segments of the media industry, including entertainment. Currently, Gazprom-Media owns seven broadcast TV channels (five of them are devoted exclusively to entertainment), 28 thematic TV channels, ten radio stations (with seven of them devoted to music and entertainment), three internet companies, one satellite TV provider, four magazines and 33 websites and online platforms. Gazprom-Media also owns four film production and distribution companies.

The second corporation, Perviy Kanal (Channel One), owns and runs one of the most popular television channels in Russia – Channel One. The channel is available to 98.8 percent of Russians free of charge. The channel also claims to have a global Russian speaking audience of more that 250 million (Pervivy Kanal, 2018). Perviy Kanal inherited its infrastructure from the Soviet All-Union State TV and Radio Company (Gosteleradio) and has changed multiple owners since 1991. Currently, 38.9 percent of the channel belongs to the Russian state agency Rosimushestvo (the same agency that owns Russia Today), 24 per cent to Roman Abramovich, a Russian billionaire loyal to Vladimir Putin, and the controlling share belongs to the National Media Group, another major corporation. Channel One's entertainment programs – films, serials, entertainment-oriented talk shows, game shows and reality shows – regularly make up at least a half of the top ten most popular television entertainment programs in Russia (Mediascope, 2017).

The third company, Vserossiyskaya Gosudarstvennaya Tele Radio Kompaniya or VGTRK (All-Russia State Television and Radio Broadcasting) belongs entirely to the Russian government and owns several television channels, with two highly popular ones – Rossiya 1 (Russia 1) and Rossiya 24 (Russia 24) – among them. Rossiya 1 regularly tops the ratings of all Russian TV channels. Since 2016, it has been steadily holding the first place in ratings, having pushed a long-time leader, Pervyi Kanal, into second place. The difference between the two channels' ratings is small, however; together, the two typically have the largest share of the daily television audience. Additionally, the entertainment programming from these two channels regularly tops the ratings of the most popular television programs (Mediascope, 2017).

The forth company, National Media Group, was formed in 2008 as result of a merger of the media assets of three large financial and industrial groups. The group owns a diverse set of media assets and partners with such international giants of subscription television as Discovery, Viasat and Turner. After a new media law prohibiting foreign companies from owning more that 20 percent of any Russian media company passed in 2014, the National Media Group quickly came to dominate Russia's subscription television market with 20 percent market share.

Finally, CTC-Media is a smaller company that nevertheless owns and runs CTC Channel, one of the leading television channels in Russia devoted exclusively to entertainment. The channel "strives to achieve the perfect combination of Russian and foreign programs, series, sitcoms and other content ... The channel's lineup includes its own in-house series and shows, as well as adaptations of some of the best international formats" (CTC, n.d.). CTC-Media owns three more entertainment channels: Domashny, branded as "targeting the specific interests of women aged 25–59" (Domashny, n.d.); CTC Love, aimed at "young girls and women [between 11 and 34 years old], who make up the main audience for programs about love and romance" (CTC Love, n.d.); and Che, "an action entertainment channel ... with a modern approach to spectacular entertainment" (Che, n.d.). In addition to some of its own programming like the reality show *Reshala* (*Solver*), the car show *Utilizator* (*Utilizer*) and the extreme travel show *Put' Bazhenova: Naprolom* (*Bazhenov's way: Straight through*), the channel recently broadcast such highly popular foreign TV series as *Westworld, House of Cards, The Young Pope, Mr. Robot* and others.

While Russian television entertainment is fairly consolidated, the film industry is much more fragmented, though most recent industry reports indicate a trend toward consolidation (Vsemirniy obzor, 2017). An important player in the production of Russian film is the Russian Ministry of Culture. In the past several years, the Ministry, along with such state agencies as the Federal Film Foundation, has been developing new incentives for the development and popularization of Russian film. The initiatives often go hand in hand with various strategies of state protectionism. For example, one of the most recent initiatives is a program aimed at the opening of more movie theaters across Russia. As part of this program, 70 regions in Russia received funding for the modernization and opening of 437 movie theaters, of which 174 were opened in 50 regions in 2016 (Vsemirniy obzor, 2017). The key requirement for the theaters that received the funding is that Russian films make up no less than 50 percent of all films shown. Other recent initiatives included legislative updates like a more comprehensive anti-piracy law, the decision to designate 2016 the Year of the Cinema, and new regulations on film release dates (Film production, 2016).

Cross-Border Links and Connections

Russia's Key Import-Export Markets and Strategies

As discussed earlier in the chapter, the Russian entertainment industry relied heavily on imported content throughout the 1990s, and in later decades the amount of domestic as well as co-produced entertainment started to grow. Nevertheless, the amount of imported entertainment remains high, and foreign films (especially Hollywood productions) and music (American and Western European) remain highly popular.

This tendency is particularly noticeable in the film industry, where foreign films always generate more in ticket sales than domestic ones (InterMedia Agency, 2015). For example, in 2016, U.S. and foreign films made up 82 percent of box-office takings in Russia (Holdsworth & Kozlov, 2017). The lack of popularity of domestic films among Russian audiences has become a point of concern for the Russian state and the Russian Ministry of Culture, leading to the emergence of various initiatives (discussed earlier in the chapter) aimed at boosting domestic film production and distribution, on one hand, and at state protectionism, on the other.

While the reception and consumption of foreign entertainment by Russian audiences has been very successful, Russian domestic entertainment has struggled to attract the attention and interest of audiences abroad, aside from the former Soviet states, particularly Kazakhstan, Ukraine and Belarus. Here too, the Russian state has been investing significant resources into the popularization of Russian films abroad. The strategies included reducing prices, stimulating co-productions, improving the quality of Russian films by training professionals abroad and allocating funds for dubbing, subtitling and marketing of Russian films (Duvernet, 2012; Kozlov, 2018). So far, these strategies have had mixed results. For example, the number of co-productions had grown between 2011 and 2014 but dramatically decreased in 2015, from between 24 and 32 films per year to 13 (European Audiovisual Observatory, 2016). On the other hand, some of the Russian animation films and series have been internationally successful. For example, the two animation films *Snezhnaya Koroleva* (*The Snow Queen*) and *Snezhnaya Koroleva 2: Perezamorozka* (*The Snow Queen 2: The Snow King*) have been successful in Asia and Latin America (European Audiovisual Observatory, 2016). Additionally, Russia sees China as one of the most promising foreign markets, although here the results have also been mixed. On the one hand, in 2017 China "accounted for the lion's share of Russian movies' foreign gross, $12 billion" (Kozlov, 2018). On the other hand, the most recent Russian movie, *Viking* (*The Viking*), released in China in the fall of 2017, only grossed $2.2 million. Nevertheless, the two countries still see potential in entertainment partnerships. For example, in 2016, one of the Russian media giants, Gazprom-Media, signed strategic cooperation agreements with such Chinese media companies as Shanghai Media Group, People's Daily Online and China Central Television (CCTV). The agreement focuses on production, development and distribution of TV, film and digital content in both countries. One of the first steps of this agreement was the selling of the format of the original Russian series *Interny* (*The Interns*) to Jiangsu Broadcasting Corporation, making it the first-ever adaptation of the Russian series in China (Our History, 2017).

Interestingly, one recent Russian entertainment product that became very popular globally, including in North America and Western Europe, was produced and marketed without the assistance of either the Russian state or Russian media conglomerates. The Russian animated series *Masha i Medved* (*Masha and the Bear*), which has been translated into 25 languages and broadcast in more than 100 countries (Vasilyeva, 2016), received critical acclaim and has become commercially successful, with a 40 percent annual revenue increase (Vasilyeva, 2016). The cartoon's YouTube channel was in the top ten most viewed YouTube channels in 2016. One the series' episodes had a sixth place in the top ten most-viewed videos on YouTube, with over a billion views in September of 2017 (Top ten, 2017). It was also the only non-music video on the list. According to the series creators, two thirds of the YouTube royalties come from views outside Russia (Vasilyeva, 2016). In 2016, *Masha and the Bear* became available to U.S. viewers on Netflix. Netflix also recently bought five television series produced by a small independent Russian studio, Sreda, and, according to Sreda's founder, there are agreements about future series as well (How Alexander Tsekalo, 2017).

Impact of the Digital Revolution

The advance of information and communication technology had a significant impact on the development of Russian entertainment. The digital revolution posed serious challenges for certain entertainment media and formats but also presented the industry with multiple new opportunities.

For example, for many years, television was the chief source of entertainment for most Russians but as the number of Russian Internet users has rapidly grown in the past decade, television has started to lose ground, particularly among younger audiences. To address this problem, television channels launched digital platforms and mobile device applications for some of the most popular programs. For example, Channel One's website features about 280 thousand videos, and the website's audience consists of more than 15 million unique users monthly (History, n.d.). Still, with 71 percent of the Russian population having access to the Internet in 2017 (Auditoriya, 2017), and over 95 percent of Russians aged between 12 and 34 using the Internet at least once a week (Mediascope, 2017a), the competition becomes more and more challenging. The trend is reflected in the dynamics of advertising as well with Internet advertising showing faster growth rates than TV advertising and the market shares of the Internet advertising quickly catching up with the market shares of TV advertising (Summarnyi ob'yem, 2017).

The digital revolution strongly affected the Russian music industry, particularly its reliance on sales of CDs. While by the mid-2000s Russia had made it into the top ten countries by volume of music CD sales, by 2012 these had fallen by 30% (Kuznetsova, 2013). The chief reason for this shift was the online piracy that flourished especially on one of the biggest Russian social networks, VKontakte (often referred to as "Russian Facebook"). Users could download pirated music from numerous VKontake pages without any restrictions or consequences. By 2014, CD sales became almost completely irrelevant for the Russian music industry, and the industry started transitioning to digital-only formats such as legal downloads and streaming (InterMedia Agency, 2015).

Online piracy became a challenge for the film industry as well, although new technologies allowed Russian filmmakers to experiment with new funding models such as crowdfunding, especially for independent and lower-budget projects (Kraudsorsing, 2016). Additionally, projects like Dubl' Dv@ (Take Two) became possible. Dubl' Dv@ is an online film festival aimed at showing a variety of Russian films that have not made it to mass release. The columnist of *Rossiyskaya Gazeta* Valeriy Kichin came up with the idea several ideas ago and launched the first festival in 2011. For 48 hours, the films, most of them with English subtitles, become available for viewing free of charge on the website of *Rossiyskaya Gazeta* newspaper. The viewers select the winner by rating films on a numeric scale; viewers can also leave comments and the most insightful reviews automatically enter the viewer reviews contest. Since 2011, more than 130 films have been shown at the festival and the website received more than 4,000 viewer reviews (O festivale, 2017). While the festival's popularity has not reached a mass scale yet, it nevertheless serves as a good illustration of the possibilities for the film industry opened up by the digital revolution.

Television Versus YouTube

A Case Study of the Russian Battle Rap Project, Versus Battle

If in the late 1990s and early 2000s MTV Russia was the primary source of music-centered entertainment in Russia, today this source is YouTube. YouTube consistently makes up the top ten Internet projects in Russia in terms of daily, weekly and monthly audience reach (Mediascope, 2017a), particularly among younger audiences.

One genre of entertainment that has grown rapidly in popularity on Russian YouTube in recent years is battle rap. Since 2013, the *Versus Battle* project became the leading battle rap platform attracting Russian rap and hip-hop artists, corporate sponsors and most importantly millions of viewers. The numbers alone are striking. In 2015, a battle between the Russian rappers Oxxxymiron and Johnyboy became the first rap battle in the history of global battle rap to receive one million views within the first 24 hours. A year later, a battle between rappers Oxxxymiron and ST received more views than the most popular rap battle in the United States. In April of 2017, the battle between video bloggers El'dar Dzharakhov and Dmitriy Larin received 7.7 million views within the first 24 hours. Finally, in August of 2017 the battle between rappers Oxxxymiron and Gnoynyi received 9.1 million views within the first 24 hours. At the time of this chapter's writing, the battle had received over 30 million views. Such explosive popularity of Russian battle rap attracted the attention of battle rappers abroad, leading to the first Russia–USA rap battle that took place in Los Angeles (USA) in October of 2017 between the American battle rapper Dizaster and the Russian rapper Oxxxymiron (rapping in English). The battle received over one million views on YouTube in less than 8 hours and was named the Battle of the Year by *HipHopDX* (The 2017 Breakdown, 2017) – one of the leading online magazines of global hip-hop music news and criticism.

What makes the case of the Russian battle rap fascinating in the context of the discussion of the Russian entertainment industry is that the emergence and the rapid development of the Russian YouTube-based *Versus Battle* project points to the changing dynamic of the Russian entertainment industry as a result of disruptive effects caused by the advent of digital technologies. As Jenkins, Greene and Ford (2013) remarked, in today's digital media environment, there is "an emerging hybrid model of circulation, where a mix of top-down and bottom-up forces determine how material is shared across and among cultures in far more participatory (and messier) ways" (p. 1). The *Versus Battle* project is an example of a site where one can witness a complex interplay of the top-down and bottom-up forces that mediate the cultural, technological, and business dimensions of a popular entertainment product.

Versus Battle was started in 2012 by then-23-year-old Aleksander Timartsev, or as he is commonly known, Restorator, who had no experience of, or serious connections in, the entertainment industry. Restorator came up with the idea while working two part-time jobs in the service industry. He befriended two music-video makers at a party and the three decided to launch a YouTube channel where they would upload videos of rap battles that they would also organize and film. The project required minimum investment of technology or money but a lot of networking, most of which was done via social media. Running on the pure enthusiasm of its developers, *Versus Battle* was not conceived of as a business project. Artists volunteered to take part in the battles, and the physical space for filming the battles was provided free of charge by the restaurant where Restorator worked. The project rose to fame so quickly that, as one journalist remarked, "it seemed like there was a team of talented marketing professionals behind it" (Nikitin, 2014), soon attracting a flurry of corporate sponsors.

Such success did not go unnoticed by the key players of the Russian entertainment industry. Different television channels approached *Versus Battle* with suggestions to adapt the format for television. However, *Versus* is a decidedly anti-television project. As Restorator himself remarked, "The format [of *Versus*] would definitely lose. TV is artificial . . . there will be people sitting in those little nice chairs there . . . [that's] disgusting. We stand. We all stand until the battle is over. We are part of an underground scene" (Restorator, 2017). At the core of *Versus'* success is a large degree of authenticity and a connection with the battle rap fans that can be easily maintained on YouTube given the platform's interactivity. Thus, in an industry historically dominated by television entertainment produced by large media corporations, *Versus* serves as a vivid example of a successful entertainment project that utilizes the opportunities opened up by the digital revolution and relies on an alternative business model to remain independent financially and keep its format and content relevant for its multi-million audience of (mostly) young Russians.

Most importantly, the success of the *Versus Battle* project points to important shifts in the Russian entertainment industry that mirror most of the global trends. At the same time, Russia's increasing authoritarianism and periodic conversations at various levels of the government about stricter Internet regulation pose a potential challenge for a future of projects like *Versus*, especially if the rappers address political topics more frequently. As Restorator remarked in an interview, answering the question about his biggest dream: "My dream is that YouTube doesn't close in Russia" (Restorator, 2017). It remains to be seen how the project develops within the environment of shrinking freedom of speech in Russia.

Given the project's incredible popularity, especially among younger audiences, it will nevertheless remain a critical site of power negotiation among such forces as the Russian state, Russian domestic business interests, the global technology and business giants, and grassroots initiatives at local and global levels.

References

Arutunyan, A. (2009). *The Media in Russia*. Maidenhead: McGraw-Hill Education.

Auditoriya pol'zovatelei Interneta v Rossii v 2017 godu sostavila 87 mln chelovek. (2017) [The audience of Russian Internet users in 2017 consisted of 87 million people]. *RussianInternetforum.ru*. Retrieved from http://2017.russianinternetforum.ru/news/1298/

Beumers, B. (2008). Killers and gangsters: The heroes of Russian blockbusters of the Putin era. In S. White (Ed.), *Media, Culture and Society in Putin's Russia* (204–225). New York: Palgrave Macmillan.

Beumers, B. (2009). The serialization of culture, or the culture of serialization. In B. Beumers, S. Hutchings & N. Rulyova (Eds.), *The Post-Soviet Russian Media: Conflicting Signals* (159–177). New York: Routledge.

Che (n.d.). CTC-Media. Retrieved from www.ctcmedia.ru/business/our_channels/che/

CTC (n.d.). CTC-Media. Retrieved from www.ctcmedia.ru/business/our_channels/ctc/

CTC Love (n.d.). CTC-Media. Retrieved from www.ctcmedia.ru/business/our_channels/ctclove/

Domashny (n.d.). CTC-Media. Retrieved from www.ctcmedia.ru/business/our_channels/domashniy/

Duvernet, P. (2012, April 30). Russian films look abroad. *Russia Beyond the Headlines*. Retrieved from www.rbth.com/articles/2012/04/30/russian_films_look_abroad_15441.html

European Audiovisual Observatory (2016, December 9). Industry report: Market trends. *Cineuropa*. Retrieved from http://cineuropa.org/dd.aspx?t=dossier&l=en&tid=1967&did=315300#cm

Film production and co-production in Russia, and the export of Russian films abroad (2016). A report by European Audiovisual Observatory. Retrieved from www.obs.coe.int/documents/205595/552774/RU+Film+Production+and+Co-Production+in+Russia%2C%20and+the+Export+of+Russian+Films+Abroad+2016+EN/cbd71dc6-a3ef-402f-808a-52e975eda13c

Frumes, H. (1999). Motion pictures in Russia. *Whittier Law Review*, 20, 839–851.

Holdsworth, N. & Kozlov, V. (2017, October 13). Russia ditches plan to boost exhibition fees after outcry, considers levy system. *The Hollywood Reporter*. Retrieved from www.hollywoodreporter.com/news/russia-ditches-plan-boost-exhibition-fees-outcry-considers-levy-system-1048472

How Alexander Tsekalo and Russian TV series conquered Netflix and the world (2017, May 10). *Russia Beyond the Headlines*. Retrieved from www.rbth.com/arts/2017/05/10/how-alexander-tsekalo-and-russian-tv-series-conquered-netflix-and-the-world_759916

Hutchings, S. & Rulyova, N. (2009). *Television and Culture in Putin's Russia: Remote Control*. New York: Routledge.

InterMedia Agency. (2015, September 11). Kul'turno-zrelishnaya industriya RF v 2014 godu [The entertainment industry in Russian Federation in 2014]. InterMedia agency report. Retrieved from www.intermedia.ru/news/283591

Jenkins, H., Ford, S., & Green, J. (2013). *Spreadable Media: Creating Value and Meaning in a Networked Culture*. New York: NYU Press.

Kozlov, V. (2018, January 12). Russia to provide funds to boost homegrown movies' exhibition abroad. *The Hollywood Reporter*. Retrieved from www.hollywoodreporter.com/news/russia-provide-funds-boost-homegrown-movies-exhibition-1074238

Kraudsorsing: osnovnye ploshadki v Rossii i ikh analogi na zapade. (2016, September 14) [Crowdsourcing: the main platforms in Russia and their equivalents in the West]. *Towave.ru*. Retrieved from www.towave.ru/pub/kraudsorsing-osnovnye-ploshchadki-v-rossii-i-ikh-analogi-na-zapade.html

Kuznetsova A. (2013). Amerikantsy obvinili "VKontakte" v unichtozhenii legal'nogo rynka muzyki [Americans accused VKontate of destroying the legal music market]. *Kommersant*. Retrieved from www.kommersant.ru/doc-y/2128880

Mediascope. (2017). Dannyie po auditorii [Audience metrics]. Mediascope agency. Retrieved from http://mediascope.net/services/media/media-audience/tv/national-and-regional/audience/?arrFilter_pf%5BCITY%5D=5096&arrFilter_pf%5BPERIOD%5D=18%2F12%2F2017+-+24%2F12%

2F2017&arrFilter_pf%5BTYPE%5D=66&captcha_code=0584651765906b4f8ab7100234180047&captcha_word=P8JHD&set_filter=Y

Mediascope. (2017a). Internet. Mediascope agency. Retrieved from http://en.mediascope.net/services/media/media-audience/internet/information/?arrFilter_pf%5BYEAR%5D=2017&set_filter=Show&set_filter=Y

Mikhailova, N. (2010). Modern Russian entertainment TV: "Live well now – ask me how!" In A. Rosenholm, K. Nordenstreng & E. Trubina (Eds.), *Russian Mass Media and Changing Values* (175–192). New York: Routledge.

Muravina, E. (1999). The structure of the Russian entertainment industry. *Whittier Law Review*, 20, 825–830.

Nikitin, A. (2014, February 4). Boytsovskiy klub [Fight club]. *Colta*. Retrieved from www.colta.ru/articles/music_modern/1912-boytsovskiy-klub

O festivale "Dubl' Dv@." (2017) [About the "Take Two" festival]. *Rossiiskaya Gazeta*. Retrieved from https://rg.ru/2014/04/02/d2-aboutfest-site.html

Our History (2017). Gazprom-Media. Retrieved from www.gazprom-media.com/en/page/history?change_lang=1

Perviy Kanal (2018) Perviy Kanal – 20 Let v Efire [Channel One – 20 years on air]. Perviy Kanal. Retrieved from www.1tv.ru/20years/

Preobrazhenskiy, D. & Latov, Y. (n.d.). Shou-biznes [Show business]. In *Encyclopedia Krugosvet* online. Retrieved from www.krugosvet.ru/enc/kultura_i_obrazovanie/teatr_i_kino/SHOU-BIZNES.html?page=0,1#part-3

Restorator – ob Oximirone, tsenzure i bable. (2017) [Restorator on Oxxxymiron, censorship and dough]. Interview with Yuriy Dud'. *VDud'*. Retrieved from www.youtube.com/watch?v=baLHI-u8h5g

Sukhanov, V. (2012). Fenomen muzykal'nykh leyblov v sovremennoi Rossii [The phenomenon of music labels in contemporary Russia]. *Vestnik SPBGUKI* (online). Retrieved from http://cyberleninka.ru/article/n/fenomen-muzykalnyh-leyblov-v-sovremennoy-rossii

Summarnyi ob'yem reklamy v sredstvakh ee rasprostraneniya za pervyie tri kvartala 2017 goda. (2017) [The summary of advertising market share for the first three quarters of 2017]. Association of Communication Agencies of Russia (ACAR). Retrieved from www.akarussia.ru/knowledge/market_size/id7558

Top ten most viewed YouTube Videos with over a billion views right now (2017, September 2). YouTube video. Retrieved from www.youtube.com/watch?v=BdMfEtQOj4Y

The 2017 Breakdown. (2017). *HipHopDX*. Retrieved from www.youtube.com/watch?v=-2LbEqHZUVM

Vartanova, E. & Smirnov, S. (2010). Contemporary structure of the Russian media industry. In A. Rosenholm, K. Nordenstreng & E. Trubina (Eds.), *Russian Mass Media and Changing Values* (21–40). New York: Routledge.

Vasilyeva, N. (2016, April 12). Russian cartoon bear takes the world by storm. *The Associated Press*. Retrieved from https://apnews.com/9a3807793f2e4a398257d8b5c005dc97

Vsemirniy obzor industrii razvlecheniy I SMI: prognoz na 2017–2021 gody. (2017) [Global overview of entertainment and media industry: forecast for 2017–2021] PricewaterhouseCoopers report. Retrieved from www.pwc.ru/outlook2017

Yarotskiy, Y. (2000, May 24). O chem molchat fonogrammy [What the phonograms are silent about]. *Kommersant*. Retrieved from www.kommersant.ru/doc/24399

11 The Entertainment Industry in Spain

Juan Pablo Artero Muñoz

Introduction

What in the USA is understood as the entertainment industry, in Spain is usually labeled the audiovisual industry, an important part of the media, cultural or creative industries (García, Fernández & Zofío, 2003; Rodríguez Ferrándiz, 2011). Academic studies on that topic have been diverse in the last two decades, especially by authors like Artero, Herrero and Sánchez-Tabernero (2008), Bustamante and Álvarez Monzoncillo (1999) and Fernández-Quijada (2009).

A recent concentration analysis of the Spanish media market concluded that content industries are moderately but increasingly concentrated, while technology industries are highly but decreasingly concentrated (Artero & Sánchez-Tabernero, 2015). Other studies have implemented European comparisons, where differences among big countries are not huge (Sánchez-Tabernero & Artero, 2008).

This chapter gives a situational overview of the main segments of the entertainment industry in Spain: free-to-air television, pay television, video, film, videogames, radio and recorded music. As a data-driven study, it relies on the last available figures from industry associations (AEVI, 2017; Promusicae, 2017), regulatory bodies (CNMC, 2017), authors' coalitions (SGAE, 2017) and consulting firms (PwC, 2017).

Free-To-Air Television

The television industry was a public service monopoly in Spain till 1990. That year, Antena 3 and Telecinco started competing for audience and advertising with state-owned TVE and other regional public service broadcasters. Since that moment, free-to-air television has followed a path to more competition with the entrance of new players in the market as well as more consolidation among them, as can be seen in Table 11.1.

In audience terms, Italian-owned Mediaset is the market leader with a share of 30% in 2016. This conglomerate is the result of the merger of Telecinco and Cuatro in 2010 and includes a total of seven different national channels. The same thing holds true with Atresmedia, the result of the merger of Antena 3 and La Sexta in 2012. It obtains 27% of the audience with its six channels. Public service RTVE reached 16% of the market with five channels. All three companies constitute the basic television oligopoly that has been dominant in the last three decades. Apart from that, a second tier of the market can be defined as a monopolistic competition structure. This second-level industry accounts for less than 10% of the total audience and includes six small players. They received broadcasting licenses from government in 2002 (Vocento and Unidad Editorial) and 2015 (13TV, DKiss, Ten and Real Madrid TV).

This dual-market structure is even clearer in advertising terms. Atresmedia and Mediaset concentrate 89% of all advertising revenues of television industry in Spain, a 1,765 million

Table 11.1 Audience Share of National Television Groups (in bold) and Channels in 2014–2016

Group/Channel	2014	2015	2016	Group/Channel	2014	2015	2016
Mediaset	30.7	31.0	30.2	**RTVE**	16.7	16.7	16.8
Telecinco	14.5	14.8	14.4	La 1	10.0	9.8	10.1
Cuatro	6.7	7.2	6.5	La 2	2.8	2.7	2.6
FDF	3.5	3.5	3.2	Clan	2.3	2.4	2.2
Divinity	2.1	2.3	2.3	Teledeporte	0.9	0.9	0.9
Energy	1.5	1.5	1.9	24 horas	0.8	0.9	0.9
Boing	1.7	1.6	1.5	**Vocento**	3.5	3.4	2.9
Be Mad	–	–	0.4	Paramount	1.9	2.0	1.8
Atresmedia	27.7	26.8	27.1	Disney	1.5	1.4	1.1
Antena 3	13.6	13.4	12.8	**Unedisa**	3.6	4.2	3.2
La Sexta	7.2	7.4	7.1	Discovery Max	2.1	2.1	1.9
Neox	2.6	2.6	2.5	Gol	–	–	0.2
Nova	2.5	2.4	2.2	**13TV**	1.6	2.0	2.1
Mega	–	0.9	1.8	**DKiss**	–	–	0.4
Atreseries	–	–	0.8	**Ten**	–	–	0.3
				Real Madrid TV	–	–	0.2

Source: CNMC (2017, p. 187). Figures in percentages.

euros market in 2016 (CNMC, 2017, p. 185). The third main player in audience terms (RTVE) does not participate in the advertising market as a public service broadcaster, apart from having a small income from sponsoring. Other small private competitors (Vocento and Unidad Editorial) and regional public service broadcasters (TV Catalunya and Canal Sur) have a very limited access to the main national advertisers, so that the dual-market structure is even deeper in advertising than in audience figures. Atresmedia and Mediaset form an advertising duopoly while the rest are a second stream that can be defined as a monopolistic competitive sub-industry.

Pay Television

The pay-television industry also started in Spain in 1990, when the government gave Canal Plus one of the new private channels' licenses. That offer was a single terrestrial channel and obtained a significant number of subscribers for more than 15 years. In 1997 its owners (Spanish Prisa group and French Canal+) launched a new satellite multi-channel offer called Canal Satélite Digital. That platform competed with Vía Digital/DTS till their merger in 2003 as Digital Plus and its full acquisition by Telefónica in 2015. Additionally, since 1995, cable telecommunications had started to develop in Spain. The vast majority of the companies that received cable licenses merged around Ono in 2005, purchased by Vodafone in 2015. Apart from satellite and cable, the emergence of IPTV in the last few years has also changed the ways the Spanish receive pay-television content.

In 2012, satellite was still the leading technology to distribute pay television in Spain, with cable and IPTV as followers in a total number of 4 million subscribers. But five years later, IPTV is the main technology, while cable is second and satellite is third in a total base of more than 6 million subscribers. The pay-television market has grown since: a volume of 1,622 million euros in 2012 to 1,884 in 2016. Satellite TV represented 60% of all income in 2012, while in 2016 it reached half of it. On the other hand, IPTV includes 55% of revenues in 2016, while it was only 17% of the market in 2012 (CNMC, 2017, p. 190). Terrestrial and mobile TV never had an

Table 11.2 Pay-TV Subscribers and Revenues by Companies 2012–2016

	2012	2013	2014	2015	2016
Movistar	815,357	811,096	1,881,457	2,551,697	3,646,984
	247.01	227.40	304.79	597.77	1,579.28
Vodafone	58,422	0	0	964,299	1,278,793
	3.91	0.00	0.00	163.00	178.88
Orange	102,603	124,015	152,440	308,332	493,272
	12.28	14.42	14.49	23.09	56.48
Euskaltel	136,186	106,768	110,399	115,811	269,708
	18.68	19.46	21.51	21.49	28.76
Wuaki	0	0	0	115,830	148,260
	0	0	0	n.a.	n.a.
TeleCable	134,456	125,963	129,891	131,833	126,633
	35.06	30.15	25.33	6.31	9.55
R	103,333	98,009	94,608	122,559	0
	21.46	16.57	14.22	12.78	0.00
Digital Plus	1,733,752	1,649,031	1,696,585	1,317,690	0
	983.24	964.23	937.45	826.79	0.00
GolTV	290,604	237,178	231,414	0	0
	80.16	62.09	57.95	32.14	0.00
Ono	872,608	789,841	785,552	0	0
	184.74	149.19	133.23	0.00	0.00
Others	120,082	115,725	101,570	167,378	183,402
	36.27	29.80	2.97	14.30	31.94
Total	4,367,403	4,057,626	5,183,916	5,795,429	6,147,052
	1,622.79	1,513.29	1,511.95	1,697.66	1,884.89

Source: CNMC (2017, p. 192–193). Revenue figures in million euros.

important role, while cable has been losing part of its television revenues. The reason behind that is that cable operators obtain most of their income from telecommunications services (fixed line, mobile phones, ISP) and not from television content. As a result of that, the main players in pay TV are listed in Table 11.2.

Movistar is the clear market leader with 59% of all subscribers in 2016. Its owner is Telefónica, the former state-owned telecommunications company. Most of its customers came from the acquisition of satellite platform Digital Plus in 2015, as well as its own cable and IPTV previous subscribers. British-owned Vodafone is the second player and also acquired most of its 1.2 million clients after its merger with the leading cable operator Ono in 2015. French-owned Orange is the third telecommunications competitor in Spain and also the third in pay television, but with less than half a million subscribers. It also made an important corporate operation purchasing Jazztel in 2015. Euskaltel is a cable company only located in the north of Spain that has recently acquired TeleCable and R, while Wuaki is a small IPTV company.

Differences are significant in subscription numbers, but even more in revenues. As can be seen in Table 11.2, Movistar concentrates 83% of all pay-TV revenues in Spain. That can be explained by the previously mentioned acquisition of Digital Plus, a base of customers used to pay just for TV content. However, customers of Vodafone, Orange and Euskaltel pay mostly for telecommunications services and television represents a small share of their invoices. These companies use television more as a way to complement their triple-play services than as a business by itself. Consequently, pay television is almost a monopoly of the telecommunications leader Telefónica.

Video

With new digital platforms such as YouTube and Netflix, video is emerging as a new industry independent from both television and film, even if companies from both traditional sectors participate within it. First, it is important to highlight the clear decline of physical video rental and sales in Spain. Between 2012 and 2016 video rental units has been reduced by two thirds, while sales have diminished by half. In total revenue, the reduction of that market has been 28% (SGAE, 2017, p. 7). Most of the videos come from the film industry.

That important decline may come from the changing consumption patterns, given that most customers are migrating from physical to online video, in all its feasible devices. In 2016 the Spanish watched 910 million of downloading videos and 10,597 million of streaming videos, most of them for free and only 13% from paying platforms (SGAE, 2017, p. 28–33). It is obvious that streaming is becoming the dominant technology, that the dominant business model is free supply and that cell phones and tablets are beating computers as the favorite device. Table 11.3 supplies some insights into the video genres preferred by the audience.

As can be seen in Table 11.3, in 2015 and 2016 short videos were the favorite content of online watchers. It can be deduced that the vast majority of these videos were consumed within platforms like YouTube. Short videos are watched by more than half of the audience. After that, series and movies account for almost half and one third of the video consumption. In this case, it can be inferred that many of them were accessed through platforms like Netflix. After that, family and friends videos reach roughly 30% of the audience, news and sport are almost on 20% and online documentaries are liked by more than 15% of Internet video users. Table 11.3 includes the most important pay video platforms in the Spanish market.

In 2016, Yomvi was still the market leader for online pay video, with a penetration of 7.6% of all households with Internet access. Yomvi is the online application to access content from Movistar+, the pay television offer from Telefónica, so that the telecommunications, pay television and online video leaders are logically the same company. But this fact might be changing dramatically with the entrance of Netflix to the Spanish market in 2015. In a very short time, 3,4% of households have subscribed to Netflix. The third most important player is Wuaki (around 1%), while Bein and Filmin reach significantly fewer subscribers (SGAE, 2017, p. 37). Though the position of YouTube as the dominant free video platform is very strong, regarding streaming

Table 11.3 Online Video Genres in 2015–2016.

	S1 2015	S2 2015	S1 2016	S2 2016
Short videos	53.7%	55.4%	54.3%	58.2%
Series	45.4%	42.0%	49.2%	47.6%
Movies	33.6%	30.1%	34,2%	36.2%
Family/Friends videos	37.5%	35.5%	30,8%	29.0%
News	17.5%	14.7%	20.5%	19.7%
Sports	22.0%	20.9%	21,7%	19.0%
Documentaries	14.3%	15.3%	16.8%	16.9%
Other	18.2%	18.1%	16.1%	15.4%

Source: SGAE (2017, p. 36). Individuals who watch online video once per week.

pay video the market situation is still highly volatile, with the recent entrance of HBO, Amazon Prime Video and Sky.

Film

Theatrical film is still an important industry in Spain even though its social penetration was much higher in past decades. The current revenue volume is above 600 million euros per year and figures are coming back to pre-crisis (i.e. pre-2008) standards. The number of movies released between 2012 and 2016 has been fluctuating between around 1,500 and 2,000 titles. But the significant figure is that sold tickets were above 100 million in 2016, which situates the Spanish market well above two tickets per head and year. Prices are reducing slightly due to special sales and promotions, but it has always been around 6 euros per ticket. The total revenue is above 600 million euros both in 2012 and 2016, while the other three years in-between were worse from a box office viewpoint (SGAE, 2017, p. 8).

The American film industry dominates the Spanish theatrical market, with 31% of all movies released, 63% of theaters' sessions and 68% of both sold tickets and total revenues. On the other hand, 25% of titles released were Spanish, but they represent only 18% of sessions, tickets and revenues. In total, all European movies account for 58% of the releases, but they only obtain around 30% of sessions, tickets and revenues. Latin America and other industries produce less than 10% of movies released in Spain, but the sessions, tickets and revenues are less than 2% of the market (SGAE, 2017, p. 43).

The Spanish film production industry can be defined as both competitive and weak. It is not concentrated, as many different companies participate in the market and none has got a dominant position; it is also weak, given that most firms produce just a few movies, or even just one movie, per year. The film divisions of strong television groups like Atresmedia, Telecinco or Telefónica are an exception to this. Apart from them, other important film production companies include Apaches, Nostromo, Kowalski and Morena, all of them with above 10 million euros of box office sales in 2016 (SGAE, 2017, p. 69). But, as seen earlier, they altogether obtain just 18% of total

Table 11.4 Main Film Distribution Companies in 2016.

	Company	Movies	Tickets	Revenue
1	The Walt Disney Company Iberia	33	19,110,751	110,564,606
2	Universal Pictures	83	18,725,399	108,586,102
3	Hispano Foxfilm	57	15,733,430	93,853,329
4	Warner Bros Entertainment	82	14,944,243	90,401,721
5	Sony Pictures Releasing España	56	8,985,119	52,419,279
6	Aurum Producciones	51	6,602,650	39,236,121
7	Paramount Spain	21	3,196,532	19,621,941
8	DeaPlaneta	26	2,286,434	12,716,851
9	Nostromo Pictures	1	1,973,340	12,471,763
10	Vértigo Films	48	2,107,588	12,231,390
11	A Contracorriente Films	77	1,218,191	7,393,283
12	Tripictures	11	1,220,261	7,177,032
13	Castelao Pictures	18	764,469	4,401,397
14	Golem Distribución	88	720,125	4,061,590
15	Caramel Films	21	508,260	2,992,781

Source: SGAE Cine (2017, p. 54).

market revenues, with American movies representing 68%. That can be illustrated by taking a look at distribution companies in 2016 (Table 11.4).

The top four film distribution companies in Spain are American. Disney, Universal, Fox and Warner sell around 100 million euros of box office sales each per year by distributing mainly American movies. The fifth corporation is Sony, technically Japanese. Including Paramount in seventh place, only four Spanish firms are included in the top ten: Aurum, DeaPlaneta, Nostromo and Vértigo. Unlike the highly competitive national film production industry, distribution is highly concentrated around the top five international film companies. After them, a second-tier market adopts a structure of monopolistic competition, with a high specialization of distribution labels.

Finally, the top two proprietors of film theaters in Spain are foreign: American Cinesa and Mexican Yelmo, a subsidiary of Cinépolis since 2015. They own more than 500 and 400 screens respectively. Three other companies – MK2-Cinesur, Ocine and Kinépolis – control around 100 screen. But the exhibition market is very competitive in general, with only 12 firms operating more than 25 screens and almost 2,000 screens out of a total amount of around 3,500 in the hands of small local operators (SGAE, 2017, p. 11).

Videogames

The videogames industry has developed sharply in Spain in the last three decades. As in most countries in the world, the market is currently dominated by platforms Play Station (Sony), Xbox (Microsoft), Wii and DS (Nintendo), as seen in Table 11.5.

In total, videogames reached sales of 1,163 million euros in 2016, with more than one million consoles, nine million games and four million accessories sold. One third of all revenues were digital and two thirds were physical. Japanese Sony and its PlayStation platform

Table 11.5 Videogames Industry in 2016

Platforms	Hardware		Software		Accessories	
	Units	Sales	Units	Sales	Units	Sales
Play Station		229		229.9		50.5
PS4	0.65	215	4.15	199.1	0.97	42.8
PS3	0.06	1	0.90	26.2	0.36	6.9
PS2			0.02		0.05	
PSP			0.01		0.08	0.8
PS Vita	0.02	4	0.17	4.6	0.08	
Nintendo		64		90.2		11.1
Wii	0.01		0.40	11.6	0.12	2.2
WiiU	0.04	13	0.44	16.5	0.12	3.2
DS			0.01	0.1		
3DS	0.35	48	1.77	62	0.54	5.7
Microsoft		22		25.4		10.1
Xbox 360	0.03		0.27	7.2	0.07	2
Xbox One	0.07	22	0.43	18.2	0.16	8.1
Other	0.05	3	0.03	0.1	0.07	0.1
Computer			0.51	15	0.20	8.9
Multiplatform					1.62	31.5
Total	1.2	308	9.11	361	4.29	113

Source: AEVI (2017, p. 30–32). Figures in million units and million euros.

represents around two thirds of all sales of hardware, software and accessories. Nintendo, also a Japanese corporation, is second, far from the market leader with two platforms: Wii and DS. Finally, American Microsoft and its Xbox is the third player, with less than 10% of the market. It is important to note that all hardware and most accessories revenue goes to the platform's manufacturers, but not necessarily software income, given that independent developers produce videogames for different platforms.

Radio

Radio in Spain is a small industry financed only by advertising expenditures, but it is very important in terms of social penetration and influence. The main radio groups include both music- and talk-radio networks. They are listed in Table 11.6.

From an audience viewpoint, the clear market leader is Prisa, which includes the top talk-radio network Cadena Ser and the top music-radio network 40 Principales, along with four other music channels. The second position is usually occupied by Cope, a property of the Catholic Church, including their news radio network and three other music channels. Atresmedia, also present in television, is the third competitor, with news network Onda Cero and two music channels. Finally, Radio Nacional, owned by public service corporation RTVE, holds four national networks. After that oligopoly, other national and regional offers can be found, such as music group Kiss, sports network Radio Marca or news channels EsRadio or Intereconomía.

As with audience figures, Prisa is also the market leader, selling in most years more than 150 million euros worth of advertising. Cope is second, with around 100 million euros and Atresmedia is the third radio group, with around 80 million euros worth of advertising sales (CNMC, 2017, p. 196). Consequently, the advertising oligopoly is made up of just three main players that share a market of around 350 million euros per year. Public service RTVE and other regional public service broadcasters include very little or no advertising at all.

Table 11.6 Audience of National Radio Groups (in bold) and Channels in 2014–2016

Group/Network	2014	2015	2016	Group/Network	2014	2015	2016
Prisa				**RTVE**			
Cadena Ser	4.4	4.2	4.0	Radio 1	1.2	1.2	1.1
40 Principales	3.1	2.9	2.7	Radio 3	0.4	0.4	0.4
Dial	2.2	2.2	2.0	Radio 5	0.3	0.3	0.3
Máxima FM	0.6	0.5	0.4	Radio Clásica	0.1	0.1	0.1
M80	0.5	0.5	0.4	**Kiss Media**			
Radiolé	0.5	0.5	0.4	Kiss FM	0.8	0.9	0.9
Cope				Hit FM	0.1	0.1	0.2
Cope	1.7	2.5	2.5	**Radio Marca**	0.5	0.6	0.5
C100	1.6	1.6	1.7	**EsRadio**	0.3	0.3	0.3
Rock FM	0.8	0.9	1.0	**Intereconomía**	0.1	0.1	0.1
Megastar FM	0.2	0.3	0.2				
Atresmedia							
Onda Cero	2.3	1.7	1.8				
Europa FM	1.9	1.7	1.7				
Melodía FM	0.2	0.2	0.2				

Source: SGAE (2017, pp. 55–62). Figures in million of listeners at end of each year.

Table 11.7 Recorded Music Industry in 2016

	Sales	Label	Market Share
Digital	100.2		61.2
Downloading	10.2	Universal	32.5
Mobile products	2.4	Sony	29.7
Streaming subscriptions	62.2	Warner	27.6
Streaming advertising	25.3	Discmedi	3.5
Other		Blanco y Negro	1.8
		Nuba	1.7
		Avispa	1.5
		Música Global	1.1
Physical	63.5		37.8
	Units	Universal	33.2
Singles	0.01	Sony	29.3
LP	0.43	Warner	27.1
CD	8.01	Discmedi	3.7
DVD	0.16	Blanco y Negro	1.9
Other	0.13	Nuba	1.7
Total	8.75	Avispa	1.5
		Música Global	1.1

Source: Promusicae (2017, pp. 1–2). Figures in million units and euros and percentages.

Recorded Music

As in many other countries, digitalization has created deep transformation in the music industry in Spain that has only recently been overcome. With more than one million subscribers to streaming music, mostly to Spotify, digital revenues are nowadays more important than physical sales, as Table 11.7 shows.

In fact, digital music sales (mostly streaming income from both subscriptions and advertising) reached 100 million euros in 2016, while physical music sales (mostly CDs) were slightly above 60. Regarding music labels, the global oligopoly of Universal, Sony and Warner concentrate around 90% of the market, both digital and physical. As in other industries, after them a second-tier stream includes small independent labels such as Discmedi, Blanco y Negro, Nuba, Avispa and Música Global. But unlike in movies, big global labels produce much music in Spain that becomes a leading product in Spanish-speaking markets.

Conclusion

The market structure of the entertainment industry in Spain is generally oligopolistic. That is the clear situation in segments like free-to-air television, pay television, film distribution, videogames, radio and music. Other more competitive sectors include film production and exhibition as well as online video, still in their infancy in the Spanish market. But even in these new segments, the danger of monopolization by global entrants such as YouTube, Netflix or Spotify is present.

Cross-ownership within different industry segments sometimes occurs, and relevant examples can be found. Atresmedia participates significantly in television, radio and film production. The same thing holds true with Italian Mediaset, but with no radio operations. Public service RTVE participates in television and radio segments. All three are also willing to have a stake in the free

Table 11.8 Revenue Forecasts for the Entertainment Industry in 2017–2021

Segment	2017	2018	2019	2020	2021	CAGR 2016–2021
TV advertising	2,127	2,120	2,121	2,140	2,165	0.4%
Pay TV subscriptions	1,950	2,047	2,106	2,159	2,205	4.2%
Videogames	932	967	1,000	1,032	1,067	3.5%
Film box office	616	635	656	678	702	3.2%
Radio advertising	477	493	507	521	534	3.1%
Recorded music	228	243	261	278	291	6.1%
Online video advertising	169	190	208	222	237	10.3%
Online video subscriptions	114	137	158	174	185	15.4%
Online TV advertising	49	55	60	64	69	10.3%
Physical video	67	65	63	62	61	−2.2%
Total video	399	447	489	522	552	
Total	6,729	6,952	7,140	7,330	7,516	

Source: PwC (2017, p. 74–79). Figures in million euros.

online video market. Telefónica-Movistar is almost monopolistic in pay television and is also important in pay-online video and film production. Japanese Sony is present in movies and music and it is very dominant regarding videogames. American Universal and Warner are also strong in both film distribution and music. The future evolution of the different entertainment segments is expected to be unequal (Table 11.8).

As shown in Table 11.8, revenue forecasts for the entertainment industry in Spain are promising except for television advertising (the biggest sector) and physical video (the smallest). Pay television, videogames, film, radio and music will develop at good compound annual growth rates (CAGR) in the next five years. Finally, the still small industry of online video will grow at rates of 10% (advertising) or even 15% (subscriptions). At that point, video will become the fifth most important industry segment after free television, pay television, videogames and movies. Radio and recorded music are thought to become less strategic sectors in the years to come.

References

AEVI (2017). *Anuario de la industria del videojuego*. Retrieved from www.aevi.org.es/web/wp-content/uploads/2017/06/ANUARIO_AEVI_2016.pdf

Artero, J. P., Herrero, M., & Sánchez-Tabernero, A. (2008). Monopolio, oligopolio y competencia en los últimos quince años de televisión en España. *Sphera Publica, 5*, 83–98.

Artero, J. P., & Sánchez-Tabernero, A. (2015). Media and telecommunications concentration in Spain (1984–2012). *European Journal of Communication, 30*(3), 319–336. doi: 10.1177/0267323115577307

Bustamante, E. & Álvarez Monzoncillo, J. M. (1999). España: la producción audiovisual en el umbral digital. *ZER, 7*, 45–64.

CNMC (2017). *Informe económico sectorial de las telecomunicaciones y el audiovisual*. Retrieved from www.cnmc.es/sites/default/files/1880454_3.pdf

Fernández-Quijada, D. (2009). The Spanish independent production market in view of the appearance of Cuatro and la Sexta. *Communication & Society, 23*(1), 59–87.

García, M. I., Fernández, Y., & Zofío, J. L. (2003). the economic dimension of the culture and leisure industry in Spain: National, sectoral and regional analysis. *Journal of Cultural Economics, 27*, 9–30.

Promusicae (2017). *El mercado de la música grabada en España en 2016*. Retrieved from www.promusicae.es/estaticos/view/4-informes-promusicae

PwC (2017). *Entertainment and media outlook 2017–2021. España*. Retrieved from www.pwc.es/es/publicaciones/entretenimiento-y-medios/assets/gemo-espana-2017-2021.pdf

Rodríguez Ferrándiz, R. (2011). From cultural industries to entertainment and creative industries. The boundaries of the cultural field. *Comunicar, 18*, 149–156. doi: 10.3916/C36-2011-03-06

Sánchez-Tabernero, A., & Artero, J. P. (2008). Competition between public and private television in the European market. *Palabra Clave, 11*(2), 343–354.

SGAE (2017). *Anuario de las artes escénicas, musicales y audiovisuales*. Retrieved from www.anuariossgae.com/anuario2017/home.html

12 Entertainment

The Golden Resource of Italian Cultural and Media Industries

Mario Morcellini, Mihaela Gavrila and Simone Mulargia

Entertainment is, even prior to representing a form of cultural production, and subsequently a market (i.e. in many ways a measurable economic system), above all a platform for communicative innovation. But there is more: it is highly revealing of the anthropological changes of the modern subject.

We will therefore try to briefly examine the dynamics and speed with which entertainment, which has now become fundamental in the media system, has grown exponentially in modern times at the expense of the other two containers through which we usually read the contemporary communication triptych: fiction in all its forms, on the one hand, and journalistic information (news, current affairs), on the other.

Observing the main contents of the principal media systems that, for the moment, and certainly in the short term, are substantially stable, the tripartition, which has become familiar (though excessively taken for granted), consists of information, entertainment and fiction. This is a modern division, which is now familiar both to broadcasters and to analysts, and follows a canonical doctrine inspired by the BBC. Indeed, it acts as the effective and definitive handbook which accompanied the birth of the great European television systems, and, with some exceptions, the American market[1] as well.

Over time, however, the practice of the tripartition of dominant communicative genres became established with the invaluable advantage of allowing some essential change indicators to appear: first of all, the ability of these three key areas to highlight their overwhelming part in the programming of television, radio and now even multimedia; a substantial balance between the three macro-genres, formerly defined as "expressive areas"; and finally, a simplified but essential theory of human needs to which communication lends its sensitive and intelligent response interface (Morcellini & Bentivegna 1989; Gavrila 2010).

Here, however, we need to introduce the comparative dynamic, that is, a minimum of historical contextualization, because this tripartition is indeed quite modern and dates back to the second half of last century. Therefore, the history of the most "radical" fibres that make up communication have not always been like this, and it is an interesting exercise to briefly explore this history here.

Within the communicative cultures of the past there were essentially two great communicative dimensions: education and entertainment. On the one hand, the educational dimension was symbolized by the school, even though it also had the ability to go beyond the temporal confines of the school itself. In other words, we are dealing with what in contemporary media linguistics would be called "culture", with in-depth information and the discussion of current events clearly becoming a variant.

On the other hand, everything else was understood as entertainment and fun. However, it should be pointed out that this creative aspect can also effectively include both narration and storytelling. In fact, this becomes clear when we focus for a moment on such an important term in history as that of "comedy". Beyond the philological disputes, however incredibly specific these may be, "comedy" originally alludes to the Bacchic procession grounded in songs, witticism and mocking, and inspired by licentious and burlesque content.

More generally, over the course of history, communication and its essential functions became established, and, well before the extraordinary analysis of Roman Jakobson (1966), were essentially polarized: on the one hand, training, information and, in other words, commitment; on the other, fun, invention, and therefore dreams and the spectacle.

We are dealing with a very interesting structure which allows us to detect some of the overbearing dimensions of human imaginary and symbolic values which are always revealing of profound changes in individual expectations. In other words, there were two main functions of what we identify today as communication, which is to say, nothing but the communicative exchange of symbols and messages between human beings, and then between men and machines (as Bacon reminds us, "Homines [. . .] per sermones sociantur[2]").

With the arrival, and the impetuous development, of the proto-cultural industries in the nineteenth century and at the beginning of the twentieth century, the entertainment world became progressively more and more recognizable in two dimensions: on the one hand, amusement, which was soon to become a variant of shows, quizzes, musicals and comedy – programs which, both separately and taken together, were defined as "evasive"; and on the other hand, everything that relates to *invention* and therefore to a detachment from reality (or so it was believed), which was later to be effectively defined by the term "storytelling".

Even before dealing with problems in the philology of communication, it must immediately be said that this progressive specialization of functions is the main feature of mass cultural production systems, in the precise sense of indicating a phenomenon under which the moments of commitment and disengagement are no longer in balance in the communicative lexicons of modernity. The specialization of entertainment into *fiction* and entertainment (two terms that, not by chance, have known derivations, blossoming terminology and impressive definitions, ranging from *talk-show* to *TV serials* and other TV-related terms) has in fact multiplied the supply and consumption of that world which the classical authors of the American Communication Sociology labelled "evasion"[3].

Seen as a snapshot of the interaction between man and media, *fiction* is, in all its subtle forms, definitely the area in which contemporary man's projection of identity needs, reassurance and recognition appears most immediate. This is even more evident for those most affected by the convulsion of the crises of the modern individual, particularly the young. So far, we are in the field of communication genres that men have always known and chosen, from the classical world of tragedy and Greek comedy to their cultural variations.

However, the entertainment show has become more overwhelming in contemporary communication, and it is to be wagered that it will continue to do so progressively, even in digital communication (many data already indicate this today). It is interesting to reflect on the semantic aspect of words that refer to the entertainment world; almost all allude to the *gap* between life and symbolization, between the routine of everyday life and the de-anchoring song from the burden of everyday life.

In almost all modern languages, and in any case in those of Latin derivation, it is interesting to note that *dis-traction* and *e-vasion* emphasize a dimension of escape and difference with respect to life, while initiating a path of dis-assignment, *dis-engagement* and progressive *un-reality*; all founded on and fuelled by the increasing share of available free time of modern subjects.

Moreover, it cannot be a coincidence that many of these nouns are preceded by privative or negative suffixes, which make us understand the progressive dilatation of the medial and hypermedial virtual dimension with regard to concrete experience. Reasoning in modern terms about the fortunes of entertainment, it is interesting to recognize that it is composed of other more or less reasonable myths of the contemporary: from the decline decrease of facts to the weakening of critical thinking, from dis-intermediation that obviously stresses the quality of individualism to opinion experts. If one thinks about it, entertainment, like a parasite, feeds off disintermediation and indeed becomes its soundtrack.

The Entertainment Market in Italy: Strong Viewers, Weak Producers

According to a recent PricewaterhouseCoopers (PwC 2017) report, the turnover of the market identified by the label "entertainment and media" (E & M) saw a growth of 5% in 2016, a revenue increase from 30 billion euros to 31.5 billion. In general terms, therefore, the sector is showing some signs of recovery when compared to the crisis that began in 2008. As often happens, Italy (compared to its European partners) has shown itself to be slower to reverse the trend when compared to the economic crisis and its consequences on the E & M market. A forecasted time horizon up to 2021, shows a Compound Annual Growth Rate (CAGR) for the media and entertainment sector to be around 3,9% with a total value of about 38 billion euros in revenue (PwC 2017).

While remaining within the ambit of entertainment, we may draw attention to several specific considerations with regard to the relative weight of the different sectors. From this point of view, when considering the revenue indicator, the Internet and TV remain the most significant segments; more specifically, following the indications of PricewaterhouseCoopers, 68% of the revenues of 2021 will come from these two sources (PwC 2017). For the Internet in particular, higher revenues are expected in terms of access, with the CAGR of mobile devices reaching 11%. The penetration will exceed 90% in 2021. At the same time, internet advertising, linked above all to mobile platforms, is expected to grow significantly, with a €1.6 billion stake in 2021 (PwC 2017).

Also with regard to TV, Italy seems to have emerged from the crisis, as is evidenced by a new increase in subscriptions to paid services. With 6.9 million households having pay-TV services in 2016, the number is expected to grow to 7.5 million in 2021. Internet video will also continue to grow at a rapid pace (PwC 2017). As for the advertising market, although there are weak signs of a change of orientation towards the online, the Italian scenario is and will still be dominated by the free-to-air model and the duopoly Rai and Mediaset in the near future, despite the significant decrease in the audience and the progress of the other TV channels in terms of TV/share ratings (see Figure 12.1).

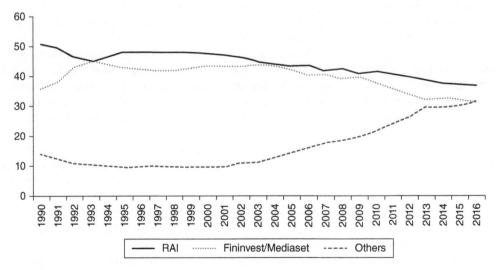

Figure 12.1 Italian TV audience's evolution (%).
Our elaboration on Auditel data 1990–2016.

Compared to this overall positive picture, there are still areas of difficulty, regarding, for example, the publishing segment, even though there is some element of optimism related to the possibility of exploiting the opportunities offered by digital readers. As for books, the sector as a whole continues its negative trend. From this point of view, in spite of some interesting signs relating to children's books and digital professional books, the trend does not change.

The performance of the cinema sector is indicative of the complex nature of the media vis-à-vis entertainment, forever located at the intersection of global economic dynamics and local specificities. While 2016 was a positive year, thanks to the extraordinary success of a film played in by a famous Italian comedian, 2017 turned out to be a veritable debacle: −46.3% compared to 2016 for number of appearances and −44.2% for the number of tickets sold (ANICA-Cinetel 2018).

In spite of this fluctuating evolution in numerical terms of the Italian entertainment industry, the data remain significant and confirm some irrefutable characteristics of this market.

A metric by which to understand the economic value of a sector of the cultural and media industry has always been constituted by the interest aroused in relation to advertising investors.

In fact, historically one of the characteristics of the media industry and Italian entertainment, known as the "Italian anomaly" (Morcellini, 2015, De Domenico, Gavrila, Preta, 2002) is precisely that of seeing advertising investments concentrated in television, which has tended to cannibalize resources to the detriment of the development of other media industries.

Taking a historical view, we can see how, in the 20 years between 1975 and 1995, advertising expenditure in Italy increased from 396 to 5790 billion Lire, with the share of investment in television broadcasters going from 16.1% to 58.9%. In 2001 the TV advertising share decreased to 51.22% and, starting from the 2008 economic crisis, and, above all, with the progressive transformation of traditional media and the digital revolution, there has been a redistribution of resources allocated by businesses to promotional campaigns. In this sense, the expansion of new media in terms of advertising revenue inevitably subtracts resources from traditional media. All this does not necessarily affect the turnover of publishing companies, where product differentiation policies have been activated to allow the presence on several platforms, both traditional and digital. In numerical terms, according to the Nielsen Media Research data, the analysis of the Italian market has highlighted an overall decline in advertising investments related to the totality of the media in question, with the exception of the Internet.

In terms of revenue, the entertainment market distribution in Italy continues to assign a lead position to television and, in particular, to private and international media companies. For some years now, Sky Italy, which combines advertising resources to those coming from subscriptions, has ranked in first place. Following Sky Italy is Fininvest/Mediaset and Rai, the public service media company, which, on April 28, 2017, obtained the renewal of the public radio, television and multimedia service concession for the decade 2017–2027.

Table 12.1 Distribution of Advertising Revenue (Mil €)

	2011	2012	2013	2014	2015	2016
Tv	4.221	3.621	3.266	3.220	3.248	3.456
Radio	566	493	460	451	482	486
Newspapers	1.359	1.132	941	871	817	754
Periodicals	1.291	1.011	784	694	678	651
Internet	1.408	1.503	1.483	1.624	1.660	1.905
Total	**8.844**	**7.760**	**6.933**	**6.860**	**6.884**	**7.252**

Source: Annual report AGCom 2017.

Table 12.2 Share of the Main Subjects Operating in the Integrated Communications System (%)

	2015
21st Century Fox	**15.4**
– *Sky Italia*	15.1
– *Fox Networks Group Italy*	0.3
Fininvest (*)	**14.9**
– *Mediaset*	1.3
– *Arnoldo Mondadori editore*	1.4
Rai Radiotelevisione Italiana	**13.7**
Gruppo Editoriale L'Espresso	3.3
Google	3.2
RCS MediaGroup	3.0
Seat Pagine Gialle	1.4
Facebook	1.3
Gruppo 24 Ore	1.3
Cairo Communication	1.3
Others	41.2
Total	**100.0**

*The share relating to Fininvest also includes the revenues generated by the Mediamond company.
Source: AGCom 2017 Annual Report.

The Italian entertainment market, never considered a mature market, and always, almost totally, identified with mainstream television, is facing some radical changes today which go far beyond technological issues and the multiplication of players currently involved in the production and distribution of content entertainment.

First, the bringing in of the law "Discipline of the cinema and the audio-visual" of November 14, 2016 (published in the *Official Gazette* on November 26, 2016), has been considered the first organic law to deal with the entire audio-visual sector. This includes all its sectors, all operators and the entire supply chain. The new law comes at a time of crisis for Italian cinema, as already mentioned in the previous paragraph, and the results will not be visible in the short term. However, there are many elements of innovation:

- promoting and facilitating investments in cinematographic and audio-visual productions in distribution and promotion with various concrete instruments;
- enhancing public investment by 60%, tying up available resources to a minimum of 400 million euros;
- allocating specific incentives for start-ups and new talent/creativity;
- obliging broadcasters to program the viewing of Italian works, stimulating co-productions, increasing the number of theatres and the penetration in foreign markets;
- creating facilitation tools for access to credit;
- identifying specific support tools for the training and cultural growth of the public, as well as for all promotional activities;
- developing an extraordinary plan for the digitization of the entire existing audio-visual assets;
- defining selective contributions (for all production phases) and automatic contributions granted according to more complex criteria and with the obligation of productive reinvestment;
- expanding tax credit instruments;

- abolishing censorship and creating new tools to protect minors, with the responsibility of operators for distributed content;
- establishing the Superior Council of Cinema and Audio-visual, an advisory body of the Ministry of Cultural Heritage and Activities and Tourism, composed of experts in the sector and representatives of trade associations.

All this should also, according to impact simulations carried out by the Ministry of Cultural Heritage and Activities, have repercussions on television: both in terms of Italian and European film content to be included in the schedules, and as an investment of public and private TV in the production of films, fiction, animation and TV programs of Italian and European production.

However, by distinguishing between a noble up-market and supportive role on the one hand, consisting of cinema and quality serials, and a trash and cheap part on the other, made up of fiction and entertainment programs such as game shows and talent shows, variety, reality shows and factual entertainment, this norm seems to replicate a typically European attitude to the entertainment industry.

While public policies and financial investments are aimed at the cinema and the so-called "educated" audio-visual sector, it nevertheless does seem to delay serious investment aimed at activating a creative system focused on "Made in Italy" ideas, formats and pilot productions that can also circulate outside Italy and are able to generate significant returns in terms of the diffusion of Italian culture; that is, in addition to necessary economic capital, as well as real social and cultural capital. The birth of a genuine "conceived in Italy" entertainment industry could be a challenge for the future, but it would need adequate support strategies to significantly enhance and encourage the production of multi-platform content by national companies.

Currently, considering the research data "Il valore della produzione. L'intrattenimento come risorsa economica e culturale" ["The value of production. The entertainment as an economic and cultural resource"] (APT- Ce.R.T.A. 2016), about 8,500 people were employed in the production and post-production television sector in 2014. Of these it is estimated that the entertainment area activates 3,800 contracts annually. However, the number of full-time employees in production companies in the entertainment sector is limited to about 614 employees.

In 2015 this industry produced 290 programs, for a total of 13,850 hours of programming, with a concentration on the prime segment of prime time. However, most of these consist of imported formats, while only 5% are from original Italian formats (MIBACT 2015). These latest data clearly demonstrate the extent to which strong investment is necessary in the production of content made in Italy in order to create wealth and value to an industry that would otherwise risk cannibalization by the great global giants and lead to the generation of a tendential cultural and economic colonization by large multinational productions[4].

In fact, the production of Italian entertainment is not immune to the changes that are affecting the entire global audio-visual market, in particular to the rapid change in the current scenario in which the big global players act, accelerating strategic alliances to overcome crises by recovering or expanding markets. The market and organizational assets are disrupted and redesigned very quickly and this reality would require immediate action and above all the capability of anticipating the future, rather than reacting to it. For example, Disney's recent acquisition of most of Fox will undoubtedly also have consequences on the Italian entertainment market. This move, which concentrates an immense productive and commercial potential in the hands of a single operator, effectively forces operators, and not only Europeans and Italians, to come up with, and implement, new strategies to face the competition (D'Ascenzo 2017).

In support of this need to strengthen the national entertainment system, the "Italia Creativa 2015"[5] report demonstrates the strategic value of this sector in Italy: culture and creativity are worth 2.9% of the Italian national GDP, placing itself above telecommunications and immediately behind the automotive industry. In terms of total value, the first three sectors are: television and home entertainment (12.2 billion), visual arts (11.2 billion) and advertising (7.4 billion). In addition, videogames (+10.3%), the visual arts (+3.9%) and the cinema (+3.4%) recorded growth and led the sector between 2012 and 2014. However, what is difficult to implement in Italy is the possibility of collaboration between the various operators, with a configuration of a compact, united and strong system able to compete at the global level as well. International dynamics show just how important it is to set up a system and to produce and encourage the national and international circulation of contents, also by exploiting digital platforms. To this we should add the delicate and complex issue of the protection of original ideas and copyright within the evolutionary framework of the digital ecosystem. In fact, one of the most powerful drivers for the circulation of all entertainment products (ranging from audio-visual to music and publishing) is represented by mobile platforms, particularly suited to current lifestyles with their increasing mobility and connectedness. These platforms are also strategic for a rejuvenation of entertainment and for the adaptation of advertising messages to the behaviour of new viewers.

Digital Transformation in Italy

The impact of digitization can be read on at least three levels: content, distribution and business models (Sigismondi 2011). In terms of content, digital technologies have allowed not only the modification of some production processes related to analogue media, but have also, in fact, imposed new standards of audio-visual representation, as, for example in the case of 3-D animation films. Furthermore, with regard to the impact of digitization on content, the entertainment sector is today characterized by new media objects, such as videogames (Mulargia 2016). As for distribution, the most significant changes are related to the availability of broadband networks capable of enabling the terminals of private individuals to use streaming services, both with regard to the world of music consumption and the related audio-visual sector. As for business models, enabling digital transformations has led to a significant acceleration of the time horizon in which a specific business model is able to function. Recent developments in the music segment are indicative: after decades in which the main economic subjects and business models remained unchanged, digitization at first introduced a crisis into the content market (also due to illegal downloading). However, since then digitization has contributed to the creation of a new system for downloading legal content on large platforms (such as iTunes), and, more recently, to moving business boundaries once again with music streaming subscriptions (e.g. Spotify).

These general changes can be contextualized with respect to Italy by analyzing some significant data. As for the new contents of entertainment, videogames have now been confirmed as a stable segment. Although the Italian context has witnessed a significant presence of smartphones, the volume of business generated by casual games specifically designed for these platforms, does not exceed that of traditional video games. More specifically, even if this sector of the entertainment industry has already exceeded the symbolic revenue share of one billion euros, it will tend to grow even further in the future, and indeed double by 2021 (Pwc 2017). Again, with reference to PricewaterhouseCoopers' data, the new virtual reality and e-sports sectors will be protagonists of very high growth rates (74.5% and 35.3%, starting, however, from very low absolute values) (Pwc 2017).

On the network infrastructure side, Italy still shows some signs of weakness compared to other countries in the European context. The rate of broadband penetration in Italy is lower than the European average and lower than countries such as the United Kingdom, Germany, France and Spain (Eurostat 2016) (see Figure 12.2).

Although some specificities related to Italian geography and delays resulting from archaeological digs help to explain this lag, the delay in the implementation of a stable, fast and efficient network infrastructure nevertheless does have a considerable impact on the possibility of a greater diffusion of the entertainment media.

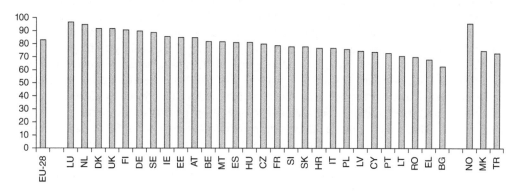

Figure 12.2 Households with broadband access, 2016 (as % of all households).
Eurostat 2016.

With regard to business models, and in line with emerging globally trends, the Italian context of digital transformation is characterized by the definition of new business models, especially in the video sectors (with Netflix) and music (Spotifiy). Subscriptions which are not overly expensive (when compared to the offers of traditional operators), and less characterized by time constraints, are meeting the needs of the subjects, allowing for the audience expansion of users of paid services.

As highlighted by PricewaterhouseCoopers (2017), these cases are particularly significant with regard to the new strategies for content monetization. More specifically, both Netflix and Spotify possess high-quality content which, in the past, had been the most relevant resource through which to attract the public as a function of advertising procurement. Today, payment of a subscription functions as a mechanism that allows people to access the content without being bombarded by unsolicited advertising. The drive for a differentiation of offer, based on quality content, is currently also influencing the other players in the market. From this point of view, the case of YouTube is emblematic. This platform was born as the very symbol of participatory culture (Jenkins 2006) as well as focusing on amateur content produced by common users. Under the competitive drive of the new digital scenario, YouTube is also diversifying its business model by going through processes of institutionalization and professionalization of user-generated content (professionally generated content) (Kim 2012; Morreale 2014). In general terms, therefore, it is reasonable to expect the development of a new stage of web entertainment, characterized by the professionalization of content producers.

For now, though, the weight of low-quality click-baiting is still very high. This phenomenon is an example of the intersection between entertainment and the political dimension, as, for example, in the case of fake news. Although the production and dissemination of fake news at present can be linked to an attempt to field alternative narratives carried out by cultures opposing the establishment (Starbird 2017), one of the main drivers of this phenomenon is economic, in a historical phase in which this type of investment is, in the short term, more profitable than that linked to quality entertainment (Pwc 2017).

In general terms, although content is central to characterizing the level of a nation's cultural debate, the economic development of the entertainment industry, especially when we consider the size of content digitization and the use of platforms for access to content, moves towards the centrality of the user's experience (Pwc 2017) and data flow (Swan 2012) within the so-called "platform society", as defined by Jose van Dijk in her speech at the AoIR 2016 (Leurs & Zimmer 2017).

From this point of view, the fact that few platforms have achieved a central position and, in some respects, a dominant position in their role as content distributors, redefines the balance of power in the field in a way that tends to be independent of content. To give an example: the next video to reach record views in Italy could very well be an international video, but it could also be a video conceived and realized in Italy. The Italian origin of this hypothetical video will contribute to the wealth increase in the entertainment content of the country and, by extension, the overall wealth in terms of language and imagination. This same video, however, will most likely be hosted and distributed by a digital platform that belongs to a foreign company and will be viewed through a device that is not produced in Italy. The data produced by the views, which will help to understand consumer behaviours and offer them a better user experience (in terms of new content and a more precise advertising communication), will not be owned by Italian companies. This is why, from the point of view of the advertising market, it is conceivable that the video will produce value for non-Italian entrepreneurial subjects. It will depend on Italy's ability to influence these processes as to whether it will be able to play a role as protagonist in the transition to full digitalization with regard to the Media and Entertainment sector. From what has been said so far, it is clear that there is much to do in this regard and that the game at stake is wider than just the entertainment universe.

Notes

1 The formula by which the Public Telecommunications Service is defined by Parliament in the Authorization and the Statute of the BBC has remained unchanged since 1925, the year of the Crawford Commission Report (Crawford Committee), which drafted the BBC Constitution, recognizing the Government as having the power of a final check on transmissions. According to this documentation, the BBC is defined as "telecommunications service operation and means of information, education and entertainment" (Burns 1977, p. 37).
2 We are referring here to the famous aphorism number 43 (Bacon 1902) where the Author claims that "it is by discourse that men associate".
3 To the point that Robert Merton applies the powerful interpretative label of *apathy effect* to entertainment (for a contextualization see Statera 1972).
4 The founding act of the pact between Italians and RAI, represented by the Service Contract, also goes in the direction of enhancing national production. The most recent Service Contract, valid for the five-year period 2018–2022, provides, in Article 8, for the "Audio-visual Industry".

   1 RAI enhances the productive, entrepreneurial and cultural capacities of the country in order to favour the development and growth of the system of independent audio-visual productions, both Italian and European, promoting their efficiency and pluralism, as well as the search for new production models as well as new languages including multimedia.
   2 Rai [...] also ensures adequate support for the development of the national audio-visual industry, also with reference to the production of documentaries and animation films, through the acquisition or co-production, within the framework of transparent procedures, of high quality products, made by or even with independent companies that have stable representation in Italy, for their valorisation in foreign markets.
   3 For the purposes of achieving the objectives referred to in paragraph 2, Rai undertakes to:

      a) create audio-visual products of Italian nationality within national borders, except for artistic needs;
      b) promote international co-production projects, which enhance the national product and facilitate its commercialization abroad, and of documentary production, also in order to strengthen the image, the artistic and cultural heritage and the landscape wealth of the country. "

5 The study was carried out by Ernst & Young with the support of all the major trade associations and guidance by the Ministry of Cultural Heritage and Activities and Tourism and by the Siae-Società Italiana Autori e Editori/The Italian Society of Authors and Publishers.

References

AgCom. (2017). *Relazione Annuale 2017*. Available at: www.agcom.it/documents/10179/8078012/RELAZIONE+ANNUALE+2017_documento+completo.pdf/2021e7ba-8250-4239-9a46-5d82fdbf702c

ANICA-Cinetel (2018). Il cinema in sala nel 2017: i dati del Box office, available at: www.anica.it/allegati/Box%20Office%202017%20Italia.pdf

APT- Ce.R.T.A. (2016). Il valore della produzione. L'intrattenimento come risorsa economica e culturale, available at: www.primaonline.it/wp-content/uploads/2016/06/Executive-summary_APT.pdf

Bacon, F. (1902). Novum organum (1620). New York: PF Collier & Son.

Burns, T. (1977). *The BBC: Public Institution and Private World*. London: Macmillan.

D'Ascenzo, M. (2017). Disney acquista 21st Century Fox per 52,4 miliardi di dollari, (2017, December 14), *Il Sole 24 Ore*, available at: www.ilsole24ore.com/art/finanza-e-mercati/2017-12-14/disney-acquista-21th-century-fox-524-miliardi-dollari-131905.shtml?uuid=AEcfOKSD

De Domenico, F., Gavrila, M., & Preta A. (eds) (2002). *Quella deficiente della Tv. Mainstream Television e Multichannel*. Milano: FrancoAngeli.

Eurostat (2016). Households with broadband access. Available at: http://ec.europa.eu/eurostat/statistics-explained/index.php/File:Households_with_broadband_access,_2016_(as_%25_of_all_households).png

Gavrila, M. (2010). *La crisi della Tv. La Tv della crisi. Televisione e Public Service nell'eterna transizione italiana*. Milano: FrancoAngeli.

Jakobson, R. (1966). *Saggi di linguistica generale* (a cura di Luigi Heilmann). Milano: Feltrinelli.

Jenkins, H. (2006). *Fans, bloggers, and gamers: Exploring participatory culture*. New York: New York University Press.

Kim, J. (2012). The institutionalization of YouTube: From user-generated content to professionally generated content. *Media, Culture & Society, 34*(1), 53–67.

Leurs, K., & Zimmer, M. (2017). Platform values: an introduction to the# AoIR16 special issue. *Information, Communication & Society, 20*(6), 803–808.

MIBACT (2015). *Italia Creativa. Studio sull'Industria della Cultura e della Creatività in Italia*. Second edition available at: www.italiacreativa.eu/wp-content/uploads/2017/01/ItaliaCreativa_SecondaEdizione.pdf.

Morcellini, M. (ed.) (2015). *Il Mediaevo italiano. Industria culturale, tv, tecnologie tra XX e XXI secolo*. Roma: Carocci.

Morcellini, M., & Bentivegna, S. (1989). *L'obbligo del nuovo: televisione e spettacolo tra innovazione e tradizione*. Torino: Rai Eri.

Morreale, J. (2014). From homemade to store bought: Annoying Orange and the professionalization of YouTube. *Journal of consumer culture, 14*(1), 113–128.

Mulargia, S. (2016). *Videogiochi. Effetti (sociali) speciali*. Milano: Guerini e Associati.

PricewaterhouseCoopers Advisory SpA (PwC) (2017). Entertainment & media outlook in Italy 2017–2020. Executive summary. Available at: www.pwc.com/it/it/publications/entertainment-media-outlook/2017/doc/pwc_emoi_es_en.pdf

Sigismondi, P. (2011). *The digital glocalization of entertainment: New paradigms in the 21st century global mediascape*. New York: Springer.

Starbird, K. (2017). Examining the alternative media ecosystem through the production of alternative narratives of mass shooting events on Twitter. Paper presented at the 19th Iinternational AAAI Conference on Weblogs and Social Media, Venice, Italy.

Statera, G. (1972). *Società e comunicazione di Massa*. Palermo: Edizioni Palumbo.

Swan, M. (2012). Sensor mania! the internet of things, wearable computing, objective metrics, and the quantified self 2.0, *Journal of Sensor and Actuator Networks, 1*(3), 217–253.

13 Turkey in Global Entertainment
From the Harem to the Battlefield

Senem B. Çevik

Introduction

Turkey is amongst the many new players in the global entertainment scene that have slowly gained recognition for their cinema and television. Turkey's appearance in the world entertainment scene has been a gradual process – so much so that it has moved from being an importer of media productions to being an exporter of them in a matter of only two decades. Significant advances in media technology, Turkey's growing economic stability, and its full integration into the liberal economic order have been the key determinants of the evolution of Turkey's media industry. The 1990s marked a time period in which privatization created a thriving television industry and Turkey broke away from state-run programs. Shortly after this period, Turkish films, by world-renowned directors, won awards in film festivals. As Turkish cinema saw an upward trend, Turkish television was also making strides by the mid-2000s. By 2017, Turkey began exporting both content and its own formats. Acting as a bridge between the East and the West, Turkey has been able to appeal beyond its borders due to its transnational character and a growing distribution network. The Middle East, which lies in Turkey's approximate neighborhood, has been a natural market for its content. This era also coincides with Turkey's rise on the international scene. Turkey has been applauded for its domestic reforms, growing freedoms, and its ambitious yet multi-tract foreign policy. However, domestic political turbulences have turned the tide around and created a less-open space for freedoms in the media industry. The government's heavy hand in controlling the discourse on social and political issues, as well as a general political climate that rewards self-censorship, have caused alarming trends in Turkey's entertainment industry. Following the Gezi Park protests in 2013, the ruling AKP government has been exercising more control over the media, as well as putting further pressures on producers and media conglomerates. Over the course of the last three consecutive AKP governments, media ownership in Turkey has been consolidated. However, even though political pressures on the media and the entertainment industry exist, Turkey continues to be a major actor in global entertainment. Turkey's position as a major content exporter in the future will be dependent on whether the industry will be able to keep producing creative content rather than government-sanctioned content. Thus, as the drivers of Turkey's growth – such as democracy and freedom – see a reversal, Turkey's entertainment industry may experience heavy set-backs.

The Emergence of Television in Turkey

Television broadcasting in Turkey started in 1964 with the establishment of the state television network called Turkish Radio and Television (TRT). Until the early 1980s, there was only one channel, due to the lack of technology, human resources, and economic means to broadcast multiple channels. More importantly, television sets did not become household items until after the mid-1970s. During this early era of television, Turkey imported content from the United States. Alongside these, there were a number of locally made drama series and sitcoms, as well as Brazilian and Mexican telenovelas that were imported by TRT in the mid-1980s.

In the late 1980s, Turkey experienced an era of liberal economic politics introduced by former Prime Minister Turgut Özal. The privatization of radio and television was a significant turn in Turkey's broadcasting industry, thanks to Özal's policies. The economic crisis of 2001 and the political repercussions following this crisis overwhelmingly changed media ownership. The decline of the former media empires gave rise to new ones such as Sancak Group, Albayrak Group, and Zirve/Kalyon Group. With the advances in satellite and digital technologies, Turkey's television networks grew exponentially. Hundreds of television channels, all catering to different demands, are currently available on digital and satellite platforms. However, even with the high number of available channels, the major networks continue to belong to media empires, specifically the new media empires of the twenty-first century. In essence, the actors have changed from the 1990s to the 2010s but the structure itself has not changed much. There is still a close relationship between business and media. However, in contrast to the media empires of the 1990s, the government exercises much more control over the media (Yeşil, 2016).

With the AKP's rise to power, the new political elite put their foreign policy vision into action. This vision established relations with Turkey's neighbors and former Ottoman territories. Simultaneous with the developments in media privatization and the emergence of new actors, the public broadcaster TRT also expanded its services to reach audiences abroad. The Turkic nations of the former Soviet Union and the Turkish diaspora in Europe were the two major audience groups for TRT. International broadcasting has been a cornerstone of Turkey's global engagement and multi-faceted foreign policy. The consecutive AKP governments oversaw the establishment of TRT channels that were specifically geared toward the Middle East and Asia. TRT Avaz and TRT Al-Arabiya are examples of channels that were created as a result of Turkey's foreign policy goals. The creation of TRT Kurdi was a groundbreaking step in Turkish broadcasting history and it was launched as a result of the policy changes in regard to the Kurdish question in Turkey. The channel, also known as TRT 6, is Turkey's first national television broadcast in the Kurmanji, Sorani, and Zazai dialects of Kurdish. With the goal of reaching out to Turkey's Kurdish population, as well as to Kurds across the Middle East, TRT Kurdi has been instrumental for Turkey in approaching the Kurdish question (Yeşil, 2016). With the launch of this channel, the state of Turkey officially recognized the presence of a distinct Kurdish identity within Turkey and the need to communicate with them. In summation, domestic issues and Turkey's foreign policy objectives are what motivated TRT's expansion.

One of the most notable challenges Turkey has faced has been its global reputation since the Gezi Park protests in 2013. The increasingly negative media coverage, which came as a result of the domestic turbulence and mounting international pressure from the global community, caused Turkey to seek new methods of communication via TRT. The launch of TRT World, Turkey's 24-hour English language news channel, came about at a time during which critical discussions regarding Turkey were taking place across the globe. These discussions followed the government crackdown on the opposition and on the failed coup attempt.

TRT, as Turkey's public broadcaster, provides an exclusively Turkish perspective on global issues. In this regard, TRT World follows the tradition of international broadcasters such as Al Jazeera of Qatar, Russia Today of Russia, CCTV of China, and NHK TV of Japan. Turkey's move to launch TRT World came in response to the competition among nations regarding global public opinion, as well as the external pressures on Turkey and its goals to expand its sphere of influence. The recently launched English language channel aims to deliver original content from underrepresented parts of the world, particularly Africa and the Middle East. However, TRT World faces many challenges in gaining popularity, one of the main challenges being Turkey's track record in press freedoms. TRT World's editorial line will determine its credibility in the long run.

The evolution of television broadcasting Turkey over the last four years has been rapid. Due to the influence of domestic demands and external pressures, Turkey's television broadcasting has shifted from international to domestic markets. Turkey's television industry during its early stages was directly under government control, with the state-owned television channel TRT.

Privatization has provided a variety of outlets for audiences, but the close ties between business and government has always been, and continues to be, a serious obstacle in reporting and program content. This can be clearly seen under the consecutive AKP governments, under which media consolidation has increased, thus causing the ties between the government and the media to intensify. This results in self-censorship and the monitoring of content. The future of Turkish broadcasting to domestic and international markets will depend on how much control the state exercises over its public broadcasters.

Turkey's Drama Power

The United States has dominated the entertainment industry for decades and it continues to hold its place as global leader. However, despite their domination of quantity, in terms of quality, U.S.-based content has become increasingly disconnected in a cultural sense. The decline in the appeal for American television in local markets has paved the way for new formats and content from underrepresented countries (Bayles, 2014). In the last few decades, Bollywood from India (Thussu, 2013), telenovelas from Mexico and Brazil (Straubhaar, 2007), Nollywood from Nigeria (Ojo, 2017; Gloria, 2013), and K-dramas from South Korea have challenged the U.S. entertainment hegemony (Kim, 2007; Hong, 2014). Turkey, with its drama industry, is also amongst the new global actors in world entertainment (Bilbassy-Charters, 2010; Yanardağoğlu & Karam, 2013). According to Eurodata TV statistics, Turkey and India are emerging actors in global TV in response to a demand for original dramas (Cassi, 2012). For instance, in 2017 Turkey had the largest number of top ten drama exports around the world (Clarke, 2017).

Turkey is still a relatively new actor in the global television market compared to more established content producers. However, the success of the Turkish drama series can be attributed to decades-long production and practice. Since the production of the first local series in the 1970s, Turkish series have come a long way in terms of quality, quantity, and exposure. In the past 20 years, what once started as a local market has slowly morphed into a global phenomenon. Turkey's first international content export was to the Soviet Union with *Çalıkuşu* (1986). During that time, Turkey was importing foreign content. Turkish drama series and media productions have witnessed an era of unprecedented success by way of expansion into global markets during the late 1990s. The international exposure of Turkish soap operas began with the export of the 1999 production *Deli Yürek* [*Crazy Heart* in English] to the Caucasus (Matthews, 2011). Within the next five years, Turkish television productions had become a global competitor in the cross-cultural entertainment industry. The ascendance of the AKP and Turkey's relative economic progress during the last 15 years has facilitated the media sector's expansion into new markets, particularly in the Middle East. There are currently 19 prominent production companies in Turkey who are distributing their series to different television networks. D Yapım, Ay Yapım, and Tims Production are among the most successful production companies to have reached international markets.

The popularity of Turkish drama series first started in the Middle East when Middle East Broadcasting (MBC) broadcast *Gümüş* (*Noor* in Arabic), a romantic soap opera depicting a young couple, in 2005. In spite of the fact that it was not a huge success in Turkey, this Turkish drama became the highest-rated program throughout the Middle East for its cast, story, quality of production, and colloquial use of Arabic (Buccianti, 2010; Salamandra, 2012). Soon after the success of *Noor*, MBC imported a number of other popular Turkish dramas.

There are two main arguments in regard to Turkish drama series. The first argument proposes that Turkish drama series, due to their romantic appeal, inspire women, particularly those in the Middle East. In fact, previous literature (Salamandra, 2012) has analyzed the romantic component of Turkish dramas and their appeal to female audiences, which she has coined as the Muhanned effect (Salamandra, 2012). In the Arab Middle East, friction has been created between Muslim religious clergy and Turkish drama series that are providing a new set of dynamics for everyday social conduct, especially concerning the social roles of women. In 2009, a Saudi Islamic cleric declared it was permissible to kill the owners of satellite television stations who showed immoral content, in reference to Turkish drama series (Henderson, 2009). Similarly, in Afghanistan, the religious *ulema* called for the cancellation of *Forbidden Love* on the grounds that it was corrupting youth (International Religious Freedom Report 2011).

The second argument proposes that Turkish drama series are a projection of neo-Ottomanism and that they are also Turkey's soft-power resources. Some scholars (Öktem, 2012; Kaynak, 2015; Al Ghazzi & Kraidy, 2013) have critically analyzed Turkey's soap opera exports as neo-Ottoman projections or components of Turkey's expansionist vision. According to these scholars, Turkey's drama series have helped shape Turkey's image and have complemented the government's foreign policy ambitions throughout the Middle East.

Ghazzi and Kraidy (2013) suggest that the Turkish state has been using popular culture to encourage their business ties with Egypt, which they describe as the repercussions of the neo-Ottoman cool. There have been several cases where the state has capitalized on soap-opera power, such, as hiring Kıvanç Tatlıtuğ as a brand ambassador for Turkish Airlines (Kimmelman, 2010). However, these initiatives do not necessarily constitute a broad strategy, such as the strategy that is used in South Korea, where the state is directly involved in promoting the television industry as part of Korea's national image (Park, 2010). In fact, Turkey's state institutions have not capitalized on drama power; rather it has been the entertainment industry that has managed to find success in global markets. Therefore, the Turkish state is not active in promoting drama series and in turn does not have any particular policy in regard to pushing a neo-Ottoman agenda by way of drama series. Nonetheless, drama series, especially in the historical genre, could provide an impression of the exotic.

As a result of this global cultural expansion, Turkish soap operas and their actors have become cultural ambassadors and the shows themselves have become a cultural powerhouse. To illustrate, celebrities have used their popularity in the Middle East in order to promote local brands and have also become spokespeople for companies such as Turkish Airlines (Kimmelman, 2010). The actors in these dramas, who could not have otherwise gained fame, are not only celebrities but they are also using their fame to sign product endorsement deals in Turkey and other countries. For instance, Kıvanç Tatlıtuğ, the leading actor in some of the most notable TV shows, was featured in a TV commercial for cologne in the Middle East as well as in a music video by the Lebanese singer Rola Saad.[1] Another famous actress, Tuba Büyüküstün, starred in a shampoo commercial that aired in the Arab world in 2011. Beren Saat starred in a Turkish soap commercial that was aired on Arabic TV channels.[2] Yörük and Vatikiotis assess that the popularity of a cultural product may not directly translate to soft power, which points to the shortcomings of Turkish soap-opera power.

Nonetheless, more than 100 Turkish soap operas have been exported globally with a revenue exceeding 100 million dollars in 2013. Today, Turkish drama series are reaching audiences in over 130 countries in Africa, the Americas, Europe, and Asia (Candemir, 2013). Audiences from Colombia all the way to Djibouti tune in to the romantic Turkish series.

The New Entertainment Landscape in "New Turkey"

Turkey's increasingly turbulent political climate has left deep scars on its entertainment landscape. In 2013, Turkey was enjoying relative popularity across the Middle East (Öktem, 2012) and the drama series they exported were still quite popular (Yanardaoğlu & Karam 2013). In May of 2013, mass protests, widely known as the Gezi Park Protests, took place. The surge of anti-government protests had emerged from a series of confrontations between the ruling AKP government and the opposition on social and cultural grounds. However, the protests were violently crushed by the government. In December of 2013, a massive "graft probe" (an investigation into corruption and/or bribery) against the political elite erupted, which involved the top echelons of the ruling AKP. The graft probe became the final breaking point in the political alliance between the AKP government and the Gülenists, who are a cult-like organization with ties to a self-exiled Turkish clergyman by the name of Fethullah Gülen. Following the volatile political climate in 2013, the AKP government unleashed a series of repressive measures through legislative action; these began limiting social media access and started a series of extensive purges within academia, government, and the media. The efforts to eliminate Gülenist civil servants from the state apparatus has evolved into a witch hunt that some scholars see as a means to punish the opposition. The Gezi Park Protests and the graft probe were both contributors to Turkey's slip into a more authoritarian state. As a result of this, populism is increasing at an alarming rate (Aytaç & Öniş 2014; Tekmen 2017). The presidential elections of 2014, which carried the then Prime Minister Erdoğan to the presidency seat, further facilitated this process and empowered the strongman in Turkish politics.

Furthermore, the parliamentary elections in the summer of 2015 resulted in increased confrontations in an already polarized country, and following the snap elections in the fall of 2015, the AKP tightened its grip on Turkish politics. Consequently, in the summer of 2016, Turkey faced a coup attempt, which was successfully rebutted by the people and the government. The failed coup attempt galvanized support for President Erdoğan and the AKP and paved the way for a referendum that had the goal of Turkey transitioning to a presidential system. Since 2013, Turkey has increasingly turned inwards, scapegoating domestic and international adversaries while simultaneously focusing its energy on security demands. In doing so, President Erdoğan and the AKP political elite have employed more polarizing discourse.

Rising authoritarianism and populism in Turkey have had a direct impact on the media system. Today, Turkey is one of the most repressive countries for media production, especially for journalists. Press and media freedoms in Turkey, as well as freedom of expression, have been on a significant downward spiral throughout the past four years, which also coincides with the third AKP term in office. According to Reporters Without Borders (RSF), political control over media funding, media outlets, and distribution networks in Turkey is at high risk (RSF, 2017). The RSF's 2017 report ranked Turkey one hundred and fifty-fifth out of 180 countries in press freedom, placing Turkey amongst the least free, along with countries such as Russia, China, Mexico, India, and a number of African countries. This ranking demonstrates the fragile media structure in Turkey. Similarly, Freedom House, in its latest report (2017) labeled Turkey "partially free", with ratings in political rights and civil rights declining over the past few years. Human Rights Watch (2017), in its report on Turkey's press freedoms, argues that crackdowns and assaults on journalists critically declined in 2014 and then accelerated after the failed coup attempt in 2016. Over the past few years, the government has taken over and closed privately owned media networks while appointing government owned trustees to them instead. Pen International's 2014 report indicates that the government crackdowns on the media have had repercussions on freedoms and have been driving journalists to self-censor their reporting. These international rankings are indicative of the erosion of civil liberties and the growing influence of the government on the media structure. The media and journalists in Turkey experience judicial suppression, online banishment, surveillance defamation, accreditation discrimination, and conglomerate pressure as part of neoliberal government pressures (Akser & Baybars-Hawks, 2012).

In relation to these five systemic pressures (Akser & Baybars-Hawks, 2012), domestic politics have also shaped corporate media. There is a strong state presence and clientelism in Turkey and conglomerates run corporate media with business interests in non-media sectors. As of 2017, Turkuvaz/Kalyon Group, Demirören Media, Ciner Media, and Doğuş Media are major conglomerates controlling the Turkish media. These media owners have investments in at least three other media sectors, as well as with other businesses, which are mainly in construction, mining, energy, banking, and tourism industries (Media Ownership Monitor, 2017). As they rely on government contracts, they are vulnerable to political and economic pressures. As a result, such ties shape their editorial lines and compromise their neutrality (Yeşil, 2014). The business investments of media conglomerates extend to government contracts that are both in and outside of Turkey, which puts more pressure on these businesses to toe the government line and employ self-censorship.

As a result of the current media structure in Turkey, the production and distribution systems of television series have also changed dramatically. Two production companies have demonstrated a shift towards the government's role in shaping the media structure and their productions. Es Film, the producer of *Filinta* and *Abdülhamit: The Last Emperor*, has emphasised historical dramas. Tekden Film, the producer of Resurrection, was established by Mr. Kemal Tekden, who is a member of the ruling AKP parliament. The productions of both companies are aired on the public broadcaster channel TRT, which is indicative of clientelism in Turkey. Moreover, the surge of historical drama series that are broadcasted on TRT reflects a government agenda to shape television content that reinforces AKP's social policies.

To conclude, there is a tight-knit connection between business and politics, which poses a limitation to the citizens right to access unbiased and accurate information. In addition, this tight connection limits the direction of drama series that are produced by state television and private production companies who may feel pressured by the political climate. As a result, the current media structure has become conducive towards pleasing the government and its political discourse. With this trend, the role of drama series as soft-power resources has slowly been shifting towards drama series as instruments legitimizing the political discourse.

Ottoman Dreams: From the Harem to the Battlefield

When *Muhteşem Yüzyıl* (*Magnificent Century* in English) was first aired on a private network in 2011, it drew significant negative attention from conservative circles. The success of *Muhteşem Yüzyıl* (*Magnificent Century*) is a watershed moment in the rise of historic TV dramas. As Turkey was shaken by its many crises, the success of *Muhteşem Yüzyıl* inspired the production of other historical drama series that emphasized Turkish political history.

The government's heavy hand in controlling the television industry has had a direct impact on media production through the self-selection of drama series that are aired on TV. TRT's wide array of historical dramas is reflective of this tight control. In addition, government involvement has had an indirect impact on promoting self-censorship, which has resulted in screenplays being molded into more desirable topics (Zalewski, 2013). Due to the sexual scenes and the Ottoman Sultan's harem life that were depicted in the show, *Magnificent Century* drew much criticism and disapproval from the then-Prime Minister Erdoğan who stated that "we don't recognize these ancestors" (Batuman, 2014; NPR, 2013). Soon enough, the AKP media apparatus began designing its own drama series such as, *Filinta, Diriliş (Resurrection), Bir Zamanlar Osmanlı (Once Upon a Time: The Ottoman Empire), Osmanlı Tokadı (The Ottoman Smack), Osmanlı'da Derin Devlet (Deep State in the Ottoman Empire), Payitaht: Abdülhamit (The Last Emperor)*, while also giving rise to *Kösem* and *Fatih: Fetih Bir Başlangıçtı (Fatih: Conquer Was the Beginning)* on private TV networks.

The themes of these historical drama series carry the undertones of Turkey's current political climate, with messaging geared toward domestic audiences. As a result, historical dramas are becoming instrumental in legitimizing the AKP government's policies by drawing parallels between past and present instances. The growing presence of historical dramas, specifically on state television, demonstrates the increased role that domestic politics plays in shaping the content of drama series and the transition of their role as Turkey's soft-power resources to instruments of domestic politics.

The most widely received amongst the historical drama series has been *Diriliş: Ertuğrul* (*Resurrection*), which draws parallels with the current political climate. *Resurrection* has aired on state TV TRT since 2014; it narrates the establishment of the Ottoman Empire in the thirteenth century through tribal leaders and the warrior Ertuğrul. The series depicts Ertuğrul as a righteous and fierce warrior who stands against injustices and foreign invasions. *Filinta: The Dawn of the Millenium*, another historical drama depicting the last stages of the Ottoman Empire on state TV TRT, is a thriller. *Filinta* takes part during the reign of Abdülhamid I, a period that is highly cherished amongst Islamist circles in Turkey. *Filinta* is the nickname of Mustafa, an Ottoman detective who is trying to save his nation from foreign enemies and who emphasizes the rule of law. *Filinta* was followed by another series that takes place in the same time period, *Payitaht: Abdülhamid*, which portrays the reign of Sultan Abdülhamid. In 2018, TRT is scheduled to air a new production by the same producers of *Diriliş* that it has titled *Mehmetçik: Kut'ul Amare*.

The shift in Turkish drama series from harem stories to the Ottoman battlefield represents the relevance and weight of politics over cultural affairs. More importantly, the direct and indirect encouragement of the political elite in the production of historical dramas creates an agenda for the government AKP.

Conclusion

Turkey, as a newcomer, has swept into the global entertainment industry. With content exports in hundreds of countries and revenue surpassing 100 million dollars, Turkey's entertainment industry, mainly dominated by television drama series, has been growing exponentially. While Turkey's renowned directors and producers are gaining global recognition for their work in international film festivals, Turkish drama series are adopting digital platforms as a way of reaching global audiences. Aside from video platforms such as YouTube, Turkish drama series have found their way into Netflix. Despite the growing interest in Turkish drama series, domestic political developments in Turkey are resulting in an increasingly oppressive nature where self-censorship is limiting the creative capacity of television producers. The highly concentrated media ownership of private television networks and government's tight grip on the state television network TRT have spurred a wave of historical dramas that emphasize various eras of the Ottoman Empire. As Turkey struggles with institutionalizing a Western democracy and battles with the memory of the fall of the Ottoman Empire, the country's entertainment industry is also at a crossroads.

Notes

1 Cologne commercial: Mohannad and Lemis; Music Video: Rola Saad, Nawyahalo, 2008.
2 Tuba Büyüküstün for Pantene, Beren Saat for Duru.

References

Akser, M. & Baybars-Hawks, B. (2012). Media and Democracy in Turkey: Toward a Model of Neoliberal Media Autocracy. *Middle East Journal of Culture and Communication*, 5, 302–321.

Al-Ghazzi, O. & Kraidy, M. (2013). Neo-Ottoman cool 2: Turkish Nation Branding and Arabic-Language Transnational Broadcasting. *International Journal of Communication*, 7, 2341–2360.

Aytaç, S.E. & Öniş, Z. (2014). Varieties of Populism in a Changing Global Context: The Divergent Paths of Erdoğan and Kirchnerismo. *Comparative Politics*, 47 (1), 41–59.

Batuman, E. (2014, February 17 and 24). Ottomania: A Hit TV Show Reimagines Turkey's Imperial Past. *The New Yorker*, 50–58.

Bayles, M. (2014). *Through a Screen Darkly: Popular Culture, Public Diplomacy, and America's Image Abroad*. New Haven, CT: Yale University Press.

Bilbassy-Charters, N. (2010). Leave It to Turkish Soap Operas to Conquer Hearts and Minds. *Foreign Policy*. Retrieved from http://foreignpolicy.com/2010/04/15/leave-it-to-turkish-soap-operas-to-conquer-hearts-and-minds/

Buccianti, A. (2010). Dubbed Turkish Soap Operas Conquering the Arab World: Social Liberation or Cultural Alienation. *Arab Media and Society*, 10, 4–28.

Candemir, Y. (2013). Turkish Soap Operas: The Unstoppable Boom. *Blogs WSJ*. Retrieved from http://blogs.wsj.com/middleeast/2013/04/29/turkish-soap-operas-the-unstoppable-boom/

Clarke, S. (2017). Turkey, Russia Edge out US in Drama Exports League. *TBI Vision*. Retrieved from: http://tbivision.com/news/2017/03/turkey-russia-edge-us-drama-exports-league/735672/

Freedom House Report. 2017. Freedom of the Press 2017: Press Freedom's Dark Horizon, April 2017. *Freedom House*. Retrieved from: https://freedomhouse.org/sites/default/files/FOTP_2017_booklet_FINAL_April28.pdf

Gloria, F. (2013). Nollywood: A viable vehicle of public diplomacy in Nigeria. *New Media and Mass Communication*, 11, 21–24.

Henderson, S. (2009, February 18). Saudi Arabia Changes Course Slowly. *The Washington Institute Policywatch 1479*. Retrieved from: www.washingtoninstitute.org/policy-analysis/view/saudi-arabia-changes-course-slowly

Hong, E. (2014). *The Birth of Korean Cool*. New York: Picador.

Human Rights Watch World Report. 2017. HRW World Report 2017: Events of 2016. HRW Report. Retrieved from www.hrw.org/sites/default/files/world_report_download/wr2017-web.pdf

International Religious Freedom Report for 2011, State Department, www.state.gov/documents/organization/193129.pdf, p.11

Kaynak, S. 2015. Noor and Friends: Turkish Culture in the World. In S.B. Çevik & P. Seib (Eds.), *Turkey's Public Diplomacy* (233–259). New York: Palgrave Macmillan.

Kim, K. (2007). The Rising East Asian Wave: Korean Media Go Global. In D. Thussu (Ed.). *Media on the Move: Global Flow and Contra-Flow* (135–152). London: Routledge.

Kimmelman, (2010, June 17). Soap Operas in the Arab World Yield Their Own Soft Power. *NY Times*. Retrieved from www.nytimes.com/2010/06/18/arts/18abroad.html?_r=0

Matthews, O. (2011). Turkish Soap Operas Are Sweeping The Middle East. *Newsweek*. Retrieved from www.newsweek.com/turkish-soap-operas-are-sweeping-middle-east-67403

Media Ownership Monitor. 2017. *Media Ownership Monitor: Turkey*. Retrieved from http://turkey.mom-rsf.org/en/.

NPR. 2013. Prime Minister Finds Soap Operas Turkish Delights in Bad Taste. *NPR*. Retrieved from www.npr.org/2013/01/03/167981036/prime-minister-finds-soap-operas-turkish-delights-in-bad-taste

Ojo, T. (2017). Nigeria, Public Diplomacy and Soft Power. In N. Chitty, L. Ji, G.D. Rawnsley & C. Hayden (Eds.), *The Routledge Handbook of Soft Power* (315–325). London: Routledge.

Öktem, K. (2012). Projecting Power: Non-Conventional Policy Actors in Turkey's International Relations. In K. Öktem, A. Kadıoğlu & M. Karlı (Eds.), *Another Empire?: A Decade of Turkey's Foreign Policy Under the Justice and Development Party (77–108)*. İstanbul: Bilgi University Press.

Park, S. (2010). Transnational Adoption, "Hallyu", And the Politics of Korean Popular Culture. *Biography*, 33 (1), 151–166.

Reporters Without Borders. RSF (2017). Reporters without border: Turkey. *RSF*. Retrieved from https://rsf.org/en/turkey.

Salamandra, C. (2012). The Muhannad Effect: Media Panic, Melodrama, and the Arab Female Gaze. *Antropological Quarterly*, 85 (1): 45–77.

Straubhaar, J. (2007). *World Television: From Global to Local*. Thousand Oaks: Sage.

Tekmen, H. (2017). Populism and Closing Civic Space: A Post-Truth Challenge. *Turkish Policy Quarterly*, 16 (1): 105–112.

Thussu, D.K. (2013). *Communicating India's Soft Power: Buddha to Bollywood*. New York: Palgrave.

Yanardağoğlu, E. & Karam, I. (2013). The Fever That Hit Arab Satellite Television: Audience Perceptions of Turkish TV Series. *Identities: Global Studies in Culture and Power*, 20 (5): 561–579.

Yeşil, B. (2014). Press censorship in Turkey: Networks of State Power, Commercial Pressures, and Self-Censorship. *Communication, Culture & Critique*, 7, 154–173.

Yeşil, B. (2016). *Media in New Turkey: The Origins of an Authoritarian Neoliberal State*. Urbana, IL: University of Illinois Press.

Zalewski, P. (2013). *As Turkey Turns: Soap Operas as Power. Roads and Kingdoms*. Retreieved from http://roadsandkingdoms.com/2013/as-turkey-turns-soap-operas-as-power/.

14 Entertainment Media Industry in Egypt
Overview, Challenges and Future Performance

Rasha Allam

Introduction

Media entertainment in Egypt has been a leading industry in the Arab world since the introduction of cinema in 1896 to the introduction of radio in 1926, and the introduction of television in 1960 (The Report, 2016a). Egypt has a population of almost 102 million people, the majority of whom consider radio and television the most popular and dominant media platform (Gallup, 2014). Egyptian media products were the primary influencer in the Arab world, transmitting Egyptian culture, dialect and political messages throughout the region (Amin, 2002).

Since 2015, the Egyptian media industry has started to place emphasis more on entertainment and less on the political programs and talk shows that had dominated the airwaves since 2011 (The Report, 2016b). Egyptian media is facing new challenges in reaching younger audiences, with rapid changes in programming style and popular media platforms.

Radio and Television Industries

Radio

Egypt has the largest and most reputable radio broadcasting system in the Arab region. There are an estimated 18,000,000 radio sets in the country. Entertainment broadcasting is the primary form of programming enjoyed by the Egyptian radio audience. The most common language used on Egyptian Radio is Arabic and accounts for 86% of the broadcast content, while English accounts for 17% and French 4% (MENA Media Guide, 2015).

Since control of Egyptian radio has been closely held by the government as a tool to help it achieve its political, social and economic agenda, there is substantial resistance to complete privatization. Proposals for partial privatization must undergo the very gradual process Egypt must undertake since its ratification of the General Agreement on Tariffs and Trade (GATT).

Entertainment programming is the highest in terms of the average daily broadcasting hours by type of program (excluding programs broadcast from Egypt and directed to another country in their own language) in 2015–2016, scoring 87.21, even after a slight dip compared to 2005–2006. The average daily broadcasting hours for cultural programs has also increased, in addition to sports programming, where both are considered to be different kinds of entertainment content (ERTU, 2016).

Egyptian radio successfully used a combination of propaganda, culture and entertainment in the 1950s and 1960s to promote pan-Arabism and Nasserism and in the 1970s, through the 1990s to promote and support the causes of Palestinian rights and regional cooperation. In addition, Egyptian radio used an extra tool represented by the Quran Station and the overseas network in using religion as a point of attraction and a bridge to other Islamic and non-Islamic countries.

Egypt took the next step toward partial privatization of radio and in May 2003 two new stations were launched: Nejoum 100.6 FM, an all-Arabic music format, and Nile 104.2 FM, an all-Western music station broadcasting in English 24 hours a day. Both popular stations actively seek advertising and have given a tremendous boost to the radio advertising industry. Other were launched later, such as Radio 9090, and in 2017 another two were launched: Radio NRJ, and Radio DRN.

Television

Public and state-owned television channels as well as private television networks constitute the major television media industries in Egypt. The state owns two national terrestrial channels, six local channels and a network of satellite channels (Amin, 2004). The television sector operates under "Law 92 for 2016" that states the establishment of the Supreme Council for Media Regulation (SCMR) that regulate public and private media sector. The National Media Council (NMC) is responsible for all state radio and television broadcasting. A third entity is the National Press Council, which is responsible for national newspapers and magazines.

Although Egyptian terrestrial broadcasting is government-owned and controlled, it relies heavily on advertising revenues from national and international product commercials aired on Egyptian channels. The main channel – Channel 1 – provides the public programming, offering news, soap operas, films, sport and other general interest programs. Channel 2 provides more entertainment-oriented programs and devotes more broadcast time to music, arts and cultural programs. Local stations, in different governorates, provide news, religious, cultural, and entertainment programs from a local perspective (Boyd 1999).

Nearly all (98.8%) Egyptians have television sets in their homes (Central Agency for Public Mobilization and Statistics [CAPMAS], 2017). Television is by far the most common source of news for Egyptians, as nearly all Egyptians (94.1%) use the TV to get news at least once a week, and 84.2% use it daily or most days a week (Gallup, 2014).

Political content makes up the highest average of television transmission hours in central and local channels (22.65). Entertainment is the second highest (16.3) program subject in both central and local channels. This percentage excludes other sources of entertainment programs,

Table 14.1 Daily Average of Television Transmission Hours, in Central and Local Channels, by Subject of Program (2005–2016) – Unit: Hour

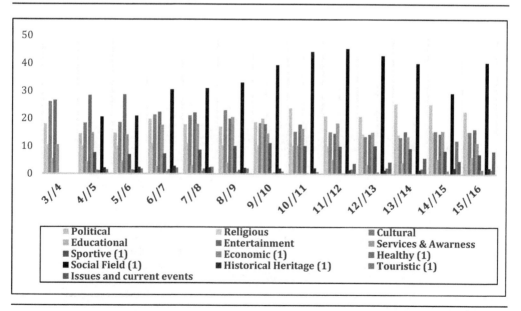

Source: Egyptian Radio & Television Union (2016)

such as cultural programs that are aired for an average of 15.31 hours, sports programs for 7.24 hours, tourism programs for 1.57 hours and health programs for 0.20 hours.

Production and Distribution

- The Egyptian Media Production City (EMPC)
  - The Egyptian Media Production City (EMPC) is the main center platform and the hub for entertainment media production in the region. It was established in 1997 to provide production companies with all essential information, production services and equipment, whether for shooting purposes or for pre- and post- production with regard to cinema and TV. The EMPC has a variety of production tools, and around 64 studios that have lots of attributions with the highest quality.
- The Nilesat
  - The Egyptian Satellite channels, the Nile specialized channels and the private satellite channels are broadcast on the Nilesat satellite that was launched on April 28, 1999. Nilesat is the second major arm of the media industry after the EMPC. Nilesat launched a second satellite in August 2000, with more than 1,200 television stations and more than 100 radio stations. Nilesat is a successful project that is playing a major role in distributing media products to all Egyptian and Arab satellite households. Its aim is offering reliable, secure, high-quality digital television, radio and data services to inform, educate and entertain viewers throughout the Middle East and African areas (Egyptian Radio and Television Union [ERTU], 2016). The Nile specialized channels were launched in 2005 offering a range of seven channels for different genres of entertainment content (Nile Drama, Nile Cultural, Nile Sport, Nile Life, Nile Cinema, Nile Comedy, Family and Child).

Table 14.2 Daily Average of Television Transmission Hours of Nile Specialized Channels (2005–2016)

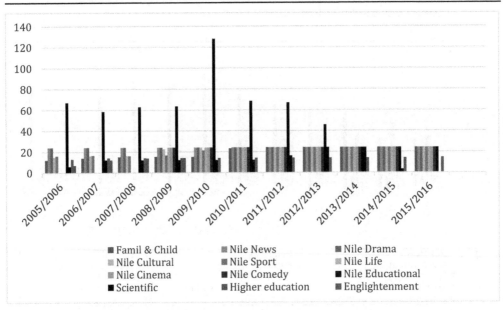

Source: Egyptian Radio & Television Union (2016).

Most of the Nile specialized channels offer a daily average of 24 hours of programming, except for two education channels ("Manara for Scientific Research" and "Enlightenment") that were shut down due to lack of funding and the financial crisis of the ERTU at the time (ERTU, 2016).

Besides the satellite and Nile Specialized channels that are state-owned, private satellite television networks were launched and have a very high reach. The first private satellite channel was launched in 2004 (Dream TV), followed by El Mehwar, Al Hayat network and ON network; other stations were launched after 2011, and the dissolution of the Ministry of Information, namely CBC network, DMC network, Al-Nahar network; others went through restructuring, such as ON network, which started to be more entertainment-oriented than news-oriented, and launched a specialized sports channel, which is DMC network. CBC took another track and launched the first specialized cooking channel, CBC Sofra. All the private satellite channels take their licenses from the GAFI (General Authority for Foreign Investment).

Drama in Egyptian Media

Drama in Egypt has always reflected political, economic and cultural changes. It is considered the largest in terms of production in the Arab region and the most popular. It managed to build up a loyalty of viewers until it became the number one source of entertainment in Egypt (Gallup, 2014). Egyptian drama productions were, and are still, exported to most Arab countries and constitute a main component of overall content on Arab media channels (Abdulla, 2014).

It is estimated that 96.6% of Egyptian families own a television set as per year 2017 (CAPMAS, 2017). The first Egyptian production for a television series was in 1962, and it was the first in the Arab region. Most of the TV series in the 1960s were adaptations of novels written by veteran Egyptian novelists like Nagib Mahfouz, Youssef Idris and Ihsan Abdel Quddos. At that time, the writing focused on literature, and the "directing styles and acting were theatrical and static" (Schwartz, Kaye, & Martini, 2013). During the 1970s, drama began to portray the social segmentation that had started to prevail in society, particularly the social and financial gaps that reflect the difference between the socialist system under President Gamal Abdel Nasser and the capitalist system under the later president Anwar Al Sadat. Many of the popular productions at that time used to question the viability of authoritarianism and economic development versus state autonomy and capitalism, and this reflected political changes as well (Schwartz et al., 2013). The late 1980s saw a different series taken from the records and files of the Egyptian intelligence, telling stories of Egyptian war heroes. Unfortunately, the 1990s brought with it the money-hungry businessmen and corporations that wanted the "soap opera topics to focus more on the interest of the investors or even sponsor" .

A change was witnessed after the mass demonstration in 2011 where scriptwriters began to tackle issues that were previously taboo (Abdel Rahman, 2012). The cultural norms and traditions have been always mirrored in Egyptian drama, especially in the 1980s and 1990s, where the middle classes, with their social and economic concerns, were very present. Yet, starting with the political upheavals in 2011, and the dissolution of the Ministry of Information, some unusual trends started to appear in TV series, such as strong, offensive language, vulgarity and high levels of violence (Al Abaseery, 2016); the wealth gap became clearly represented in TV series with a decline in middle class representation (Abdel Rahman, 2015.) As for the corporations that produce drama in Egypt, there are many. The two public entities in Egypt that produce TV series is the production sector of the Radio and Television Union, and the Egyptian Media Production Company (EMPC), while content control is in the hands of the Central Administration for the Control of Artistic Works, which ensures that there are no violations with regard to cultural norms and the politics of the governing regime.

EMPC provides many advantages to investors and to those interested in producing drama and other media forms. Other private corporations that produce drama include El Adl Group, El Sherouk for Media Production, T-vision and I-productions. T-vision has the highest number of distributed shows in the Middle East. As for I-productions, it is looking to collaborate with international TV companies and invest in productions throughout the Arab world, especially the Saudi Arabian and Jordanian productions.

Egyptian consumers are also avid watcher of foreign dramas from India and Turkey. The multi-channel environment made transnational and Egyptian drama always available and accessible to Egyptian audiences through websites like Panet.com, Shahid.com and YouTube.

The holy month of Ramadan is considered a fifth broadcast season with approximately 100 TV series (Asaad, 2017).

Fashion, Health and Beauty Programs

The Egyptian media industry has been always concerned with fashion, starting from magazines such as *Hawaa (Eve)*, *Nisf EL-donia (Half of the World)* and *Al Kawakeb (The Planets)*, which focused on celebrities and fashion. National newspapers have specialized pages for women that encompass information about fashion and health. Magazines usually cover fashion shows and beauty pageants that take place either in Egypt or abroad. For health care only, there was *Tabibak Al-khas (Your Private Doctor)* magazine, while health care was a subtopic in other magazines.

Digital technology has made revolutionary changes in the world of Egyptian fashion media. Blogs, websites and online fashion magazines were established, such as the Egyptian online fashion and lifestyle magazines *Identity* and *Cairo Scene*, which offer beauty and healthcare tips; radio started including some special programs that concentrate on health such as *Eyadet Misr (Egypt's Clinic)*. Social media platforms, such as Facebook and Instagram have taken the place of the traditional magazine industry to some extent. Instagram and Facebook accounts of famous figures and fashionistas have become more popular ways of spreading fashion trends and healthy lifestyles (Rahhal, 2014; Rizk, 2014).

Economic and political factors have affected fashion media through the years; in the 1950s and at the beginning of the 1960s, fashion and beauty media were prevalent due to the flourishing economy and the stable political situation (Attia, 2017; Khalaf, 2017), which included the blooming of the textile and cosmetics industry besides healthcare products. Consequently, a stable flourishing media for fashion, beauty and healthcare emerged through the magazines and even international magazines were prevalent, such as *Burda*, because the public atmosphere was calm and people had high per capita income (Cochrane, 2010; Douglas, 2013). Later, in the 1970s and the 1980s, Egypt went through economic recession (Attia, 2017) and the attention of the media was directed less toward fashion, beauty or healthcare. The 1990s and 2000s were relatively more stable economically and politically, where the magazine industry carried on flourishing.

Regarding cultural characteristics, in the 1950s through to the 1970s, English colonialism influenced Egyptian culture. The Egyptians implemented a European lifestyle, which persisted despite the revolution. During the last period of the 1970s and the beginning of the 1980s, religious groups such as the Muslim Brotherhood started spreading their ideologies as a response to the immense liberation movements during the 1970s (Ibrahim, 1982). Consequently, the fashion industry was affected despite the modernized lifestyle and the economic openness initiated by the late president Al Sadat. During the 1990s and until today, a religious background persists among most Egyptians. The trend in the production of local brands has started to expand recently and has its footprints in the media; some of these are competing with international brands, such as Oktein, Azza Fahmy and Temraza (Young, 2014).

The Movie Industry

Egyptian cinema is the largest and the oldest cinema industry in the Arab region. It is known as the "Hollywood of the Arab World". The film production industry began to appear in 1896, in Alexandria, the second largest city in the Mediterranean and known to be a cosmopolitan hub.

By 1908, Egypt had ten movie houses, and by 1917, the industry had grown to about 80 theatres throughout Egypt. In 1925 a royal decree was passed for the establishment of "The Egyptian Company for Acting and Cinema" by Bank Misr (The Egyptian Bank), and the greatest move was realized by the great Egyptian economist, Talaat Harb, who founded Studio Misr, in 1936. The first law to regulate the movie industry was a censorship law that was passed in 1923 by the Egyptian government. In 1927, the first full-length silent movie, *Layla*, was produced. Studio Masr was usually compared to Hollywood because of their similar functions and influence. The Egyptian film production industry was very prosperous from the 1940s to the 1960s, and is known as "the Golden Age".

After the 1952 revolution, the political changes affected the industry. Leaders of the revolution believed in the importance of the cinema industry and its influence on the audience, and they started issuing laws to support the film industry. Seven years after the revolution, the High Cinema Institute was established. Yet, because of the revolution, the cinema was nationalized, making government intervention inevitable. As a result, talented actors and directors traveled to Lebanon where there was more freedom. Moreover, audience numbers fell drastically. In 1967, after the setback of the Six-Day War, Egypt shifted its spending on the military, which affected spending on movies and the entire industry. Movie theatres were subsequently reduced from 354 in 1945 to 255 in 1966 (Amin and Fikry, 2001).

After the 1973 Arab–Israeli War, several movies were made to record the event such as *Al Nasr Al Azeem* (*The Great Triumph*) and *Al Rosasa La Tazal Fi Gaybi* (*I Still Have the War Bullet*). Yet, when Egypt signed the peace treaty with Israel, it led to the closure of the Arab markets for Egyptian products and film, which in return led to a loss in production from 1978 to 1983. Later, the movie industry witnessed a growth after the introduction and proliferation of video cassette tapes in Egypt; moreover, Arabs began investing in Egyptian cinema with the help of Hussein Al Qalla, a producer, who funded the industry and helped in production (Rashid, 2015).

In the 1990s, the Egyptian film production industry plummeted, and was labeled as the "Hidden Death of the Egyptian Cinema". Cinemas and movie theatres decreased in number drastically from 255 cinemas in 1966 to 62 in 1992. In 1994, the movie production industry was near death as the number of films produced in a year was in single digits. The introduction of specialized movie channels on the satellite had affected the number of visitors to the movie theatres, and it had an impact as well on the video rental shops.

The film industry is still in decline. According to the Central Agency for Public Mobilization and Statistics (CAPMAS), only 20 movies were produced in 2016, half of them being social drama and the other half, comedy movies. Of the English movies that are locally distributed in the Egyptian movie theatres, there was a total of 24 movies (4 drama, 6 comedies, 3 action and 11 falling into other categories); of the Egyptian movies that are distributed outside its borders, they were a total of 5 movies before 2016, and this went up to 19 movies in 2016, where Lebanon is considered the largest market for consuming Egyptian movies (CAPMAS, 2017). Yet, this is considered an improvement compared to the period after the Arab Spring in 2012 and 2013, where cinema was facing a real crisis and most of the production companies were shutting down (Mahmoud, 2013).

Movie theatres in Egypt are very popular among the citizens; although the number of movie theatres and audiences has declined dramatically since 2011, until reaching its lowest point in 2015, the number of audiences has been only slightly affected.

Egyptian Movie Production and Distribution

The distribution of Egyptian movies is an important component in the value chain that aims towards maximizing revenue. It is done through both the public and the private sector. The distribution of Egyptian movies by the public sector locally and to Arab countries is higher than the private sector as of 2016. Genres that are mainly distributed are drama, comedy and historical movies.

The digital revolution companies are trying to get the maximum out of the present dynamics, with more movies being digitally produced and distributed. Video on demand (VOD) also became another source of revenue for movie producers. Digital technology enables movie producers to implement new techniques to diversify their risks and maximize their profit.

Music

Egypt is widely considered to be the centre of Middle-Eastern classical, traditional and modern musical forms and had a vital role in transmitting music to different cultures. Many iconic composers and singers appeared between 1920 to 1970, such as Saad Darwish, the father of Egyptian popular music. In his music, he truly expressed the yearnings and moods of the masses, as well as recording the events that took place during his lifetime. The dazzling Najat El Saghira, Shadia, Sabah (a Lebanese singer) and many other singers were part of the Egyptian golden age. Moreover, there was the iconic legendary queen Om Kalthoum, who was one of the most influential Arab singers of the twentieth century (Al Gammal, 2006).

Music in Egypt has always been a tool to express and document political change, and sometimes to mobilize people. Many songs were composed during the 1952 revolution when Abd El Halim Hafez, a famous Egyptian singer, brought hope to Egyptians during the war and sang for the revolution. He, with other popular singers such as Shadia, produced several national songs that are still sung today (Kamel, 2012). After 2011, underground music appeared to express the demands of young people and the political changes at that time, for example, "Cairokee", "Salalem", "West El Balad", "Masar Egbary". Some people refer to "Cairokee" as "the sound of the revolution" (Swedenburg, 2017)

Music Production was mainly performed at Alam El Phan, or the Art World, a major corporation that has been distributing music in Egypt since the early 1920s. The best, most successful notable musicians have all recorded through Alam El Phan at one point in their careers. Yet, recently there have been new alternative record labels that produce different types of music, like house, trance, techno and jazz. Kultkairo, Besworx and Noizem records are examples of these contributors to the new-school era.

Artists can now be discovered and go viral because of the digital platforms that surpass many traditional structural barriers, and many bands are brought into the light through the help of the social media (Underground music flourishes, 2016).

Specialized television musical programs in Egypt are not very successful. They started to appear in the media scene in 2006, for example, *X-Factor Arabia*, an Arabic version of the Western program. *X-Factor Arabia* originally aired on March 26, 2006 with the name *Xseer AL Najah* which means "the essence of success". Yet, its appeal fell drastically with the flourishing success of its rival, Star Academy on Lebanese Broadcasting Corporation (LBC) and *XSeer Al Najah* was taken off after its second season (Haddad, 2013). In 2012, however, CBC, a private Egyptian satellite station, announced its return in 2013, and the show changed its format, but still struggled against its rival shows, MBC's *Arab Idol* and *The Voice* (Estrin, 2017).

Sports Media Industry

There is no doubt that the Egyptian media has increased the popularity of sport to a peak, especially in the age of satellite channels, which started in the late 1990s and early 2000s. Sports content is important for the media as it captures audiences and generates income. All public and private newspapers have a specialized sports page. Sports programs on radio and television have a wide appeal and reach.

The sports media industry went into a critical stage as of 2011 as most of the sports activities froze due to the political unrest that Egypt witnessed after the 2011 revolution. Yet during 2016, newspapers witnessed an increase in the number of sports pages; the national Nile sports channel, and the specialized sports channels on the private broadcast networks are among those with the highest viewership (Al Ahly TV, ON Sport, DMC Sport, etc.). Digital specialized sports news websites, such as Yalla Kora, Filgoal, and goalfmradio, were also launched to offer timely local and international sport news to audiences.

The Book Industry

Egypt is one of the nerve centres of Arabic publishing. The earliest book form originated in the Egypt of the Pharaohs thousands of years before the discovery of paper (Botros, 1978).

Egypt is the home of the oldest book fair in the Arab world. Similar to other industries, it was affected by the political unrest in 2011, yet the situation has started to recover since 2014 with a remarkable increase in the number of exhibitors, coming from 24 countries (Trentacosti, 2015).

The modern book industry in Egypt started in 1789. Since then there have been two main types of publishers: the private enterprise establishments whose aim is profit and fast turnover; and the big publishing enterprises that are attached to press organizations, such as Dar al Hilal and Dar Al Maaref, which are also responsible for the printing of newspapers (Botros, 1978). The book industry in Egypt has good potential, and during the past few years young Egyptian writers have been ranked among those at the top of the market (Underwood, 2014), yet low readership and distribution across borders are among the barriers to its development.

Technological developments have affected the book industry and made room for digital distribution such as Kotobi (My Books), a platform that has agreements with about 70 publishers to offer a wide variety of content to audiences (Underwood, 2014)

Table 14.3 Number of Published and Printed Books and Booklets Written and Translated, by Subject (2013–2015)

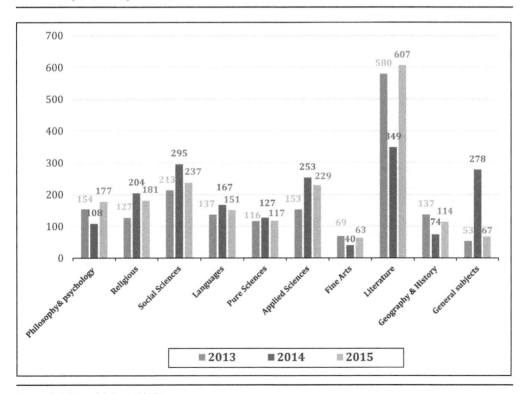

Source: Ministry of Culture (2017).

Theatres and Authentic Performance:

The introduction of theatre in Egypt started in the nineteenth century when Khedive Ismail exported theatre and opera from European civilizations to Egypt. It wasn't until the 1919 Revolution when theatres started to take a nationalistic tone in their works, providing musical theatre using colloquial language. During the 1950s and 1960s, Egyptian theatre witnessed many developments where actors persisted in providing art of high quality, and at that time the National Egyptian Theatre was inaugurated and radio plays were regulatory aired (Ismail, 2005).

A drop took place during the 1970s with the Open Door Economic Policy (ODEP) and the private sector started to focus on purely commercial content that was heavily criticisized for affecting public taste. In the 1990s, theatre was still among the most popular entertaining platforms in both the public and the private sector (Seif, 2017); after 2011 theatre witnessed a decline in the number of theatres and audiences, although since the end of 2013 it started to recover, with an increase in the number of both (Ministry of Culture, 2017).

Internet, Social Media, and Advertisments: Challenges and Opportunities

Internet penetration in Egypt reaches up to 38 million of the population; and the mobile broadband subscriptions reaches 31% of the poplulation. Internet users through mobile phones accounts for 32 million of the population. Citizens who have Internet access from home accounts for 46.5 % of the population. Social media users (Facebook and Twitter) accounts for 30.5% of the population (ICT, 2017; CAPMAS, 2017).

The average time spent online per week in Egypt has increased from 18 hours in 2013 and 23 hours in 2015, to 26 hours in 2017. Using smartphones to connect to the Internet is rising and computer use is declining. The usage of smartphones increased from 32% in 2015 to 47% in 2017, and usage of computers went down from 34% in 2015 to 20% in 2017. Egyptians increasingly embrace social media, as the use of Facebook increased by 8 points, WhatsApp by 12 points, YouTube by 13 points and Instagram by 17 points (2017: 47% Facebook, 38% WhatsApp, 35% YouTube, 21% Instagram). Twitter was only 11% in 2017 (Media Use in the Middle East, 2017).

Some of the traditional media outlets are facing challenges to generate their aimed revenue. The Internet and, specifically, social media have opened a direct relation with customers to the point that the content distributor can understand audiences' personal preferences and tailor the content according to their different interests and preferences, a technique known as micro-targeting.

Many TV stations have set up their YouTube channels to maximize their traffic and generate more advertisements, yet 45% of the online advertising goes to YouTube (Allam, 2019). The value of digital advertising in the market has reached around LE500m or 7% of total advertising expenditure. Growth rate is expected to be 50% (Allam, 2019).

There is potential for growth in the entertainment industry in Egypt, especially through digital technology and the possibility of audience analysis that opens up ways to the entertainment companies and advertisers to generate more data on consumers, their preferences, habits and geographical characteristics, to better target their audiences.

References

Abdel Rahman, Mohamed. (2012). "TV goes Dynastic". *Al Akhbar* Newspaper. July 5, 2012. http://english.al-akhbar.com/content/egyptian-tv-goes-dynastic

Abdel Rahman, Mohamed. (2015). "The Egyptian Drama after the Revolution". *Al Akhbar* Newspaper. July 5, 2015. http://www.al-akhbar.com/node/17948

Abdulla, Rasha. (2014). "Egypt's Media in the Midst of Revolution". Carnegie Endowment for International peace. http://carnegieendowment.org/files/egypt_media_revolution.pdf

Al Abaseery, Asmaa. "The Impact of January 25 Revolution on the Egyptian Drama". *Al Fajr* Newspaper. January, 21, 2106. http://www.elfagr.com/2002707

Allam, Rasha (2019). "Constructive Journalism in Arab Transitional Democracies: Perceptions, Attitudes and Performance, Journalism Practice". DOI: 10.1080/17512786.2019.1588145

Amin, Hussein. (2002). "Egypt, Status of Media". In the *Encyclopedia of International Media and Communications*. Cambridge, MA: Academic Press.

Amin, Hussein. (2004). Social Engineering: Transnational Broadcasting and its Impact on Peace in the Middle East. *Global Media Journal*, 3, 4.

Amin, Hussein and Hanzada Fikry. (2001). "Media, Sex, Violence and Drugs; Egypt's experience". In Y.R. Kamalipour and K.R. Rampal (Eds.), *Media, Sex, Violence and Drugs in the Global Village*. Lanham, MD: Rowman and Littlefield.

Asaad, Saleh. (2017). "The Egyptian Drama Faces a Real Crisis". Al Wasat. May 12, 2017. www.elwatannews.com/news/details/2575257

Attia, Sayed. (2017). "A History of the Economy". *Al-Ahram Weekly*. www.google.com.eg////#q=a+history+of+the+econmoy+ala+hram+wweekly&spf=73

Botros, Salib. (1978). Problems of Book Development in the Arab World with Special Reference to Egypt. *Library Trends*, 26, 4, 567–573, Spring.

Boyd, Douglas A. 1999. *Broadcasting in the Arab World: A Survey of the Electronic Media in the Middle East*, edited by Douglas A. Boyd. 2nd ed. Ames, IA: Iowa State University Press.

Central Agency for Public Mobilization and Statistics (CAPMAS) (2017). Year Book. Cairo, Egypt.

Cochrane, Paul. (2010). "Egypt's Clothing Industry Starting To Bloom". *Just-Style.Com*, 2010, www.just-style.com/analysis/egypts-clothing-industry-starting-to-bloom_id109855.aspx.

Douglas, Kate. (2013). "Analysis: What Are The Market Opportunities For Beauty Companies In North Africa?". *How We Made It In Africa*, 2013, www.howwemadeitinafrica.com/analysis-what-are-the-market-opportunities-for-beauty-companies-in-north-africa/.

"Egyptian Fashion Social Network Slickr Integrates E-Commerce | Digital Media Junction". *Digitalmediajunction.Com*. (2015). http://digitalmediajunction.com/egyptian-fashion-social-network-slickr-integrates-e-commerce/.

"Egyptian Ready-Made Garment Industry's 'Road Show' Hits Manhattan". *Apparel.Edgl.Com*, (2014), http://apparel.edgl.com/news/Egyptian-Ready-Made-Garment-Industry-s--Road-Show--Hits-Manhattan90888

Egyptian Radio and Television Union (ERTU) (206). Year Book. Cairo Egypt.

El Gendi, Yosra. "Social Media and Economic Development in Egypt". *Middle East Institute*, 2014. www.mideasti.org/content/article/social-media-and-economic-development-egypt

Estrin, Daniel. (2017). "Seven Fun Facts About 'Arab Idol'". *NPR*. 26 Feb, 2017. Web. 22 May. www.kpbs.org/news/2017/feb/26/seven-fun-facts-about-arab-idol/

Gallup. (2014). Contemporary Media Use in Egypt. Broadcasting Board of Governance.

Haddad, Vivian. (2017). "Middle East Eagerly Awaits X Factor Arabia."*ASHARQ AL-AWSAT English*. N.p., 27 Feb, 2013. Web. 22 May. https://eng-archive.aawsat.com/vivian-haddad/lifestyle-culture/middle-east-eagerly-awaits-x-factor-arabia-2

Ibrahim, Saad. (1982). An Islamic Alternative in Egypt: The Muslim Brotherhood and Sadat. *Arab Studies Quarterly*, 4 (1982): 75–93. www.jstor.org/stable/41857618?seq=1#page_scan_tab_content

sICT Indictors in Brief. Monthly Brief, November 2017. Ministry of Communication and Information Technology (MCIT), and Central Agency for Public Mobilization and Statistics (CAPMAS), *Year Book*, 2017. Cairo, Egypt.

Ismail, Sayed (2005). *History of Theatre in Egypt in the 19th Century*. The National Public Entity for Book. Egypt, 2005.

Kamel, Mahmoud (2012). *The Taste of Egyptian Music*. The National Public Entity for Book. Egypt, 2012.

Khalaf, Rayana. "This Egyptian Fashion Designer Is Putting Egypt Back On The Map". *Stepfeed*, 2017, http://stepfeed.com/this-egyptian-fashion-designer-is-putting-egypt-back-on-the-map-8242.

Mahmoud Sayyed. (2013). *The Cinema Industry Crisis Exacerbating. . .Production Companies are Shutting Dow."*. October 26, 2013. http://www.ahram.org.eg/News/984/68/239150/-نجوم-وفنون/أزمةالسينما-وشركات-الإنتاج-تغلق-أبوابها-F8%80%E2%F8%80%E2%تتفاقم.aspx

Media Use in the Middle. East (2017). *A Seven-Nation Survey*. Northwestern University in Qatar. Mediastmedia.org

MENA Media Guide. (2015). Retrieved from www.mediasource.me

Ministry of Culture. (2017). Derived Files. Cairo, Egypt.

Rahhal, Noha. (2014). "Meeting Up with Egyptian Beauty Blogger Menna Amin". *Sans Retouches*, 2014, http://sansretouches.com/meeting-egyptian-beauty-blogger-menna-amin/

Rashid, Eman. (2015). "The Egyptian Cinema: The industry of changing society". *The Middle East Observer*. October 23, 2015. www.meobserver.org/?p=2852

Rizk, Sandra. (2014). "8 Egyptian Fashionistas Everyone is Talking About Right Now". *Identity*, http://identity-mag.com/10-egyptian-fashionistas-everyone-talking-right-now/

Schwartz, L., Kaye, D., & Martini, J. (2013). *Artists and the Arab Uprisings*. RAND Corporation. Retrieved from http://www.jstor.org/stable/10.7249/j.ctt3fgzkf

Seif, Nesma. (2017). "Theatre and the Development of Egyptian Society in the First Half of the Twentieth Century". August 7, 2017. www.shomosnews.com/المسرح-وتطور-المجتمع-المصري-في-النصف-ا/

Swedenburg, Ted. (2017). *Egypt's Music of Protest | Middle East Research and Information Project*. N.p., n.d. Web. 22 May. www.merip.org/mer/mer265/egypts-music-protest

The Report: Egypt (2016a). Oxford Business group. Advertising expenditure on the rise in Egypt. https://oxfordbusinessgroup.com/analysis/bouncing-back-after-difficult-period-advertising-expenditure-once-again-rise

The Report: Egypt (2016b). Oxford Business group. Technological advances pushing Egyptian media sector to adapt. https://oxfordbusinessgroup.com/overview/rising-competition-technological-advances-are-pushing-sector-adapt

Trentacosti, Giulia. (2015). "The Egyptian Book Industry: A Changing Reality". *2seasagency*. July, 2015. http://2seasagency.com/egyptian-book-industry-a-changing-reality/

"Underground music flourishes in post-revolution Egypt". (2016). *The National*. N.p., 23 Nov. www.thenational.ae/world/underground-music-flourishes-in-post-revolution-egypt-1.214929?videoId=5587173

Underwood, Alexia. (2014). "Young Readers Transform Egypt's Book Inudstry". Business Monthly. August 2014.

www.amcham.org.eg/publications/business-monthly/issues/224/August-2014/3181/young-readers-transform-egypts-book-industry

Young, Robb. (2014) "All Eyes on Egypt". *Business Of Fashion*. https://www.businessoffashion.com/articles/market-gps/eyes-egypt.

15 Nollywood
Prisms and Paradigms*

Jude Akudinobi

The emergence in the 1990s of Nollywood, the iconoclastic Nigerian popular film culture, was met with ambivalence, even derision, in normative African cinema circles partly because of its rough-and-ready production practices, stylistic mélanges, humdrum soundtracks, stilted dialogue, prevalent technical lapses, chaotic straight-to-video distribution, commerce-driven ethos, and proclivity for melodrama, the supernatural, and occult horror.[1] However, in melding various film genres and establishing diverse representational registers, narratives, and themes; by exploring global popular cultural forms but emphasizing stories that ordinary Africans can identify with; and by allowing wellsprings of talent to emerge and develop, it has created critical spaces and reference points for the reappraisal of African cinema, of its history and future.

Remarkably, without critical sustenance, plaudits in Western festival circuits, government support, or international funding schemes, Nollywood's eclecticism has inspired a renascent filmmaking movement across Africa, as illustrated by the number of "woods" springing up across the continent: for example, Riverwood (Kenya), Ghollywood (Ghana), and Bongowood (Tanzania), all enkindling prospects for national cinemas.[2] Deeply plugged into the dynamics of contemporary African cultural formations and eschewing orthodox expectations, in establishing thriving continental and global markets, Nollywood has transcended a long-standing challenge for African cinema.

Whether seen as a touchstone or a scourge for African cinema, Nollywood is a complicated cultural, artistic, commercial, and transnational phenomenon. Whereas African cinema emerged during the era of anti-colonial nationalism, Nollywood, in a "postcolonial" milieu, embraces "globalized" popular cultures, creatively linking them to local concerns and purposes and engendering vibrant hybrid cultures and identities.[3] In breaking the mold of African cinema, through the formulation of unique, vernacular grammars of representation, Nollywood challenges conceptualization of the former through erstwhile, ostensibly inviolate categories, even approximating Djibril Diop Mambety's vision of *films de poche* (pocket films).[4]

Emerging out of a tense Nigerian social milieu and heady entrepreneurial culture, Nollywood's commercial pressures engendered, in a self-reflexive way, an enduring palimpsestic framework; in its formative era, unsold VHS copies of Nollywood films were simply taped over, and proven formulas, or successful narratives, still see seemingly endless cycles of repetition and permutation. The focus in this essay is on the institutional, social, and economic configurations that shape its creative thrusts, modes of production, and consumption; as Nollywood, given the relentless dynamics that drive it, is always in a state of flux, constantly reworking proven formulas and reformulating conventions of the "popular."

Not surprisingly, Nollywood's breakout production, *Living in Bondage* (Chris Obi Rapu, 1992), with its pact-with-the-devil premise, is a melodramatic narrative about social ambiguities, cultural and moral fragmentation, juxtaposed to elements of Pentecostalism, the arcane, and critiques of materialism that laid tracks for a popular cinema culture that attracts and sustains its audiences by exploring the shadows and paradoxes of the quotidian.

It merits underscoring how decades of social, cultural, and political upheavals provided ready indexes and a nexus for Nollywood narratives and offered frameworks of engagement with the complicated tangents and trajectories of the everyday. These narratives, whether spurred by the rise of the tabloid press in Nigeria or rumors and gossip floating in the social imaginary, were often presented as "true stories" or "based on a story." With such intertextual resonances, the narratives' relationship between "the real" as source or inspiration and its reworking—with dramatic twists or even commentary—is very significant. Nollywood's penchant for the quotidian and its focus on life lessons inevitably intervene in the social and political imaginaries not just through its narrative premises but also in terms of how its narratives unfold as bearers of meanings. Its practitioners and producers, aiming for profit, often abdicate intricacies. Remarkably, no sooner had an Ebola outbreak in West Africa been reported in March 2014, and the abduction of school girls in Chibok, Nigeria, by Boko Haram a month after, all causing global consternation, than some Nollywood titles ostensibly on the subjects emerged, even though neither issue had been resolved and that some Nollywood practitioners joined the ensuing wave of social activism.

The contemporary was and continues to be integral to Nollywood diegetic realms, even though one of its unique genres, the "epic," usually set in indeterminate times or places, mixes elements from oral traditions, folk theaters and idioms, headlines, hearsay, speculations, and horror with invented "traditions" (manifest in costumes and makeup) and special effects to forge its own representational repertoire and conjure distinctive worlds. Hence, in epics like *Igodo* (Andy Amenechi and Don Pedro Obaseki, 1999), special effects merge with indigenous epistemological systems to map social realities and assert ostensible realities beyond the material, eliciting an intricate interplay of cultural, aesthetic, technological, and commercial discourses.

Furthermore, the oscillation between commerce and art has seen Nollywood productions also run the gamut of conventional genres, including the musical (*Inale*; Jeta Amata, 2010), dance (*I Will Take My Chances*; Desmond Elliot, 2011), sci-fi (*Kajola*; Niyi Akinmolayan, 2010), psychodrama (*Tango with Me*; Mahmood Ali-Balogun, 2010), history (*Invasion 1897*, Launcelot Imasuen), and comedy (*Osuofia in London*; Kingsley Ogoro, 2003). Even so, most Nollywood productions are inordinately lengthy and open-ended narratives, shot often as two-, three-, or even four-part films, with insubstantial relationships, if any exist, between the original and its ostensible "sequels." While this may be attributable to the technical limitations of the VHS format earlier, and now the more popular, cheaper VCD format, it also derives, arguably, from narrative styles lacking in vitality and purpose other than commercial inclinations. While this may also be reflective of the to-be-continued serial TV roots of Nollywood, it is a peculiar marketing strategy, because, unlike sequels, these Nollywood productions usually have no cliff-hanger endings or proven commercial success to exploit. In another unique trade practice, unsold films are underpriced and liquidated in the "oil market," Nollywood parlance for the closeout phase of surplus inventory—metaphorical of the inscrutable and volatile dynamics of the nation's economic mainstay, the oil sector.

Central to advertising strategies and often plastered over public spaces, the ubiquitous posters of Nollywood productions uniquely constitute part of its visual and commercial cultures. These posters engender a unique street culture, function as semiotic bait to arouse curiosity, capture the imagination, generate buzz, and offer points of entry and identification to Nollywood's diffuse audiences, which cut across geographical locations, gender, ethnicities, cultures, and social classes. With an emphasis on visual impact, the posters' layouts, which prominently feature stars, are often spiced with a collage of scenes, usually of spectacular dramatic moments and emblematic of themes and genres.

On a related note, Nollywood titles, like the posters, open up diegetic vistas and are integral to establishing a film's distinctiveness, genre, cast, interpretive frame, and a broad range of tropes through which the narrative is imagined. In such an inchoate market, titles become significantly strategic and evocative. Generally, Nollywood titles range, irrespective of thematic congruence, from the sappy—*End of Facebook Love* (Yomi Adejumo, 2014), *Emotional Blunder* (Ikechukwu Onyeka, 2014)—to the sensationalist, like *Hottest Babes in Town* (Charles Inojie, 2013). Others are declarative, such as *Career Woman* (Chidi Anyanwu Chidox, 2014); contemplative, such as *Through the Glass* (Stephanie Okereke, 2008); titillating, such as *Mad Sex* (Ifeanyi Ogbonna, 2010); poetic, such as *Dazzling Mirage* (Tunde Kelani, 2014); or even cryptic, such as *Native Fowl* (Tchidi Chikere, 2014).

Films such as *Beyonce and Rihanna* (Afam Okereke, 2008), *Sharon Stone in Abuja* (Adim Williams, 2003), *Gangnam Style Reloaded* (Ejike Chinedu Obim, 2014), *Lady Gaga* (Ubong Bassey Nya, 2011), *Margaret Thatcher* (Prince Iyke Olisa, 2012), *Hoodrush* (Dimeji Ajibola, 2012), and *Girls in the Hood* (Fred Amata, 2005) are not biographies, spoofs, or mere attempts at cosmopolitan narratives. They point to the many possible conjugations of fame, stardom, and fandom arising out of global popular cultural exchanges and, crucially, Nollywood's openness to global cultural traffic.[5] While they may derive from commercial calculations, they are significant, too, in terms of intertextuality, cultural discourses, and contexts, particularly how they acquire new meanings and how specific lived experiences or inspirational sources can be reconfigured and used to unsettle boundaries and subvert expectations.

In a broader context, the contradictions and tensions intrinsic to Nollywood's commercial culture coalesce vividly around women and their relationship to the dynamics of contemporary Nigerian society in titles like *Mrs. Somebody* (Desmond Elliot and Tom Robson, 2012), *Mr. and Mrs.* (Ikechukwu Onyeka, 2013), *Glamour Girls* (Chika Onukwufor, 1994), *BlackBerry Babes* (Sylvester Obadigie, 2011), *Barren Women* (Morgan Ukaegbu, 2013), *Games Women Play* (Launcelot Imasuen, 2005) and its corollary *Games Men Play* (Launcelot Imasuen, 2005), *Today's Women* (Chidi Anyanwu Chidox, 2013), *Swagger Mamas* (Ifeanyi Azodo, 2013), *The Widow* (Aquila Njamah and Kingsley Ogoro, 2007), and *The Pastor and the Harlot* (Charles Novia, 2002). Remarkably, although patriarchal values are critiqued, and even parodied, in Nollywood, they remain part of its fundamental assumptions and derivative stereotypes. To a great extent, such representations navigate the variegated cultural and ideological terrains intrinsic to the nation's cultural diversity, indigenous patriarchal traditions, and the values—literally and metaphorically—of the marketplace. In that sense, Nollywood shows women negotiating new subjectivities, identities, roles, positions, and even sexualities. For instance, *Lagos Cougars* (Desmond Elliot, 2014), produced by one of Nollywood's doyennes, Emem Isong, is about desire, age, and sexuality. However, "nonnormative" sexualities, as defined by Nigeria's stringent legislation, present representational debacles within the conceptual, creative, cultural, and commercial matrices of Nollywood, as shown by *Emotional Crack* (Launcelot Imasuen, 2003), involving a lesbian relationship, and *Girls on Fire* (2013), which makes it part of an initiation ritual.[6] Ultimately, Nollywood's women are diverse but often framed within dilemmas, relationships, transgressions, and patriarchal forms.

Nigeria's belated recognition of Nollywood in April 2014 as contributing $5.1 billion dollars to the nation's economy is of strategic significance and has raised hopes of investments, capital, and infrastructural boosts, as well as concerns about whether such investments would come from the domestic private sector, government, or global financial institutions. Their interests, it is feared, may be at odds with those of the industry and its proven constituencies in ways that may compromise its creative autonomy and redefine its trajectories and configurations. In 2001, for instance, the "marketers," Nollywood's de facto producers and distributors, went on "strike" for about three months, shutting down production and threatening a ban on all who breached their efforts to clear the stock and streamline releases. Facing the prospects of corporatization and conglomeration, however faint on the horizon, issues such as scrupulous market research, budget, and criteria for credit (like collaterals, interest rates, and track records) have become worrisome factors for the practitioners, who are mostly struggling independents. Overall, these changes may establish new criteria for entry into the field where, arguably, none had ever existed.

So, while the recent government support of Nollywood—for instance, a loan scheme, the Entertainment Industries Intervention Fund, in 2010, through the Nigerian Export-Import Bank, and Project ACT-Nollywood in 2013, with grants for production, distribution, and capacity building through the Bank of Industry—appears primarily economic, even altruistic, there are also ideological stakes that may present challenges. Nigeria's most expensive production to date, *Half of a Yellow Sun* (Biyi Bandele, 2013), which won the 2014 Golden Dhow in the Zanzibar International Film Festival and is an adaptation of Nigerian Chimamanda Ngozi Adichie's multiple- award-winning book, had its release in Nigeria suspended by the Nigerian Film and Video Censorship Board (NFVCB), due not to questions of propriety but to "national security concerns," even though the book is widely available in the country.[7] Arguably, the government envisions a cinema of public good, a grandiose project embodying the ethos of nation, heritage, cultural conservation, and even tourism, and may conflate nationalist sentiments with artistic merits.

More than twenty years after its dawn, Nollywood is in the process of renewal and rebuilding at the goading of the Nigerian government which, to date, has no co-production treaty with any country or tax incentives for prospective investors. Its regulatory agency—notably, the Nigerian Film and Video Censorship Board, whose attempted market reforms in 2006 to establish formal structures, lure prospective investment partners through international "road shows," and from a more practical side, curb endemic piracy were largely ineffectual. Remarkably, the censorship board, whose operative principles evolved from colonial censorship laws to the postindependent Cinematographic Act of 1963, was established in 1993.

The *Half of a Yellow Sun* imbroglio has significant implications for understanding the relationship, even tensions, among the government, its regulatory and cultural institutions, and Nollywood, especially in light of the latter's progressive affinities to technologies of production and consumption, from TV, VHS, VCD, and DVD to the Internet and cell phones. In a way, and owing to the pressures of the marketplace, the relationship between digital media technologies and Nollywood can be said to be reflexive, insofar as each is constantly changing and yielding dynamics for regeneration and networks of possibilities. With profound implications for the commercial logic that drives Nollywood, digital platforms not only decentralize existing channels of distribution but also destabilize power relations inscribed within the governmental and institutional gatekeeping systems, which may in turn circumscribe economic opportunities.

Lately, prolonged saturation of the domestic market, widespread piracy, and the emergence of other continental commercial film cultures has to some degree spurred Nollywood's search for new thresholds and further growth, particularly a drive to go beyond formula and transcend genericness. The increased casting of Ghanaian stars and collaborative exchanges are examples of such practical initiatives with accompanying commercial interests. Furthermore, production partnerships with corporations, like Globacom for *Phone Swap* (Kunle Afolayan); a Nigerian pharmaceutical firm for *Musical Whispers* (Bond Emeruwa, 2014), a film on autism, family, and stigma; and an aggregation of state government and private-sector backing for *Dazzling Mirage*, which deals with sickle-cell anemia, love, and self-affirmation, are auspicious for Nollywood. Notwithstanding, Nollywood is at a juncture where it needs to "reinvent" itself or re- define its relationship with its disparate publics. In the emerging scenario, production values have improved considerably, production rates and numbers have slowed, global attention has been sustained, and new talents and diverse styles are enriching the industry's creative palette.[8] In uniquely reflexive trajectories, Nollywood has inspired a controversial photo-essay and, since 2008, a popular M-NET produced soap opera, *Tinsel*, with the industry as a backdrop.

Nollywood has not only been the subject of international documentaries;[9] it is also establishing a steadfast presence in international film festivals. Burgeoning film festivals in Nigeria, like Africa International Film Festival, Abuja International Film Festival, and Zuma International Film Festival—run by the Nigerian Film Corporation, which has also established the Nigerian Film Institute—augur well, too, for Nollywood. Pertinent, as well, are Nollywood-inspired BOBTV's

African Film and Television Programmes Expo and Market, and African Movie Academy Awards. Moreover, the resurgence and refurbishment of cinema theaters, often multiplexes, in Nigeria indicate a renewed cinemagoing culture with potential for the industry's growth. The current trend for theatrical releases, coupled with the "eventness" and prestige of theatrical premieres, usually in Lagos, to build up buzz ahead of the DVD release, help stem piracy and engender greater financial returns. The revival of the cinema theaters and their Nollywood roster, however sparse, provides a framework for a "new-and- improved," "upmarket" Nollywood and significant reference points to gauge through box-office returns and exhibition records the relationships between the industry and its crucial home market. The choice of Nigerian-born Parisian Newton Aduaka, a remarkably brilliant auteur whose *Ezra* (2007) won FESPACO's most coveted trophy, as the jury chair of the 2014 Zuma International Film Festival, underscores the need for Nollywood's creative ferment to engage other global, particularly diasporic, markets and film cultures, as the success of iROKOtv indicates.

Jason Njoku, the British-born founder of iROKOtv, considered the "Netflix of Africa" and the largest archive of Nollywood films, was inspired by his relatives' enthusiasm, in London, for Nollywood.[10] In this case, issues of origin, "home," belonging, identity, and memory—common to diaspora subjects—evoke channels of identification, provide reference points for a sense of community, and assuage feelings of alienation. Crucially, these issues also underscore Nollywood's positioning, especially through technologies of communication, at the interstices of the local and global, the national and transnational marketplaces. As veritable digital platforms like iBAKATV, Buni TV, Pana TV, and Afrinolly, among others, thrive, flourishing online communities devoted to Nollywood create new forms of interaction, circuits of circulation and consumption, and, inevitably, provinces for piracy.[11] Remarkably, Afrinolly even offers the Afrinolly Master Class to train budding filmmakers, and the Afrinolly Short Film Competition to exhibit their films.

With respect to diaspora narratives, however, the challenge for Nollywood is to find a representational middle ground, one where these narratives affirm certain specificities but, importantly, generate points of identification with other constituents and navigate a more complex global marketplace. Films like *Anchor Baby* (Lonzo Nzekwe, 2010), *Mother of George* (Andrew Dosunmu, 2013), *Onye Ozi* (Obi Emelonye 2013), *Dr. Bello* (Tony Abulu, 2013), *Man on Ground*, (Akin Omotoso, 2011), *Ijé: The Journey* (Chineze Anyaene, 2010), and *Through the Glass*, are in different ways intricately linked to Nollywood through casting, opportunities for coproduction, thematic overlaps, and the directors' origins in Nigeria.

Nollywood's efflorescence has led to the development, in Nigeria, of film education workshops, symposia, and production infrastructure, like Tinapa Studios—where *Half of a Yellow Sun* was largely shot—with the growing number of youths seeking formal training or education in drama, film, and media constituting a new vanguard. With filmmaking now considered a viable career and with the rise of professional guilds, practitioners have enjoyed unprecedented social respectability, including national honors. Whereas the founding talents came, chiefly, from television and indigenous theatrical traditions, new talent now emerges constantly from the drama or theater arts programs of Nigerian universities, from reality TV shows, like *Project Fame* (MTN, 2010–), *Big Brother Africa* (M-Net, 2003–), and *The Gulder Ultimate Search* (Nigerian Breweries, 2004–), and elsewhere, including the ranks of extras (*waka pass*, or roughly, passersby, in Nollywood pidgin idiom), with many becoming institutional or corporate brand ambassadors. For example, actress Omotola Jalade Ekeinde, named in 2003 as one of *Time* magazine's one hundred most influential people in the world, is a UN goodwill ambassador. Others parlay their stellar status in a dynamic celebrity culture where, in addition to founding private businesses outside of the industry, such as in fashion, beauty, and event planning, they are coveted as emcees, or star attractions, at private and public events and as voice-over artists on commercials. In this context, *Ladies Secret* (Donkollins Onuekwusi, 2014), an aspirational narrative on fame, and

Last Celebrity (Launcelot Imasuen, 2009), a meditation on stardom, aging, and social worth, acquire a particularly self-reflexive significance.

Insofar as Nollywood is a convenient but contested term, given its erroneous conflation with national cinema and its use as an umbrella term for diverse expressive practices, it may be best understood as a heuristic rather than a self-evident category.[12] Its openness to the dynamics of appropriation and transformations makes it critical in exploring the interstitial spaces of African modernities.[13] Its prodigious productions are also valuable as cinematic and cultural archives. In many respects, Nollywood practitioners have entered a phase of critical self-consciousness: redefining the scope of their creativity, adopting more pragmatic approaches, seeking to refine modes of production, and aiming at structural changes essential to the industry's sustenance.

Notes

1. For detailed histories of Nollywood beyond this survey, see Jonathan Haynes, "A Literature Review: Nigerian and Ghanaian Videos," *Journal of African Cultural Studies* 22, no. 1 (2010): 105–120.
2. See Gaston Kabore, "The African Cinema in Crisis," *UNESCO Courier*, July–August 1995, 70–73; see also Mbye Cham, "African Cinema in the Nineties," *African Studies Quarterly* 2, no. 1 (1998): 47–51. Ghanaian video remarkably, predated Nollywood. See Carmela Garritano, *African Movies and Global Desires: A Ghanaian History* (Athens: Ohio University Press, 2013); Mahir S͏aul and Ralph A. Austen, eds., *Viewing African Cinema in the Twenty- First Century: Art Films and the Nollywood Video Revolution* (Athens: Ohio University Press, 2010).
3. Manthia Diawara, *African Film: New Forms of Aesthetics and Politics* (Munich: Prestel, 2010); Akin Adesokan, *Postcolonial Artists and Global Aesthetics* (Bloomington: University of Indiana Press, 2012); Françoise Ugochukwu, *Nollywood on the Move: Nigeria on Display* (Trier: Wissenschaftlicher Verlag Trier, 2013).
4. See N. Frank Ukadike, "The Hyena's Last Laugh: A Conversation with Djibril Diop Mambety," *Transition* 78 (1998): 136–153.
5. See Matthias Krings and Onookome Okome, *Global Nollywood: The Transnational Dimensions of an African Video Film Industry* (Bloomington: University of Indiana Press, 2013).
6. See Lindsey Green-Simms and Unoma Azuah, "The Video Closet: Nollywood's Gay-Themed Movies," *Transition* 107 (2012): 32–49; Lindsey Green-Simms, "Hustlers, Home-Wreckers and Homoeroticism: Nollywood's Beautiful Faces," *Journal of African Cinemas* 4, no. 1 (2012): 59–79. See also Phil Hoad, "How Does Nollywood Picture Its LGBT Community?," *Guardian*, August 1, 2013, http://www.theguardian.com/film/fi-lgbt-community.
7. Tambay A. Obenson, "Half of a Yellow Sun STILL Has Not Been Released in Nigeria—Director Biyi Bandele Addresses Delays in Op-Ed," Shadow and Act (blog), May 21, 2014, http://blogs.indiewire.com/shadowandact/half-of-a-yellow-sun-still-has-not-been-released-in-nigeria-director-biyi-bandele-addresses-delays-in-op-ed. Remarkably, the Nigerian theatrical release eventually occurred on August 01, 2014, days after its DVD release in the US. Even then, its opening weekend broke domestic box office records. Notably, an earlier film Across the Niger (Izu Ojukwu, 2004) with similar political edges and love-in-the-time-of-crisis resonance set against the Nigerian civil war, did not generate such censorial scrutiny, anxieties or controversies.
8. See Pieter Hugo, *Nollywood*, (Munich: Prestel, 2010); also, Nomusa Makhubu, "Politics of the Strange: Revisiting Pieter Hugo's Nollywood," *African Arts* 46, no.1 (2013): 50–61. In another momentous twist, a Nollywood actor, Femi Ogedegbe, caused a stir in June 2014 when his newborn twins, a girl and boy, were christened Nollywood and Hollywood, respectively, among other names.
9. For example, *Nick Goes to Nollywood* (Alicia Arce and Brenda Goldblatt, 2004); *This is Nollywood* (Franco Sacchi, 2007); *Welcome to Nollywood* (Jamie Meltzer, 2007); *Nollywood Babylon* (Ben Addelman and Samir Mallal, 2008); *Nollywood Lady* (Dorothee Wenner, 2008); *Nollywood Abroad* (Saartje Geerts, 2008).
10. Teo Kermeliotis, "'Netfl of Africa' Brings Nollywood to World," *CNN*, July 5, 2012, http://edition.cnn.com/2012/07/04/business/jason-njoku-iroko-nigeria/.
11. Piracy has been an endemic issue for Nollywood. For instance, see Brian Larkin, "Degraded Images, Distorted Sounds: Nigerian Video Industry and the Infrastructure of Piracy," *Public Culture* 16, no. 2 (2004): 289–314.

12 The term was first used in Norimitsu Onishi, "Step Aside, L.A. and Bombay, for Nollywood," *New York Times*, September 16, 2002, http://www.nytimes.com/2002/09/16/international/africa/16NIGE.html; see also Jonathan Haynes, "Nollywood: What's in a Name?," *Film International* 5, no. 2 (2007): 106–108.
13 Emerging scholarship on Nollywood may be found in the "special issues" of the following journals: "Close-up: Nollywood—A Worldly Creative Practice," *Black Camera* 5, no. 2 (2014): 44–185; "Nollywood's Unknowns," *Journal of African Cinemas* 6, no. 1 (2014); and, earlier, "Nollywood and the Global South," *Global South* 7, no. 1 (2013).

* First published as the article: "Nollywood: Prisms and Paradigms" by Jude Akudinobi from *Cinema Journal* 54:2, Winter 2015, pp. 133–140. Copyright © 2015 by the University of Texas Press. All rights reserved.

Reproduced with permission of the copyright owner. Further reproduction prohibited without permission.

16 Entertaining the Nation
Incentivizing the Indigenization of Soap Opera in South Africa

Sarah Gibson, Lauren Dyll and Ruth Teer-Tomaselli

Television entertainment in South Africa is dominated by the soap opera genre. Although, globally, soap operas are the most popular television form (Corner 1999: 59), they are frequently dismissed as "only entertainment" (Gledhill and Ball 2013: 336). However, within the South African context they play an important part in the imagining of a post-apartheid national identity and culture. Locally produced soap operas in the 1990s, such as *Generations* and *7de Laan*, focused on representing multicultural South Africa, and there has been extensive scholarship on this "soap opera era" in South Africa (Barnard 2006; Ives 2007; Ives 2009; Lockyear 2004; van der Merwe 2005, 2012, 2015; Meijer and de Bruin 2003). This chapter examines current South African soap opera that is broadcast on public service television, known as the South African Broadcasting Corporation (SABC). Each channel has its own flagship soap opera/s; SABC1 (*Uzalo* and *Generations: The Legacy*), SABC2 (*Muvhango* and *7de Laan*) and SABC3 (*Isidingo*). The popularity of these soap operas is equated with their cultural proximity and the "ease with which audiences are able to identify with the characters, contexts and situations portrayed" (Teer-Tomaselli 2005: 568).

These productions can be categorized as prime time, public service, realist and community model soap opera. While in the immediate post-apartheid context soap operas were associated with "nation building" and the discourse of the rainbow nation (Barnett 1999), today this genre of television entertainment also includes stories that reflect local South African community cultural identities and stories. This chapter centres on *Uzalo: Blood is Forever*, a recent South African soap opera, first broadcast on 9 February 2015. It has the largest audience viewership in South Africa today and recently won the South African Film and Television Award (SAFTA) for the most popular soap/telenovela as voted for by the public in 2018.

In the 1990s, television became a "key site for nation-building cultural strategies" (Barnett 2000: 54) in South Africa, and earlier soap operas focused on how "different communities can enter into exchange, fostering mutual cross-cultural understanding and encouraging tolerance of cultural diversity" (Barnett 2000: 54). Flagship soap operas such as *Generations, Isidingo* and *7de Laan* represented multiracialism, multiculturalism and multilingualism in the post-apartheid "rainbow nation" (Barnard 2006; Barnett 1999; Lockyear 2004; Tager 2010; van der Merwe 2015).

The notion of "community" is still essential in defining South African soap opera. Whereas in the past, the community was the rainbow nation as presented within individual productions, today storylines that focus on local communities with unique cultural identities and practices have started to problematize the previous message of a "happy multiculturalism" (Ahmed 2007). Whereas these productions were multilingual and multicultural, today single language productions, encouraged by the 2016 Independent Communications Authority of South Africa (ICASA) local content regulations are the norm.

This chapter explores the shift away from a generic national identity towards the showcasing of specific, local cultural identities and places. The television industry itself supports the concept of "cultural proximity" (Straubhaar 2007: 26) through incentivising local content in terms of language, dress, humour, ethnic appearance, style, historical references and social issues. Cultural proximity incorporates "educative, cognitive and emotional elements and aspects related to the audience's immediate surroundings" (Castelló 2010: 207; Roome 1997).

South African prime-time soap operas are "striking political documents in genres usually known for their apolitical insistence" (Barnard 2006: 42). In contrast to the global format of soap operas that focus on the domestic and personal sphere, South African soap operas are political in the sense that they are central to the discourse of nation-building and have to conform to ICASA's regulations. Public television translates the discourse of nation building through stipulating local content and language requirements and incentives (Bradfield 2013: 2). South African soap opera functions as both a "barometer" and a "vehicle of change and consistency" (Tager 2010: 100; Cardey, Garforth, Govender, and Dyll-Myklebust, 2013; Govender, Dyll-Myklebust, Delate, and Sundar, 2013).

Soap Opera as Global Entertainment

Television entertainment is defined as programming that is produced with the deliberate intention of entertaining the audience (Gray 2008: 3). While entertainment may appear as a common-sense term, it actually comprises "a complex condensation of individual gratifications, textual forms and industrial organisation" (Hartley 2002: 83).

Soap opera is "the perfect television form" (Hobson 2003: xi-xii) and "the paradigmatic television genre" (Brunsdon 1997: 120) and as such is a genre worth studying in order to explore entertainment programming on South African television. Soap opera is culturally significant as it is

> part of the history of broadcasting and an important part of the economy of broadcasting as well as being part of popular culture, a major dramatic form, a purveyor of ideological messages and a source of great pleasure to audiences.
>
> (Hobson 2003: 1)

Soap opera on television follows a serial format that is broadcast daily in a set time slot. It is guided by a linear narrative structure with intermittent cliff-hangers that creates suspense. The storylines include melodrama that is played out by a community of central characters in a core location where action occurs in both domestic and public settings.

> It is based on fictional realism and explores and celebrates the domestic, personal and every day in all its guises. [. . .] Through its characters the soap opera must connect with the experience of its audience, and its content must be stories of the ordinary.
>
> (Hobson 2003: 35)

Soap opera is defined as global in two senses: as a narrative form that is produced in different national contexts, and as an exported televisual text that is consumed in a range of different cultural contexts (Barker 1997: 75). While Barker argues that the "global appeal" of soap opera is its "long-running serial form with interweaving multiple story strands . . . set in distinct geographical locations" (Barker 1997: 92), the local appeal of soap operas is "the possibilities offered to audiences of engaging in local or regional issues" (Barker 1997: 93). Soap operas have the "unique potential to combine local appeal and universal characteristics" (Franco 2001: 450; Dunleavy 2005). National television programmes cannot be separated from global models, and so the local soap opera's role in national programming must instead be understood as offering a "new hybrid or glocal" form within specific local, regional or national contexts (Straubhaar 007: 3), as will be discussed though our example of *Uzalo* in South African.

Soap Opera as Local Entertainment

The local appeal of soap opera relates to the "indigenization" of the global genre (O'Regan 2004; Buonanno 2009; Moran 1996). This indigenization refers to the way in which global expressions are adapted in accordance with local cultures and "homegrown systems of meaning" (Buonanno 2008: 88). Soap operas in South Africa are culturally proximate and are "a daily record of the concerns, obsessions, ethos, and values of the society that produces it" (Teer-Tomaselli 2011: 414). The soap opera is able to offer "stories that authenticate the audience's world by reflecting that world back to them" (King'ara 2013: 90). Straubhaar (2007) argues that in South American telenovelas cultural proximity is a condition of television production whereby certain local audiences prefer local or regional productions with which they share cultural elements. In this way audiences relate to cultural similarities that are not necessarily part of the general national expression. The 2016 South African broadcasting regulations show a similar phenomenon. Based on the fact that the 2016 policy incentivizes stories that emanate from particular locales and champions minority languages, it could be argued that South African television now encourages cultural proximity. In fact, the current dominance of cultural proximity in South African soaps makes them "difficult to on-sell into other markets" (Teer-Tomaselli 2005: 571). The financial rewards of exporting television products for a global market is deprioritized over the requirements for local production and consumption.

The local production of television programmes like soap operas reinforces national identities through elements including language, humour and social issues (Castelló 2010: 208). The local productions indigenize the "community model" of soap operas, which is most commonly associated with British soap operas (Liebes and Livingstone 2005). This "community model" centres on multi-generational families and characters who all live within one neighbourhood and belong to the same community (Liebes and Livingstone 2005: 237). This broadcasting model of television promotes "cultural citizenship" (Hartley 1999: 155) in teaching "cultural *neighbourliness*" (Hartley 1999: 172). This "community soap" model incorporates social realism together with public service (Castelló 2010: 208). South African soap opera can be situated within the contrasting model of the "public-service soap opera" (Moran 1996: 168). This is shown through the range of locally produced soap operas on South African television. These soap operas "tackle social issues and problems but they also focus on the maintenance of everyday relations" (Moran 1996: 174).

Today "rainbow TV" (Andersson 2003: 151) is no longer only presented within individual soaps but is also presented across the range of soap operas being broadcast on the different SABC channels, which represents specific cultural communities. The range of SABC flagship soaps across the different channels reflects South African diversity, but not necessarily as an "assimilation into a single, unified culture of previously separated communities" (Barnett 2000: 54). *Uzalo* is one such flagship production.

Television in the South African Mediascape

The South African television landscape is made up of public, community, commercial and subscription sectors. The South African Broadcasting Corporation (SABC) is a public service broadcaster that originated in the mould of the British Broadcasting Corporation (BBC) in 1936 (Teer-Tomaselli, 2016:60). Initially confined to radio, television was introduced in 1976 (Teer-Tomaselli 2015). At first a single channel, SABC-TV evolved to the present three free-to-air channels (SABC 1, SABC 2 and SABC 3) and two 24-hour channels (one news and one a selection of local drama) hosted on the DStv (MultiChoice) subscription bouquet.

Unusually, for a public service broadcaster, the SABC has two public service channels, SABC 1 and SABC 2 (that nevertheless broadcast advertisements), and one, SABC3, that is dubbed a "commercial public service". Following the abolition of apartheid in the mid-1990s, the SABC "relaunched" its inherited channels along a "language-based model" that took as its starting point the view that South Africa was a multilingual society with eleven official languages, all of which had to be accommodated. The eleven languages were grouped in four clusters, according to a presumption of mutual intelligibility.

Under this model, SABC 1, with the largest footprint, broadcasts most of its prime-time programming in the Nguni group of languages, isiZulu and isiXhosa, which are also the most widely spoken languages in the country. isiNdebele and Tshivenda, spoken by a smaller number of people, is also accommodated here. SABC 2, with the second largest footprint, carries seSotho, seTswana and seSwati that alternates with Afrikaans during prime time. This policy saw the significant downgrading of Afrikaans from being a language that prior to 1994 was co-equal with English, to a minor language, given a greatly reduced allocation of broadcast time, on a par with other African languages. SABC 3, which was later defined as a "public commercial channel", uses mainly English, and is aimed at the "professional and specialised viewer", a euphemism for the middle class, mainly urban population of all races and languages. Scheduling was and remains arranged according to blocks of same-language programming back-to-back. Languages with smaller speaking-communities were accommodated on an ad hoc basis. While the language model ran the risk of maintaining apartheid perceptions and promoting ethnic divisions, it had the advantage of being predictable and "viewer friendly", as well as rationalizing the question of language equity.

etv is a commercial, free-to-air channel with an additional feed that is also broadcast on the DStv/MultiChoice platform. DStv/MultiChoice is part of the mega-corporation Naspers media stable. Multichoice is the subscription and distribution arm of the corporation, while DStv is responsible for the acquisition, commissioning and scheduling of content. While the majority of their television programming is imported either as whole self-standing global brands or for scheduling on curated channels, there is a significant amount of locally commissioned programming available on DStv's own branded (curated) channels. Historically the space of the wealthy and privileged, DStv has extended their local offerings through a dedicated channel, "Mzanzi Magic" (South African Magic) that broadcasts only in South African indigenous languages. There is a significant amount of content produced for this channel, all commissioned from independent production companies.

The three SABC channels command the greatest share of audience, commanding approximately 60% of market share overall, while etv is in the region of 30% and DStv plays out the remaining 10%. However, in terms of socioeconomic trends, the order is reversed: DStv caters to the top economic brackets; SABC 3 and etv sit in middle-class and upper middle-class brackets; while SABC 1 and SABC 2 cater for the lower- and middle-class audiences. The significant expansion of Mzanzi Magic, which is also available on less expensive "compact" bouquets, is changing this situation, and making subscription television more accessible to a larger part of the population (Pendoring Newsletter, 2017).

Broadcasting Legislation

Broadcasting in South Africa is governed by the South African Broadcasting Act (Act 4, 1999, as amended)[1] and the Electronic Communications Act (EC Act) (Act 36, 2005, as amended).[2] The latter legislation was promulgated in 2006 (amended in 2007) with the purpose of promoting convergence across the broadcasting and telecommunication platforms. The Act incorporated many of the provisions of the previous Broadcasting Act. Together the two Acts cover five specific areas of broadcasting policy: diversity, universal access, public interest, the promotion of a South African cultural identity, and the empowerment of previously disadvantaged persons. These two latter areas speak directly to the centrality of cultural proximity in Broadcasting. By "diversity", the Acts refer to a range of ownership and of programming content across genres, audiences and regions (EC Act, Section 2(i)). "Public interest" is a broad category of concerns, although for the purposes of this chapter, the provision of programming in all 11 official languages is paramount (EC Act, Section 2(u)). The "promotion of a South African cultural identity" is designed to promote specifically South African content as well as South African cultural industries (EC Act, Sec 62). "Empowerment and redress" aims to reconstruct ownership and production capacity, as well as the output programming of broadcasting to needs of "historically disadvantaged groups and individuals", that is, "black people, women and people with disabilities" (EC Act, Section 2(h)).

One of the primary objectives of the Broadcasting Act was to "establish and develop a broadcasting policy [. . .] in the public interest [that would] contribute to democracy, development to society, gender equality, nation building, provision of education and strengthening the spiritual and moral fibre of society" (Broadcasting Act, Section 2(a)). From the outset, then, the legislation and regulations that govern South African broadcasting, including entertainment broadcasting, have been underpinned by strongly normative values and purposes. This section of the chapter outlines the main regulatory framework that guides entertainment television, particularly as shown on the SABC.

Broadcasting, and specifically broadcasting content, is regulated by the Independent Communications Authority of South Africa (ICASA). Two of the most far-reaching sets of ICASA's regulations refer specifically to language use and the broadcasting of locally produced television programming, known in the regulations as "local content". In keeping with the enabling legislation outlined above, the purpose of ICASA's local content policies are twofold: to promote a sense of "South African identity and belonging"; and to promote a thriving, diversified and sustainable independent audio-visual production section that is "effectively controlled by South Africans" (EC Act, Section 2(v)).

ICASA first introduced national local content regulations for both radio and television in 2002 (ICASA formalised in the Broadcasting Amendment Act of 2002). These regulations were reviewed in 2016 (ICASA, 2016a). The 2016 regulations were far more complex than their predecessors. The outcome was an intricate matrix of different factors, based on broadcast minutes, production and acquisition spend, as well as by whom and where the productions were made. The primary distinction was made between different genres of programming (drama, informal knowledge building, children's education, documentary and current affairs) Different requirements were set out according to broadcasting platforms (specifically public and commercial broadcasters as well as those employing a free-to-air dissemination compared to a closed subscription platform). Time slots were also taken into consideration, with a different set of requirements in "prime time", defined as "the period between 18H00 and 22H00 every day" (ICASA 2016a) and television performance period ("ppt") defined as the hours in air.

Local Content Regulations

The 2016 local broadcasting regulations have a two-fold purpose. The first is to incentivize a greater use of South African languages and to foster a sense of national identity using South African localities and themes. This is to engender a sense both of nationalism and local identity that champions the promotion of specific unique cultures within South Africa instead of a generic national identity. There is a sense in which it is important for South Africans to see themselves in what they see, to experience a sense of cultural proximity. Viewers, when watching programmes, should be able to say "I recognize that!" The second purpose is driven by economic and capacity-building ambitions that will help grow the South African production industry, especially startup companies and those owned, operated and controlled by previously disadvantaged persons, a code-phrase for Black South Africans who were excluded from the mainstream South African economy prior to the fall of apartheid in 1994.

The regulations measure, monitor and incentivize local content through three mechanisms. For subscription television, with their large array of curated and self-standing channels, it is mostly through a percentage of monetary value of programme commissioning and acquisition through local South African companies as described eaerlier (ICASA, 2016b, Section 3). For both commercial and public service channels, there is a complicated matrix of broadcast time and "value added" points.

Broadcast time is measured in absolute minutes, calculated in hours per week; the first repeat (usually during the morning hours of the following day) is credited at 50% of time, with the "omnibus edition" (repeat of entire week's production back-to-back, usually over the weekend) awarded a further 50% of the hours. Repeat broadcasts do not attract value-added "production points" (see later).

A number of "format factors" were introduced in the 2016 regulations that were not available in the previous regulations. This was done "in order to assist broadcasting services licensee[s]" (ICASA, 2016a) to meet the requirements of local content. These factors work by adding weight to tactically identified aspects of productions, thus driving the national strategy outlined in the Broadcasting Act. While different "weightings" for the various genres are included in the regulations, this chapter will consider only those relating to "drama", using *Uzalo* as an illustrative case.

Various sub-genres of drama are weighted according to both their perceived cultural value and their production costs, with "one-offs" (including feature films, telemovies and mini-series) as the highest with a weighting of 4 out of a possible 4 (Section 9.1(a)). Serials that are produced at the rate of no more than one hour a week are rated at 3 (Section 9.1.(b)), while those that run over an hour a week, which includes most programmes that fall into the "soap opera" description including *Uzalo*, are given 2 points (Section 9.1.9c)). In order to incentivize the use of indigenous South African languages, a further 4 points are awarded to productions in any of the official African languages, including isiZulu (section 9.2(a)). Local geographic diversity is rewarded on a sliding scale, with production in KwaZulu-Natal being valued at 2 points (Section 5(b)); while "diversity of ownership", by which is meant that the programme is produced by an "independent production company controlled by historically disadvantaged persons" garners further points (Section 5(c)).

Applying these criteria to *Uzalo*, it is clear that the programme is strategically well-placed to make the most of the local content incentives. Time wise, it is broadcast during prime time for 30 minutes a day, five days a week. It is rebroadcast the following morning in the general production period, and again back-to-back as an omnibus block on Sunday afternoons. This gives the programme a total broadcast time of five hours a week (2.5 for initial broadcast and a further 1.25 each for the rebroadcast and the omnibus). In terms of the "format factors", additional value is also created. As a locally produced isiZulu-language programme made in Durban, rather than the industrial heartlands of Johannesburg or Cape Town, produced by an independent company (Stained Glass Productions) headed by a team all of whom qualify as "previously disadvantaged", the programme is able to garner a significant number of value-added points for its broadcaster, SABC1. Arithmetically, this amounts to

Drama sub-genre	2
African language	4
Local geographic diversity	2
Independent production company owned by PDP	3
Cumulative total	10

Multiply by initial broadcast time $10 \times 2.5 = 25$ points = 2.5% per week for 52 broadcast weeks.

A further 1% of the total local content requirement is allocated for each 10 incentive points gathered on weekly basis. At the rate of 2.5% per week over a period of 52 weeks *Uzalo* helped the SABC fulfill its local content obligations substantially. Thus, the production makes good monetary, regulatory and ideological sense.

Uzalo: The Community Soap

Uzalo is selected as this chapter's illustrative example as it demonstrates the way in which the shift to representing unique cultural identities and locales has become paramount in the "new" South African mediascape.

Genre

Uzalo was first broadcast on 9 February 2015. Initially conceived as a telenovela, it is currently in its fourth season. Its first two seasons (2015 and 2016) were broadcast three days a week. Since its initial broadcast, *Uzalo* has quickly become the flagship programme and ratings leader for SABC 1. The latest audience numbers from the broadcast Research Council of South Africa for *Uzalo* in February 2018 were 949,761 viewers with an audience share of 71.9%[3]. One reason for its success is that individuals in South Africa are possibly beginning to resonant with stories that are generated from Durban (Manda 2015), and that are possibly more "gritty" and "localized" than the glamorous aspirational soap operas, usually set in Gauteng.

Due to its popularity *Uzalo* is now broadcast as 30-minute episodes five days a week during the prime-time slot of 20:30. It is repeated the following day at 13:30 on SABC2. There is an omnibus at 12:30 on Sunday broadcast in SABC1. It runs for all 52 weeks of the year.

Ownership

First conceptualised by Gugu Zuma-Ncube and her executive co-producers, Duma Ndlovu and Pepsi Pokane, *Uzalo* was commissioned as part of SABC1's remit to produce high-quality local programmes and to foster local production industries.

Stained Glass Productions, a South African production company, responded to the SABC's call for proposals from the independent production sector to achieve its goals as a Public Service Broadcaster. The Request for Proposals clearly stipulated how bidders could provide content ideas that were inspiring, informative, educational and entertaining (SABC RFP 2014). Stained Glass Productions successfully bid on a story of two prominent families in the Durban township of KwaMashu whose sons are switched at birth in 1990, on the day Nelson Mandela was released from prison. The *Uzalo* narrative follows their fortunes 20 years later.

Uzalo is funded by the SABC, as well as the KwaZulu-Natal Film Commission (KZNFC), which was established in 2010. The KZNFC's objectives are similar to those of both the ICASA and SABC; however, it operates at a provincial level to facilitate effective support throughout the value chain to local and international film makers by creating opportunities in order to grow the KZN film industry[4]. As part of this process, Stained Glass Productions and the Durban Film Office have partnered to provide training and job creation via trainee programmes for Durban youth in a number of areas of film-making on the *Uzalo* set[5].

Language

One of the reasons for the production's "localised identity" as contributing to its popularity is that it is an isiZulu soap opera with English subtitles. *Uzalo* is "monolingual (isiZulu), and represents a distinct cultural identity ('Zuluness'), and is set within a specific community (KwaMashu, and more broadly KwaZulu-Natal)" (Gibson 2018). Executive Producer Mmamitse Thibedi confirms that this choice was to meet the SABC's mandate. Despite it being broadcast in isiZulu, the scripts are written in English. The scripts are given to the isiZulu-speaking actors who then workshop them in accordance with the nuances of the isiZulu language. *Uzalo* producers believes that this lends itself to the social realism of the production. In explaining how language assists in the characterisation of the two matriarchs, executive producer Mmamitse Thibedi explained:

> I think with language, the actors themselves played huge parts in that their interpretation and their understanding of the characters led to how the character is translated. So, everybody speaks Zulu but what type of Zulu, how harsh is it, so where MaNzuza is modest even her language in a sense is more traditionally modest whereas MaNgcobos' is hasher, she is more . . . crass . . . in terms of language.
>
> (Thibedi 2016)

Location

Uzalo meets the 2016 incentives in that it is entirely produced and shot in Durban, KwaZulu-Natal, "with an emphasis on using local talent, and the Province's infrastructure to create a true-to-life depiction of South African families and community dynamics in a way that hasn't been portrayed on local television before".[6] The *Uzalo* narrative is pronounced "unique to itself" as it tells "a specific story, which happens in a specific place" (Ferreira, 2015). The shooting of *Uzalo* in a township location like KwaMashu, described as "poor but vibrant" (Ferreira 2015), subverts the often-typical glamorous setting of many other South African soap operas which are usually shot on set in Johannesburg. *Uzalo* producers explain that "[KwaMashu] is a very specific place with its own type of feel, and its own characters. In the story, we really try to weave in KwaMashu as its own character so it's not just a story that could be set anywhere" (Ferreira 2015:1). The township is a uniquely South African space created in apartheid (Gibson 2018; Mbembe 2003). KwaMashu, located in the north of Durban, was built between 1957 and 1970 following the 1950 Group Areas Act, with its residents having been forcibly removed from Umkhumbane (Cato Manor). Together with Inanda and Ntuzuma townships, KwaMashu is part of one of the largest African residential areas in South Africa, known as the INK area (Godehart 2006).

Being set and filmed on location in the township, lends itself to social realism and cultural proximity. Thuli Zuma, one of the *Uzalo* directors elaborated:

> I think one of the really cool things about being in KwaMashu is that it makes it more relatable. Like *Generations* is great . . . they have opened up more but for, for a while a large part of their world was of high flying which is really entertaining and fun to watch but is not necessarily the lead experience of a lot of people watching the show . . . But being set in townships . . . I think that's another way in which the audience is able to relate to the world and to our characters.
>
> (Zuma 2016)

The location is also important in distinguishing *Uzalo* as a contributor to the aestheticization of the township in South African film and television (Ellapen, 2007). Sarah Gibson (2018) argues that the social realism is complemented through the distinctive aesthetic of *Uzalo* that foregrounds the spectacular realism of landscapes of KwaZulu-Natal and KwaMashu.

Conclusion

Writing in 2011, noted South African academic, Musa Ndlovu (2011: 279) remarks that despite the increasing strategic importance of isiZulu media, this has surprisingly "not resulted in any exclusively Zulu soap operas". This prescient comment underlines the importance of locality, authenticity and genuine commitment to cultural proximity, all factors that have propelled *Uzalo* to both commercial and cultural success

This chapter has argued that the success of this programme is not serendipitous but is the consequence of legislation, regulation and funding, all of which have acted in unison to promote a genuine South African experience in the realm of television entertainment, of which *Uzalo* is a prime example.

Notes

1 www.gov.za/sites/www.gov.za/files/a4-99.pdf
2 www.gov.za/sites/www.gov.za/files/a36-05_0.pdf
3 www.brcsa.org.za/wp-content/uploads/2018/03/SABC-1-Feb-2018-Primetime-1.pdf
4 www.kwazulunatalfilm.co.za/about-us/
5 www.durbanfilmoffice.co.za/NewsArticle?news=121
6 www.mytvnews.co.za/uzalo-omnibus-to-premieres-this-sunday-february-14/

References

Ahmed, Sara (2007), "Multiculturalism and the Promise of Happiness", *New Formations*, 63: 121–137.
Andersson, Muff (2003), "Reconciled Pasts, Fragile Futures, Parallel Presents: Chronotopes and Memory Making in *Isidingo*", *African Identities*, 1: 2, 151–165.
Barker, Chris (1997), *Global Television*, Oxford: Blackwell.
Barnard, Ian (2006), "The Language of Multiculturalism in South African Soaps and Sitcoms", *Journal of Multicultural Discourses*, 1: 1, 39–59.
Barnett, Clive (1999), "Broadcasting the Rainbow Nation: Media, Democracy and Nation-Building in South Africa", *Antipode*, 31: 3, 247–303.
Barnett, Clive (2000), "Governing Cultural Diversity in South African Media Policy", *Continuum*, 14: 1, 51–66.
Bradfield, Shelley-Jean (2013), "'Unity in Diversity?': South African Women's Reception of National and Global Images of Belonging", in Radhika Parameswaran (ed.) *The International Encyclopedia of Media Studies*, Oxford: Blackwell, pp. 1–22.
Brunsdon, Charlotte (1997), *Screen Tastes*, London: Routledge.
Buonanno, Milly (2008), *The Age of Television*, Bristol: Intellect Books.
Buonanno, Milly (2009), "*A Place in the Sun*: Global Seriality and the Revival of Domestic Drama in Italy", in Albert Moran (ed.) *TV Formats Worldwide: Localising Global Programs*, Bristol: Intellect, pp. 255–270.
Cardey, Sarah, Garforth, Chris, Govender, Eliza, and Dyll-Myklebust, Lauren (2013), "Entertainment Education Theory and Practice in HIV/AIDS Communication: A South Africa/United Kingdom Comparison", *Critical Arts*, 27: 3, 288–310.
Castelló, Enric (2010), "Dramatizing Proximity: Cultural and Social Discourses in Soap Operas from Production to Reception", *European Journal of Cultural Studies*, 13: 2, 207–223.
Corner, John (1999), *Critical Ideas in Television Studies*, Oxford: Oxford University Press.
Dunleavy, Trisha (2005), "*Coronation Street, Neighbours, Shortland Street*: Localness and Universality in the Primetime Soap", *Television & New Media*, 6: 4, 370–382.
Ellapen, Jordache Abner (2007), "The Cinematic Township", *Journal of African Cultural Studies*, 19: 1, 113–137.
Ferreira, Thinus (2015), "SABC1's New Uzalo: 'We're Not Generations'", www.channel24.co.za/TV/News/SABC1s-new-Uzalo-were-not-generations-20151210. Accessed 22 March 2016.
Franco, Judith (2001), "Cultural Identity in the Community Soap: A Comparative Analysis of *Thuis* (*At Home*) and *Eastenders*", *European Journal of Cultural Studies*, 4: 4, 449–472.
Gibson, Sarah (2018), "The Landscapes and Aesthetics of Soap Opera: Townships, Television and Tourism", *Journal of African Cinemas*, 10, 1–2, 95–110.
Gledhill, Christine and Ball, Vicky (2013), "Genre and Gender: The Case of Soap Opera", in Stuart Hall, Jessica Evans and Sean Nixon (eds.), *Representation*, 2nd ed, London: Sage, pp. 335–384.

Godehart, Susanna (2006), *The Transformation of Townships in South Africa: The Case of kwaMashu, Durban*, Dortmund: SPRING Centre, University of Dortmund.

Govender, E., Dyll-Myklebust, L., Delate, R., and Sundar, T. (2013), Social networks as a platform to discuss sexual networks: *Intersexions* and Facebook as Catalysts for Behaviour Change, *The African Communication Research Journal: Using Entertainment Formats in Educational Broadcasting*, 6(1): 65–88.

Gray, Jonathan (2008), *Television Entertainment*, London: Routledge.

Hartley, John (1999), *The Uses of Television*, London: Routledge.

Hartley, John (2002), *Communication, Cultural and Media Studies: The Key Concepts*, London: Routledge.

Hobson, Dorothy (2003), *Soap Opera*, Cambridge: Polity.

ICASA (2016a), Regulations on Local Television Content Gazette 39844 No345, Pretoria: Government Printers. Available at: www.icasa.org.za/legislation-and-regulations/icasa-regulations-on-local-television-content-2016

ICASA (2016b), South African Local Content Reasons Document, March 2016, Government Gazette No. 342

Ives, Sarah (2007), "Mediating the Neoliberal Nation: Television in Post-Apartheid South Africa", *ACEME: International E-Journal for Critical Geographies*, 6: 1, 153–173.

Ives, Sarah (2009), "Visual Methodologies through a Feminist Lens: South African Soap Operas and the Post-Apartheid Nation", *GeoJournal*, 74: 3, 245–255.

King'ara, G.N. (2013), Mining Edutainment from Mainstream Soap Operas. *The African Communication Research Journal: Using Entertainment Formats in Educational Broadcasting*, 6(1): 89–110.

Liebes, Tamar and Livingstone, Sonia (2005), "European Soap Operas: The Diversification of a Genre", in Denis McQuail, Peter Golding and Els de Bens (eds.), *Communication Theory & Research*, London: Sage, pp. 235–254.

Lockyear, Hester (2004), "Multiculturalism in South African Soap Operas", *Communicatio: South African Journal for Communication Theory and Research*, 30: 1, 26–43.

Manda, S. (2015), R5m handed to Zuma daughter's soapie, *Tonight*, 12 June 2015. Available at www.iol.co.za/tonight/tv-radio/r5m-handed-to-zuma-daughter-s-soapie-1.1870666

Mbembe, Achille (2003), "Necropolitics", *Public Culture*, 15:1: 11–40.

Meijer, Irene Costera and de Bruin, Joost (2003), "The Value of Entertainment for Multicultural Society: A Comparative Approach Towards 'White' and 'Black' Soap Opera Talk", *Media, Culture & Society*, 25: 695–703.

Merwe, Nadia van der (2005), "*Isidingo* as Entertainment-Education: Female Viewers' Perceptions", *Communicare: Journal for Communication Sciences in Southern Africa*, 24: 2, 47–65.

Merwe, Nadia van der (2012), "The Appeal of *7de Laan*: Selected Viewers' Self-Identified Reasons for Watching", *Communicare*, 31: 1, 36–57.

Merwe, Nadia, van der (2015), "'We Are All Equals There': Selected Viewers' Reception of Multiculturalism in *7de Laan*", in Michele Tager and Colin Chasi (eds.), *Tuning In: Perspectives on Television in South Africa*, Cape Town: Pearson Education, pp. 95–112.

Moran, Albert (1996), "National Broadcasting and Cultural Identity: New Zealand Television and *Shortland Street*", *Continuum*, 10: 1, 168–186.

Ndlovu, Musa (2011), "The meaning of post-apartheid Zulu media", *Communicatio: South African Journal for Communication Theory and Research*, 37: 2, 268–290.

O'Regan, Tom (2004), "Australia"s Television Culture", in Robert C. Allen and Annette Hill (eds.), *The Television Studies Reader*, London: Routledge, pp. 79–91.

Pendoring Newsletter (2017), Mzani Magic Continues to Delight Viewers with Prime Time Content, Available at: www.mediaupdate.co.za/marketing/142629/mzansi-magic-sponsors-the-2017-pendoring-advertising-awards.

Republic of South Africa (2005), *Electronic Communications Act*, Act No. 36 of 2005, Pretoria: Government Printer.

Republic of South Africa (1999), Broadcasting Act, Act No. 4 of 1999, Pretoria: Government Printer.

Republic of South Africa (2002), Broadcasting Amendment Act, No. 64 of 2002, Pretoria: Government Printer.

Roome, Dorothy (1997), "Transformation and Reconciliation: 'Simunye', a flexible model", *Critical Arts*, 11: 1–2, 66–94.

Straubhaar, Joseph D. (2007), *World Television: From Global to Local*, London: Sage.

SABC Request for proposal (RFP) (2014), Book 9 RFP/FY 2014 – 15/01.

Tager, Michele (2010), "The Black and The Beautiful: Perceptions of (a) New *Generation*(s)", *Critical Arts*, 24: 1, 99–127.

Teer-Tomaselli, Ruth (2005), "Change and Transformation in South African Television", in Janet Wasko (ed.) *A Companion to Television*, Oxford: Blackwell, pp. 558–579.

Teer-Tomaselli, Ruth (2011), "Legislation, Regulation, and Management in the South African Broadcasting Landscape: A Case Study of the South African Broadcasting Corporation", in Robin Mansell and Marc Raboy (eds.), *The Handbook of Global Media and Communication Policy*, Oxford: Wiley-Blackwell, pp. 414–431.

Teer-Tomaselli, Ruth (2015), "In the Beginning: Politics and Programming in the First Years of South African television", in Michele Tager and Colin Chasi (eds.), *Tuning In: Perspectives on Television in South Africa*, Cape Town: Pearson, pp. 1–17.

Thibedi, Mmamitse (2016), Interviewed by Janet Atinuke Onuh (with supervisors Lauren Dyll and Sarah Gibson) at Stained Glass Productions Studio, Riverhorse Road, Durban on 26 August 2016.

Zuma, Thuli (2016), Interviewed by Janet Atinuke Onuh (with supervisors Lauren Dyll and Sarah Gibson), at Stained Glass Productions Studio, Riverhorse Road, Durban on 22 August 2016.

Part III
Asia And Oceania

17 Media Culture Globalization and/in Japan

Koichi Iwabuchi

While the rise of South Korea, China and India are attracting more academic attention with regard to media culture production and its international circulation, Japan, together with Hong Kong, is a pioneering country in Asia in the development of domestic production and the international export of media cultures. The high time of Japan's export of media culture might have culminated around the beginning of the new millennium (except, perhaps, for manga, animation and games), but Japanese media culture still has ample presence and involvement in the global media culture arena. This chapter will sketch the evolution of Japanese media culture under cultural globalization processes, which generate intricate interactions of global, regional and local. It will discuss the significance of examining Japanese media culture to comprehend the localization process, a prominent role Japanese media culture plays in the activation of regional flows and connections, and the recent development of the "cool Japan" policy, which is symptomatic of the global promotion of national culture. Japanese cases indicate, it will be suggested, that these developments have been further advanced by the growing corporate-state alliance that governs market-driven global entertainment business.

Global-Local Interactions

The history of media culture production in Japan, like many countries, cannot be traced without attending to deep influences by American media culture, especially after the end of the war. Yet, in Japan there has not been any regulation policy to counter the influx of American media culture by imposing any quota on foreign media culture or policy to support media culture production until recently. This is mostly due to the negative appraisal of rigid state control of culture in the prewar era. Cultural policy in postwar Japan has been predominantly concerned with the construction of a creative environment and infrastructure and the evaluation of artistic activities (mostly handled by the Agency for Culture), refraining from being involved with cultural creation processes and their products. Nevertheless, Japan localized American influences through emulation and appropriation of the original, and domestic production of Japanese media culture has relatively quickly advanced rather than being dominated and "colonized" by America.

The Japanese film industry flourished as early as the 1930s and enjoyed a golden age in the 1950s after the end of occupation. Around 1960, the market share of domestic films was nearly 80%. From the start of Japanese TV broadcasting in 1953, Japanese TV programming also relied enormously upon imports from Hollywood until the mid-1960s. However, the imbalance has drastically diminished since then. As early as 1980, Japan imported only 5% of all programs and this trend has still continued (Kawatake and Hara 1994). There were several socio-economic reasons behind this rapid evolution, such as: two national events around 1960 contributing to the ascendancy of TV's popularity—the crown prince's wedding in 1959 and the Tokyo Olympics in 1964; the prosperity of the film industry sustaining the swift growth of the TV industry at the cost of its own decline—movie attendance decreased from 1.1 billion in 1958 to 373 million in

1965 (Stronach, 1989, p. 136); and remarkable economic development since the 1960s and the large size of the domestic market with a population of more than 100 million. However, the localization of American media culture is also a major factor that facilitated the asecndancy of Japanese media production. Needless to say, this is not unique to Japan but is reminiscent of a globally observed trend. As Tunstall (1995) suggests, regarding the relative decline of American media power in the world, the Japanese mode of indigenization of American original media culture can be seen as a pattern of the development of non-Western TV industries which, he predicts, other non-Western countries such as China or India will follow.

Such a view of Japan's experience of localization as a model to be followed attracted wider attention with the increasing concern with cultural globalization processes in the 1990s. The Japanese capacity for localizing or indigenizing the foreign has been evaluated as innovative and universal not just for other non-Western countries but also for global media industries. The Japan-originated marketing strategy of "global localization" or "glocalization" has come to be credited as a leading formula for global corporations in the 1990s in place of "global standardization". Thus, Sony's strategy of global localization was regarded as a kind of "Japanization", which is "a global strategy which does not seek to impose a standard product or image, but instead is tailored to the demands of the local market" (Featherstone, 1995, p. 9). Referring to *The Oxford Dictionary of New Words* (1991, 134) acknowledging that "global localization" and the new word "glocal" originate in Japan, Robertson (1995, p. 28) explicates that it aims to be

> simultaneously global and local; taking a global view of the market, but adjusted to local considerations ... Formed by telescoping global and local to make a blend; the idea is modelled on Japanese *dochakuka* (derived from *dochaku* 'living on one's own land'), originally the agricultural principle of adapting one's farming techniques to local conditions, but also adopted in Japanese business for global localization, a global outlook adapted to local conditions.

This dynamic of localization indigenization is what media industries have become keen to produce in global markets and the subtle mingling of being at once global and local is considered to be marketable in the age of globalization.

The prevalence of the remaking and formating business in the film and TV industries is one exemplar of such practices. While buying formats from the US and Europe such as *Who Wants be a Millionaire*, Japan is also an exporter of formats to many parts of the world. Format business has been considered effective to export Japanese TV culture, especially to profitable Euro-American markets where TV programs, except animations, were not circulating well. TBS, a leading exporter of TV programs and format in Japan, started a format business when it sold the format of *Wakuwaku Animal Land*, a quiz show about animals, to Holland in 1987 and the format has been sold to more than 20 countries. NTV, another commercial TV station, has also sold several formats of quiz show, such as *Show-by Show-by*, to Spain, Italy, Thailand and Hong Kong in the 1990s. The format of a video-game-like amateur game contest, *Takeshi Castle*, which was broadcast in the late 1980s in Japan, has also been exported to several Western countries such as the US, Germany and Spain. A globally adapted TV format of *America's Funniest Home Videos* is originally a part of a TBS variety show (*Katochan Kenchan Gokigenn Terebi*, January 1986 to March 1992) and ABC bought the format in 1989 and since then has globally exported the amateur video show format. Fuji TV's *Ryouri no Tetsujin* (*Iron Chef*), a cooking contest program, was first exported to a U.S cable network, but the popularity of the program has urged the US TV producers of Paramaount Network to make an American version by purchasing the format in 2001. Many Japanese films, such as *The Grudge, Shall We Dance, Godzilla, The Ring*, also have been remaded by Hollywood. This reflects an international strategy that Hollywood has been adopting with the rise of Asian media culture production and lucrative markets. In addition to remaking, Hollywood has been actively employing directors and actors such as John Woo, Ang Lee, Jackie Chan, Zhang Ziyi and Lee Byung-hun, and (co)producing and distributing Asia-related films such as *Hero, Crouching Tiger, Hidden Dragon, Kung Fu Hustle, The Last Samurai* and *Memoirs of a Geisha*. This shows how Hollywood itself needs to accommodate itself to global–local interactions with the rise of East Asian media culture production, at the same time as Japanese and other Asian counterparts are actively getting involved in the reconfiguration of glocalized entertainment business, which has been driven by the partnership of transnational media industries of developed countries.

Regional Flows and Connections

Regionalization has been another conspicuous trend of global entertainment business in the last few decades. Since the mid-1990s, East Asian media flows and connections have been intensified with the developlent of media culture production and the expansion of media markets in the region. The circulation of media culture is no longer limited to national borders but finds a broader transnational acceptance in the region, leading to the generation of cross-border exchanges among people in East Asia. It can be argued that this trend testifies to the decentering of US-dominated media and cultural flows and regionalization is a sign that some changes are occurring in the structuring force of cross-border cultural flows and connections since the mid-1990s. The globalization of culture has accelerated through astonishing advances in communications technology, which instantaneously connects the world, the integration of markets by transnational media industries, and the dynamics process of localization. The interaction of these factors has made transnational flows of culture more complex and multi-directional.

Japan has been one of the key players in cultural regionalization process in East Asia. East Asian countries have been most receptive to a variety of Japanese media culture such as animation, comics, characters, computer games, fashion magazines, pop music and TV dramas. Japan has actually long been exerting cultural influence in East Asia, not just as the former colonial power but also as a producer of media culture, at least since the 1970s. The spread of Japanese media culture took a step further in the mid-1990s. Initially, this was something the producers did not expect in the production process, since media cultures are produced chiefly for national audiences. However, media cultures have transcended national boundaries to reach unforeseen audiences via free-to-air channels, cable and satellite channels, pirated VCD and DVD and Internet sites. Accordingly, Japanese and other media industries in Asia are collaboratively promoting a wider range of Japanese media cultures in various markets for routine consumption in East Asia. In the late 1990s we observed the emergence of those young people named as *harizu* (Japan tribe) who love Japanese pop culture and follow it keenly in Taiwan (Iwabuchi, 2002). The boom in popularity of Japanese media culture has been surpassed by that of Korean media culture, as will be discussed, but the penetration of Japanese media cultures in East Asian markets is still far-reaching in the region.

Regionalization is also closely associated with and generated under globalization processes. The "distinctive" appeal of the media culture of East Asia is the product of global–local interactions in terms of representation and consumption as well as production. Many people in the region identify themselves more sympathetically with media cultures from other parts of the region, as they lucidly show the sense of "being modern" in East Asian contexts, which is articulated through the intertwined global–local configuration. During my research I often heard audiences in East Asia express that Japanese TV dramas, for example, represent something culturally closer, more familiar, more realistic, and therefore easier to relate to than American counterparts (Iwabuchi 2002). Yet this does not mean the cultural homogenization of East Asia. East Asian viewers tend to relate to Japanese media culture because it shows that Japan is similar but different, different but the same. The perception of closeness suggests comfortable difference that audiences perceive from other cultures and societies in East Asia. Similar and dissimilar, different and the same and close; all of these intertwined perceptions arouse a sense of identification, relatedness and sympathy in the eyes of people in East Asia (Iwabuchi, 2004a). It can be argued that the comfortable sense of familiarity that East Asian audiences feel when consuming Japanese media culture is founded on a sense of coevalness (Fabian, 1983) or contemporaneity, but it has been generated by globalized experiences of urban dwellers such as simultaneous distribution of information and media culture, the spread of common consumerist culture and lifestyles, the development of the media industry and market and the emergence of young middle-class people with considerable spending power (Iwabuchi, 2002).

In the new millennium, we have observed the further intensification of East Asian mediated connections. Many East Asian players are creating their own cultural forms within the social and cultural contexts specific to their countries of location, and media flows are becoming more and more multilateral. The most conspicuous trend is the popularity of South Korean media culture, a phenomenon which is called "Korean Wave" or "*Hallyu*". Although Korean television drama production has been in no small way influenced by Japanese TV dramas (Lee, 2004), the Koreans have produced drama series portraying Asia's here and now with their own appeal, which are being circulated in Asian markets. Korean television series and pop music are now receiving an even warmer welcome in places like Taiwan, Hong Kong and China than their Japanese equivalents (Chua and Iwabuchi, 2008; Kim, 2013). With the rise of media culture production in many parts of Asia, the co-production of media culture has also become active, with the growing collaboration and close partnerships among media culture industries in the region with the aim of pursuing international marketing and joint ventures spanning transnational markets, as a term such as "Asiawood" indicates (Beals and Platt, 2001). Indeed, so many films have been co-produced within East Asia, such as three-language films like *Seven Swords* (Hong Kong/China/Korea), which was produced in Cantonese, Mandarin and Korean; a US$35 million budget film *Promise* (China/Korea/Japan); *Daisy* (Korea/Hong Kong with a Japanese music director); a trilogy horror film *Three* (Korea/Hong Kong/Thailand) and its sequel *Three . . . Extremes* (Hong Kong/Japan/Korea), to mention just a few (Jin and Lee, 2007). East Asian markets have become increasingly synchronized, and producers, directors, actors as well as capital from around the region have been engaged in various creative activities that transcend national borders.

Remakes of successful TV dramas and films from other parts of East Asia are frequently produced, especially between Japanese, South Korean, Hong Kong and Taiwanese media texts, and Japanese comic series are often adapted for TV dramas and films outside of Japan. A prominent example is *Meteor Garden* (*Liuxing Huayuan*), a Taiwanese TV drama series that adapts a Japanese comic series. The drama series became very popular in many parts of East and Southeast Asia, so much so that Japanese and South Korean versions were later produced (and an unofficial Chinese version was also created). A chain of adaptations of the same story of a girls' comic series (*shojo manga*), *Hana yori dango*, which has been widely read in East Asia, shows some kind of regional sharedness. It is a story about confrontation, friendship and love between an ordinary female high-school student and four extraordinary, rich and good-looking male students. While the representation of beautiful boys in each version is a very important factor for its popularity (Jung, 2010), the common motif—the narrative of *shojo*—travels well across East Asia and Southeast Asia (Le, 2009). It is "an ambivalent and resistant genre that narratively and stylistically defers incipient womanhood—and its attendant responsibilities—by maintaining the open-ended possibility of adolescence" (Le, 2009, p. 82). While there are intriguing differences in the representation of the agency of the adolescent heroine according to the country's specific sociohistorical context (e.g., the South Korean version depicting the agency of the young female more passively), each drama "remains definitely Asian in its inflection", as all versions still share "the imagery of Asian modern" that is narrated through the experience of female adolescence (Le, 2009, p. 115). Trans-Asian localization and remaking work as a channel through which the intricate juxtaposition of specificity and commonality of East Asian modernities is freshly articulated.

Global Promotion of "Cool Japan"

While even in the late 1990s it was stated in an influential book on media globalization that "Japan is supplying capital and markets to the global media system, but little else" (Herman and McChesney, 1998, p. 104), such a view fails to realize the rise of Japanese cultural export to the world beyond Asian regions. The spread of Japanese media culture, especially animation, into the US and Europe has been a gradual and steady phenomenon but "Japanese media culture goes global" came to the fore in at least the 1980s. In this period, the focus was on the cultural influence of "made-in-Japan" communication technological products such as the Walkman and Japanese manufacturers' inroads into the global entertainment business, as exemplified by Sony and Matsushita's buyout of Hollywood studios, Columbia and MCA, in the late 1980s. It sought to gain access to the huge archives of Hollywood movies and other media culture rather than producing them in Japan, but the significant increase in Japanese exports of popular cultural products was occurring in the same period. Following the success of Ôtomo Katsuhiro's popular animation film, *Akira* (1988), the quality and popularity of "Japanimation" came to be recognized by the US market. Oshii Mamoru's animated film, *The Ghost in the Shell*, was shown simultaneously in Japan, America and Britain in 1995 and its sales turned out to be number one in the US video charts (Billboard, 1996). Furthermore, the popularity of Japanese games software is demonstrated by the phenomenal success of Super Mario Brothers and Sonic. Pokémon's penetration into global markets exceeds even that of Mario. As of June 2000, sales of Pokémon games software had reached about 65 million copies (22 million outside Japan); trading-cards about 4.2 billion (2.4 billion outside Japan); the animation series had been broadcast in 51 countries; the first feature film had been shown in 33 countries and its overseas box-office takings had amounted to $176 million; in addition, there had also been about 12,000 character merchandises (8,000 outside Japan) (Hatakeyama and Kubo, 2000). These statistics clearly show that Pokémon has become a "made-in-Japan" global cultural phenomenon (Tobin, 2004). Furthermore, Miyazaki Hayao's animation films are now widely respected and *Sen to Chihiro no Kamikakushi* won the best film award at the Berlin Film Festival in 2002. According to Sugiura (2003), industry estimates Japanese exports of popular cultural products nearly tripled, from 500 billion yen in 1992 to 1.5 trillion yen in 2002. Hello Kitty, a cat-like character produced by the Japanese company Sanrio also earned $1 billion a year outside Japan (Sugiura, 2003).

Accordingly, Japan's media culture has become recognized domestically and internationally as a global culture and Euro-American media paid attention to the phenomena: "During the 1990's, Japan became associated with its economic stagnation. However, what many failed to realize is that Japan has transformed itself into a vibrant culture-exporting country during the 1990s." (New York Times, 2003); "Japan is reinventing itself on earth—this time as the coolest nation culture" (Faiola, 2003). These reports sparked off Japanese discussion, publication and symposium on its "cool culture" and the potential for enhancing Japan's soft power. These American observations are still crucial for the confirmation of the "cool Japan" phenomena within Japan. It can be thus argued that Japanese fascination with "cool Japan" shows its reliance on the Western gaze in the assessment of the value of Japanese culture, as was the case with traditional culture such as Ukiyoe (Iwabuchi, 1994). In this sense, Cool Japan is basically a Western phenomenon.

The Japanese embracing of Cool Japan with the Western endorsement in the twenty-first century marked a crucial difference from previous cases, in that it is not just limited to a celebratory nationalistic euphoria. It eventually has accompanied the active development of cultural policy discussion and implementation aimed at further enhancing Japan's cultural standing in the world. This is a significant shift in Japan as there had been no cultural policy to boost media culture production and export before then, as mentioned earlier. This development is in line with the growing policy concern in the world with the enhancement of national interests in terms of both economy and foreign policy through cultural export—be it called soft power, creative industries, cultural diplomacy, nation branding (Iwabuchi, 2015). In Japan, too, several terms such as Cool Japan, soft power, content industries and creative industries have been used by different actors of the cultural policy discussion. Soft power is concerned with the enhancement of Japan's international standing and promotion of cultural diplomacy, and the Ministry of Foreign Affairs (MOFA) mostly uses it.

The Ministry of Foreign Affairs (MOFA) also became active in incorporating the uses of media culture for the advancement of cultural diplomacy and adopted a policy of Pop Culture Diplomacy in 2006. It appointed popular animation character, *Doraemon* as Anime Ambassador in 2008 and three young female fashion leaders as Ambassadors of Cute. They are assigned to travel the world to promote Japanese culture abroad. MOFA also support the World Cosplay Summit, which has been held annually in Japan. Content business is discussed in terms of the increase of exports of media and cultural products, mostly used by the Ministries of Economy, Trade and Industry (METI). More recently METI established the Cool Japan promotion office in June 2010 by adopting the term "creative industries" for English translation. Although no one body makes a coherent and substantial cultural policy due to the vertically dividing administrative structure, Cool Japan has gradually become an umbrella policy term and METI has been taking the initiative in the implementation of Cool Japan policy. In 2013, the Cabinet Secretariat also set up "the Council for the Promotion of Cool Japan" and 50 billion yen was allocated in the national budget for infrastructure promoting Japanese content overseas to spread the charm of Japanese culture internationally (which also includes food, fashion, tourism and traditional crafts).

Inspired by the Korean success, METI has become keener to generate a bigger Japan boom through the international expansion of Japanese content, which should lead to more selling of other consumer goods such as fashion, foods, consumer technologies and crafts. This reflects their belief that Japanese content industries have already achieved great appeal in the world: "these Japanese contents are acclaimed as 'cool Japan' overseas and thus has a promising future of further development by international expansion"[1]. METI's key policy strategy focuses on the support for the international expansion of content industries rather than planning a comprehensive cultural policy for developing content industries in Japan. The main discussion is about how to make the best use of the existing production strength of media culture for exporting contents and enhancing national brand images, and the key strategy is creating new platforms, distribution networks and exhibition events that promote Japanese contents overseas, which will lead to an increase in tourists in Japan.

Japanese media industries and creators are skeptical of the Cool Japan policy initiative to further advance the export of media cultural products, not least because it is not concerned with the improvement of domestic production environments such as the training of creators and the improvement of labor conditions. Policy makers and politicians much praise the creativity of Japanese animation and manga, as they are believed to significantly elevate Japan's brand image, but they are not much concerned with the actual working conditions of animation subcontractors in Japan. The labor conditions of Japanese animation and game industries are likewise infamous and many young people leave the industries due to low wages. According to *Yomiuri Newspaper* (Yomiuri Newspaper, 2013), the average annual income for workers in their twenties is 1.1million yen, in their thirties, 2.14 million yen and in their forties, 4.01 million yen. All figures are far below the national average, especially for those in their twenties (just a third of the national average). This testifies that Cool Japan is an effortless nation-branding policy whose key aim is opportunistically to utilize the established appeal of Japanese media cultures for the purpose of promoting a good image of Japan in the international arena without engaging with the improvement of the infamously poor working conditions of media creators.

Globalized Governance of the Entertainment Business

The development of Japanese media culture shows some ways in which globally shared trends are articulated in a specific socio-historical context: global–local interactions, regionalised cultural flows and connections and global promotion of national culture. These trends are structurally pushed forward by the complicated process of de-centering and re-centering of America-centered global cultural power configurations and the growing interests in policy concern with the uses of media culture for national interests. The decentralization of power configurations can be seen in the emergence of (transnational) media corporations that are based in Japan and other non-Western countries as global players.

While we cannot deny the enormity of American global cultural influence, it is no longer convincing to automatically equate globalization with Americanization. To explain the uneven structure of global cultural connections as bipartite, with one-way transfers of culture from the center to the periphery, is not productive, for cultural power has been decentered through the web of corporate alliances in a globalized world. Cross-border partnerships and cooperation among local and transnational corporations and capital involving Japan and other developed countries are being driven forward, with America as a pivotal presence. The spread of Japanese anime and video games throughout the world has also been underpinned by the stepping-up of mergers, partnerships and other forms of cooperation among multinational media corporations based in developed countries, principally the United States. It is American distribution networks that help Pokémon (distributed by Warner Brothers) and the anime films of *Hayao Miyazaki* (distributed by Disney) to be released worldwide. The Pokémon anime series and movies seen by audiences around the world—with the exception of those seen in some parts of Asia—have been "Americanized" by Nintendo of America, a process that involves removing some of their Japaneseness to make them more acceptable to American and European audiences (Iwabuchi, 2004b).

In turn, as discussed earlier, Hollywood becomes more inclined to internationally oriented film production as it realizes the profitability of non-Western markets and the usefulness of collaborating with non-Western films, as shown by remakes of Japanese and Korean films and employment of directors and actors from China, Hong Kong and Taiwan. Regional flows are not free from this corporate-driven recentering force either. As exemplified by STAR TV and MTV ASIA, global media giants have been penetrating regional media flows by deploying localization strategies. It should also be noted that the activation of regional media flows and connections has also been pushed forward by major media corporations in the region, which have been forging transnational partnerships and facilitating mutual promotion and co-production of media culture. These trends in the region indicate the activation of de-Americanized multi-directional flows, but the mode of media production has eventually been recentered by the advancement of a market-oriented and corporate-driven trans-Asia media culture network shaped between regional sub-centers such as Tokyo, Seoul, Hong Kong, Taipei and Shanghai.

A growing interest in Japan's Cool Japan policy is reminiscent of what Raymond Williams (1984, p. 3) calls "cultural policies as display", which is "the public pomp of a particular social order." This kind of cultural policy is typically put on display by a given national event and ceremony in order to achieve "national aggrandizement", but it also takes the form of an "economic reductionism of culture" that aims to promote domestic business opportunities and economic growth. While cultural policy can no longer effectively be developed without considering the role played by commercialized cultures in the public sphere, the two forms of cultural policy as display have been well integrated inasmuch as the state is trying to claim its regulating power by collaborating with media corporations. An issue at stake here is whether and how the advancement of cultural policy as display discourages the engagement with "cultural policy proper". As Williams (1985) suggests, it is more concerned with social democratization in terms of support for art and media regulation designed to counter the kind of penetrating market forces that tend to marginalize unprofitable cultural forms and the expressions of minority groups. And I would add that social democratization encompasses efforts aimed at the construction of open and dialogic cultural identities that go well beyond the constraints of the national imaginary. The discursive formation focusing on the utilization of media culture to enhance national interests tends to put in the background the imperative issues to be tackled. As market-driven governance of media culture has been pushed forward by corporate-state alliance, it is imperative for researchers to take seriously a question of "the public good—this, understood as distinct from the political objectives of governments or the commercial objectives of the cultural industries" (Turner, 2011, p. 696) in the study of the global entertainment business.

Note

1 www.meti.go.jp/policy/mono_info_service/contents/downloadfiles/121226-1.pdf

References

Beals, Gregory and Kevin Platt (2001). The birth of Asiawood. *Newsweek*, May 21, pp. 52–56.
Billboard (1996). *Billboard*, 24 August.
Chua, B. H. and K. Iwabuchi. (Eds.). (2008). *East Asian pop culture: Approaching the Korean Wave*. Hong Kong: Hong Kong University Press.
Fabian, Johannes. 1983. *Time and the Other: How anthropology makes its object*. New York: Columbia University Press.
Faiola, Anthony (2003). Japan's empire of cool: Country's culture becomes its biggest export". *Washington Post*, 27 December.
Featherstone, M. (1995). *Undoing Culture: Globalisation, postmodernism and identity*. London: Sage.
Hatakeyama, K. & M. Kubo. (2000). *Pokemon Story*. Tokyo: Nikkei BP.
Herman, E. and R. McChesney. (1998). *The global media: The new missionaries of global capitalism*. London: Cassell.
Iwabuchi, K. (1994). Complicit exoticism: Japan and its Other. *Continuum* 8(2), 49–82.
Iwabuchi, K. (2002). *Recentering globalization: Popular culture and Japanese transnationalism*. Durham, NC: Duke University Press.
Iwabuchi, K. (2004a). (Ed.). *Feeling Asian modernities: Transnational consumption of Japanese TV Drama*. Hong Kong: University of Hong Kong Press.
Iwabuchi, K. (2004b). How "Japanese" is Pokémon?. In J. Tobin (Ed.), *Pikachu's global adventure: the rise and fall of Pokémon* (pp. 53–79), Durham, NC: Duke University Press.
Iwabuchi, K. (2015). *Resilient Borders: Internatonalism, brand nationalism and multiculturalism*. Lanham, MD: Lexington Books.
Jin, D. Y. and D. H. Lee. (2007). The Birth of East Asia: Cultural regionalization through coproduction strategies. Paper presented at the annual meeting of the International Communication Association. San Francisco, CA, 23 May.
Jung, S. (2010). *Chogukjeok* pan-East Asian soft masculinity: Reading *Boys over Flowers, Coffee Prince* and Shinhwa fan fiction. In D. Black, S. Epstein and A. Tokita (Eds.), *Complicated currents: Media flows, soft power and East Asia* (8.1–8.16). Melbourne: Monash University ePress.
Kawatake K. and Y. Hara. (1994). *Nihon o chûshin to suru terebi bangumi no ryûtsû jôkyô* (The international flow of TV Programmes from and into Japan), *Hôsô Kenkyû to Chôsa*, November, 2–17.
Kim, Y. (Ed.). (2013). *The Korean wave: Korean media go global*. London: Routledge.
Le, L. X. (2009). Imaginaries of the Asian modern text and context at the juncture of nation and region. MA thesis, Massachusetts Institute of Technology.
Lee, D. H. (2004). Cultural contact with Japanese TV dramas: Modes of reception and narrative transparency. In B.bH. Chua and K. Iwabuchi (Eds.), *East Asian pop culture: Analysing the Korean wave* (pp. 157–172), Hong Kong: Hong Kong University Press.
New York Times (2003). *New York Times*, November 23.

Robertson, R. (1995). Glocalisation: Time-space and homogeneity-heterogeneity. In M. Featherston (Ed.), *Global modernities* (pp. 25–44), London: Sage.

Stronach, B. (1989). Japanese television. In R. Powers and H. Kato (Eds) *Handbook of Japanese popular culture* (pp. 127–165), Westport, CT: Greenwood Press.

Sugiura, T. (2003). *Hi wa mata noboru: Pokemon kokokuron* [On Pokémon prospering the nation], *Bungei Shunju*, October, 186–193.

The Oxford Dictionary of new words. (1991). Compiled by S. Tulloch. Oxford: Oxford University Press.

Tobin, J. (Ed.) (2004). *Pikachu's global adventure: The rise and fall of Pokémon*. Durham, NC: Duke University Press.

Tunstall, Je. (1995). Are the media still American?, *Media Studies Journal*, Fall, 7–16.

Williams, R. (1984). State culture and beyond. In L. Apignanesi (Ed.), *Culture and the State* (pp. 3–5), London: Institute of Contemporary Arts.

Yomiuri Newspaper (2013), *Yomiuri Newspaper*, 20 March.

18 China's Entertainment Industry

Ying Zhu

At the core of the entertainment industry is so-called show business, which includes theater, motion pictures, and television. The arrival of digital media adds new layers to the traditional ways of entertainment creation and distribution for popular consumption. In China, the entertainment industry mostly refers to film, television, and online media that creates entertainment for mass consumption. This chapter focuses exclusively on China's film, television, and online video industry. Documentaries and news programs are not for popular entertainment in China, so will be excluded from my discussion. The Chinese government considers the film and media industry, what they call the "cultural industry," an important component of its push for national development, or "national rejuvenation," to use the Chinese party chief Xi Jinping's term, and for projecting China's soft power globally. China has subsequently invested heavily in the industry. State subsidies in the form of low taxes, direct investment, and land usage at a discounted price for building cinema houses stimulated the growth of the cinema sector. Similar policies have allowed TV and Internet sectors to grow at a rapid pace. China's entertainment industry has been booming in the past decade and has become one of the core revenue-generating economic engine in China. An industry whitepaper (Deloitte, 2015) calls the period since the 2000s the Golden Age of China's entertainment industry, with a projected revenue of RMB one trillion by 2020. In cinema, China boasts the fastest growth in box-office receipts, with a projection of 200 billion by 2020. The Chinese film market is expected to surpass North America in both revenue and viewership to become the world's largest. Sony Pictures' *Resident Evil: The Final Chapter* (2017) for instance, received more than 50% of the film's ultimate worldwide gross in China, which generated six times more box office for the film than North America did (Cain, 2017). In television, China produces the largest quantity of TV dramas and is eyeing the global market for exports, though there is little demand for Chinese entertainment content in the rest of the world, a cultural deficit that China is eager to overcome. Finally, the rise of China's Internet companies is rapidly transforming traditional media in speed and scale.

The Chinese Film Industry

The Chinese film industry was nationalized in 1953 under the direct guidance of Soviet film experts and followed the Soviet-style command economy model whereby the state owned and subsidized production, and the studios produced ideologically motivated films that serve to ensure the Party's political control (Zhu, 2003). The Ministry of Culture's Film Bureau was put in charge of such planning. A system for film licensing was promulgated in the mid 1950s, which stipulated that both domestic and imported films must obtain approval for exhibition by the Film Bureau. The Bureau's Film Exhibition Management Department oversaw film distribution and exhibition. The National Film Management Company (NFMC) was formed in Beijing in February 1951 to take over film distribution from Film Bureau's distribution division. NFMC (which later changed its name to China Film Distribution and Exhibition Company and finally to China Film) purchased original film prints from studios at a flat rate, regardless of quality or popularity. The multi-layered distribution network was configured at four levels, with China Film perching on top at the national level, and distribution companies at provincial, municipal, and county level forming a cumbersome vertical administrative chain. Studios and theaters had to share box-office revenue with all the distribution layers, which took a lion's share of revenue. This distribution and profit-sharing model benefited affiliated local administrative departments.

The central government kept Hollywood and West European imports at bay, thus keeping China's large film market exclusive to the domestic film industry. As such, Chinese cinema witnessed a period of prosperity that lasted until the outbreak of the Cultural Revolution. The Cultural Revolution, from 1966 to 1976, virtually collapsed film production. The end of the Cultural Revolution ushered in an era of economic reform that introduced growth and consumption-based market mechanisms, which led to reform in the film industry. Film reform began with distribution reform to grant the local distributors more economic autonomy and hence financial responsibilities, which led to a surge in production outputs and theater attendance. Encouraged by the uptake in film attendance and the growing revenue of the distribution-exhibition sector, studios lobbied for a direct cut of box-office receipts. Unfortunately, few studios produced films that made any real profits, which exposed the gap between audience taste and studio productions under the party's mandate. Film attendance began to dip as television took off and alternative entertainment options opened up. The financial trouble of the film industry deepened by the late 1980s. The shortage of production capital became apparent by the early 1990s, which led to further audience erosion. As domestic pictures lost audiences, co-productions began to take off.

In 1992, the year when Chinese cinema was at its lowest ebb, international co-productions were exceptionally active. 1992 to 1993 witnessed the first wave of international co-production, mostly with Hong Kong film companies. Film production retreated into co-production by 1993, with studios merely collecting licensing fees from overseas producers. In 1993, nine out of the ten best box-office performers were co-productions, mostly with companies from Taiwan and Hong Kong. Since only the 16 state-run studios were allowed to produce films and the distributors could only distribute studio films, an outside investor had to be attached to a studio in order to obtain production and distribution license. Termed as "co-production," the studios were in essence "selling" production rights to wealthy investors. Studios collected a flat "management fee" for co-producing and a cut of the profits at the rate of 40%. Co-production was extended to international co-productions that used overseas investment while employing domestic labor and facilities. International co-production utilized studios' existing production capacity, helping to pay for the otherwise dormant talent and equipment. Though co-productions only accounted for a small proportion of the total number of productions in the Chinese film market, they contributed a significant%age of total box office revenue. Co-produced films are considered as domestic films and thus enjoy unfettered domestic distribution. Efforts have been made in recent years to make co-productions targeting the international market as part of China's global soft-power push, which brought Chinese investment to Hollywood (Zhu, 2017).

Production reform in the early 1990s did not lead to better box-office performance. Hoping to improve the situation, the Ministry of Radio, Film, and Television (RFT) issued a policy revision in early 1994, approving the importation of ten international blockbusters annually, primarily big-budget Hollywood films such as *Natural Born Killers* (dir. Oliver Stone, 1995), *Broken Arrow* (dir. John Woo, 1995), *Twister* (dir. Jan De Bont, 1997), *Toy Story* (dir. John Lasseter, 1995), *True Lies* (dir. James Cameron, 1995), *Waterworld* (dir. Kevin Reynold, 1995), *The Bridges of Madison County* (dir. Clint Eastwood, 1995), and *Jumanji* (dir. Joe Johnston, 1995). Banned since 1950 amidst the Korean War, Hollywood reentered the Chinese market and has henceforth profoundly altered the course of Chinese cinema. The imports generated huge box-office revenues, totaling 70 to 80% of the total box office in 1995 (Zhu, 2008). The ten big imports introduced to China a Hollywood-style distribution method that divides profits as well as the losses among the producer, the distributor, and the exhibitor. The Chinese film industry began to experiment with this new distribution method in the mid-1990s. The State Administration of Radio, Film, and Television (SARFT) dispatched a delegation of theater managers to the United States and Singapore between September and October of 1997 to conduct filed observation on how theater chains operated in both countries.

Suggestions to the SARFT was made upon return that the Chinese film industry should establish transregional shareholding theater chains, form film groups that would integrate production, distribution and exhibition, and build multipurpose theaters along freeways while renovating old theaters in urban centers. The delegation further lobbied the SARFT to allow foreign investment in both film production and theater construction and for more-relaxed content regulation for domestic productions (China Film Yearbook, 1998/1999). In June 2000, the SARFT and the Ministry of Culture jointly issued Document 320 (SARFT & MC, 2001), "Some Opinions About Carrying Out Further the Reformation in the Film Industry," proposing the establishment of film groups and the implementation of a theater-chain system. On December 18, 2001, the two administrations jointly promulgated Document 1519, "The Detailed Regulations to Implement the Structural Reformation of the Mechanism of Film Distribution and Exhibition" (SARFT & MC, 2002) to stipulate that the China Film Export & Import Corporation (CFEIC), an affiliated company to the newly established China Film Group, be the sole shareholding company in charge of film importation, and that a second shareholding company, Huaxia Film Distribution Company, be established to distribute domestic movies overseas. The two companies would work in tandem to promote domestic films by utilizing revenues from imports. Document 1519 further required that the theater-chain system be implemented to streamline distribution networks and remove administrative and regional barriers. The Document permitted private capital, including foreign capital for investing in theater renovations, which led to a rapid rise of private film companies such as Bona, and the emergence of large-scale film-exhibition groups such as Wanda.

The flourishing theater-chain system created a huge demand for Hollywood imports, which have maintained a strong foothold in the Chinese market, creating anxiety for both policy makers and industry practitioners. Under the current five-year agreement signed by former vice president Joe Biden and Chinese president Xi Jinping in February 2012, China accepts 34 imports per year, 14 of which are 3-D or large-format movies. Foreign studios are allowed up to 25% of the box-office revenue while the standard global practice is 50% in the US and 40% in most other countries. Nonetheless the 25% was an increase from the previous 13%. The Film Bureau continues to enact measures to ensure that Hollywood's annual China intake amounts to less than 50% of the total Chinese market. The period reserved exclusively for domestic movies from June 20 to the end of July was extended to the end of August in 2012 (Zhang, 2012). A value-added tax system was rolled out in 2013 to impose tax directly from the revenue share of foreign producers instead of taxation imposed on gross box-office revenues, which led to an 8% decrease in foreign producers' shared revenue. Foreign studios must also pay administrative fees to China Film Group. These restrictive measures cut into Hollywood's China revenues. The 32 films imported into China in 2016 generated a total of $6.5 billion in revenue worldwide, but they generated only $500 million in China, which was less than 8% of the total (Horwitz, 2017). Hollywood lobbied for more relaxed policies as the new round of negotiation over WTO membership ensued in 2016. The industry analysts and Chinese state-media outlets have predicted a loosening of China's import quota and an increase on the existing 25% cap on the box-office take to the international average of 40% for foreign studios (Brzeski, 2017). Regardless of the outcome of the new negotiation, the Chinese government is determined to cap Hollywood's market share at below 50%. A government-mandated incentive starting on January 1, 2018 rewards theaters whose intake is over 55% from local pictures. Led by the megahit Chinese action movie *Wolf Warrior 2*, which collected $854 million in its PRC run, Chinese movies dominated the top of the box-office charts in 2017, with Hollywood films grossing a combined

$3.4 billion, a 25% increase over $2.7 billion in 2016 (Cain, 2017). Yet Chinese movies are unable to compete overseas. *Wolf Warrior 2*, the top gross Chinese movie, collected a grand total of only $4.3 million outside China.

The TV Industry

Initiated in 1958, television in China has transformed itself over the past several decades from a state propaganda organ to a profit-generating media juggernaut. Atop China's TV pyramid is China Central Television (CCTV), the only network TV in China, which was funded entirely by the state from 1958 to 1978 and served at the party's pleasure. Economic reform reprising commercialization and marketization played a major role in the rapid development of the Chinese television industry during the post-Mao era. As China sped up its overall marketization and decentralization drive in the 1990s, state funding gradually diminished and was dropped entirely by 1997. Though CCTV now operates as a commercial enterprise abiding by market principles, its fundamental party-mouthpiece function remains. As such, it retains its protected status as China's monopoly national television broadcaster. Yet the relationship between CCTV and local stations is not without friction. Commercialization and decentralization led to the initiation in 1983 of a four-tier TV system that had TV stations set up at the national, provincial, county, and city levels. Both national and local regulators operated their own TV stations and served audiences within their own administrative boundaries. The policy was aimed at getting local communities and authorities involved in local broadcasting so as to lessen central control. The change coincided with the upgrading of the Central Broadcasting Administrative Bureau to the Ministry of Radio and Television in 1982. The agency was further upgraded to the Ministry of Radio, Film, and Television in 1985. The policy did not dismantle CCTV's monopoly in news, which was to be integrated into local program flow, but it did grant local stations the autonomy for financial management and program development. Such an ecosystem ensures that television stations, broadcasting bureaus, and governments at the same administrative level are closely linked in economic and political patronage. TV stations seek respective government and broadcasting bureaus' protection to maintain their grip on regional markets while government and broadcasting bureaus count on television stations to propound their political influence and to also generate revenue. Since the early 1990s, TV stations have become important economic engines to local governments and their broadcasting bureaus. This is particularly evident in affluent regions where local channels competed with CCTV-1's terrestrial channel for advertising revenue.

In the 1990s, although MRFT reiterated the "must carry" policy, many local stations ignored these directives. To ensure local compliance, MRFT (later SARFT) issued several policy documents, demanding that local terrestrial, cable, and retransmitting stations carry CCTV-1's programs in full, including commercials. SARFT emphasized that guaranteeing CCTV-1's national coverage is a political mission, an "undeniable" obligation and responsibility of local broadcasting bureaus and television stations. MRFT blamed the four-tier system for the chaos and disorder and thus launched a campaign to recentralize China's TV system. In 1996, it ordered the closing down of unapproved TV outlets across the country. Following this, it merged county-level cable, terrestrial, and educational television and radio stations and city and provincial cable and terrestrial TV stations and tightened control over program sources, requesting that county TV stations allocate most of their airtime to transmit central and provincial TV stations' programs. But major provincial TV operators, who had by then managed to extend their regional reach via independent satellite and cable distribution deals with other provincial broadcasters, thus continued their challenge to CCTV's monopoly. A small number of well-resourced satellite channels such as CCTV Channel 1, Hunan Satellite TV, Zhejiang Satellite TV, and Beijing Satellite TV have dominated the market by cultivating their trademark programming.

The best-known provincial channel is Hunan Satellite Channel, a part of Hunan provincial media group known as the Hunan Broadcasting System (HBS, formerly the Golden Eagle Broadcasting System).

CCTV now has 50 channels broadcasting different programs and is accessible to more than one billion viewers. The monopoly of news program has turned CCTV news into a lucrative profit-generating vehicle, with massive annual auctions for advertising spots. Advertising is not allowed during news bulletins, so spots immediately before and after are well sought after. Another monopolistic program of CCTV is the annual Spring Festival Gala, which was watched by hundreds of millions in the domestic Chinese audience and accessed by Chinese diaspora around the world. TV drama is another area where stations can fetch sizable price tags for commercial spots, though the rise of reality shows since the mid-2000s has threatened to challenge its dominance. The popularity of entertainment shows, especially dating shows such as Jiangsu Satellite TV's *If You Are the One*, led SARFT to issue an edict in 2010 to stipulate that dating shows "shall not insult or slander participants or discuss sex in the name of love and marriage, shall not display or sensationalize unhealthy, incorrect outlooks on love and marriage such as money worship" (Bai, 2014). Censorship remains the most serious obstacle to competitiveness. Between May 1994 and February 1995, following party orders, the MRFT undertook a comprehensive analysis of broadcasting in China, culminating in the "Report to Further Strengthen and Improve Radio, Film and TV Work," which stipulated major objectives for Chinese media: retaining correct opinion guidance, improving program quality, enhancing government oversight, and promoting technological development. "Quality" was defined as content that would promote patriotism, socialism, and collectivism. "Diversity" promoted "richer," more "colorful," and "creative" content to compete with the rising tide of East Asian popular culture for viewership. SARFT and the General Administration of Press and Publications (GAPP) merged into the State Administration of Press Publications Radio Film and Television (SAPPRFT) in 2013 to streamline regulatory control and content oversight. SAPPRFT is responsible for drafting the laws and regulations that provides "supervision and management" of radio and television programs. Such laws and regulations are to be ratified by the State Council. SAPPRFT can suspend or cancel programs and revoke license of stations/companies that do not adhere to Party directives.

CCTV began to import serial dramas from the United States, Japan, Hong Kong, and South America in the early 1980s (Zhu, 2008). *Iron-Armed Atongmu* and *Doubtful Blood Type* from Japan, *Dynasty* and *Dallas* from the United States, *Huo Yuanjia* from Hong Kong, *Woman Slave* from Brazil, and *Slander* from Mexico became popular hits. Between 1982 and 1984, CCTV signed contracts with six American television companies. Between 1985 and 1986, national and local stations were said to be getting as many as 750 television dramas and telefilms from overseas (Keane, 2015, p. 38). The government eventually stepped in to reign in the explosion of foreign programs on Chinese TV. In 1995, SARFT implemented a regulation limiting imported dramas to 25% of overall broadcast time and no more than 15% of prime time. The popularity of the imports nonetheless helped to redefine both the story structure and the program format of China's domestic television drama, encouraging experimentation with multiple-episode dramas. Single-episode anthology dramas dominated prime-time television in China throughout the 1980s. Serial dramas didn't begin to outnumber anthology dramas in prime time until after the debut of China's first long serial drama, *Yearnings* (*kewang*) in 1990, which marked the turning point for multi-episode, hour-long drama. *Yearnings*' sweeping success firmly established the multi-episode serial as a commercially viable format in Chinese prime-time television. While more evident in the film industry, co-productions have taken off in the TV industry as well, with Chinese companies collaborating with Hong Kong, Taiwanese, and Korean companies to produce serial dramas. Co-productions benefited local producers by bringing in knowledge and skills and at the same time allowed their East Asia counterparts a foothold in the Chinese market.

Online Media and Overseas Expansion

In recent years, the rapid expansion of digital media has accelerated the development of China's entertainment industry. Many young viewers now access entertainment content via online devices. Indeed, content is watched, or rather accessed, most online in China (Consumers viewing, 2012). A slew of digital media companies such as Youku-Tudou, Sohu, Baidu, IQiYi, LeTV, BesTV, PPS, and PPTV have joined the Chinese media market both in content creation and distribution. This led to the proliferation of over- the-top (OTT) content. The OTT content providers have in turn transformed China's entertainment industry. The presence of online players has expanded the industry from "network television" dominated by the big commercial networks to "networked television" where viewing is connected to devices and networks other than television (Holt & Sanson, 2014). With the rise of revenues from online distribution, the Ministry of Industry and Information Technology (MITT) is getting involved in the regulation of the television sector, as MIIT must remit profits to SAPPRFT. As Michael Keane (2015) observes: "Turf wars have ensued between SAPPRFT and MIIT over the past decade regarding disputes over who controls the coaxial cable for basic fixed-line services."

Current Internet behemoths in China include the leading search engine Baidu, the world's biggest e-commerce business Alibaba, and the world's largest online games distributor with nearly 800 million social media subscribers Tencent (Frater, 2015). Integrators of major components along the movie life cycle through acquisition or alliance, the vast assets of Baidu, Alibaba, and Tencent (BAT) give them the ability to attract audiences across every major media platform. Tencent owns the messaging services QQ and WeChat, which is the online messaging app with over 980 million monthly active users. Baidu owns iQIYI, a video platform known for professionally generated as well as high-premium self-made content. iQiyi's top rival is Youku Tudou, an online video platform owned by Alibaba, known for amateur or user-generated content. Alibaba and Baidu have major stakes in two of China's top three online video companies that have become China's leading film producers. With $21.1 billion available in cash, Alibaba's market capitalization of $246 billion is bigger than Disney and Time Warner combined, though the recent acquisition of 21st Century Fox by Disney might change the equation. The three companies are involved in the commercial cycle of just about every film released in China, with Alibaba through its stake in Youku functioning as producer, ticket vendor, and promotional partner, Baidu through iQIYI as a marketing conduit and online video platform, and Tencent through WeChat as social media vector that provides audiences with the most comprehensive content including exclusive copyright content from HBO and the like. Online video, with a wider program selection and shorter commercial breaks, had drawn an estimated 439 million users by mid-2014. The five largest online players are Youku (21.3%), Tencent video (20.2%), iQIYI (19%), LeTV (11.9%) and SOHU (6.7%), which together accounted for 79.1% of China's market share. With film and TV fans as their core audience, Chinese OTTs screen hundreds of trailers and teasers and produce their own TV shows.

Chinese Internet companies have been involved in making top-grossing movies since 2014, serving as producers, distributors, exhibitors, and ticket vendors. In August 2015, *Monster Hunt*, a Chinese fantasy film mixing live-action and animation became the highest-grossing Chinese movie in history, with US$257.6 million in box-office within its three weeks debut. Costing US$56.35 million to make, *Monster Hunt's* smashing success reportedly owed much to the financial and marketing support of Tencent. Originally scheduled for release at the end of 2014, production plans and promotional campaigns came to an abrupt halt after the movie's lead actor was arrested along with Jackie Chan's son for possession of narcotics, which led to a ban on the actor. With the financial backing of Tencent and Youku Tudou, the producer retooled the story line and cast actors popular with China's Internet users. They changed the plot to further match the tastes of the Internet-based audiences. Chinese Internet companies' ability to consolidate the local market for maximum profits has attracted US entertainment firms eager to attract as many Chinese eyeballs as possible. Bypassing traditional film studios in China, Hollywood is partnering up with leading video firms for the post-theatrical ancillary market as well as pre-release marketing platforms.

BAT and other Internet companies have eroded the dominance of traditional film and TV companies in China, forcing them to diversify. Film distribution is shifting from a supply-led to a demand-led market. The traditional singular value chain is being replaced by niche market business that can be tailored to the demand of each individual film release. Meanwhile modern economies have moved from the sale of goods and services to the sale of experiences in the Internet era. The new era of ubiquitous, interactive, "always on," and instantaneous media enhance the value of unique experiences. Offering premium individual experiences has become the motto for Chinese companies. The number of Internet video subscribers in China exceeded 500 million by 2015, and competition for exclusive film content led copyright royalties to rise accordingly, providing a reliable source of income for film producers. Chinese Internet companies have in recent years aggressively made inroads into overseas markets. Baidu have their offices in Silicon Valley and draw talent from the US. Alibaba has set up branch offices in overseas locations, appointing foreigners as managers, and recruiting the best bilingual talent. Alibaba partnered with Lionsgate in 2014 to launch Lionsgate Entertainment World, a streaming service exclusively available on Alibaba's set-top boxes. Alibaba also ventured into film production, establishing Alibaba Pictures in 2014 to create customized movies and TV programs while marketing and distributing them across Alibaba's platforms. Alibaba Pictures entered into a partnership with Steven Spielberg's Amblin Entertainment in October 2016 (Brzeski, 2016).

Yet the leading Chinese firm that has made big splashes in recent years is not an Internet company. It is Dalian Wanda, China's largest real-estate developer and owner of the world's largest cinema chain. Wanda has set up shop in Hollywood's front yard by acquiring foreign entertainment assets including the US AMC Theaters chain in 2012 for $2.6 billion, the Australian cinema chain Hoyts in June 2015, and the Legendary Entertainment (with credits to *Godzilla, Pacific Rim*, etc.) in 2016 for $3.5 billion. Wanda further ventured into overseas film production by taking a minority stake in September 2016 in Sony Pictures Entertainment's upcoming China related films. In October 2016, Wanda came under scrutiny from 17 Washington lawmakers who wanted the company investigated for possible violations of the Foreign Agents Registration Act. The US lawmakers were worried that a company closely aligned with the Chinese government might wield too much control over the content and distribution of American movies. Ironically, it was China's domestic politics that put a stop to Wanda's overseas shopping spree financed by cheap loans from the Chinese banks. Chinese companies and their growing investments in the entertainment industry faced greater scrutiny in 2017 by the Chinese government. In July 2017, the Chinese Government introduced measures to bar state-owned banks from providing new loans to private Chinese firms seeking foreign expansion, which led to the evaporation of deals and Dalian Wanda publicly losing its balance. Speculations abounded that Wanda might sell AMC, as the company outlined in December 2017 a plan to focus on domestic investment by building 1,000 Wanda Plaza shopping centers in China within the next ten years. China and US relations stumbled as a result of a new administration in the White House and the Chinese government's effort in pulling back on investment overseas. As 2018 kicked in, both sides were keen on a new agreement regulating media imports. As China's media market continues to grow and Chinese entertainment turns inward, Hollywood is expected to focus on locally geared movies catering specifically to the Chinese market.

Conclusions: The Chinese Entertainment Industry at the Mercy of the Party-State

As I discussed in *Two Billion Eyes: The Story of China Central Television* (Zhu, 2014), cultural policy in China follows directives issued by the party's Propaganda Department, which is embedded at all layers of government, from the national level all the way down to the local. These party propaganda departments, along with the party committees within media institutions, act as censors and set the policy and propaganda tone according to the directives of the Ministry of Central Propaganda. The local Propaganda Department operates mainly behind the scenes and in broad strokes, except for editorial content (news and information), which it manages very closely via secret weekly instructions to the media. In the past, the Propaganda Department also actively directed the variety, quantity, and content of cultural products. In the reform era, however, self-censorship by media professionals has been the principal mode of control. While the party-state must now attend to markets and their systems of rules, it still exercises what often amounts to ad hoc control over China's entertainment industry. The state government establishes laws, but because the party apparatus ranks above the state government, party directives trump everything else. For the entertainment industry, this amounts to an informal regulatory practice that results in often disruptive regulatory fiddling. For entertainment industry professionals, it creates a climate of constant uncertainty and self-censorship. Meanwhile, economic logic continues to encourage entertainment programs of popular appeal, which will inevitably exert pressure for censors to loosen their grips. These contradictory mission statements and swings—from forays into market reform to retreats to conservatism, from initiatives to commercialize to those attacking the concept—have been typical of media regulation in the post-Mao era, and they have contributed to the on-the-job training of a new generation of media professionals thoroughly steeped in the fine art of intuiting what their overseers want. It may involve self-censorship, the primary mechanism of cultural control in contemporary China, or at times out-and-out censorship. Under this environment, the development of Chinese entertainment industry must reconcile the party's demand for loyalty and stability and the market's demand for profits and popular appeal. China's film division was moved in March 2018 from the State Administration of Press, Publication, Radio, Film and Television to the Central Propaganda Department, which means that all imported and co-produced films now need that ministry's approval. The Party's tight grip over China's cultural and entertainment affairs sees no signs of loosening up.

References

Bai, R. (2014). Curbing entertainment: television regulation and censorship in China's disjunctive media order. In R. Bai & G. Song (Eds.) *Chinese Television in the Twenty-First Century: Entertaining the Nation* (pp. 67–68) London: Routledge.

Brzeski, P. (2016, December 28). China's Alibaba to invest $7.2B in entertainment over three years. *Hollywood Reporter*. Retrieved from www.hollywoodreporter.com/news/alibaba-invest-72b-entertainment-three-years-959747

Brzeski, P. (2017, February 9). China's quota on Hollywood film imports set to expand, state media says. *Hollywood Reporter*. Retrieved from www.hollywoodreporter.com/news/chinas-state-media-says-quota-hollywood-film-imports-will-expand-974224

Cain, R. (2017, December 27). China 2017 box office wrap-up: Hollywood movies grab $3.4 billion, Universal rules. *Forbes*. Retrieved from www.forbes.com/sites/robcain/2017/12/27/china-2017-box-office-wrap-up-hollywood-movies-grab-3-4-billion-universal-rules/#3bb251d9233e

Cain, R. (2017, October 8). To Get a China save "Blade Runner 2049" must play more like "Resident Evil," less like "Arrival". *Forbes*. Retrieved from www.forbes.com/sites/robcain/2017/10/08/to-get-a-china-save-blade-runner-2049-must-play-more-like-resident-evil-less-like-arrival/#69d45d211f5a.

China Film Yearbook. (1998/1999). When can we see the arrival of China's own "aircraft carrier"? (Heshi caiyou zhongguodianying de hangkongmujian?). Beijing: *China Film Yearbook*. pp. 435–436.

Consumers viewing more online video content on TVs. (2012, August 23). *The NPD Reports*. Retrieved from www.prweb.com/releases/NPD/DisplaySearch/prweb9829010.htm

Deloitte (2015). China culture industry forecast: A new era for film" (中国文化娱乐产业前瞻电影新纪元). https://www2.deloitte.com/content/dam/Deloitte/tw/Documents/technology-media-telecommunications/tw-entertainment-movie.pdf

Frater, P. (2015, February 3). China rising: how four giants are revolutionizing the film industry. *Variety*. Retrieved from http://variety.com/2015/film/asia/china-rising-quartet-of-middle-kingdom-conglomerates-revolutionizing-chinese-film-industry-1201421685/

Holt, J. & Kevin Sanson. (2014). Introduction: getting connected. In J. Holt & K. Sanson (Eds.) *Connected Viewing: Selling, Sharing and Streaming Media in the Digital Era*. London: Routledge.

Horwitz, J. (2017, May 11). The "Fast & Furious" franchise is huge in China, but probably isn't making much money there. *Quartz Media*. Retrieved from https://qz.com/981277/the-fast-furiohttp://variety.com/2015/film/asia/china-rising-quartet-of-middle-kingdom-conglomerates-revolutionizing-chinese-film-industry-1201421685/

Huang, Y. (1994). Peaceful evolution: the case of television reform in post-Mao China. *Media, Culture and Society* 16 (2), 236.

Keane, M. (2015). *The Chinese Television Industry*. London: BFI.

SARFT & MC (2001). Ideas about carrying out further reform in the film industry. *China FilmYearbook*, pp. 1–3

SARFT & MC (2002). Specific regulations governing the structural reform of the mechanism of film distribution and exhibition. *China Film Yearbook*, pp.15–16.

Zhang, Y. (2012, July 31). The gap between box office and word of mouth: The immature development of Chinese film market. *Xinmin Wanbao*. Retrieved from http://news.entgroup.cn/movie/3114327.shtml

Zhu, Y. (2003). *Chinese Cinema During the Era of Reform: The Ingenuity of the System*. Westport, CT: Praeger.

Zhu, Y. (2008) *Television in Post-Reform China: Serial Dramas, Confucian Leadership and Global Television Market*. London: Routledge.

Zhu, Y. (2014). *Two Billion Eyes: The Story of China Central Television*. New York: The New Press.

Zhu, Y. (2017, July 5). Film as soft power and hard currency: The Sino-Hollywood courtship. *The Online Journal of the China Policy Institute*. Retrieved from https://cpianalysis.org/2017/07/05/film-as-soft-power-and-hard-currency-the-sino-hollywood-courtship/

19 Beyond *Hallyu*
Innovation, Social Critique, and Experimentation in South Korean Cinema and Television*

Jeongmee Kim, Michael A. Unger and Keith B. Wagner

Over the past 20 years or so, "in vast swathes of the world," South Korean (hereafter *Korean*) culture "has become a byword for all that's cool and cutting edge" while the country has seen itself transformed from "Third World backwater to First World powerhouse."[1] The meteoric rise of Korean popular culture is a result of a soaring cultural phenomenon known by its all-encompassing neologism *Hallyu* (which roughly translates as *flow of Korea* or *the Korean Wave*). The country's televisual output, beginning with popular drama series such as *Autumn in My Heart* (KBS 2000), *Winter Sonata* (KBS 2002) and *Jewel in the Palace* (MBC 2003), has been successfully exported *en masse* to numerous East and South East Asian countries including Japan, China, Singapore, the Philippines, Vietnam, and Taiwan, creating international celebrities out of many of its stars. Hallyu has also become an integral part of the Korean national export industry and plays an important part in its cultural policy in promoting a positive image of Korea overseas. The Korean Wave, however, is not a one-sided phenomenon as the name suggests; it also encompasses transnational exchanges of cultural content to and from Korea that have achieved great significance in other countries, populations, and markets. For example, one aspect of Hallyu is dependent on the recalibrating and remaking of popular and successful Japanese and American television series for Korean audiences. Korea's EnterMedia Pictures is to produce a Korean localized version of *Suits* (USA Network: 2011–present),[2] and this production is just the latest in a list of imported formats and dramas given a Korean makeover that includes *Korea's Next Top Model* (On Style 2010–present) from the United States and *Boys Over Flowers* (KBS 2009) from Japan. Likewise, several critically and commercially successful Korean films from the Korean Wave have been, or are in the process of being, developed for Hollywood remakes: Park Changwook's revenge thriller *Oldboy* (2003), which won the Grand Prix at the 2004 Cannes Film Festival, was remade a decade later by New York director Spike Lee in 2013. Kwak Jae-Yong's blockbuster screwball comedy *My Sassy Girl* (2001) was transplanted into an idealized New York City setting by Yann Samuell in 2008. And New Line Cinema has acquired remake rights to Lee Jeong-beom's 2010 Korean action film *The Man From Nowhere*.[3]

In addition to film and television, the Korean Wave has grown to encompass a growing constellation of products, consisting today of pop-music, fashion, musical theater, modern dance, literature and art, cuisine, cosmetics and other consumable goods. Some of the products, rather than being promoted overseas as generically "Korean," have also been marketed in numerous different ways to appeal to niche markets. For example, in the film industry, Park Chanwook's three critically acclaimed films in his *Vengeance Trilogy* (*Sympathy for Mr. Vengeance* in 2002, *Oldboy*, and *Lady Vengeance* in 2005) have been linked to what has been billed as "Asian extreme cinema."[4] Such marketing gave a second lease of life to risqué Korean films in countries such as Britain, where Chanwook's films were released on DVD by Tartan Films. While the success of this marketing strategy in reaching international audiences has proven significant, the reductive nature of such branding has also been problematic. While Tartan helped raise viewership of, and bring awareness to, Korean revenge, horror, and thriller films for an international audience (in addition to films from Japan, Hong Kong, Thailand and other countries in the Pacific Rim released under the same brand), the emphasis on the extreme violence, outrageous gore, and the perceived erotic and exotic nature of these films through Tartan's marketing focus on "Asian Extreme" often overshadowed other nuanced and critical aspects of Korean life portrayed in them. This type of "extreme" branding has, according to Chi-Yun Shin, fostered and re-enforced in Western audiences' perceptions an image of the East as strange and exotic.[5]

Whether targeted at mass or niche audiences, Hallyu cultural products have succeeded in achieving growing popularity in diverse and different territories outside of Asia such as the Middle East, Latin America and Africa, as well as having a noteworthy impact in areas of the United States and Europe, exemplifying Hallyu's planetary reach. Undoubtedly, this Korean Wave has subtly contributed to decentering processes of globalization one television series, film, or music track at a time. To quote *The South China Morning Post*, Hallyu products have long been "kicking up a cultural storm" and proven responsible for "elevating South Korea in the consciousness of Asia and the world."[6]

Park Jae-Sang or Psy's music video "Gangnam Style" (2012), which parodies the materialistic lifestyle of Seoul's affluent neighborhood "Gangnam-gu," is arguably the most well-known Hallyu media artifact in the world. Upon its release, the music video spread like wildfire over the internet and became a global sensation, inspiring flash dance mobs in public places in the Global North including Chicago, London, and Berlin. It also holds the Guinness World Record for the most globally "liked" song ever.[7] Its parody of Korean consumption and K-pop music video conventions ironically became overshadowed by its overwhelming international success and is now perceived as a symbol of the triumph of Hallyu with Psy as one of its global ambassadors rather than a one-time critic of Korea's materialism. The KTO (Korea Tourism Organization) opportunistically utilized Psy's global profile for the purposes of attracting visitors to Seoul and the Gangnam district and in doing so "conveniently ignored the song's strong criticisms of Gangnam."[8] The shifting of "Gangnam Style" from its critical sensibility of initially being situated "beyond Hallyu" to becoming one of Hallyu's centerpiece texts reveals the fluid nature of what constitutes a Hallyu product, and how its reception in the Korean and international markets is largely contingent on audience appeal, local critical reception, marketing and social media presence. With the growth of the latter, fans globally are ever more actively participating in the promotion of Hallyu. As Youna Kim explains, "social networking services and video-sharing websites such as YouTube and Twitter are now playing a primary role in expanding 'digital Hallyu' to Asia, the U.S., Europe and elsewhere."[9] Even pre-modern Korean culture is utilized in taking advantage of today's modern social media environment, as demonstrated through the hyper-production of *sageuk* or costume dramas such as *Maids* (JTBC 2014) and *Six Flying Dragons* (SBS 2015). The domestic conditions that allow Hallyu to flourish are due in large part to the creative industry's conflation and control via the oligopolic conglomerates (*chaebols*) such as CJ Group and LG Corp. This cultural infrastructure is largely responsible for Korea's national institutional *Hallyu-hwa* or *Hallyuization*, the media machine that engages critics, fans and consumers in a local and global context.[10]

Hallyu, as a reflection of Korea and its cultural infrastructure, is not a static concept or entity. The dominance of English language work on Hallyu reveals the extent to which it needs to be considered as "multi-layered and multi-directional," to use Eun-young Jung's words, given that it creates so many socio-cultural contacts that take "place across, beyond, and outside national and institutional boundaries."[11] Just a small snapshot of some recent English language academic work reveals that Hallyu is currently being explored in relation to an ever increasing array of sociocultural, econopolitical and technological aspects including its impact on cultural[12] and gender identity,[13] social impact in Asia[14] and beyond in countries such as America[15], Argentina,[16] the Czech Republic,[17] Israel,[18] Poland,[19] Romania,[20] and the United Kingdom.[21] Its dissemination and use in online participatory cultures and via social media is also a current focus[22] as is its utilization as a tool of soft power and cultural policy.[23] Hallyu's multi-layered and multidirectional nature is also exemplified by the various stages and rapid transformations cultural critics have already identified in its development and marketing of various cultural products: For example, "Hallyu 1.0" is commonly used to define the initial wave of the success of Korean television dramas and feature films, as mentioned earlier in this article, that occurred prior to the turn of the millennium and the first decade after. "Hallyu 2.0" is used to distinguish a perceived second phase that followed from the first in which Korean music or "K-pop" was seen to be driving the Korean Wave through the international success of K-pop groups such as *Girls Generation, 2NE1*, and *Big Bang* to name but a few. "Hallyu 3.0" is the latest phase being promoted and disseminated and is a government-led initiative. The Korean Cultural Ministry has "put almost all areas with which the cultural ministry is concerned—except religion—under the umbrella of the Korean Wave and gave them the fashionable prefix 'K': K-fine art, K-traditional arts and K-literature and so on." This has been done in the belief that "many areas of 'Kculture' can ride the Korean Wave" and bring "Korean people's distinct spirit, identity and character" across national borders.[24]

While these categorizations denote a linear, progressive development of Hallyu that in itself can be disputed (K-pop was hugely important in "Hallyu 1.0," television drama remains hugely important in the era of "Hallyu 3.0"), the expansion and dominance of Hallyu into so many different aspects of the Korean cultural and media industries, and the amount of capital invested by the Korean government in the process, have increased to the point where now the term begs the question: what aspects of Korean popular culture are beyond its grasp or influence?

We suggest in this article that some form of qualification or "disclaimer" is required to distinguish what is still unclaimed by Hallyu and we propose "beyond Hallyu" as a term to assist in achieving this. Clearly, what comprises Hallyu (or the Korean Wave) is as fluid and changing as a wave itself and so "beyond Hallyu" is a fluid addition to a fluid definition that serves to aid in identifying what still lies beyond the borders of the growing, ever more encompassing Korean Wave classification. What we find pertinent in our coinage "beyond Hallyu" is that it offers a much-needed corrective to demarcate the continuing, but changing, dynamic cultural forces in Korea that have been so overshadowed in the past two decades by the Hallyu phenomenon. We define "beyond Hallyu" as an auxiliary type of cultural flow, exemplified often by lower and micro budget productions of film, television and art with an independent sensibility not beholden to the machinations of Hallyu production and representations; beyond Hallyu can also be unconventional and at times subversive in the topics it presents, measured in large part by its participation in Korea's creative and culture discourses *from below* in the vein of the History Workshop and its key thinkers: Raphael Samuel, Raymond Williams, E. P. Thompson, and Christopher Hill. These British historians of a Marxian predisposition sought to excavate local histories from common people—usually concerning the social histories of miners' unions, amateur clubs, extracts of pauper letters, and oral recounts of folklore and customs of the British working class—to shift emphasis away from institutional or political histories of great men or global events. Such new histories go beyond state controlled authorized versions of the past and ensure that authentic working class social and cultural history rather than ideological narratives constructed on behalf of this social class are recorded and find a place. To find such a place is what many beyond Hallyu texts warrant as they often, in filmic and televisual terms, present Korea's society and culture, past and present, from below, but in new ways. Many beyond Hallyu texts deal with urban poverty and have not "abandoned the poor in favor of the glittering lives of the better off," in the words of Tim Hitchcock,[25] whilst others concentrate on issues relating to sexual identity, regional intellectual traditions, and middle-class non-conformity in ways that are specific to contemporary Korea.

One television example of a beyond-Hallyu text with an "independent sensibility" is *Life is Beautiful* (SBS 2010), which explores the lives of gay Koreans and Korean homophobia; this point is discussed at length in Glynn and Kim's article within this special issue.[26] In regards to cinema, a prominent and recent example of a beyond Hallyu film is the controversial documentary *The Truth Shall Not Sink With Sewol*, perhaps better known as *The Diving Bell*, directed by Lee Sang-ho and Ahn Hae-ryong in 2014. This film concerns the tragic sinking of the Korean MV Sewol ferry on April 16, 2014, in which more than 300 passengers perished. What made this event all the more shocking was that the majority of passengers were high school students on a school trip and were instructed by the crew to stay onboard the capsized vessel to await rescue before the captain and the majority of the crew proceeded to abandon the ship. The remaining passengers as a consequence perished within a matter of hours as they sent farewell text messages, phone calls, and pictures to their family and friends. In the days and weeks following the incident, outrage spread across Korea over the widespread corruption and ineptitude revealed at all levels that lead to, and resulted in, the tragic sinking: the cargo in the ferry had been overloaded on the part of the owners to maximize profit; collusion and then a blind-eye had been turned by government regulators, evidenced through their failure to report this oversight through proper channels; a poorly trained captain and many crew members abandoned both the ship and its passengers who they left behind to drown; an apparently unprepared Korean coast guard failed to rescue any survivors after the initial capsizing of the vessel. . . and the list went on. Compounding this tragedy was the Korean government's late and confused responses to the crisis that publicly exposed the corruption and culpability of various government agencies who were covering up for one another, ultimately resulting in the resignation of Korea's prime minister Jung Hong-won. Completed within only six months of the sinking, *The Diving Bell* does not at all seek to incorporate different points of view but rather intends to create moral indignation and outrage through its guerilla style shooting that follows one man's attempt to help in the rescue attempt and then to seek answers afterwards about the tragedy from the authorities. Its screening at the Busan International Film Festival (BIFF) in 2014, arguably Korea's largest and most prestigious international film festival, created a conflict over control concerning what content could and could not be viewed at the festival between its organizers who screened *The Diving Bell* and the Busan city government and its mayor and festival chairman, Seo Byung-soo, who sought to prevent it from being screened. As of this writing, the repercussions of this conflict continue still in 2016 with a threatened boycott over the BIFF by a number of filmmakers and artists after the city government forced its co-executive director Lee Yong-Kwan to resign. The film's bold critique of the Korean government and the pressure placed on those who screened it by governmental forces continue to directly impact the discourse over the freedom of expression in Korean film exhibition to this day. The film itself offers a political and social "oppositional" or "counter" reading that is beyond the state-sanctioned Korean positivism implicit in much of the Hallyu cultural branding. Another aspect of *The Diving Bell* that places it in our category of beyond Hallyu is that its creators worked independently in terms of the production of the project rather than working for a corporate or state-sponsored film studio or production company.

The Diving Bell is emblematic of oppositional documentary cinema in Korea that has existed long before Hallyu. For example, the Korean *Minjung* documentary film movement (discussed by Park, Lee and Wagner in this special issue[27]) was another form of cinema from below that existed in the 1980s that challenged the political status quo at that time and also faced censorship. Beyond Hallyu, however, also encompasses work that confronts not just regimes but also challenges, or goes beyond, accepted cinematic and televisual aesthetics, genres, and terminologies and is independent in spirit by representing marginal viewpoints and experiences outside the domain of the Hallyu consciousness. The term *Hallyu* inevitably raises the question of what constitutes a Korean experience in its various manifestations.

One noted filmmaker who embraces a marginal viewpoint is Kelvin Kyung Kun Park who studied in the United States for a number of years before returning to Seoul to make his experimental documentaries *Cheonggyecheon Medley* (2010) and *A Dream of Iron* (2013), which premiered at the Berlinale in 2014 and then screened at New York's Museum of Modern Art

(MoMA). His documentaries consist of collages of different documentary conventions or film styles used to document the social subject, or what Bill Nichols categorizes as the poetic, expository, observational, participatory, the reflexive, and performative modes in his seminal book *Introduction to Documentary* (2001).[28] Using iron as a metaphor, *Cheonggyecheon Medley* combines observational footage of a group of iron workers from Seoul's *Cheonggyecheon* neighborhood facing gentrification and who struggle to make ends meet in their marginal existence within Korea's neoliberal economy. In the film Park uses found and archival footage from Korean and Japanese newsreels, feature films and television shows to help articulate the development of Korea's "compressed modernity" through its iron and steel industries. Park rewrites and intertwines these social/industrial histories with his own voice-over that consists of a one-sided dialogue with his deceased grandfather who also made a living working with metal during the Japanese occupation of Korea and thereafter. Park evokes his personal thoughts and fears as he describes himself as being "haunted" by iron in the form of a reoccurring nightmare presented via montages, animation, and Paulo Vivacqua's industrial musical score that are all interlaced throughout the film. Park's collage of these different documentary modes reveals how each depicts or represents the social subject of iron in a different cinematic manner—as a way of life in the observational mode, as a vital economic force in Korea's modernity in the archival footage, and as representing a close bond between grandfather and grandson in his voice-over. In sum: Park creates an alternative, subjective history of these ironworkers as well as foregrounding his own marginal subjectivity as a former Korean ex-patriot through the use of his fractured and evocative approaches to filmmaking.

A Dream of Iron is a more expansive documentary, an essay film that combines found footage of the lives of whales, observational footage of a Hyundai industrial facility contrasted with archival footage of its construction, Vivacqua's hypnotic score, and Park's voiceover that opens the film reading aloud a letter from a former girlfriend who is seeking a form of spiritual nourishment, suggested visually within the documentary through archival footage of religious ceremonies. Park, as in his former documentary, juxtaposes these various different documentary modes to create an open-ended, fractured, experimental documentary that can also be considered contemporary art and visual anthropology. Park belongs to a recent generation of Korean documentary filmmakers, such as Lee Kang-hyun (who directed *The Color of Pain* [2010]) and Moon Seung-wook (who directed *The Watchtower* [2014]), who are pushing the aesthetic and critical boundaries of visual ethnography well beyond that offered by the mainstream Korean media industry, albeit primarily in the venues of film festivals, museum screenings, and art houses.

While these are only a couple of documentary examples that we consider beyond Hallyu texts, there are a whole range of feature films and television shows that also embody similar independent sensibilities: *Jiseul* (2012), for example, is an independent feature directed by Jeju native O Muel that depicts the 1948 Jeju massacre of locals by Korean government forces from the point of view of the local islanders, portraying another marginal Korean experience that has seldom been given expression. Shot in black-and-white, and featuring a cast of local actors speaking in their Jeju dialect, the film had a small budget of 210 million won ($190,000) that was partly crowd funded,[29] circumventing state or corporate sponsorship or input. It became the first Korean film to win the prestigious Grand Jury Prize at the Sundance Film Festival. Based largely on word of mouth dissemination, it screened in more than 60 theaters in Korea and eventually became the most viewed independent dramatic film ever in Korea, replacing Yank Ik-June's independent hit *Breathless* (2008) which had held the record since 2008.[30]

It may seem as though we are advocating a binary cultural nexus here: on the one side, government-supported, heavily financed and groomed Hallyu, while, on the other side, cultural producers who seem to purportedly avoid spectral-like hype, have failed to ascend the ladder of Korean media (that is endemic to the industry), or denounce the institutional hegemony of Hallyu altogether. In short: *Hallyu* versus *anti-Hallyu* or *non-Hallyu*. However, to put the cultural flow of Korea in a larger comparative context with other national film industries, for a moment, we consider China's post-Tiananmen underground and independent scenes, the subjects of Paul G. Pickowicz and Yingjin Zhang's 2006 anthologized *From Underground to Independent*, as a pertinent parallel exploration of other Asian underground or non-mainstream cultural production occurring in the region. Its editors call for more scholarship devoted "to the immensely rich materials produced by Chinese underground films, whose social, ideological, and aesthetic significance calls for in-depth investigation."[31] Like Pickowicz, and Zhang, we believe cultural productions of an independent ilk reveal alternative voices and often telling perceptions about our societies under increased monetization, corporatization and in many cases political censorship; though, of course, such work in Korea can still be understood occasionally as lighthearted, idiosyncratic or solipsistic in their narrative footprint and inexorably tied to, or affected by, mainstream cultural forces even when operating as counterforce. Thus, as with the case of *Life Is Beautiful* discussed elsewhere in this issue of the *Quarterly Review of Film and Video*, a text can be beyond Hallyu even when produced within established cultural industries.

Nevertheless, the divisible aspects of work we associate as beyond Hallyu seem one practicable means to historicize and conceptualize the expansion of independent moving image culture in Korea since at least the 1980s. *Beyond Hallyu* as a definition articulates creative success beyond financial metrics and proprietary consciousness in and outside of Korea. While Hallyu products, through various approved "productive, distributive and cultural processes" have become at the very least "a semi-global phenomenon,"[32] beyond Hallyu products receive an evident lack of promotion and marketing or support with production processes (MediAct and Wildflower being two examples of only a very few cultural infrastructures operating in the country that support very low-budget film production). While many of those who produce work of an independent sensibility operate in a smaller scale of production with more modest aspirations to see work circulate on their own terms often within their civic, class and social circles, this article and others within this special issue ultimately encourage a greater seeking out and identification of important independent work often falling below the media parapet, both regionally and globally; it is here that we draw attention to the scale and importance of beyond Hallyu products to allow them to orbit not just beyond but also to parallel Hallyu's production, and to encourage further scholarship, awareness, and support for these vital works and their creative producers.

Notes

1 Thomson, "A Very Good Korea Move," in *Mail on Sunday Event*, p. 36.
2 Lee, "USA's 'Suits' to Get South Korean Remake," in *Hollywood Reporter*.
3 McNary, Korean Action-Thriller 'Man From Nowhere' Getting Remake from New Line in *Variety*.
4 Park, "Transnational Adoption, *Hallyu*, and the Politics of Korean Popular Culture," in *Biography*, p. 159.
5 Shin, "Art of Branding: Tartan 'Asia Extreme' Films," in *Jump Cut: A Review of Contemporary Media*.
6 "How Korean Culture Stormed the World," in *South China Morning Post*. <http://www.scmp.com/news/asia/article/1094145/how-korean-culture-stormed-world2_
7 "Gangnam Style becomes YouTube's most-viewed video," in *BBC News*.
8 Glynn and Kim, "'Oppa'-tunity Knocks: Psy, 'Gangnam Style' and the Press Reception of K-Pop in Britain," in *Situations: Cultural Studies in the Asian Context*, p. 12.
9 Kim, "Introduction: Korean Media in a Digital Cosmopolitan World," in *The Korean Wave: Korean Media Go Global*, p. 2.
10 Choi, "Hallyu versus Hallyu-hwa: Cultural Phenomenon versus Institutional Campaign," in *Hallyu 2.0: The Korean Wave in the Age of Social Media*.
11 Jung, "Transnational Korea: A Critical Assessment of the Korean Wave in Asia and the United States," in *Southeast Review of Asian Studies*, p. 70.
12 Yoon, "Cultural Identity and Korean Historical Television Drama," in *The Global Impact of South Korean Popular Culture: Hallyu Unbound*.

13 Chan, "'Like a Virgin:' Sex, Marriage and Gender Relations in the Korean TV Drama *Wedding*," in *Reading Asian Television Drama: Crossing Borders and Breaking Boundaries*; Epstein and Turnbull, "Girls Generation? Gender, (Dis)empowerment, and K-Pop," in *The Korean Popular Culture Reader*; Jung, "K-Pop Female Idols in the West: Racial Imagination and Erotic Fantasies," in *The Korean Wave: Korean Media Go Global*; Oh, "The Politics of the Dancing Body: Racialized and Gendered Femininity in K-Pop," in *The Korean Wave: Korean Popular Culture in Global Context*.
14 Kuwahara, Yasue. *Hanryu*: Korean Popular Culture in Japan," in *The Korean Wave: Korean Popular Culture in Global Context*; Nugroho, "Hallyu in Indonesia," in *The Global Impact of South Korean Popular Culture: Hallyu Unbound*; Takeda, "Japanese-Korean International Marriages through the Korean Wave in Japan," in *The Global Impact of South Korean Popular Culture: Hallyu Unbound*.
15 Lee and Nornes, *Hallyu 2.0: The Korean Wave in the Age of Social Media*; Molen, "A Cultural Imperialist Homecoming: The Korean Wave Reaches the United States," in *The Korean Wave: Korean Popular Culture in Global Context*; Park, "Negotiating Identity and Power in Transnational Cultural Consumption: Korean American Youths and the Korean Wave," in *The Korean Wave: Korean Media Go Global*.
16 Iadevito, "Hallyu and Cultural Identity: A Sociological Approach to the Korean Wave in Argentina," in *The Global Impact of South Korean Popular Culture: Hallyu Unbound*.
17 Mazaná, "Cultural Perception and Social Impact of the Korean Wave in the Czech Republic," in *The Global Impact of South Korean Popular Culture: Hallyu Unbound*.
18 Lyan and Levkowitz, "Consuming the Other: Israeli Hallyu Case Study," in *Hallyu 2.0: The Korean Wave in the Age of Social Media*.
19 Kida, "Wind of Change: Poland is One Step Away from the Korean Wave," in *The Global Impact of South Korean Popular Culture: Hallyu Unbound*.
20 Marinescu and Balica, "Audience Perceptions and Representations of Korea: The Romanian Experience," in *The Global Impact of South Korean Popular Culture: Hallyu Unbound*.
21 Balmain, "Pop Goes Korean popular Culture: An Investigation into the Popularity of *Hallyu* Culture in the UK," in *The Global Impact of South Korean Popular Culture: Hallyu Unbound*.
22 Islam, "'I rili lyke dis:' Forum Culture and the Cosmopolitan Spacing of Asian Television Online," in *Reading Asian Television Drama: Crossing Borders and Breaking Boundaries*; Lee, "As Seen on the Internet: The Recap as Translation in English-Language K-Drama Fandoms," in *The Korean Popular Culture Reader*; Lee and Nornes, Hallyu 2.0; Sung, "Digitization and Online Cultures of the Korean Wave: 'East Asian' Virtual Community in Europe," in *The Korean Wave: Korean Media Go Global*.
23 Nye and Kim, "Soft Power and the Korean Wave." *The Korean Wave: Korean Media Go Global*; Lee, "Cultural Policy and the Korean Wave: From National Culture to Transnational Consumerism," in *The Korean Wave: Korean Media Go Global*; Walsh, "Hallyu as a Government Construct: The Korean Wave in the Context of Economic and Social Development," in *The Korean Wave: Korean Popular Culture in Global Context*.
24 Lee, Cultural Policy, p. 192.
25 Hitchcock, "A New History from Below." *History Workshop Journal*, p. 296.
26 Glynn and Kim, "*Life is Beautiful*: Gay Representation, Moral Panics, and South Korean Television Drama Beyond *Hallyu*," in *Quarterly Review of Film and Video*.
27 Park, Lee, and Wagner, "Changing Representations of the Urban Poor in Korean Independent Cinema: *Minjung* Heroes, Atomized Paupers, and New Possibilities," in *Quarterly Review of Film and Video*.
28 Nichols, *Introduction to Documentary*.
29 Park, "Arthouse Film *Jiseul* trailblazing at box office," in *The Korea Herald*.
30 Ji, "JISEUL Becomes Most Viewed Independent Film," in *Korean Film Council*.
31 Pickowicz and Zhang, *From Underground to Independent: Alternative Film Culture in Contemporary China*, p. vii.
32 Choi and Maliangkay, Introduction: Why Fandom Matters to the International Rise of K-Pop, p. 1.

Works Cited

Balmain, Colette. Pop Goes Korean Popular Culture: An Investigation into the Popularity of *Hallyu* Culture in the UK. *The Global Impact of South Korean Popular Culture: Hallyu Unbound*, edited by Valentina Marinescu (Lanham, MD: Lexington, 2014), pp. 81–87.

Chan, Brenda. "Like a Virgin:" Sex, Marriage and Gender Relations in the Korean TV Drama. *Wedding*. *Reading Asian Television Drama: Crossing Borders and Breaking Boundaries*, edited by Jeongmee Kim (London, UK: I.B. Tauris, 2014), pp. 169–189.

Choi, Jung Bong. Hallyu versus Hallyu-hwa: Cultural Phenomenon versus Institutional Campaign. *Hallyu 2.0: The Korean Wave in the Age of Social Media*, edited by Sangjoon Lee and Abé Mark Nornes (Ann Arbor, MI: University of Michigan Press, 2015), pp. 31–52.

Choi, Jung Bong and Roald Maliangkay. Introduction: Why Fandom Matters to the International Rise of K-Pop. *K-pop: The International Rise of the Korean Music Industry*, edited by Choi, Jung Bong and Roald Maliangkay (London: Routledge, 2014), pp. 1–18.

Epstein, Stephen, and Turnbull, James. Girls Generation? Gender, (Dis)empowerment, and K-Pop. *The Korean Popular Culture Reader*, edited by Kyung Hyun Kim and Youngmin Choe (Durham, NC: Duke University Press, 2014), pp. 314–336.

Gangnam Style becomes YouTube's most-viewed video. *BBC News*. December 25, 2012. <http://www.bbc.co.uk/news/technology-20483087>

Glynn, Basil, and Kim, Jeongmee. *Life is Beautiful*: Gay Representation, Moral Panics, and South Korean Television Drama Beyond *Hallyu*. *Quarterly Review of Film and Video* (2016), *34*(4), epub ahead of print.

Glynn, Basil, and Kim, Jeongmee. "Oppa'-tunity Knocks: Psy, "Gangnam Style" and the Press Reception of K-Pop in Britain. *Situations: Cultural Studies in the Asian Context* 7:1 (Winter 2013/14), 1–20.

Hitchcock, Tim. A New History from Below. *History Workshop Journal* 57 (2004), 294–298. How Korean Culture Stormed the World. *South China Morning Post*. November 30, 2012. <http://www.scmp.com/news/asia/article/1094145/how-korean-culture-stormed-world>

Iadevito, Paula. Hallyu and Cultural Identity: A Sociological Approach to the Korean Wave in Argentina. *The Global Impact of South Korean Popular Culture: Hallyu Unbound*, edited by Valentina Marinescu (Lanham, MD: Lexington, 2014), pp. 135–148.

Islam, Maimuna Dali. "I rili lyke dis:" Forum Culture and the Cosmopolitan Spacing of Asian Television Online. *Reading Asian Television Drama: Crossing Borders and Breaking Boundaries*, edited by Jeongmee Kim (London, UK: I.B. Tauris, 2014), pp. 75–100.

Ji, Yong-jin. JISEUL Becomes Most Viewed Independent Film. *Korean Film Council*, 24 April 2013. <http://www.koreanfilm.or.kr/jsp/news/news.jsp?modeDVIEW&seqD2435>

Jung, Eun-young. K-Pop Female Idols in the West: Racial Imagination and Erotic Fantasies. *The Korean Wave: Korean Media Go Global*, edited by Youna Kim (London, UK: Routledge, 2013), pp. 106–119.

Jung, Eun-young. Transnational Korea: A Critical Assessment of the Korean Wave in Asia and the United States. *Southeast Review of Asian Studies* 31 (2009): 69–80.

Kida, Pawel. Wind of Change: Poland is One Step Away from the Korean Wave. *The Global Impact of South Korean Popular Culture: Hallyu Unbound*, edited by Valentina Marinescu (Lanham, MD: Lexington, 2014), pp. 65–74.

Kim, Youna. Introduction: Korean Media in a Digital Cosmopolitan World. *The Korean Wave: Korean Media Go Global*, edited by Youna Kim (London: Routledge, 2013), pp. 1–27.

Kuwahara, Yasue. Hanryu: Korean Popular Culture in Japan. *The Korean Wave: Korean Popular Culture in Global Context*, edited by Yasue Kuwahara (New York, NY: Palgrave McMillian, 2014), 213–221.

Lee, Hye-Kyung. Cultural Policy and the Korean Wave: From National Culture to Transnational Consumerism. *The Korean Wave: Korean Media Go Global*, edited by Youna Kim (London, UK: Routledge, 2013), pp. 185–198.

Lee, Hyo-won. USA's "Suits" to Get South Korean Remake. *Hollywood Reporter*, June 2, 2015 <http://www.hollywoodreporter.com/news/suits-get-south-korean-remake-799436>

Lee, Regina Yung. As Seen on the Internet: The Recap as Translation in English-Language KDrama Fandoms. *The Korean Popular Culture Reader*, edited by Kyung Hyun Kim and Youngmin Choe (Durham, NC: Duke University Press, 2014), pp. 76–97.

Lee, Sangjoon, and Nornes, Abé Mark, eds. *Hallyu 2.0: The Korean Wave in the Age of Social Media* (Ann Arbor, MI: University of Michigan Press, 2015).

Lyan, Irina, and Levkowitz, Alon. Consuming the Other: Israeli Hallyu Case Study. *Hallyu 2.0: The Korean Wave in the Age of Social Media*, edited by Sangjoon Lee and Abé Mark Nornes (Ann Arbor, MI: University of Michigan Press, 2015), pp. 212–228.

Marinescu, Valentina, and Balica, Ecaterina. Audience Perceptions and Representations of Korea: The Romanian Experience. *The Global Impact of South Korean Popular Culture: Hallyu Unbound*, edited by Valentina Marinescu (Lanham, MD: Lexington, 2014), pp. 89–103.

Mazaná, Vladislava. Cultural Perception and Social Impact of the Korean Wave in the Czech Republic. *The Global Impact of South Korean Popular Culture: Hallyu Unbound*, edited by Valentina Marinescu (Lanham, MD: Lexington, 2014), pp. 47–63.

McNary, Dave. Korean Action-Thriller 'Man From Nowhere' Getting Remake from New Line. *Variety*, June 26, 2016. <http://variety.com/2016/film/news/man-from-nowhere-remake-korean-new-line-1201806149/>

Molen, Sherri L. Ter. A Cultural Imperialist Homecoming: The Korean Wave Reaches the United States. *The Korean Wave: Korean Popular Culture in Global Context*, edited by Yasue Kuwahara (New York, NY: Palgrave McMillian, 2014), pp. 149–187.

Nichols, Bill. *Introduction to Documentary* (Bloomington, IN: Indiana University Press, 2001). Nugroho, Suray Agung. Hallyu in Indonesia. *The Global Impact of South Korean Popular Culture: Hallyu Unbound*, edited by Valentina Marinescu (Lanham, MD: Lexington, 2014), pp. 19–32.

Nye, Joseph and Kim, Youna. Soft Power and the Korean Wave. *The Korean Wave: Korean Media Go Global*, edited by Youna Kim (London, UK: Routledge, 2013), pp. 31–42.

Oh, Chuyun. The Politics of the Dancing Body: Racialized and Gendered Femininity in K-Pop. *The Korean Wave: Korean Popular Culture in Global Context*, edited by Yasue Kuwahara (New York: Palgrave McMillian, 2014), pp. 53–81.

Park, Jung-Sun. Negotiating Identity and Power in Transnational Cultural Consumption: Korean American Youths and the Korean Wave. *The Korean Wave: Korean Media Go Global*, edited by Youna Kim (London, UK: Routledge, 2013), pp. 120–134.

Park, So Young. Transnational Adoption, Hallyu, and the Politics of Korean Popular Culture. *Biography* 33.1 (2010): 151–166.

Park, Sui. Arthouse film *Jiseul* trailblazing at box office. *The Korea Herald* March 28, 2013. <http://www.koreaherald.com/view.php?udD20130328000661>

Park, Young-a, Lee, Do-hoon, and Wagner, Keith B. Changing Representations of the Urban Poor in Korean Independent Cinema: *Minjung* Heroes, Atomized Paupers, and New Possibilities. *Quarterly Review of Film and Video, 34*(4), epub ahead of print.

Pickowicz, Paul, and Zhang, Yingjin eds. *From Underground to Independent: Alternative Film Culture in Contemporary China* (Lanham, MD: Rowman & Littlefield, 2006).

Shin, Chi-Yun. Art of Branding: Tartan 'Asia Extreme' Films. *Jump Cut: A Review of Contemporary Media* 50 (2008). <http://www.ejumpcut.org/archive/jc50.2008/TartanDist/> Sung, Sang-yeon. Digitization and Online Cultures of the Korean Wave: 'East Asian' Virtual Community in Europe. *The Korean Wave: Korean Media Go Global*, edited by Youna Kim (London, UK: Routledge, 2013), pp. 135–147.

Takeda, Atsushi. Japanese-Korean International Marriages through the Korean Wave in Japan. *The Global Impact of South Korean Popular Culture: Hallyu Unbound*, edited by Valentina Marinescu (Lanham, MD: Lexington, 2014), pp. 35–45.

Thomson, Graeme. A Very Good Korea Move. *Mail on Sunday Event* August 31, 2014, 36.

Walsh, John. Hallyu as a Government Construct: The Korean Wave in the Context of Economic and Social Development. *The Korean Wave: Korean Popular Culture in Global Context*, edited by Yasue Kuwahara (New York, NY: Palgrave McMillian, 2014), pp. 13–32.

Yoon, Sunny. Cultural Identity and Korean Historical Television Drama. *The Global Impact of South Korean Popular Culture: Hallyu Unbound*, edited by Valentina Marineu. Lanham, MD: Lexington, 2014, pp. 7–17.

* **First published as the article: "Beyond *Hallyu*: Innovation, Social Critique, and Experimentation in South Korean Cinema and Television" by Jeongmee Kim, Michael A. Unger and Keith B. Wagner, *Quarterly Review of Film and Video* (2017) 34:4, pp. 321–332. Reprinted by permission of Taylor & Francis Ltd, http://www.tandfonline.com**

20 The Marketization of Bollywood*

Somjit Barat

Who has not heard the name *Bollywood*? It boasts of a worldwide audience spanning across almost six continents (3.3 million in North America, 2.3 million in the United Kingdom, 2.6 million in the Gulf States, and 1.1 million in South Africa as its biggest markets), and produces arguably about 1000 films per year, which translates to almost three movies per day, including weekends.[1] India, at its peak film production, produced 1325 films in 2008 and 1255 films in 2011, and was way ahead of second-ranked United States (819 films in 2011).[2]

Until 2000, however, Bollywood was still entrenched in post-colonial managerial practices, run only by a handful of movie houses, production companies, and studios. Patriarchal individuals/families, such as the Kapoors and the Chopras, ran Bollywood and called the shots at each stage of movie production from ideation to commercial screening.

However, since the Indian government accorded "industry" status to the business of filmmaking in May 1998 (referred to as the "corporatization" of Bollywood by Punathambekar[3]), the entire Bollywood landscape has undergone a sea change. In the space of the past 15 years, what was so far a disjointed, casual, and largely chaotic conglomeration of powerful individuals from the movie industry, began a trajectory of transformation towards a "modern" organization... an organization that began to work in a more professional, organized, and Hollywood-based model.

The bold step of giving a corporate structure to Bollywood by the Indian government also had both short- and long-term consequences for the Indian entertainment sector in general and the film industry in particular. It changed the perception of the film world both in the eyes of the Indian populace and industrialists. The Indian intelligentsia—versus the "common man" who goes to the movie at the end of day just to relieve the stress of a hard day's work—began to take Indian movies more seriously, to care about what is good and what is not, and to contribute to the development and growth of the medium in a positive manner through constructive criticism and intellectual participation.

Needless to mention that, thus far, movie production functions consisted mainly of patchwork and ad hoc type arrangements. These responsibilities were executed by a few experienced film personalities who had been around long enough to navigate the circuitous alleys of Bollywood, and who knew to pull the right strings and grease the right palms to get things accomplished. However, once the Indian government's formal approval came through, from a business perspective, it spurred development of in-house, structured, and more professional movie establishments. These efforts included directorial, financial, technical, scripting, editorial, and other infrastructural ventures.

In contrast, this change "upgraded" the outlook of Bollywood from the perspective of the outside world. Foreign collaboration and participation in Bollywood, both in acting and otherwise, are nothing new. But what the Indian government's action did was to open up more opportunities for bigger ventures in terms of joint ventures, sharing technical expertise, distribution, and copyrights. This expansion happened both ways: foreign movie house and venture capitalists began to show interest in Bollywood operations, and, at the same time, Indian industrialists purchased stake in western companies (such as Anil Ambani's Reliance Industries partnering with Spielberg's DreamWorks Studios).

None of these changes happened overnight, nor are any "complete," by any stretch of imagination. Nonetheless, Bollywood films can no longer be considered to be a "pushover" or be discarded as a mishmash of ludicrous events interspersed with catchy songs and hysterical dancing around trees. Part of this radical transformation is reflected by several international awards bagged by Indian-based/origin movies and/or Indian film personalities: Satyajit Ray won a Lifetime Achievement Oscar in 1992 in additional to several other international awards; *Slumdog Millionaire* won eight Oscars in 2009, including three Oscars by A. R. Rahman and two other Indians, while *Life of Pi* won four Oscars in 2013.

It must be noted that the term *Bollywood* is casually used to refer to Indian cinema industry in general. Given that Indian movies are produced in upwards of 20 major languages, not all of them are as prominent and popular as those that are produced in Hindi, India's national language. As such, the context of the current research is limited to the Hindi film industry, which we will frequently refer to as *Bollywood* for the purpose of our discussion.

In this article, we first analyze the brief history of Indian cinema prior to its gaining industry status. Then we consider how this unique form of mass entertainment has influenced and was influenced by the Indian common man. Next we focus on how Mumbai is not just the center of this cinema, but also harbors links to other cinema hubs such as Hollywood, New York, and London, and how television and digital media have had their stakes changed forever by the ever-increasing push from Bollywood. We then present a discussion of how the marriage between Bollywood and the game of cricket has changed both entertainment and sports landscapes of India. The article discussion concludes with several interesting and groundbreaking ideas for future research, especially from a marketing standpoint, while outlining a detailed and realistic picture of what might be in store for the industry.

Brief History of Indian Cinema

Bombay (now Mumbai) is the heart of Indian cinema. Popularly known as *Bollywood*, it churns out several blockbusters (by Indian standards) every year. Our current research focuses on Hindi movies, which are the most popular both in India and abroad, of all the other Indian language movies produced (numbering to more than 1000 per year). In fact, India became the largest producer of films in the world, producing 433 films as early as in 1971. To date, India has given birth to about 27,000 full-length feature films, not to mention the countless other documentaries.[4]

India's first feature film was *King Harishchandra*, a silent movie released in 1913, while the first official "talkie" was *Alam Ara* in 1931.[5] The industry was worth $1.8b in 2006[6] and is expected to reach revenues of $4.5b by 2016.[7] Ironically, less than 4% of Indians go to the movies regularly. If these numbers can be increased even moderately, the revenues will also look healthier. Add to this the fact that Indian movies cost considerably less to make ($1.5 million, compared with an average Hollywood movie costing $47.7 million). Arguably, it is relatively easier for the distributors and producers to turn a profit, and the possibilities are endless. However, India has about 13,000 movie theaters versus 40,000 in the United States.[8]

Theoretical Framework

Bollywood movies have been the staple diet for entertainment both in terms of affordability and quality. Even until a decade ago, a movie visit would cost no more than a couple of dollars including concessions. Given the mass scale at which they were (and still are) being produced, there was something for everyone, irrespective of age, sex, education level, economic status, social status, or interest. Movie stars are considered larger than life, often catapulted to the same pedestal as Gods, even by the cognoscenti! Such is the fan following of the stars that people will do anything (bordering on absurd and hysterical) to catch a glimpse of the "demi-Gods." It is, therefore, only fair that we review how Bollywood has not only evolved as a major force to reckon with in the international arena but also provided positive energy and gumption to the promotion and marketing of "Brand India" to the outside world.

However, it is only in the recent years that Bollywood has attracted the attention of mainstream academics, much to the satisfaction of Indian movie buffs who have traditionally lamented the lack of serious research in this field. Nonetheless, such interest does not come even close to that of Hollywood: a quick search involving the terms *Bollywood* and *Hollywood* in the "abstract" field of ABI/INFORM complete database yield 4004 and 65,918 results, respectively.

This study draws from several theoretical underpinnings. The *globalization hybridity theory* originated in the 18th century fuelled mainly by the accusation of cultural and genetic "contamination" in several countries, including the United States. This effect was mainly accentuated by the European invasion, which basically displaced the local population in these countries. However, early in the 19th century, this theory acquired a new meaning motivated by anti-colonization movements. Several countries and/or regions experienced a strong pushback against European colonization and hegemony.

A fallout of these movements was *hybridity theory*, which emerged mainly in Africa, Latin America, Asia, and the mixed populace in the West. The fundamental characteristic of a "hybrid" population is their lack of strong attachment or adherence to any specific cultural norms. Instead, the population imbibes idiosyncrasies of the local environment, typically characterized by hybrid between the indigenous and the foreign culture.[9]

The current research also invokes the *cultural differentiation theory*,[10] which proposes that culture, over time, undergoes varying levels of metamorphosis due to both external and internal reasons, as well as evolutionary reasons. Some of these changes and metamorphoses are so extreme that traits of the original culture give ways to "morphed" versions and are hard to relate back to its roots. Such phenomena, evidently, are more common in large, cosmopolitan societies with a steady flow (both inward and outward) of multinational, multicultural, multiracial, nomadic, and opportunistic populations (such as in the United States) rather than in closely knit, conservative, and traditional societies (such as in India). Finally, our research also borrows from nuances of cultural art forms that depict, for example, media (especially films) as tools of "soft power" that mold, influence, and eventually transform people's feelings and perceptions about their self-being and the surroundings in which they thrive. Consequently, such soft power leads to the creation of social capital that "connects" the diaspora by a common theme,[11] irrespective of where they physically exist. The role of soft power becomes critical when individuals choose to live in a foreign (not a place of birth) environment for a prolonged period of time either due to immigration, educational opportunities, or employment compulsions. Under such circumstances, the individual is torn between merging with the local (foreign) culture and retaining whatever remains of the individual's indigenous culture. The end product is often a hotchpotch of both traditions and practices leading to a totally different "hybrid" culture, which is what motivates our current discussion, and is frequently referred to as the *Indian-American, Asian American*, or *Desi-American* subculture.

It is this intermingling and hybridity of cultures and their desperate attempt to cling to whatever little is left of their original "Indian" culture that binds the Indian diaspora by a common thread—which, in many cases, happens to be Bollywood. Research shows that for individuals of the Indian diaspora, no matter their age, profession, education level, marital status, income bracket or region of domicile, Bollywood is not just films, songs, and dances but almost a way of life.[12] Even so-called second-generation Indian offspring (i.e., those who were born and brought up in a foreign country) who have little, if any, direct connection to their homeland, seem to have a special liking for Bollywood. What makes our topic of discussion even more interesting and relevant is that a considerable segment of foreign nationals, especially in the former Soviet Union, the United States, many European countries, the Middle East, South Africa, and Australia who barely know Hindi (the Indian national language), seem to have a strong liking for Bollywood movies and songs. Numerous big cities and educational institutes in these countries host regular Bollywood shows and/or dance competitions, where foreigners participate more enthusiastically than their Indian counterparts.

In other words, this is a perfect example of globalization hybridity, characterized by a two-way effort of the guest and the host populations to embrace each other's cultures and mannerisms, despite the historical enmity the Indian and their British counterparts harbored towards each other. The author himself has met and interviewed several American and European individuals who regularly organize "Bollywood parties" at their private homes and who are more versed with Bollywood films, songs, and movie stars than the author himself. Despite that point, the *non-resident Indian population* (or *NRI*) strive to distinguish and distance themselves from the foreign culture that they are part of, either through their religious traditions, marriage within their own community, and emphasis on education as well as family values, which is a solid example of the cultural differentiation theory previously noted.[13]

Post-Corporatization of Bollywood

In addition, thanks to the recognition of official "industry" status to films in 1998, the sector witnessed several changes, both immediate and long term—some inconsequential, others profound. Given the vast and diverse nature of such changes, it is only appropriate we first discuss how corporatization altered the equation that Bollywood developed with international entities, and then explore the effects on the domestic entertainment scenario.

The International Perspective

As noted previously, the Indian movie industry has evolved considerably over the years, and due to the further liberalization of the government's policies since the late 1990s, a flurry of activities have involved international participation and assumed different formats, such as foreign capital injection and investment, foreign personnel participation (e.g., acting, direction, production), Bollywood awards, and the role of the Indian diaspora (e.g., shooting in foreign locales, incorporating Indian values and themes). In the following sections, we review each of these developments in brief, with appropriate anecdotes wherever applicable.

Foreign Capital Injection and Investment

One of the foremost effects of such transformation was felt in the business chemistry between Bollywood and Hollywood. To be sure, this interaction led to the flurry of foreign direct investment projects in the Indian entertainment sector. Spielberg's DreamWorks Studios, for example, got its much-needed cash ($875 million, to be precise) from India's Reliance BIG Entertainment.[14] The deal was also financed by Walt Disney and eight other multinational banks, which reflects the change in Western attitude towards Bollywood. To put it in the words of the Chairman and Chief Executive of Sony Pictures Entertainment, Michael Lynton:

The fact is that the business in India is becoming more and more like the rest of the world. It looks much more like a business that we understand than perhaps it did 10 or 15 years ago and the trend is to become more like that rather than less like that.[15]

Sanjay Leela Bhansali co-produced with Sony Pictures the film *Saawariya*, which was released worldwide in 2007 with about 1000 prints, whereas the number is on average 250. In fact, according to Kohli-Khandekar,[16] this release was the first time that one of top six

Hollywood studios produced an Indian film. Since then, Indian films have been seen in Top Ten lists of movies in the United Kingdom and United States. Percept Picture Company collaborated with Michael Douglas' production company Further Films and SaharaOne of India to co-produce the $50-million movie *Racing the Monsoon*. Recently, Sahara also announced collaboration with Hollywood producer Donald Rosenfeld in the form of the *Tree of Life* starring Colin Farrell.[17] Many entertainment companies such as Eros, Adlabs, India Film Company, and UTV are enlisted in the London Stock Exchange, all of which further vindicate global interest in the growth of Bollywood.[18]

Foreign Personnel Participation

India, being a former British colony, had considerable exposure to and intermingling with European culture, especially in the entertainment sector. Consequently, the presence of British actors and personnel both on and off the screen is nothing new for Bollywood, as far back to the very early Indian movies. The presence of foreign actors, stuntmen, technicians, and other personnel is nothing new in Bollywood, as far back to the very early Indian movies. Most of such roles, however, were for side characters, villains, vamps, or the "oppressor" of the helpless Indian common man.

The trend has continued ever since and in the most recent years, an increasing number of actors have made a beeline for Bollywood, with moderate to high levels of success: Sunny Leone (Canada), Katrina Kaif (United Kingdom), Jacqueline Fernandez (Sri Lanka), Nargis Fakhri (United States), Claudia (Poland), Elli Avram (Sweden–Greece), Barbara Mori (Mexico), Amy Jackson (Isle of Man), Giselli Monteiro (Brazil), and Yana Gupta (Czechoslovakia), to name a few.[19]

Interestingly, these actors have not only played the anchor role in multiple hit movies, but also participated in many highly popular reality shows or television shows (*Big Boss, Raw Star, CID, Comedy Nights*, to name a few of the top rated most recent ones), according to the website Bollymoviereviewz.com.[20] What is even more notable is the fact that most of these actors and film personnel have exhibited considerable ambition by learning the local language, culture, customs, and the modus operandi of the Bollywood world, not to mention their acting skills. Once again, such trends clearly indicate the growing interest in, and the increasing influence of Bollywood on the global population.

Bollywood Awards

For most major Bollywood film award ceremonies, foreign locations (rather than Indian) are the venues of choice. Such mega events as the Filmfare Awards, National Film Awards, and International Indian Film Academy Awards (IIFA) are held at exotic locales all over the world and are attended not just by "Who's Who" of the Indian film industry but also notable foreign movie celebrities and personalities, as well as local dignitaries. The last five venues for the IIFA awards, for example were Canada, Singapore, Macau, United States, and Malaysia, which provides us an idea of the clout that Bollywood has developed over the years.[21]

Such events not only draw the Indian diaspora from near and far and reflect of the ever-increasing popularity of the Indian film fraternity, but often also provide much-needed boost to the respective local economy.[22] It is, therefore, no wonder that such gala events are frequently blessed by the local government and/or administrative representative.

Role of the Indian Diaspora

Indian-origin people living abroad (popularly referred to as *non-resident Indians* or *NRIs*) have strong home ties. This characteristic is amply reflected in their penchant for imbibing Indian traditions, values, customs, and—in the present context—Bollywood. NRIs lap up every opportunity to experience the Indian movie magic by visiting movie theaters in big cities that regularly screen Indian movies, complete with ethnic fast food.[23]

This craze among NRIs for clinging on to their roots, especially Bollywood, is further exacerbated by regional cable and Internet services (often beamed from India in real-time) that feature a healthy dose of (sometimes exclusively) Indian movie-related content; Bollywood dance schools in urban areas, which also offer on-demand live entertainment at public events; copiously available films either for purchase or checkout at public libraries, and entertainment stores (e.g., retail stores such as Walmart as well as online streaming services such as Netflix, Hulu, YouTube, and Amazon Prime).

Both Bollywood and Hollywood have noticed such trend and have exploited the opportunity to the best available extent. Given the increasing numbers of NRIs, several western movies have either borrowed from, or based their creations on, Bollywood-based themes, especially the song and dance sequences. On one side, we have Bollywood movies that arouse the "Indian sentiment" among the diaspora by injecting an overdose of melodrama, twists, and turns (*Lagaan* [Land Tax], Dir. Gowariker 2001; *Kal Ho Naa Ho* [Tomorrow Never Comes], Dir. Advani 2003; *Kabhie Khushi Kabhi Gham* [Sometimes Happiness, Sometimes Sadness], Dirs. Johar and Johar, 2001).[24] For more specific numbers on the popularity of Bollywood movies in different regions, the reader may consult Abu-Lughod (Africa); Iordanova (Europe); and Rajagopalan (former Soviet Union).[25]

Recognizing the changing landscape and tastes of the Indian population (both within and outside the mainland), producers and directors have increasingly resorted to bold themes (sexual freedom and promiscuity, such as *Kama Sutra: A Tale of Love* (Dir. Mira Nair, 1996); *Dunno Y. . . Na Jaane Kyon* ([I Don't Know Why], Dir. Sanjay Sharma, 2010); *Dostana* ([Friendship], Dir., Tarun Mansukhani, 2008), and western themes and styles, spine-chiller action, including artificial intelligence (e.g., *Ra.One*, Dir. Anubhav Sinha, 2011; *Dhoom* [Storm], Dir. Sanjay Gadhvi, 2004, which also has two sequels). The success of such strategy on a global level is amply reflected in the fact that the movie *My Name is Khan* (Dir. Karan Johar, 2010) was ranked 21st among the top 30 feature films in 2010 and 2011.[26] Moreover, *My Name is Khan* is the highest ever foreign-grossing Indian film in history. Compared to other non-United States films at the top of the chart that were released by local distributors in the neighboring two to three countries, *My Name is Khan* was an exception in the sense that it was released by Fox Studios in about 30 countries worldwide.

On the other side, several western productions have borrowed from or are based on Bollywood themes (e.g., *The Best Exotic Marigold Hotel*, Dir. John Madden, 2011; *Bride & Prejudice*, Dir. Gurinder Chaddha, 2004; *Bend It Like Beckham*, Dir. Gurinder Chaddha, 2002; *Slumdog Millionaire*, Dirs. Danny Boyle and Loveleen Tandan, 2008; *Life of Pi*, Dir. Ang Lee, 2012). Most of these movies have grossed significantly at the box office by Indian standards, which have contributed to the popularity of Bollywood and overseas earnings of Bollywood movies (Table 1).

Foreign countries and tourist spots go out of their way to court Bollywood to organize their next event at those locations. Tourist agencies in countries such as Switzerland, United Kingdom, United States, South Africa, Afghanistan, and Greece (where many popular Indian movies have been shot in the recent past) are home to travel agencies who offer exclusive "Bollywood Packages" for tourists interested in "reliving" their Bollywood dreams.

The Domestic Perspective

With the Indian government's liberalization policy going into effect, several changes began to happen. Many of the movie houses (e.g., production, financing, distribution) began to enlist on

Table 20.1 Indian Movie Stats: Top Five Grossing Movies

Film	Budget ($ m)	Total Collection ($ million, domestic C overseas)
PK	19.98	103.13
Dhoom 3	27.98	86.66
Chennai Express	20.78	65.07
3 Idiots	5.59	63.16
Kick	22.38	56.76

the stock exchange. Most of the movie theaters, especially in big cities, began to be replaced by multiplexes, all of which were novelties for the populace who were still fed a staple diet of entertainment in age-old theaters, sometimes lacking even the basic facilities, such as clean restrooms and projection equipment. We will review two main aspects here: The evolving infrastructure and the Indian Premier League.

The Evolving Infrastructure

The "spanking-new" multiplexes, in contrast, not only boast of a superb viewing "experience" (thanks to fresh injection of interest and capital from different film entities), but also charge considerably higher prices, thereby effectively precluding the poor Indian from enjoying the latest advancements in the most popular form of entertainment. To be sure, per latest data available from the UNESCO Office of Statistics,[27] the number of multiplexes and movie attendance has held relatively steady over the past several years, even though overall rates have gone down, especially compared with rates in the United States. At the same time, such developments (intentional or otherwise) also helped maintain the professionalism, cleanliness, and high standards that are common in most Western multiplexes today.

Indian Premier League (IPL)

It is said that the game of cricket is *not a sport*, but *religion* in India. Just like movie stars, top cricketers in India not only make "megabucks," but they are also they are also worshipped as demi-Gods by the general population. The whole country goes into a tizzy during major cricket events, such as the recently concluded Cricket World Cup, the Champions Trophy, or the Indian Premier League (IPL), which is the latest addition to the already-cricket-crazy nation.

The IPL was designed to marry the two most popular phenomena of India: Bollywood and cricket. The league was started in 2008 along the lines of the Major League Baseball, complete with cheerleaders (a "first" in Indian sports). Cricket players from all over the world were "auctioned off" to the highest bidder, typically business conglomerates (co-)owned by Bollywood bigwigs.

Now in its seventh edition, the IPL featuring 60 matches, has emerged as one of the most glamorous, cash-rich, and glitzy events of all times. The opening ceremonies are replete with Indian and international performers (including several from United States), whereas the main league is no less than an epic event where players from all over the world clamor to join, and the fervor shows no signs of abating.[28] Players are bought and sold for astronomical amounts (Yuvraj Singh, for example, commanded a whopping $2.558 million for playing 14 matches). Once again, the IPL has only increased the international presence of Bollywood in the global arena and is the result of smart marketing tactics adopted by the cricketing and the movie fraternities. The result is not only further development of sporting talent but also circulation of billions of dollars both within and outside of India. In fact, many professional cricketers have evolved into international repute through the IPL, and have been successful in garnering multimillion-dollar endorsement contracts.

Challenges of Globalization

The supremacy of Indian movies is beyond question. Nonetheless, there are still some serious challenges that need to be overcome, should Bollywood desire to be among the top contenders when it comes to top-level entertainment. Specifically, we will review the following factors: black money; infrastructure, and movie attendance and pragmatic aspects.

Black Money

Bollywood has long been accused of hobnobbing with, and financed by (mostly illegally) the underworld both within and outside India. While there have been several attempts to extradite certain suspects and bring charges against them under the Indian Penal Code, lack of political will and clout in high places have prevented any major arrests from happening so far.[29] Such underworld dealings have had its grave effects on some popular Bollywood figures such as Sanjay Dutt (a popular actor, who is in prison), Gulshan Kumar (a popular music producer, shot and killed in 1997) and Rakesh Roshan (actor/director, who was shot in 2000) and others.[30]

While such unholy nexus has had historically prevented the government from providing moral and financial support to the film fraternity, there has been a remarkable change in stance, especially in terms of transparency, since the official recognition of the industry. Nonetheless, unless the Bollywood fraternity can distance itself from the underworld and come out clean, foreign direct investment and serious foreign participation (financial or otherwise) will always be suspect.

Infrastructure and Movie Attendance

A simple comparison of some of the basic indicators of infrastructure such as the total numbers of multiplexes, per capital multiplexes, digital screening equipment and screens, ticket prices, and box office revenues reflect the fact that Bollywood is still trailing behind its North American, Western European, or Chinese counterparts. These results can be surmised as due to several possible reasons:

- The total number of movies produced in Bollywood is simply too high to sustain a reasonable level of interest among viewers beyond a certain level (more than 1200 movies produced in 2011, with the United States in the second place at about 800 movies, according to the UNESCO Institute of Statistics.)[31]
- The average per capita gross domestic product (GDP) of the Indian viewer is a fraction of that of the United States and China, the two closest contenders to India in terms of movie production, which makes the box office receipts, production costs, payments to, for example, actors and technicians, less competitive (GDP for China $ 6807.4 million, India $ 1497.5 million, and the United States $53,042 million, per the World Bank's GDP 2013 reports.[32] Table 2 provides more data.
- Thanks to technological advancements and the way we access entertainment (e.g., DVD, streaming sources, cable, the Internet, video kiosks, on-demand and pay-per-view), viewers have naturally shifted from making that trip to the movie theater to watching the same movie in the comforts of their own homes.

A yet fourth reason might be the rampant video piracy, copying, and illegal downloading of different forms of entertainment, all of which have played their part in reducing box office earnings. In fact, several movie theaters in major Indian cities have had to shut down in recent times due to lack of footfall.[33]

Table 20.2 Total 2006–2011 Box Office Revenue for the Top Six Countries (US $ Millions)

Country	2006	2007	2008	2009	2010	2011	Variation 2006–2011 (%)	Annual Average Growth (%)	Share of World in 2011 (%)
United States	9488	9632	9635	10610	10580	10186	7.36	1.43	31.25
Japan	1745	1685	1885	2202	1347	2766	58.51	9.65	8.48
China	329	434	607	909	1502	2030	517.02	43.90	6.23
France	1475	1559	1586	1789	1745	1780	20.68	3.83	5.46
Great Britain	1402	1878	1723	1772	1526	1665	18.76	3.50	5.11
India	1371	1729	1843	1415	1356	1470	7.22	1.40	4.51

Data from UNESCO Institute for Statistics, July 2013. Reproduced with permission.

Pragmatic Aspects

The average Bollywood movie is three hours long,[34] which is almost double that of most non-Bollywood movies. In this day and age, how many of us have the luxury (patience) of watching a three-hour movie in one sitting? Plus, Bollywood movies are known to be melodramatic, often characterized by too many twisted, unrealistic, sometimes-ridiculous plots and storylines. Above all, the insertion of too many songs lip-synched by the actors in unnatural locations and without any rhyme or reason has earned the epithet "musical" in the western world for any Bollywood movie. Consequently, even movies with good story lines and commendable acting/direction have a tough time getting past the western movie aficionado.

Therefore, if Bollywood is to seriously take on the global movie stage in terms of worldwide acceptance and popularity, it has to concentrate on *quality* instead of *quantity*. Despite the giant strides towards marketization since the government's recognition of its official stature in 1998, problems of consistency, synchronization, and coherence in terms of different facets of movie creation still pose a threat. It is perhaps due to such factors that the United States invested about $150 million in the Chinese film sector, even though historically China lags behind India considerably in movie production.[35]

Conclusion

Bollywood is different from all other types and genres of entertainment (for reasons that cannot be elaborated here due to space limitations, not to mention the sheer volume and variety of movies produced, and the unfathomable number of viewers who watch them). Given the unique nature of this industry, therefore, the current research assumes great significance. The importance of entertainment in marketing and the relation between the two can hardly be over-emphasized. But the meteoric rise of the Bollywood industry assumes the case of a puzzle that has yet to be unraveled. The author strongly believes that this line of research will resonate very well with the international flavor of the readers of this journal.

Future Direction

Specifically, we leave the reader with several questions to ponder:

- Do movie theaters have a realistic chance of survival given the relentless onslaught of cable, Internet, and movie kiosks?

- Is the line between Bollywood and Hollywood getting blurry with more and more exchange of ideas, technology, ideology, and actors?
- How do we micro-market movies to niche segments in an age where information travels at lightning speed, not to mention the rampant video piracy and illegal copying of copyrighted material?
- What financial model do we follow where the Internet is no longer considered just an ancillary but a mainstream channel of distribution of entertainment?

The current project can be further enhanced and extended through data collection from academic journals, trade and industry reviews, media statistics, and the entertainment blogosphere, as well as personal and/or secondary interviews with movie buffs, actors, box office analysts, and forecasters, and movie critics.

Notes

1. Ghosh, "Bollywood at 100: How Big Is India's Mammoth Film Industry?" in *International Business Times*.
2. Gonzalez, 2013. "Emerging Markets and The Digitalization of the Film Industry," in *UIS Information Paper*.
3. Punathambekar, *From Bombay to Bollywood: the Making of a Global Media Industry*.
4. Pillania, 2008. "The Globalization of Indian Hindi Movie Industry," in *Management*.
5. Ibid.
6. Kearney, *Study on Transforming for Growth: Future of the Indian Media & Entertainment Landscape*.
7. Ghosh, Bollywood.
8. Ibid.
9. Kraidy, "Hybridity in Cultural Globalization," in *Communication Theory*.
10. Flew, *Understanding Global Media*.
11. Nye, *Soft Power: The Means to Success in World Politics, Public Affairs*
12. Karan, "Cultural Connections in a Globalized World: The Power of Bollywood in the United States," in *Bollywood and Globalization: the Global Power of Popular Hindi Cinema*.
13. Punathambekar, Bombay to Bollywood.
14. Duke, Spielberg Gets Movie Cash with India Partnership.
15. Leahy, US Studios Get Taste for Bollywood, para 3.
16. Kohli-Khandekar, "Indian Film Giants," in *Businessworld*.
17. Ibid.
18. Pillania, "The Globalization of Indian Hindi Movie Industry," in *Management*.
19. Times of India. *Top 10 foreign actresses in Bollywood*.
20. Bollymoviereviewz. *Top 10 Indian Reality TV Shows in 2014 by TRP*.
21. International Indian Film Academy (IIFA). *IIFA Through the Years*.
22. Karan, Cultural Connections.
23. Ibid.
24. As alluded to by Shaefer, Bollywood and globalization: The global power of popular Hindi cinema.
25. Abu-Lughod, "On screening Politics in a World of Nations," in *Public Culture*; Iordanova, "Indian Cinema's Global Reach: Histography Through Testimonies," in *South Asian Popular Culture*; Rajagopalan, "Emblematic of the Thaw: Early Indian films in Soviet Cinemas," in *South Asian Popular Culture*.
26. Gonzalez, Emerging Markets.
27. UNESCO Institute for Statistics.
28. For more information, see www.iplt20.com
29. Nanjappa, "Dawood Ibrahim: Political Will The Bigger Weapon To Nab Him," in
30. *OneIndia*.
31. Ibid.; DNA Webdesk, "Abu Salem Hit-Man Arrested; Says He 'Fired At Rakesh Roshan," in
32. *DNA*.
33. UNESCO Institute for Statistics.
34. World Bank. *GDP Reports, 2015*.
35. Acharya, Bollywood; Karan, Cultural Connections; Pillania, Globalization; Punathambekar, Bombay to Bollywood.

Works Cited

Abu-Lughod, Lila. On screening Politics in a World of Nations. *Public Culture* 5 (1993); 465–467. Acharya, Sharmistha. *Bollywood and Globalization*. Master's Thesis, San Francisco State Uni-versity, CA, 2004.
DNA Webdesk. Abu Salem Hit-Man Arrested; Says He 'Fired At Rakesh Roshan". DNA 2015. http://www.dnaindia.com/india/report-abu-salem-hit-man-says-he-fired-at-rakesh-roshan- 2078931
Bollymoviereviewz. Top 10 Indian Reality TV Shows in 2014 by TRP. Bollywoodmoviereviewz. com 2014. http://www.bollymoviereviewz.com/2013/10/top-10-indian-reality-tv-shows-in- 2013.html.
Duke, Alan. Spielberg Gets Movie Cash with India Partnership, CNN, 2009. http://www.cnn. com/2009/SHOWBIZ/Movies/08/17/spielberg.bollywood/index.html.
Flew, Terry. *Understanding Global Media*. (UK: Palgrave Macmillan, 2007). Indiamarks. You Know You're Watching a Bollywood Movie When. http://www.indiamarks. com/you-know-youre-watching-a-bollywood-movie-when/ Indian Movie Stats. http://www.indianmoviestats.com/index.html India Premier League website. http://www.iplt20.com
Ghosh, Palash. Bollywood at 100: How Big Is India's Mammoth Film Industry?' *International Business Times*. 2013. http://www.ibtimes.com/bollywood-100-how-big-indias-mammoth- film-industry-1236299
Gonz'alez, Roque. (2013). Emerging Markets and The Digitalization of the Film Industry, *UIS Information Paper no.* 14 August 2013. http://www.uis.unesco.org/culture/Documents/IP14- 2013-cinema-survey-analysis-en.pdf.
International Indian Film Academy (IIFA). *IIFA Through the Years*. http://www.iifa.com/iifa- years/
Iordanova, Dina. Indian Cinema's Global Reach: Histography Through Testimonies, *South Asian Popular Culture*, 4: 2006 (2), 113–140.
Karan, Kavita. Cultural Connections in a Globalized World: The Power of Bollywood in the United States in Schaefar, D. & Karan, K. (eds.), *Bollywood and Globalization: The Global Power of Popular Hindi Cinema*, pp. 146–166 (New York: Routledge Contemporary South Asia Series, 2013).
Kearney, A. T. Study on Transforming for Growth: Future of the Indian Media & Entertainment Landscape. 2007. http://cii.in/documents/executivesummarycii_atkearneyup.pdf.
Kohli-Khandekar, Vanita. (2006). Indian Film Giants. *Businessworld* 25: 2006 (33), 27–42. Kraidy, Marwan. M. 2002. Hybridity in Cultural Globalization *Communication Theory*, 12(3), 316–339.
Leahy, Joe. 2008. US Studios Get Taste for Bollywood. http://www.rediff.com/money/2008/jan/ 03bolly.htm
Nanjappa, Vicki. Dawood Ibrahim: Political Will The Bigger Weapon To Nab Him. *OneIndia 2015* http://www.oneindia.com/india/dawood-ibrahim-political-will-the-bigger-weapon-to- nab-him-1720366.html
Nye, J. S. (2004). *Soft power: The means to success in world politics*. PublicAffairs. pages 5–9 Pillania, Rajesh K. The Globalization of Indian Hindi Movie Industry. *Management*, 3: 2008 (2), 115–123.
Punathambekar, Aswin. *From Bombay to Bollywood: The Making of a Global Media Industry*. New York, NYU Press, 2013.
Rajagopalan, Sudha. Emblematic of the Thaw: Early Indian films in Soviet Cinemas. *South Asian Popular Culture* 4: 2006 (2), 83–100.
Schaefer, D. J., & Karan, K. (Eds.). (2013). Bollywood and globalization: The global power of popular Hindi cinema (Vol. 63). Routledge.
Times of India, Top 10 Foreign Actresses in Bollywood. http://timesofindia.indiatimes.com/entertainment/hindi/bollywood/Top-10-foreign-actresses-in-Bollywood/photostory/24691995. cms#24692669
World Bank. *GDP Reports*, 2015. http://data.worldbank.org/indicator/NY.GDP.PCAP.CD

* **First published as the article: "The Marketization of Bollywood" by Somjit Barat, Quarterly Review of Film and Video (2018) 35:2, pp. 105–118. Reprinted by permission of Taylor & Francis Ltd, http://www.tandfonline.com**

21 Australian Entertainment Industries

Terry Flew and Christy Collis

Introduction: Australian Entertainment Industries in Global Perspective

Australia is among the world's upper-middle countries in terms of the size of its entertainment and media industries. In 2016, entertainment and media spending accounted for $A39.5 billion, or 3.3% of GDP, and Australia is the world's fourteenth largest entertainment and media market (PwC, 2017). As a predominantly English-speaking nation, Australia has been very open to cultural imports from the United States and Britain in particular, although with an increasingly multicultural population, there is entertainment and media content from around the world (Flew, 2017). This in turn gives Australian entertainment industries a strong export orientation, and arguably an outsized influence in global entertainment. A cursory glance at the major figures of world entertainment points to a lot of internationally famous Australians in acting (Nicole Kidman, Hugh Jackman, Cate Blanchett, Chris Hemsworth, Russell Crowe), screen directing (Phil Noyce, George Miller, Baz Luhrmann), music (AC/DC, Nick Cave, Kylie Minogue, Iggy Azalea), theatre (Tim Minchin, Barry Humphries), and so on. Australia is also internationally renowned for its digital games industry, urban cultural precincts, innovative art museums such as the Museum of Old and New Art (MONA) in Hobart, and screen locations, such as the desert landscapes used for the *Mad Max* films.

Overseas media content, particularly from the U.S. but also from the U.K., has had a prominent role in all Australian media, including commercial TV, national broadcasting, radio music, cinema, games and streaming services. As a result, Australian media and cultural policy has, since the 1960s, placed a strong emphasis on promoting local (national) content production. Australian governments have applied local content quotas to television in order to stimulate Australian production of drama, children's television and documentaries, requiring the commercial TV networks to screen minimum amounts of Australian content in prime-time schedules, and acting as a catalyst for the local screen industries to produce original content. This does lead to a certain amount of "copycat TV", as local production houses adapt international formats for domestic audiences. For instance, virtually every significant reality/contest-based format developed in the 2000s has had an Australian version, from *Big Brother* and *Master Chef* to *The Voice* and *I'm a Celebrity, Get Me Out of Here*. It has also meant that local productions have developed significant international audiences: the popularity of *Neighbours* and *Home and Away* in the U.K. is a notable case in point.

The politics of representation and national identity are a recurring theme in Australia, and such debates play out strongly in the entertainment industries. It has been observed that, in spite of over 40 years of very active debate around the dominance of white Anglo-Australians in Australian television, you are still more likely to see the cultural diversity of Australia in talent and cooking shows than in dramas or as the hosts of popular programs (Screen Australia, 2016). Indigenous representation presents issues not only about race and racism, but around the construct of the Australian nation itself, and whether European settlers stole the land from the First Peoples. There has long been a strong indigenous entertainment industry presence, with leading filmmakers such as Warwick Thornton, Ivan Sen and Rachel Perkins, and prominent actors such as Deborah Mailman, Aaron Pedersen and Kylie Belling following on from pioneers such as Erne Dingo, Justine Saunders and David Gulpilil. Productions such as the TV drama *Cleverman* (featuring an indigenous superhero) and the film *The Sapphires* (about an indigenous girl group that performed for soldiers during the Vietnam War) advance indigenous representation beyond that of "standing in" for representation of social problems primarily understood from a non-indigenous perspective (Blackmore, 2015).

Australian Entertainment Institutions

The Australian entertainment industries are shaped by a mix of public- and private-sector institutions, small operations as well as giant media conglomerates, and domestic and international players. In broadcasting, the "dual system" of a strong national public service broadcaster (the Australian Broadcasting Corporation (ABC)) co-existing with significant commercial stations was replicated when television commenced in 1956. While the majority of Australians watch and listen to commercial broadcasters, the ABC accounts for about 15 to 30% of audience share, and is the leading broadcaster in genres such as arts, science, comedy, news and current affairs, documentary, and investigative journalism. It has been complemented by the Special Broadcasting Service (SBS), established in 1980 as an explicitly multicultural radio and television service, in acknowledgement of the notable lack of cultural, racial and ethnic diversity of the Australian broadcasting industry (Ang, Hawkins and Dabboussy, 2008). Both the ABC and SBS have a strong online presence, with ABC iView resembling the BBC iPlayer in the UK with its rich mix of freely available content.

There is one cable television provider, Foxtel, partly owned by Rupert Murdoch's News Corporation, which about 30% of Australian homes subscribe to. Video streaming services have proven to be extremely popular among Australians, and it is estimated that in 2017 the number of subscription video-on-demand households exceeds that of pay TV subscribers (Roy Morgan, 2016). The most popular streaming service is Netflix, which has very little Australian content, but other popular services include Stan, Quickflix, YouTube Red, Foxtel Play, and the channels of ABC, SBS and the commercial networks. Stan is proving to be particularly interesting in terms of investment in local content, having commissioned a number of local drama and comedy productions, including series based on the popular films *Wolf Creek* and *Romper Stomper*.

The Australian film industry has also benefited from strong government support since the 1970s, and the rise of cultural nationalism under the Whitlam, Hawke and Keating Labor governments. Reflecting a recurring tension between cultural policy and industry development rationales for supporting media and creative industries, there have been both film subsidies to promote "quality" Australian cinema, and various taxation and other incentives to promote avowedly commercial productions (O'Regan, 2001). Global hits such as *Crocodile Dundee, Babe* and *Mad Max: Fury Road* clearly come out of the latter tradition. The Australian screen industries have a complex and well-established network of creative talent, production infrastructure, locations, incentives and partnerships, with government at all levels playing a very active role in shaping an industry that aims to combine commercial success with a degree of "brand ambassadorship" around promoting Australia to the world.

Australia has a Federal system of government, with a national (Federal) government, six state governments, two territory governments, and many local governments for cities and regions. In terms of entertainment, this means that the regulatory powers associated with these industries sit almost exclusively with the Federal government under the Broadcasting Services Act and other related legislation, with one exception being censorship, where states retain independent powers. The Australian Communications and Media Authority (ACMA) is the principal regulator of broadcasting, telecommunications and online content. By contrast, in terms of promoting and supporting the entertainment industries, there is a complex and often competing range of Federal, state and local government initiatives. While the largest number of screen businesses are in Sydney, which also has the world-renowned Fox Studios, there are very significant screen businesses and studio complexes in Melbourne, the Gold Coast and Adelaide.

Australian arts and cultural policy has often had an ambivalent relationship to the entertainment industries. With screen industry support being undertaken by other agencies, the Australia Council has traditionally been focused upon the creative, performing and visual arts. Craik (2007) has described Australian arts and cultural policy as being "conceptually ambivalent", between promoting elite excellence and community participation, between economic and aesthetic priorities, and between a focus on national flagship institutions (such as the major performing arts companies) and developing innovative grassroots initiatives and promotion of Aboriginal and Torres Straits Islander and multicultural arts. There have been periodic bursts of enthusiasm for a national cultural policy, most notably with the Keating Labor Government's 1994 Creative Nation cultural policy statement, but also the 2013 Creative Australia national cultural policy. Cultural policy initiatives tend to broaden the remit of cultural support to digital technologies and creative industries such as video games, but have frequently been followed by periods of retreat, as with the earmarking of funding on a non-competitive basis to the major performing arts companies in the early 2000s, and the redirection of Australia Council funding away from peer review processes towards a short-lived "excellence in the arts" initiative championed by the Liberal-National Party Arts Minister George Brandis in 2014 (Eltham, 2016).

Import/Export Dynamics

An understanding of Australia's strong import/export dynamics is critical to understanding Australian entertainment industries. As a post-colonial nation with its contemporary national roots in British colonisation, Australia circulates in a global "Anglosphere" of English-language content and the strong influence of ideas and ideologies that have their roots in the United States and the United Kingdom, from neoliberalism to #metoo. A related point is that media content from the U.S. and U.K. possesses a lower cultural discount than that from non-English-speaking nations, at least for the majority of the population. There is also an unusually high degree of dominance of Anglo men in the upper echelons of Australia's media and entertainment industries, in spite of the broader society becoming increasingly multicultural (Screen Australia, 2016). But this is not simply a case of cultural imperialism. The high presence of media and entertainment content from the world's leading markets such as Hollywood has in turn acted as a catalyst for Australian entertainment industries to have strong international aspirations, complementing the comparatively small domestic market (Australia had a population of 25 million in 2017) with the opportunity for cultural product to be attractive internationally.

The import/export dynamic is particularly apparent in Australian screen industries. In film, it has been very common for Australian actors and/or directors to have a "breakthrough" success in Australia, and to use that as a launching pad for a Hollywood career. Russell Crowe's leading role in the controversial 1992 Australian film *Romper Stomper*, where he played the leader of a neo-Nazi gang, was a calling card for lead roles in films as diverse as *L.A. Confidential* (1997) and *Gladiator* (2000). Both Toni Collette and Rachel Griffiths came to prominence in the 1994 Australian film *Muriel's Wedding*, with Griffiths working with that film's producer, P. J. Hogan, on the 1997 Hollywood hit *My Best Friend's Wedding*. Australia has also been described as a good place to watch other people's television (O'Regan, 1994).

Australia is also a very popular place for the production of films and television series that are not identifiably "Australian" in theme or character. A large number of films involve production and/or post-production in Australia, but are not necessarily "Australian": examples include *The Matrix*, *Pirates of the Caribbean*, *The Great Gatsby*, *Thor: Ragnarok* and *The Lego Movie*.

Australia has long occupied a significant place within what Wang, Maxwell, McMurria, Govil and Miller (2005) termed "Global Hollywood", functioning as a desirable locale due to unique natural environments, highly skilled production crews, and a variety of tax and other incentives to bring overseas productions to Australia. But as O'Regan, Ward and Goldsmith (2010) have observed, it would be a mistake to see this as a one-way street, since so-called "offshore" productions build and retain local production capacity, and initiate local producers into global best practice.

The Australian games industry exemplifies both the opportunities and the challenges of operating in such a global market. For much of the 1990s and 2000s, Australian games developers largely undertook work for hire from U.S.-based giants such as Electronic Arts, with little original intellectual property (IP) ownership in spite of the high skills levels of local developers and the deep networks developed with associated institutions such as universities and industry training providers (Banks and Cunningham, 2016). While the Global Financial Crisis of 2007–2008 saw a shakedown of the big studios, the shift towards apps-based games opened up new opportunities for independent developers. By 2018, 55% of Australian games companies were solely based around generating their own IP, and another 37% combined developing their own IP with providing services for larger clients (Interactive Games and Entertainment Association, 2016). Brisbane-based Halfbrick Studios exemplifies this shift in the disintermediated Australian games industry: the company, started in 2001 as a developer of licenced games for Gameboy and Playstation consoles. With the rise of mobile gaming, Halfbrick created and published its own game in 2010: *Fruit Ninja. Fruit Ninja* quickly became one of the world's best-selling mobile games, reaching one billion downloads in 2015. The Australian games industry attracts less government support than comparable industries internationally, and has been prone to having funding withdrawn by governments either on the grounds that games are not "cultural enough", or that as a predominantly commercial sector, it should be expected to stand on its own (Senate Environment and Communications References Committee, 2016).

An exemplary example of the import/export dynamic in Australian entertainment industries is seen with the creative digital studio Animal Logic. Founded in 1991 and based at the former Fox Studios in Sydney, Animal Logic is one of the world's three major VFX/animation studios (along with George Lucas's Industrial Light and Magic in San Francisco and Peter Jackson's WETA Studios in Wellington, New Zealand), and has production credits including Hollywood films such as *Babe, The Great Gatsby, The LEGO Movie* and *Peter Rabbit*, and Chinese blockbusters such as *House of Flying Dragons* and *Hero*. It has expanded its global operations with studios in Los Angeles and Vancouver, but remains very much an Australian company, recently partnering with the University of Technology, Sydney in developing a joint training environment leading to graduate qualifications.

Public Service Media and Content Innovation

It is in public broadcasting that Australia has differentiated itself from more familiar global patterns of digital disruption and transformation in the entertainment industries. The national public service broadcaster, the Australian Broadcast Corporation (ABC), signalled an early ability to understand and harness digital shifts in entertainment with its iView online platform in 2008, released as an iOS app in 2010. iView offers time-shifted on-demand access to almost all of its television content, with unmetering of ABC iView content through most major ISPs since 2008, driving strong audience uptake. Commissioned online-only content, including *The Katering Show, Canberra Al Desko with Annabel Crabb, When I Get A Minute* and *DAFUQ*, for example, is also released through iView. In 2017, the iView ABC Kids' app accounted for 82% of online views of children's entertainment content in Australia (Simons, 2017, 52). In 2016, the average monthly reach of ABC Online in Australia was 7.6 million, or 38% of online Australians (ABC, 2016). The reach of iView saw steady expansion through 2016 and 2017 (ABC, 2016). The ABC has thus been a leader in the digital transformation of the Australian entertainment industry.

The ABC has not only been notable among global public service broadcasters in its early moves into the online content sphere, but also in its organisational structures. Digital transformation was particularly visible in the 2017–2018 restructure of the ABC. ABC Managing Director Michelle Guthrie, with a career background with Google as well as with commercial broadcaster NewsCorp, announced in 2017 that in order to retain and build its strong online presence and audience reach, the broadcaster would be restructured in order to become "platform agnostic". Replacing the organisational groups of "radio", "screen" and "news", around which the broadcaster had been organised since the 1930s (in the case of radio), Guthrie created three new divisions: News, Regional and Local, and Entertainment and Specialist. A Content Ideas Lab was also created to span all three divisions with a focus on content innovation. Guthrie's restructure outpaces the BBC's structure in this regard: the BBC remains organisationally structured by medium. Notable about Guthrie's restructure is not only its clear alignment with the digitally driven shift in audience preference from medium to content, but also its foregrounding of Entertainment as one of the core content foci for the broadcaster. Historically, public service broadcasters have been seen as responsible for "quality" content, while entertainment has been a largely private-sector product; the ABC's digitally driven restructure works against that conventional pattern by foregrounding entertainment as a core part of its public service mission and product.

Major Sport

Major sport—live and mediatised—constitutes a significant aspect of the Australian entertainment landscape. Australia's professional sports industry resembles those of other regions such as North America and Europe, with two key exceptions. The first of these is the diversity of football codes. Australia supports four major codes: Australian Football, Rugby Union, Rugby League, and Soccer. Australian Football dominates the major sports environment with annual spectatorship of over 7 million in 2016, one of the ten highest attendance rates for professional sport in the world. Played nowhere in the world other than Australia, Australian Football—known in Australia as Australian Rules Football, or AFL—has co-evolved with Australian television, growing from a state-based to a national league in 1990 shortly after the introduction of national television coverage enabled by Australia's first domestic satellite system, AUSSAT, in 1985.

Unlike the "free market" model of major sports broadcasting found in the U.S., in Australia there is strong legislation around the ownership of broadcasting rights. The Broadcasting Services Act allows the Federal Minister for Communications to give free-to-air broadcasters first preference in securing broadcast rights to major sporting events; the 2006–2010 list included over 1800 events. This Australian entertainment policy is referred to as "anti-siphoning" because of its prevention of sports broadcasting rights being "siphoned" away from free-to-air organisations. While some state that anti-siphoning legislation ensures that all Australians have equal access to major sports broadcasts, others argue that anti-siphoning has resulted in a concentration of sports broadcasting in the commercial networks, and a restriction on the potential growth of subscription sports TV. The ongoing popularity of Australian free-to-air TV remains reliant on major sport, with sports accounting for 50% of Australia's most-watched TV programs since 2001 (Goldsmith 2015, 70, 77).

Australian Online Entertainment

Between 2000 and 2005, broadcast hours of TV drama and the quantity of new TV documentaries being made in Australia both fell, while Australian web series episodes numbers "exploded" from 107 episodes to 3,248 (Swinburne and Fabb, 2017). This dynamic is largely in line with global shifts in entertainment. *The Katering Show* first aired in 2014 as a YouTube web series of six, seven-minute episodes. Funded by a $AUD30,000 Screen Australia Multiplatform grant, the series was written, directed, produced by, and stars Australian comedians Kate McCartney and Kate McLennan. *The Katering Show* lampoons contemporary cooking shows and trends, with one of its most popular episodes (2.5 million YouTube views) parodying the cult-like followers of the Thermomix kitchen appliance. Based on the series's surprise popularity, a second season was funded by the ABC and Screen Australia for release on ABC's iView platform; when it appeared online in 2016, it quickly became iView's most watched commissioned content (The Katering Show, 2016). It later aired on ABC's free-to-air TV station. The queer web series *Starting From. . .Now* (2014–2016) followed a similar trajectory, with its first three seasons airing on YouTube only, and its final two seasons commissioned by SBS for its youth digital channel SBS2. Unlike *The Katering Show, Starting From* received no government funding for its YouTube incarnation, relying instead on personal financing by its producer and on $AUD10,000 generated in crowdfunding through the now-defunct site Dana (Monaghan 2017, 86). Other successful Australian web series include *Bondi Hipsters, High Life,* and *Bruce*.

Some of Australia's most internationally known screen entertainment arises from what Stuart Cunningham refers to as "a new industry . . . based on previously amateur creators turning pro and working across many platforms such as YouTube and other social media" (Cunningham, 2017); this segment of entertainment production is often referred to as "pro-am" (Leadbeater, 2004). According to a 2016 Google-funded study of Australian online video content creation, 230,000 new online content creators emerged in Australia between 2000 and 2016, and these creators had a 90% international audience surplus (Alphabeta, 2016)

The extent to which this "pro-am" entertainment content is a trade surplus export industry is exemplified by the statistic that twice as much Australian online video is consumed in the United States as is consumed in Australia (Cunningham and Swift, 2017). In 2014 Screen Australia and Google initiated the Skip Ahead program to fund Australian online video creators who have either a YouTube channel with at least 50,000 subscribers, or a single YouTube video with over 1 million views; however, most Australian online video content creators rely on alternative business models including advertising revenue, live appearances, merchandise and cross-promotion. Australia's most internationally popular online entertainment content does not align with traditional genres. Australia's most popular YouTube entertainment content creator in 2017 and the overall winner of the Australian Online Video Awards in 2017, for example, was Wengie, whose videos focus on fashion and grooming; she has also released successful music videos. In 2018, Wengie had over 10 million subscribers to her YouTube channel. Other highly successful Australian YouTube creators and their genres include: Janoskians—pranks and vulgar humour; Maxmoefoe—pranks and shock humour; Natalie Tran—sketch and monologue comedy; Planet Dolan—bizarre facts; and CKN Toys—toy play, reviews, and unboxing. In 2018, each of these Australian YouTube channels had at least 5 million subscribers (Top 250, 2018). While some argue that the strong emergence of Australian "pro-am" entertainment content promotes greater representation of "Australianness" and diverse Australian voices and perspectives, there is also concern that this very diversity may undermine a sense of recognisable Australian identity. The Skip Ahead program aims to combat the latter by requiring that YouTube content funded by the program had to be recognisably Australian. Issues of national identity aside, the "pro-am" sphere is growing as an increasingly important segment of the Australian entertainment industry.

Conclusion

The Australian entertainment sector is grounded in tensions around Australia's relationship to the broader global industry, and global economics. In the global entertainment industry sector, Australia's impact outstrips its relatively small population size. Because Australia is a predominantly English-speaking country with well-developed industry infrastructure, it articulates well with global audiences and industries, particularly from the large U.S. and U.K. markets. Australian entertainment talent such as Kylie Minogue, Nicole Kidman, Hugh Jackman, Russell Crowe, Chris and Liam Hemsworth, and Mel Gibson in the film sector; Iggy Azalea, Sia, AC/DC, the Bee Gees, Olivia Newton-John and Wolfmother in music; celebrities such as Elle MacPherson, Portia De Rossi, Rebel Wilson and Steve Irwin; and Wengie, Janoskians and Maxmoefoe on YouTube have all achieved significant international success. Industrially, the film sector is strongly connected into global industry circuits: with its diverse locations—from urban to desert—, its government-support and its substantial human resource base, Australia has become an important node in the international film production industry. The emergence of the digital "pro-am" sector has seen similar substantial penetration of Australian-based content into the international sphere. Notably, this global success is not necessarily based on Australia's English-speaking majority: Australia's most globally popular YouTuber, Wengie, is a Chinese-born Australian who speaks both Mandarin and English, and has achieved entertainment success in both Australia and in China.

While Australia's ability to articulate into global markets has been one of the strengths of its entertainment industries, this ability has also generated longstanding concerns about the maintenance of a distinctive Australian identity as represented through entertainment content. These concerns revolve around the importation of international—mostly American and British—content, and around the nature of "Australianness" as it is represented in Australian entertainment exports. There is a history of tension around whether successful Australian-produced entertainment which is not recognisably Australian—*Fruit Ninja* and *The Lego Movie*, for example—should be supported in order to build the strength of Australia's entertainment economy. Since the 1960s, Australian media and cultural policy has thus placed a strong emphasis on ensuring that Australian-generated content that aligns with accepted cultural understandings of Australian national identity maintains a strong foothold in Australia. This is achieved in part by generating Australian content quotas for television and radio, and through local adaptations of successful international television formats. Historically, so-called "highbrow" content such as serious dramas and documentaries have been valorised as the genres privileged through government support as the primary content through which a distinctive Australian identity should be represented to both national and international audiences. The recent refocussing of the national public-sector broadcaster, the ABC, towards entertainment, however, signals that this generic privileging may be shifting. As the affordances of the digital further disrupt older industry patterns, the entertainment industries are one clear domain in which Australia is negotiating both its own identity, and its place in the broader global community.

References

Alphabeta Strategy Economics. (2016). Bigger picture: The new age of screen culture. Retrieved from www.alphabeta.com/wp-content/uploads/2016/12/Google_Bigger-Picture-Report_Dec2016.pdf

Ang, I., Hawkins, G. and Dabboussy, L. (2008). *The SBS Story*. Sydney: UNSW Press.

Australian Broadcasting Corporation (ABC). (2016). *From the Everyday to the Extraordinary: Annual Report*. Retrieved from www.abc.net.au/corp/annual-report/2016/c2-online.html.

Banks, J. and Cunningham, S. (2016). Games production in Australia: Adapting to precariousness. In M. Curtin & K. Sanson (Eds.), *Precarious Creativity Precarious Creativity: Global Media, Local Labor* (pp. 186–199). Berkeley, CA: University of California Press.

Blackmore, E. (2015). Speakin' out blak: New and emergent Aboriginal filmmakers finding their voices. In: W. Pearson and S. Knabe, ed., *Reverse Shots: Indigenous Film and Media in an International Context*. Waterloo: Wilfrid Laurier University Press, pp. 61–80.

Craik, J. (2007). *Re-Visioning Arts and Cultural Policy: Current Impasses and Future Directions*. Canberra: ANU e-Press.

Cunningham, S. (2017). Australia's screen future is online: time to support our new content creators. *The Conversation*. Retrieved from https://theconversation.com/australias-screen-future-is-online-time-to-support-our-new-content-creators-82638

Cunningham, S. and Swift, A. (2017). Over the horizon: YouTube culture meets Australian screen culture. In F. Collins, S. Bye, & J. Landman (Eds.), *Wiley-Blackwell Companion to Australian Cinema*. Hoboken, NJ: Wiley-Blackwell.

Eltham, B. (2016). *When the Goal Posts Move: Patronage, Power and Resistance in Australian Cultural Policy 2013-2016*. Sydney: Currency House.

Flew, T. (2017). Intercultural communication: An Australian perspective. In: S. Croucher, ed., *Global Perspectives on Intercultural Communication*. London: Routledge, pp. 58–61.

Goldsmith, B. (2015). Sport and the transformation of Australian television. *Media International Australia incorporating Culture and Policy*, (155), 70–79.

Interactive Games and Entertainment Association. (2016). Australian video game development: An industry snapshot FY 2016–2017. Retrieved from www.igea.net/2018/01/australian-game-developers-march-generating-118-5m-spite-limited-recognition-support/

The Katering Show is most watched iView original ever with over a million plays. (2016) Retrieved from www.if.com.au/The-Katering-Show-is-most-watched-iView-original-ever-with-over-a-million-plays/

Leadbeater, C. (2004). *The Pro-Am Revolution: How Enthusiasts Are Changing Our Society and Economy*. London: Demos.

Miller, T, Govil, N, Maxwell, R., McMurria, J., Govil, N., and Wang, T. (2005). *Global Hollywood 2*, 2nd ed. London: British Film Institute.

Monaghan, W. (2017). Starting From . . . Now and the web series to television crossover: An online revolution? *Media International Australia*, 164(1), 82–91.

O'Regan, T. (1994). *Australian Television Culture*. Sydney: Allen & Unwin.

O'Regan, T. (2001). "Knowing the process but not the outcomes": Australian cinema faces the millennium. In: T. Bennett and D. Carter, ed., *Culture in Australia: Policies, Publics and Programs*. Cambridge: Cambridge University Press, pp. 18–45.

O'Regan, T., Ward, S. and Goldsmith, B. (2010). *Local Hollywood: Global Film Production and the Gold Coast*. Brisbane: University of Queensland Press.

PricewaterhouseCoopers (2017). Perspectives from the global entertainment and media outlook 2017–2021 [online]. PwC. Available at: www.pwc.com/gx/en/entertainment-media/pdf/outlook-2017-curtain-up.pdf [Accessed 22 Feb. 2018].

Roy Morgan. (2016). More Australians now have SVOD than Foxtel [online]. Available at: www.roymorgan.com/findings/6957-svod-overtakes-foxtel-pay-tv-in-australia-august-2016-201609081005 [Accessed 1 Mar. 2018].

Screen Australia (2016). Seeing ourselves: Reflections on diversity in Australian TV drama [online]. Sydney. Available at: www.screenaustralia.gov.au/getmedia/157b05b4-255a-47b4-bd8b-9f.

Senate Environment and Communications References Committee (2016). Game on: more than playing around – The future of Australia's video game development industry [online]. Commonwealth of Australia. Available at: www.aph.gov.au/Parliamentary_Business/Committees/Senate/Environment_and_Communications/Video_game_industry/Report [Accessed 23 Feb. 2018]. 715555fb44/TV-Drama-Diversity.pdf [Accessed 22 Feb. 2018].

Simons, M. (2017). Are you thinking what I'm thinking?: How the ABC's diverse curiosity might conquer partisanship and bring us all together. *Meanjin*, 76(2), 44–62.

Swinburne, S. and Fabb, M. (2017). "How web series are shaking up Australia's screen industry", *The Conversation*. Retrieved from https://theconversation.com/how-web-series-are-shaking-up-australias-screen-industry-79844.

Top 250 YouTubers in Australia sorted by subscribers. (2018). *Socialblade* Retrieved from https://socialblade.com/youtube/top/country/au/mostsubscribed.

22 Conclusion

A Snapshot and a Springboard for the Exploration of World Entertainment Media

Paolo Sigismondi

If you are reading this chapter in its intended sequence, as the last one of this edited volume, you have been traveling without moving around the world and have encountered through the lenses of media entertainment some of the unique features of different cultures as these materialize in the production, distribution and exhibition of entertainment artifacts. You have met global and regional players, and the variety of local entities which thrive around the world generating entertainment stemming from and contributing to their distinctive popular cultural *milieus*. You have encountered, among others, scripted TV series as different as the South African soap opera *Uzalo*, the Brazilian telenovela *Velho Chico* and China's serial drama *Ke Wang* [*Yearnings*], the cooking contest program *Ryouri no Tetsujin* [*Iron chef*], the Australian web series *The Katering Show* and the evolving intersections and collaborations taking place between entertainment media producers and distributors from different countries (such as Russia and China, for example). You have witnessed and might have been surprised by the seemingly unexpected directions of flows of entertainment from and to places geographically and culturally distant, such as Russia's animated TV series *Masha i Medved* [*Masha and the Bear*] and Turkey's historical TV drama *Muhteşem Yüzyıl* [*Magnificent Century*], both crossing national borders without specific support from their respective nation's governments.

Limitations of This Study and Suggestions for Future Research Endeavors in Global Media Entertainment

In this volume 20 different media landscapes have been analyzed, and of course more could have been inserted to broaden the inquiry. Both mature media markets, such as those in Scandinavia or Benelux in Western Europe, for example, and a more comprehensive analysis of the complex media landscape of the greater China region, including the specific features of the media landscapes of Hong Kong and Taiwan, are missing. Nor, in this book, are the entertainment markets of some of the emerging countries, such as Indonesia or Eastern European, analyzed; these are left for future research endeavors. As the world entertainment media evolves, new regions and countries will attract the attention of scholarly inquiry, in addition to those discussed in this volume. Furthermore, the relatively short chapters in the book cannot capture in detail the complexities of the media markets illustrated, focusing as a result on specific case studies and inquiries and/or providing an overview of the major themes and features of the landscape, whereas volumes specifically dedicated to each nation's media landscape might have the necessary depth and breadth to analyze in more detail their dynamics.

A thorough investigation of the complexities of the global media entertainment landscape calls for multiple lenses of analysis, drawing on theoretical frameworks and approaches stemming from media, communication and cultural studies, political economy, international relations and media economics among others. This volume is situated within these conversations, aiming at shedding light on the creative industries around the world in the different phases of production, distribution and exhibition of media entertainment. Within the analytical framework of the book each chapter focused on some of the unique features of the country analyzed with distinct approaches. As these chapters have brought to the fore the complexities of the global media landscape, complementary theoretical lenses to analyze the evolving flows of international media content could help understand and explicate it in more depth.

The differences among the chapters underline the usefulness of comprehensive approaches within the conversations in international communication including and harmonizing economic, political and cultural dimensions, as all of them are necessary to explicate the dynamics of producing, distributing and exhibiting media entertainment, just as the specific analyses of the different media landscapes are necessary to paint a more complete picture of the global landscape. As the globalization phenomena unfold, the necessity to deepen and share knowledge as we analyze the creative industries around the world remains a central theme of investigation, in order to capture the complexity of their processes and dynamics. At stake is a better understanding of the diversities of our world, where currently about 7,000 different languages are being utilized to communicate, representing the tip of the equivalent numerous diverse cultures existing on our planet, as the phenomena of globalization unfold, driven by political, economic and fast-paced technological change, which has accelerated at the turn of a new millennium. Moreover, a constant monitoring of the dynamic, fast-moving global media landscape is necessary to bring to the fore new media landscapes, as they emerge. Notwithstanding these limitations, the preceding chapters have provided a snapshot of key media landscapes as they evolve within the changes ushered in by the unfolding digital revolution, and the evolution of the political and economic landscapes at local, regional and global level.

A Snapshot

The collection of chapters in this book brings to the fore different media landscapes with their distinct features. Local creative, cultural, political and economic forces are shaping these landscapes in conjunction with globalization drivers which increasingly provide access to entertainment content originating from abroad. The analysis of the different landscapes has unveiled established and emerging players in each country, competing with local and international ones in arenas molded by domestic and global political, economic and cultural forces. At the same time, as entertainment content travels around the world above and beyond its original borders, it reaches different cultural *milieus* with impactful consequences: Popular culture artifacts play a major role in building and sustaining the public diplomacy efforts of their country of origin and overall promoting national cultures, as illustrated for example in the case of "Cool Japan". Entertainment has become indeed the international forum and the arena for presenting and defending distinctive, if not competing, world views and ideas in the global public sphere.

This volume has utilized media entertainment, both platforms and content, as a privileged vantage point to scan the globe, and it has revealed a mosaic of different cultures, media ecologies and economies, communication infrastructures and the uneven diffusion of technologies originating within and accelerating the phenomena of globalization around the world. The analyses offered can help paint a better picture of the complex tapestry of global media focusing on local and regional analysis, providing information and reflections on 20 different media landscapes. In so doing, the book offers a snapshot of the dynamic, fast-moving phenomena of flows of entertainment around the world, introducing similarities, trends and/or uneven developments (such as the diffusion and adoption of digital platforms, regional import/export dynamics, standardization or local adaptations of entertainment artifacts, etc.).

The complex, uneven nature of world entertainment has been brought to the fore in this volume, shedding light on global, regional and local players. Media entertainment, both in terms of platforms and content, has been suggested as an optic to analyze phenomena of globalization, revealing a mosaic of different cultures, media economies, communication infrastructures and diffusion of technologies operating and thriving within (or notwithstanding) globalization forces. The level of analysis has been situated at local and regional level to shed light on the phenomena, providing updated information on a multifaceted, dynamic landscape. The analyses presented in this volume could also provide a springboard for future investigations.

A Springboard

The chapters of this volume on the world media landscape could contribute to a variety of conversations that might originate when comparing and contrasting different media landscapes: For example, what is and/or should be the role of public and private enterprises in the media ecosystem, as in most countries, with few notable exceptions such as the United States, public media entities still retain a pivotal role? Also, what role, if any, should local and/or international governments have in shaping such ecosystems? As media regulations are being scrutinized and questioned *pari passu* with the unfolding of phenomena of globalization, these chapters can offer an additional international informational background for discussions on media policies. To what extent and within what geographical boundaries should media be regulated? Within these discussions, for example, how should the concentration of ownership in media and the international limitations and protections of intellectual property rights be regulated, as these are at the center of how these industries operate? Different solutions could originate when these issues are analyzed drawing on data and analyses on a country-by-country basis or at regional level, as in the case of the European Union. Larger discussions centered on media communication could also originate, noticing how, more broadly, the intersections between political and economic forces (both local and international) yield vastly different results around the world, whereas forces of globalization (in many parts of the world deemed completely "external" to the local ecosystems) interact with local impulses and fears, and within the growing international relevance of media economy players increasingly operating informally outside of national and international regulations.

Moreover, while the global success of media entertainment originating from the West (and the US in particular) has been explicated by different, oftentimes complementary, theoretical frameworks and analyses (such as cultural and linguistic imperialism, cultural proximity, application and extension of cultivation theory over time, narrative transparency, etc.), some of which have been sketched in the brief literature review in the introductory chapter of this book, other phenomena unfolding within the international flows and contraflows of media entertainment are more difficult to categorize into and explicate within existing theoretical frameworks: For example, the global successes of popular culture artifacts not in the English language (such as Psy's *Gangnam Style* from South Korea and the diffusion of Latin music outside of the Spanish-speaking world), the international distribution of the aforementioned animated TV series *Masha i Medved* [*Masha and the Bear*] from Russia and the TV drama series *Muhteşem Yüzyıl* [*Magnificent Century*] from Turkey, or the unexpected success at the time of this writing of the feature-length motion picture *Perfetti Sconosciuti* [*Perfect Strangers*] in Chinese movie theatres, a local Italian comedy whose theatrical distribution in China was preceded and likely fueled by unauthorized copies available on the internet in the country, just to name a few. Understanding these phenomena could help us foreshadow new trajectories within the international communication ecosystem.

In a digital media landscape, new internet-based international delivery platforms, both within the formal and informal economies, are able to allow, outside of mainstream distribution, artifacts to find their audiences, facilitating their diffusion beyond the consolidated international media flows of the twentieth century, such as the Atlantic corridor between the US and Europe, for example. One the one hand, the increasingly transnational on-demand platforms, such as the US-based Netflix and Amazon Prime, which rely on both global and local media productions, could increase the domestic and international visibility of media artifacts with relatively low production budgets situated in the long tail of the international entertainment industry. On the other, platforms operating within the crevasses of international regulatory frameworks could also increase the exposure to locally produced media culture, cultivating future demand originating within formal economies.

While these platforms are increasingly relevant in the international communication landscape, what could be the drivers of an interest in foreign media artifacts outside of their original cultural *milieus*? Many hypotheses could be empirically tested: It could be the international appeal of universal themes that might resonate worldwide regardless of their origin or the desire/curiosity to explore different cultural environments above and beyond the mainstream cultural points of reference originating from the West, in addition to the expected interest in local or locally adapted productions. The unfolding phenomena of globalization have been opening the doors for internationally produced media artifacts and cultures, providing access to households all over the world and to audiences on the go, via the unprecedented ubiquitous distribution possibilities provided by the diffusion and adoption of digital mobile devices.

In addition to the aforementioned necessity to combine and harmonize different theoretical approaches comprising media and cultural studies, economics and international relations, to illustrate the complexity of different media landscapes, this volume brings to the fore new possibilities of distributing internationally entertainment media content also for players beyond the beaten paths of the entertainment import/export of the twentieth century. The new digital environment has, indeed, the potential to allow the phenomenon of international distribution of media entertainment to prosper and become a steadier reality and business practice above and beyond the "one-hit wonder" episodes. The ability to successfully do so would greatly benefit those who dare to think internationally, generating more diversified revenue streams for the very same cultural artifacts and setting the stage for more ambitious, higher production-value media entertainment artifacts originating from different cultural *milieus*, historically deemed small media cultures. As this volume has illustrated, the world landscape does not necessarily imply that the only international dimension in world entertainment media is the global one, as the title of this book suggests investigations at global, regional and local level.

The international entertainment marketplace represents a unique crossroads and it is increasingly relevant in political, cultural and economic terms, helping us decipher the uneven, contested, unfolding phenomena of globalization. As we continue to investigate these phenomena, in order to explicate the different flows inside and outside the mainstream lines of entertainment import/ export around the world, I hope you have been challenged reading this book, exploring different cultures and media landscapes, as they have been introduced (or reintroduced for some readers), by the different perspectives presented in this volume. The thoughtful and insightful analyses provided in the chapters have been crafted by outstanding international authors who have kindly shared their deep knowledge and expertise, and contributed to this book shedding light on the distinctive features of 20 different landscapes. And at the end of this intellectual journey you might feel enriched and rendered even more curious to further investigate the evolution and the fascinating features of the international media landscape, as I am and have been throughout the process of editing this volume.

Index

3-D 19, 27, 69, 112, 166
20th Century Fox 19–24, 81; 21st Century Fox 19–26, 63, 110, 169; *see also* FOX

Acir Group 32
Acorn TV 63
adaptations 5, 88–90, 127, 158, 199, 202
advertising: based media business models 11–13, 22–5, 32–6, 77–80, 96–104, 125, 108–14; regulation 51–3, revenues 53, 69–73, 77–80, 88–92, 96–104, 108–14, 132, 167–8; strategies136, 198
Agency for Culture 155
AK Parti (AKP) 116–122
Akira 159
Al Ahly TV 131
Alibaba 169–170
Altice 74–5
Amazon 1–2, 14, 22–8, 59, 63, 73–5, 80, 100, 187, 203
Amblin Entertainment 170
AMC Theaters 170
América Móvil 29–34
American Broadcasting Company (ABC) 24–5, 156
American Cinesa 101
americanization 11, 161
analog switch-off 31–6
Animal Logic 196
animation 16, 27, 91, 111–12, 155–160, 169, 177
Antena 3 96–7
Apple 2, 23–8, 49
Arab region 124–8
Arbeitsgemeinschaft der öffentlich-rechtlichen Rundfunkanstalten der Bundesrepublik Deutschland (ARD) 79–80
Asiawood 158
Asia Television Forum (ATF) 14
Asociación Mexicana de Internet (Mexican Internet Association) (AMIPCI) 29–34
Asociación Mexicana de Productoras y Televisoras Universitarias (Mexican Association of University Producers and TV Stations) (AMPTU) 37
Atresmedia 96–103

attendance: movies 155, 165, 188–9; sports 197
AT&T 20–8, 33–4; AT&T-TimeWarner merger 26–8
Audiovisual Media Services Directive (AVMSD) 50–4, 78
Australia 193–200
Australian Broadcasting Corporation (ABC) 194–8
Australian Communications and Media Authority (ACMA) 194
Australian Rules Football (AFL) 197
Avatar 19–21

Baidu 169–170
BCE 13–14
Beijing Satellite TV 167
Big Brother 139, 193
Blue Planet II 60
Bollywood 6, 118, 182–191
Bouygues Group 70
brand 119, 128, 145, 160, 174, 184; brand ambassador 119, 139, 194; nation branding 160, 184
Brexit 3, 58, 62
BritBox 63–4
British Broadcasting Corporation (BBC) 59–64, 106, 144, 194–7
broadband 27–34, 53–4, 69–73, 112–13, 132; ADSL 73
Brazil 39–46
broadcasting 12–19, 29–32, 39, 50–5, 61, 68–75, 77–80, 96, 116–18, 124–5, 143–7, 155, 167–8, 193–7; policies 12; *see also* public broadcasting
Broadcasting services act 194–7
Busan International Film Festival (BIFF) 176

cable television 12–14, 19–27, 30–4, 58, 74, 97–8, 156–7, 167–9, 187–90, 194
Call the Midwife 60
Canada 11–18
Canadian Radio-Television and Telecommunication Commission (CRTC) 15
Canada Media Fund (CMF) 16
Canadian Film or Video Production Tax Credit (CPTC) 16
Canal de las estrellas 36

Index

Canal+ 68–75, 97
capitalism 4, 127
CBS 12, 20–8
CD 73, 83, 87–92, 103
censorship 35, 77, 111, 116–22, 129, 138, 168–71, 176–8, 194
Centre for Media Pluralism and Media Freedom (CMPF) 53
center/periphery dynamics 3, 11–13, 161
chaebols 174
China 164–172
China Central Television (CCTV) 91, 117, 167–8
China Film Group, China Film Export & Import Corporation (CFEIC) 166
Chopras 182
Cinépolis 101
ClaroTV 30
Cleverman 194
CJ Group 174
comedies 14, 63, 129
co-productions 13–15, 84, 91, 110, 165–8
Comcast 12, 20–7
Comisión Federal de Competencia Económica (Federal Commission of Economic Competition) (COFECO) 29
commercialization 11, 55, 68, 89, 167
community: TV 36; soap model 142–8
concessions 30–5, 109, 183
conglomerates (media conglomerates) 2–5, 12–13, 21, 63, 77, 88–91, 96, 116–21, 174, 188, 194
content regulation 142–6, 166
contra-flows 5
Convention on the Protection and Promotion of Diversity of the Cultural Expressions (CPPDCE) 16
convergence 49–55, 79, 145
Cool Japan 155–161, 202
copyright 15, 81, 112, 169–70, 182, 191; copyright law 81–3
command economy model 164
Competitive Intelligence Unit (CIU) 33
Cope 102
creative digital studio 196
Creative Europe 50–1
creative industry 174
Crocodile Dundee 194
cross-ownership 103
CTC-Media 90
cultural: citizenship 144; diplomacy 160 (*see also* public: diplomacy); enterprise 71–2; exception 70; exchanges 72, 137; homogenization 5, 157; industry 6, 69, 164 (*see also* creative industry); imperialism 4, 11–17, 195; nationalism 194; policy 11–17, 68, 79, 155–61, 170, 173–5, 193–9; proximity 142–50, 203; revolution 165; *see also* popular culture

Dalian Wanda 166, 170
decentralization 161, 167
Degrassi: The Next Generation 14
digital: channels 25, 31; devices 22; distribution 22, 50, 58–9, 70, 83, 91, 99, 109–14, 117–22, 130–1, 138–9, 202 (*see also* platforms); revolution 2–3, 91–3, 130, 202; transformation 73; TV 30–1, 58–64, 70, 126
Digital Terrestrial Television (DTT) 31
digitalization, digitization 49, 103, 110–13
diplomacy *see* cultural: diplomacy; *see* public: diplomacy
direct address 39–45
DirecTV 25–6
Disney 4, 12, 19–28, 63, 81, 97–101, 111, 161, 169, 185
distribution *see* digital: distribution
The Diving Bell 176
Doctor Who 60–3
Document 1519 166
Doraemon 180
Downtown Abbey 63
drama series 61–3, 116–22, 158, 173, 203; *see also* historical drama
DreamWorks Studios 183–5
Dream TV 127
DStv/MultiChoice 144–5
dual system 194
dubbing 78, 91
duopoly 32–7, 70, 97, 108

Egypt 124–134
Egyptian Media Production City (EMPC) 126
Electronic communications act 145
El Diván de Valentina 37
Endemol 2, 26
Erdoğan, T. 120–1
Ermittlung des Finanzbedarfs der Rundfunkanstalten [KEF] 79
Europe 49–57
European Commission (EC) 50–4
European Economic Community (EEC) 49
European Union (EU) 2–3, 6, 49–53, 58, 72–5, 77–9, 203
exports (media exports) 4, 13–17, 63–4, 68–72, 84, 118–22, 159–60, 164, 199

FAANG 2
Facebook 1–2, 14, 23–7, 34, 49, 73, 92, 110, 128, 132, 137
fandom 137
fashion 128, 139, 157, 160, 173–5, 198
Federal Communications Commission (FCC) 25–6
fiction 32–7, 40–4, 60–3, 72, 79–84, 106–11
film market 64, 164–5
film production *see* production
Filmförderungsanstalt [federal film board] (FFA) 81
Film Funding Act 81

Fininvest/Mediaset 96–7, 103, 108–110
flagship 59, 63, 142–4, 148, 195
France 68–76
France Télévisions 70
FremantleMedia 2
foreign entertainment 87–91, 170
formats (TV formats) 5, 32–7, 40, 78–84, 88–93, 111, 116–18, 124–30, 143–7, 156, 168, 173, 193–9; format adaptations 2, 193–9
four-tier system 167
FOX 24–7, 101, 187, 195–6
Foxtel 194
freedom of expression 35, 55, 77, 120, 176
free-to-air TV 197–8
free trade 11–16
Free Trade Agreement (FTA) 16
Freeview 59
Fruit Ninja 196, 199
Fuji TV 156
future research trajectories 7

Gangnam Style 137, 174, 203
games (videogames) 13, 68–71, 78–83, 96–104, 112, 155–61, 169, 193–6
Gaumont 70
Gazprom-Media 89–91
General Administration of Press and Publications (GAPP) 168
General Agreement on Tariffs and Trade (GATT) 16, 124
General Authority for Foreign Investment (GAFI) 127
Germany 77–86
Gezi Park protests 116–120
The Ghost in the Shell 159
globalization 1–5, 11–15, 49–55, 155–61, 174, 184–9, 202–4; glocalization 156
Globo (Globo TV) 39–44
Google 2, 13–14, 25–7, 49, 70–3, 110, 197–8
Groupe Figaro 70
Grupo Imagen 30

Hachette 70
Halfbrick Studios 196
Half of a Yellow Sun 138–9
Hallyu [Korean Wave], 6, 158, 173–8; *Hallyu-hwa* [Hallyuization] 174; *Hallyu 1.0, Hallyu 2.0, Hallyu 3.0* 175
HBO 23–7, 75, 100, 169
Higher Audio-visual Council (CSA) 71
Hollywood 2–4, 14–15, 21–5, 61–4, 72, 90, 129, 155–61, 165–70, 173, 182–91, 195–6; of the Arab World 128; global 196; North 14–15
Hong Kong International Film and TV Market (HKIFTM) 14
Hoyts 170
historical drama 63, 121–2
Huaxia Film Distribution Company 166

Hulu 1, 22–4, 28, 63, 187
Hunan Broadcasting System (HBS) 168; Hunan Satellite TV 167
hybrid cultures 93, 135, 143, 184–5; hybridization/hybridity 5, 184–5

imports (media imports) 4, 63–5, 84, 155, 165–70, 193; *see also* exports
Independent Communications Authority of South Africa (ICASA) 142–8
India 182–192
Indian diaspora 184–6; Non-Resident Indian population (NRI) 185–7
Indian Premier League (IPL) 188
indigenization 144, 156
informal media 5
Information and Communication Technology (ICT) 2, 91
Instagram 128, 132
Institute for Financing Culture and Cultural Industries (IFCIC) 71
Instituto Federal de Telecomunicaciones [Federal Telecommunications Institute] (IFETEL) 29, 31, 35
Instituto Federal Electoral (Federal Electoral Institute) (IFE) 35
integration: horizontal 39; vertical 24
Intellectual property (IP) 19–22, 50, 65, 196, 203
International Indian Film Academy Awards (IIFA) 186
internationalization 2, 16
Internet: Protocol TV (IPTV) 97–8, Service Provider (ISP) 20, 98, 196
Interstate Treaty on Broadcasting and Telemedia (Rundfunkstaatsvertrag RStV) 79
iROKOtv 139
Italy 106–115; Italian anomaly 109; made in Italy 111
iTunes 73, 112
ITV 59–63
iView 194–8

Japan 155–163; made in Japan 159; Japanization 156; Japanimation 159
Jinping, X. 164–6
journalistic information 106

Kapoors 182
Katering Show 196–8
Ke Wang 168, 201
Kommission zur Ermittlung des Finanzbedarfs der Rundfunkanstalten [KEF] Commission for the Determination of the Financial Requirements of the PSBs 79
Korea 173–181; K-drama 118; Korean Wave *see Hallyu*; K-pop music 174–5
Korea Tourism Organization (KTO) 174
KwaZulu-Natal Film Commission (KZNFC) 148

Lagardère Active 70
Lang, J. 68–70
Lebanese Broadcasting Corporation (LBC) 130
legal framework 79; legislative framework 5, 35, 49–50; *see also* regulation
Legendary Entertainment 170
Ley Federal de Telecomunicaciones y Radiodifusión [Federal Telecommunications and Broadcasting Law] 29, 35
liberalization 68, 185–7
license fee 59
Life of Pi 183, 187
Lionsgate 20–1, 28, 170
Living in Bondage 135
local: content 142–8, 193–4; local production *see* production
local adaptations: localization 5, 155–61; trans-Asian localization 158; *see also* adaptations

M6 70
Marché International des Films et des Programmes pour la Télévision, la Video, le Cable et le Satellite (MIPCOM) 14
Marché International des Programmes de Télévision (MIPTV) 14
Masha i Medved 91, 201–3
Massey commission 11
mass media crisis 36
Maxdome 80
media conglomerates *see* conglomerates
media distribution 24; *see also* digital distribution
media: concentration 39; conglomerates *see* conglomerates; exports *see* exports; imports *see* imports; mergers *see* mergers; pluralism 50–3; policy 49–55, 79; regulation *see* regulation; system 20–4, 30, 51, 77, 106, 120, 159
Media-Most 89
Mediaset *see* Fininvest/Mediaset
mergers 2, 20–8, 161
Mexico 29–38
Microsoft 83, 101–2
Middle East Broadcasting (MBC) 118, 130
Ministry of Culture 68–73, 90, 164–6
Ministry of Foreign Affairs (MOFA) 160
Ministry of Industry and Information Technology (MITT) 169
Ministry of Radio, Film, and Television (RFT) 165–7
Miyazaki, H. 161
monopoly 32, 39, 68, 114, 117, 167–8; *see also* public monopoly
Monster Hunt 169
Motion Picture Association of America (MPAA) 6
movie attendance *see* attendance
movie theatres *see* theatres
Movistar 98–9, 104
MTV 25; MTV Asia 161; MTV Russia 87–8, 92
Muhteşem Yüzyıl 121, 201–3
MultiChoice *see* DStv/MultiChoice
Murdoch, R. 27, 63, 194

Museum of Old and New Art (MONA) 193
must offer/must carry 30, 167

Naspers media 145
nasserism 124
nation building 142–6; national identity 142–6, 193–9
National Association of Television Programming Executives (NATPE) 14
National Book Centre (CNL) 71–2
National Centre for Cinematography (CNC) 52, 68, 71
National Film Management Company (NFMC) 164
National Media Council (NMC) 125
National Media Group 89–90
national rejuvenation 164
NBC Universal 21, 25
neoliberalism 195
neo-ottomanism 119
Netflix 1–2, 13–14, 19, 21–8, 37, 59, 63, 72–5, 80, 91, 99, 103, 113, 122, 139, 194, 203
net neutrality 39, 72
News Corporation 194
New World Information and Communication Order (NWICO) 4
NHK 117
Nigeria 135–141
Nigerian Export-Import Bank 138
Nigerian Film and Video Censorship Board (NFVCB) 138
Nile 124–7, 130; Nilesat 126
Nintendo 83, 101–2, 161
Nollywood 6, 118, 135–141
North American Free Trade Agreement (NAFTA) 16

Observatorio Iberoamericano de Ficción Televisiva (OBITEL) 32–6, 40
online distribution *see* digital distribution
on-demand 13, 22–5, 49, 51–4, 59, 80, 187–9, 194–6, 203; *see also* Video on Demand (VOD); *see also* Subscription Video on Demand (SVOD)
Ontario Media Development Corporation (OMDC) 16
open text 39–44
Open Door Economic Policy (ODEP) 132
Orange 74–5, 98; Orange Cinéma Séries (OCS) 74
Oshii, M. 159
Ôtomo K. 159
ottoman empire 121–2
Over-the-top (OTT) 27, 37, 74–5, 169

pan-arabism 124
Paramount Pictures 20–4, 81, 97, 100–1
Pathé 70
pay-TV 25–6, 51, 69, 74–5, 79–89, 98, 108
Perfetti Sconosciuti 203
Perviy Kanal [Channel One] 89
piracy 22, 87, 90–2, 138–9, 189–191

platforms 1–6, 19–28, 29, 40, 54, 58, 89, 99–102, 108–113, 117, 122, 124, 128, 132, 145–6, 160, 170, 198, 202–4; digital platforms 22, 70, 91, 99, 112, 122, 130, 138–9, 202; platform society 113
Pokémon 159–161
policy convergence 54
Political Actions Programmes (PAP) 56
political economy 4, 11–17, 20–5, 201
popular culture 2–5, 88, 119, 135, 143, 168, 173–5, 202–3
post-apartheid 142
prime-time 61, 143–8, 168, 193
Prisa 97, 102
private channels 68, 97
privatization 55, 116–18, 124
pro-am 198–9
production: film production 16, 52–3, 64, 74, 81–2, 87–90, 100–4, 128–9, 161, 165–170, 199; local production 78, 144–8, 195–6; TV production 13–17, 80; *see also* co-productions; *see also* runaway productions
project ACT-Nollywood 138
ProSiebenSat.1 79–80
protectionism 11, 90
Psy 174, 203
public: broadcasting 53, 68–70, 196; Public Service Broadcasting – PSB 77–9, 84; commercial channel 145; diplomacy 3, 202 (*see also* soft power); funding 52–3, 70, 78, 81–2; Public Investment Bank (BPI) 71; monopoly 68; policy 54–5, 68, 71; sphere 161, 202
Putin, V. 89

Quebecor 11–13
quotas (media content quotas) 68, 75, 78, 83–4, 155, 166, 193–9
Quran Station 124

RAI 108–110
Rainbow nation 142; Rainbow TV 144
rap battle 92–3
reality TV 2, 80, 139
reform 29–35, 116, 135–8, 165–171
regionalization 157
Regulatory Authority for Electronic Communications and Post (ARCEP) 71–2
regulation 5, 15, 20–5, 32–6, 39, 51–5, 68–75, 77–83, 90–3, 125, 142–50, 155–61, 166–71, 203; *see also* content regulation; *see also* advertising: regulation
remaking 156–8, 173
repeat 147
Reporters Without Borders (RSF) 120
Rogers Communication 13
Rossiya channels 1, 24 89
Royal Charter 59
RTL-Bertelsmann 70; RTL Group 79–84
RTVE 96–103
runaway productions 14
Russia 87–95

Russian Ministry of Culture 90
Ryouri no Tetsujin 156, 201

Sancak Group 117
satellite television 20–6, 30–3, 59–63, 74–5, 89, 97, 117–19, 125–130, 157, 167–8, 197; digital satellite 58, 98
Scientific Research Programmes (SRP) 56
SFR Play 74
Shaw 13
show business 87, 164
Sistema Mexicano de Radiodifusión (Mexican Broadcasting System) (SMR) 32
Sky 26, 33, 59–63, 79, 100; Sky Deutschland 80; Sky Italy 109–110; Sky One 63
Slim, C. 29
Slumdog Millionaire 183–7
soap operas 37–40, 88, 125, 142–4 (*see also* community: soap model); South African 142–9; Turkish 118–9
social: media 1–2, 31, 50–3, 93, 120, 128–132, 169, 174, 198; network 34, 73, 92, 174
soft power 5, 119–121, 159–160, 164–5, 175, 184
Sohu 169
Sony 13, 20, 70, 83–4, 101–4, 156–9; Sony Pictures 20–8, 81, 100–1, 164, 170, 185
South Africa 142–151
South African broadcasting act 145
South African Broadcasting Corporation (SABC) 142–9
South African Film and Television Award (SAFTA) 142
South Korea 173–181
Spain 96–105
Special Broadcasting Service (SBS) 194–8
sports 23, 63, 74, 99, 102, 112, 124–131, 183–8, 197
Spotify 73, 103, 112–13
standardization 156, 202
STAR TV 161
state aid for media *see* subsidies; *see* public: funding
State Administration of Radio, Film, and Television (SARFT) 166–8
State Administration of Press Publications Radio Film and Television (SAPPRFT) 168–9
storytelling 106–7
streaming 14, 19–28, 59–63, 73, 80–3, 87–92, 99–103, 112, 170, 187–9, 193–4
Strictly Come Dancing 60
Subscription Video on Demand (SVOD) 25, 74, 80
subjective camera 39–45
subsidies 14–16, 52–5, 71, 78, 164, 194; *see also* public: funding
Super Mario 159
Supreme Council for Media Regulation (SCMR) 125

Takeshi Castle 156
talk-shows 88–9, 124

tax 68, 71, 81, 164–6, 194–6; credit 16, 52, 110; relief 64, 138
TBS 26, 156
technology 7, 19, 25–8, 37, 54, 70, 79, 91–4, 96–9, 116, 128–32, 157, 191; *see also* Information and Communication Technology (ICT)
Telecinco 96–100
telecommunications 13, 20, 29–37, 54–5, 71–4, 97–9, 111, 145
Telefónica 33–4, 97–104
telenovelas 32–7, 39–45, 116–8, 144
telephony 25, 29–34
Televisa 29–37
television: broadcasting *see* broadcasting; *see also* free-to-air TV; cable *see* cable television; community *see* community; TV; digital *see* digital (*see also* Digital Terrestrial Television (DTT)); formats *see* formats; platforms *see* platforms; networks 12, 25, 30–6, 87, 121, 193; pay *see* pay-TV; reality *see* reality TV; satellite *see* satellite; systems 30, 106; Television without Frontiers (TVwF) 50
telinha 40
Tencent 83, 169
TF1 Group 70
theaters 41, 78, 136, 173; movie theatres 22–4, 82–4, 87–90, 100–1, 139, 164–70, 177, 183–90
transmediation 39–40
translation 72, 160
transnational 4–5, 16, 20–6, 49, 68; 71–4, 116, 128, 135–9, 157–61, 173, 203; transnationalization 70
tripartition 106
Turkey 116–123
Turkish Radio and Television (TRT) 116–122; TRT Al-Arabiya 117; TRT Kurdi 117; TRT World 117
Turkuvaz/Kalyon Group 120
TV Azteca 30–7
Twitter 34, 43, 62, 132, 174

Ulitsy Razbitykh Fonarei 88
United Kingdom (UK) 58–67
United Nations Educational, Scientific and Cultural Organization (UNESCO) 4, 16, 188–190

United States (US) 19–28
Universal Studios 24, 81, 100–1; Universal Music 13, 70–2, 84, 103–4; Universal Parks 21; Vivendi Universal 69; *see also* NBC Universal
Universum Film AG (UFA) 81–2
Uzalo: Blood is Forever 142–150

Velho Chico 39–45, 201
Versus Battle 92–3
Viacom 12, 20–8, 63, 80
video rental 99, 129
video-sharing platforms (VSPs) 54
visual arts 69, 112, 195
Vivendi 69–75
videogames *see* games
Video on Demand (VOD) 51–4, 68–74, 80, 130; *see also* Subscription Video on Demand (SVOD)
Vkontakte 92
Vodafone 97–8
The Voice 62, 130, 193
Voluntary Self-Monitoring Television (FSF) 79
Vserossiyskaya Gosudarstvennaya Tele Radio Kompaniya (VGTRK) [All-Russia State Television and Radio Broadcasting] 89

Warner Bros. 20–7, 81, 100–1; Time Warner 12, 25–8, 80, 169; Warner Media 23–8; Warner Music 70, 84, 103–4
WhatsApp 34, 132
Who Wants be a Millionaire? 156
World Trade Organization (WTO) 16, 166

X-Factor 130

Yomvi 99
Youku-Tudou 169
Youth protection act 81
YouTube 1, 23, 72, 91–3, 99–103, 113, 122, 128–132, 174, 187, 194–9

Zhejiang Satellite TV 167
Zweites Deutsches Fernsehen (ZDF) 79–81